Crucible of the Jacobite '15

The Battle of Sheriffmuir 1715

Jonathan Oates

Helion & Company Limited

Helion & Company Limited
26 Willow Road
Solihull
West Midlands
B91 1UE
England
Tel. 0121 705 3393
Fax 0121 711 4075
Email: info@helion.co.uk
Website: www.helion.co.uk
Twitter: @helionbooks
Visit our blog http://blog.helion.co.uk/

Published by Helion & Company 2017
Designed and typeset by Serena Jones

Cover designed by Paul Hewitt, Battlefield Design (www.battlefield-design.co.uk)
Printed by Short Run Press, Exeter, Devon

Text © Jonathan Oates, 2017
Images © as individually credited
Maps drawn by George Anderson © Helion & Company 2017
Cover: Clansmen of the Jacobite left wing come under mounting pressure from Government dragoons. Painting by Steve Noon © Helion & Company 2017

ISBN 978-1-911512-89-9

British Library Cataloguing-in-Publication Data.
A catalogue record for this book is available from the British Library.

For details of other military history titles published by Helion & Company
Limited contact the above address, or visit our website: http://www.helion.co.uk.

We always welcome receiving book proposals from prospective authors.

Contents

List of Illustrations   iv
List of Maps   v
Acknowledgements   vi
Introduction   vii

1   The Reasons Why, 1714–1715   12
2   Countdown to the Campaign, July–August 1715   30
3   Raising the Men and the Money   44
4   The Government Strikes Back   58
5   The Campaign of the Fifteen, 6 September–8 November 1715   83
6   March to Battle, 9–12 November 1715   105
7   The Jacobite Army   115
8   The British Army   129
9   The Battle of Sheriffmuir, Opening Phases   143
10   The Battle of Sheriffmuir, Concluding Phase   173
11   The Consequences   195
12   Endgame in the Highlands   210
13   Conclusion   237

Appendices
I   British Army Casualties   241
II   Panmure's Regiment   259
III   British Army Officers Who Deserted   261
IV   Jacobite Prisoners After Sheriffmuir   262
V   Poetry and Songs Inspired by the Battle of Sheriffmuir   265

Bibliography   272
Index   278

List of Illustrations

1. Prince James Francis Edward Stuart, recognised by the Jacobites as 'James VIII and III'. (Public domain)   13
2. Edinburgh Castle, a forbidding sight to a would-be attacker. The Jacobites made a failed attempt to capture it in September 1715. (Author's photo)   84
3. The remnants of a fallen pillar known as 'the Gathering Stone': legend has it that the Duke of Argyle watched the battle from this spot. (Author's photo)   150
4. A nineteenth-century drawing of the Earl of Mar holding a council of war with his officers. (Public domain)   151
5. A mid-nineteenth century engraving of the battlefield. (Public domain)   157
6. A view of the battlefield from the Jacobite lines. (Author's photo)   158
7. Artefacts from the battle, Dunblane Museum. (Author's photo)   184
8. Memorial to members of Clan MacRae who were killed at Sheriffmuir. Erected by the Clan in 1915. (Author's photo)   187
9. Memorial cairn at Sheriffmuir, erected by the 1745 Association. (Author's photo)   189
10. A nineteenth-century engraving of the Royal Navy bombarding Jacobite positions on Burntisland. (Public domain)   206
11. Statue of Rob Roy MacGregor, Stirling. Erected by a descendant. (Author's photo)   216
12. Carlisle Castle. Jacobite prisoners were held here after the battle. (Author's photo)   234
13. The sign outside the Sheriffmuir Inn, close to the battlefield. (Author's photo)   238

List of Maps

1. The armies form up, late morning   149
2. The armies march to battle, early afternoon   155
3. The right wings of both armies attack the left wing of the other, afternoon   161
4. Final confrontation, late afternoon   167

Acknowledgements

The Author would like to express his thanks to all those who have assisted in the production of this work. First of all the staffs at the National Records of Scotland, the National Library of Scotland, the National Archives at Kew and the British Library must be thanked, as the unknown footsoldiers essential to any victory in their ceaseless production of the documentary evidence crucial to the book.

Quotations from the Clerk of Penicuik's papers (GD18, located at the National Records of Scotland) are made with the kind permission of Sir Robert Clerk, Bt. Quotations from GD 248 are reproduced by kind permission of the Right Honourable The Earl of Seafield.

Individually there are the kind historians who have spared time they can ill afford from their other endeavours: Professor Daniel Szechi, Dr Piotr Stolarski, John Coulter and wordsmith John Gauss. I would like to thank Professor Szechi, especially, for drawing my attention to his article cited in the bibliography and published in 2013, and also to a manuscript in the National Records of Scotland that alters our view of the final stage of the battle. Graham John Nicholls MBE was kind enough to send me a copy of this evidence. My thanks are also to my brother for his provision of free board and lodging at his house not far from the Earl of Mar's estate, as well as his provision of photographs of the battlefield and elsewhere. My son also walked the battlefield with me.

The book is dedicated to Graham John Nicholls, MBE.

Introduction

Britain's collective historical memory is limited. In 2015, the centennial anniversaries of Waterloo (1815) and Agincourt (1415) were marked and remembered, as was that of Magna Carta (1215). Yet two battles which also enjoyed centennial anniversaries went by little remarked upon in the public mind; there was no national remembrance of them. All three of the events commemorated are always in school and popular histories of England/Britain. Waterloo was the battle which ended the long Napoleonic wars, but Agincourt, though a great victory for England over France, did not lead to a lasting peace, though was celebrated by one of Shakespeare's plays over a century later and so has won undying fame. The two neglected battles, both fought on British soil, also had crucial results in confirming existing trends rather than initiating them. These were the battles of Preston and Sheriffmuir in 1715.

That year saw a major military campaign launched in Scotland, and later England, to overthrow the newly established Hanoverian dynasty in the shape of George I and to replace him with the exiled son of the late James VII of Scotland and II of England and to reverse the controversial Act of Union. In terms of manpower, it garnered more support in both countries than did the more famous attempt of 1745, and the armies it faced were far smaller than they were to be 30 years later. It should have had a greater chance of success, therefore. The fate of the campaign was decided in battle in Scotland and this book is the story of the campaign leading up to that encounter, the Battle of Sheriffmuir itself and its aftermath.

That battle was the largest in Scotland to have been fought between Dunbar in 1650 and Falkirk in 1746. It was known to contemporaries as Dunblane, that being the nearest sizeable settlement, rather than the geographical feature where the battle occurred. It had, perhaps, the potential to alter both Scotland's and Britain's history, and that of Europe, too. Unlike the battles of the 'Forty Five', no one full length book has focused solely on the campaign in Scotland in which it was the central and defining feature. The majority of those few authors writing on the 'Fifteen' have seen it as one part of the larger campaign waged in Britain, which it was. Generally, though, relatively few have paid much attention to the Fifteen, certainly not when compared to the treatment of the Jacobite campaign of 1745, which continues to attract a flood of books (at least six being published or appearing heavily revised in 2015–2016).

In the three centuries since the end of the Fifteen, there have been a number of studies of this important episode. These were firstly written by contemporaries such as

Robert Patten and Peter Rae, both clergymen, as well as by two anonymous writers in the immediate aftermath of the fighting.[1] These were both valuable works, the first two written from the viewpoints of an English Jacobite turned Whig and that of a Whig Lowlander, but they were not the complete story. Later significant works included a study of the campaign in Lancashire, published in the nineteenth century, as well as a book in 1936 that was as much a series of biographies of the campaign's leading Scots as a chronological account.[2] The first study in modern times was by a former soldier (John Baynes), who produced a narrative study of the military campaign in England and Scotland, though the sources it drew on were limited.[3]

Whilst there are numerous published primary sources, such as the histories alluded to, as well as memoirs, letters and diaries from contemporaries, the rich seam of archival sources has been not fully tapped. These include the papers created by the British state – military, political and diplomatic – most of which are held at the National Archives at Kew. Papers of Scots involved are to be found both here and in the National Records and National Library of Scotland in Edinburgh. Other published material, such as newspapers and the papers calendared by the Historic Manuscripts Commission, have also been underused.

For some decades after John Baynes' *The Jacobite Rising of 1715*, published in 1970, it could be said that no one study had been published since about the campaign to restore the exiled Stuarts in 1715. Despite a surge of academic interest in Jacobitism and the Jacobite campaigns from the 1970s onwards, much of it focused on the events surrounding 1745, as it had always done. There had been part studies in more general works, such as those by Bruce Lenman and Jonathan Oates, as well as more general studies of the Jacobite campaigns from 1689–1746 and a number of articles and essays.[4]

All that changed in the last decade when there has been a relative veritable flood of books concerning the topic – four in all (a fraction of those published in the same years about the Forty Five, it is true). The first was Professor Szechi's all-encompassing study covering the events leading up to the military campaign, the action itself and then chapters dealing with the aftermath of the conflict. It is a very detailed and extensively researched work, and concerns political, religious and social history as well as matters military.[5] Hot on the heels of this was a study about the Jacobites taken prisoner after the battles of 1715; as with Szechi's breaking new ground by bringing a

---

1   Robert Patten, *History of the Rebellion* (London: J Baker & T. Warner, 1745); Peter Rae, *History of the Late Rebellion* (London, 1746); Anon, *A Compleat History of the Late Rebellion* (London: Hinchliffe, 1716); Anon, *A Faithful Register of the Late Rebellion* (London: T. Warner, 1718).

2   Alastair and Henrietta Tayler, *1715: The Story of the Rising* (London: Thomas Nelson & Sons, 1936); Samuel Hibbert-Ware (ed.), 'Memorials of the Rebellion of 1715', Chetham Society, 5 (1845).

3   John Baynes, *The Jacobite Rising of 1715* (London: Cassell, 1970).

4   Jonathan Oates, *Responses in the North East of England to the Jacobite Rebellions of 1715 and 1745* (Reading University PhD 2001); Bruce Lenman, *The Jacobite Risings in Britain and Europe, 1688–1746* (London: Methuen, 1980); Michael Barthorp, *The Jacobite Risings, 1689–1745* (London: Osprey Publishing, 1982); Christopher Stevenson-Sinclair, *Inglorious Rebellion: The Jacobite Risings of 1708, 1715 and 1719* (London: Hamish Hamilton, 1971); Jonathan Oates, *The Jacobite Campaigns* (London: Pickering and Chatto, 2011); John Roberts, *The Highland Wars: Scotland and the Military Campaigns of 1715 and 1745* (Edinburgh: Polygon, 2002).

5   Daniel Szechi, *1715: The Great Jacobite Rising* (New Haven, CT: Yale University Press, 2005).

rigorous and extensive academic examination to a topic often dealt with superfluously in previous studies.[6]

Explicitly military history has not been neglected either. Stuart Reid, who has written extensively on Scottish military history, especially a number of groundbreaking studies of the 1745 campaign, brought out a book titled *Sheriffmuir: 1715*. It was, despite its title, an account of the campaign in its entirety, with a very similar format to that used by Baynes in 1970, with chapters covering the English dimension, though with little about the events following the battle in Scotland. Despite showing an impressive knowledge on tactical military matters and detailing the units which fought on both sides at Preston and Sheriffmuir, it had several limitations. It did not show the same degree of research that Szechi and Sankey (author of the said book discussing the prisoners) had done, and in some ways was very similar to Baynes' work of four decades previously in its restricted view of military history, as well as drawing on a limited range of almost wholly published sources, so could not be as revolutionary in its treatment of the episode as his work on the Forty Five had been. Unlike the other authors cited, Reid seemed not to fully appreciate the context of the campaign outside Scotland that had a considerable influence on it.[7]

The four books in the last century which cover the campaign of the Fifteen, excluding that by Sankey as it does not discuss the campaign in Scotland nor the Battle of Sheriffmuir, deal with it in ways which are both similar and different. All are essentially narrative. Yet the Taylers' book is made up of a fairly lightweight narrative and then over a dozen miniature biographies. Reid and Baynes provide straightforward accounts, though Reid has very little to say about the campaign following the Battle of Sheriffmuir, which Baynes covers in three chapters. Reid also includes a chapter about each army, which is a novelty hitherto. Szechi's book is as much interested in the run up to the campaign and its aftermath; in fact in terms of pages the campaign (three chapters out of nine) is overshadowed by its origins and the activity afterwards. Szechi is concerned as much with economic, social, political and religious history as he is with matters military and thus this academic history is the antithesis of the more popular works of Reid and Baynes (both former soldiers). Analysis as well as action is provided, which is not the case with his rivals.

In addition to his heavyweight book already referred to, Szechi has also broken new ground with his strategic and tactical analysis of Mar's army in a journal article. Here, a model to study military effectiveness of twentieth century armies is used to analyse the Jacobite military effort in Scotland in 1715. Put simply, the model used has four main components. These are the acquisition of men and material needed for operations, the direction of force to secure strategic goals, planning, preparation and conduct of specific operations and finally tactical ability in battle and skirmishes.

---

6   Margaret Sankey, *Jacobite Prisoners of 1715: Preventing and Punishing Rebellion in Early Hanoverian England* (Farnham: Ashgate, 2005).

7   Stuart Reid, *Sheriffmuir, 1715: The Jacobite War in Scotland* (London: Frontline Books, 2014).

Szechi concludes that of these four areas, the Jacobites in 1715 did moderately well, but that this was not enough vis-à-vis their opponents.[8]

Another book considering military matters in 1715, albeit not in Scotland, but the north of England, was by the present author in the year after Reid's.[9] This detailed the events leading up to and including the Battle of Preston, though it did not neglect civilian responses, and drew on extensive primary research, as well as dealing with the aftermath in northern England and the significance of the battle. There have also been two small books about the Battle of Sheriffmuir, one published in 1898 and a more recent and far better one with pages covering the campaign and the leaders, as well as its aftermath, drawing on many primary sources from Scotland and England, not all of which had been hitherto seen in print.[10] It was a competent and sensibly argued work and curiously unknown, apparently, to Reid.

General histories of Britain and Scotland in particular usually spend a little time on the Fifteen, but these accounts are inevitably limited in scope. They tend to downplay it in comparison with the Forty Five and tend to stress the ineptitude of the Jacobite leadership in turning what could have been a successful campaign into a dismal failure. It is customarily stated that forces were amassed at Perth in September 1715 and then did nothing aggressive until early November, by which time it was allegedly too late. As Professor Plumb wrote, 'The Fifteen has been too readily dismissed as a fiasco'.[11]

Historians of Jacobitism often stress the crucial what if of the Jacobite campaigns as being the decision of the Jacobite council at Derby in December 1745, when a march on London was contemplated but not taken. For Bruce Lenman, though, there was a greater opportunity had Mar been successful at Sheriffmuir 30 years previously:

> Once Argyll had been brushed aside, the prospects facing the Jacobite army would have been spectacular. There was more than enough sympathy and support in southern Scotland to enable local Jacobite regimes to take over and secure a broad passage to England where the rebellion in the north eastern area was more than matched in potential by latent Jacobite sympathies in Lancashire. To turn latent into active sympathy in this, as in all rebellions, military victory was essential. Forty eight hours of conflict around Stirling would have seen Mar through to Derby with over 20,000 men behind him and a disreputable and a deservedly discredited regime before him, Foreign aid was unnecessary.[12]

How much likelihood there would have been of such a diagnosis being accurate is another question and the reader can ponder it as he progresses through this book.

---

8   Szechi, 'Towards an Analytical Model of Military Effectiveness for the Early Modern Period: the Military Dynamics of the 1715 Jacobite Rebellion' in *Militargeschichtliche Zeitschrift*, 72 (2013), Heft 2.

9   Jonathan Oates, *The Last Battle on English Soil: Preston, 1715* (Farnham: Ashgate, 2015).

10   Anon, *The Battle of Sheriffmuir* (Stirling: Eenas MacKay, 1898); William Inglis, *Battle of Sheriffmuir* (Stirling: Stirling Council Libraries, 2005).

11   John Plumb, *The First Four Georges* (Glasgow: William Collins and Sons, 1956), p. 46.

12   Lenman, *Jacobite Risings*, p. 153.

Its centrality to the restoration attempt, though cannot be underestimated. The importance of the battle's potential has also been recently stressed by Professor Szechi: 'The central theatre of operations was where the '15 would be won or lost, if for no other reason than that the main government army was encamped there at Stirling. If the Jacobites could defeat it and either take Stirling castle...they would be well on their way to taking control of the whole of Scotland'.[13]

Novels and films occasionally feature the Fifteen. There is a brief reference to it at the onset of *Chasing the Deer* (1994) and a reference at the end of Sir Walter Scott's *Rob Roy* (1817). At least, however, the battlefield of Sheriffmuir is marked by two monuments (two more than that for Preston); one commemorating the MacRaes in 1915 and a more recent one erected by the 1745 Association. There have been some, albeit limited, archaeological assessments of the site (although, unlike the nearby Bannockburn battlefield, there is no museum or visitor centre, however). Dunblane Museum does, however, have some relevant artefacts. And, unlike some of the battles of the Jacobite campaigns there have been a number of poems and songs about Sheriffmuir, including two by Scotland's national bard, Robert Burns.

None of the books mentioned has exhausted the source matter covering this campaign. It is vast. This book, then, focuses on the part of the campaign of which the Battle of Sheriffmuir is central, which is necessarily treated as but one part amongst many by Baynes, Szechi and Reid (it is referred but briefly in the two other recent works just cited). It is chiefly a military history and makes no apology for this. But it takes as its definition military history in its wider capacity; finance, supply, political and diplomatic considerations, as well as looking at the rank and file of the armies and the officers. Strategy as well as tactics are important. Taking a more analytical view of the campaign, and setting it in its European and British context, and drawing on a wide range of primary source material, some hitherto never used previously, it will present a more considered view of the military theatre which played the decisive role in the struggle between Stuart and Hanover, Jacobite and Whig, Scot versus Scot and Scot versus Englishman. It will also show one of the campaign's most prominent individuals in a more sympathetic light.

The book begins with a chapter explaining why the rebellion took place when it did. The next chapter deals with the build-up towards the open declaration of Jacobite intent. In chapter three we examine the formation of the Jacobite war effort. The steps taken by the government and particularly its strategy against the Jacobite insurrection, as well as the steps taken on the ground by its commander, the Duke of Argyle make up chapter four. Chapters five and six give a narrative account of both the campaign and then the immediate period before the battle. Chapters seven and eight deal with the generals, officers and men in the two armies. There are then two chapters on the battle itself, before rounding off the campaign with its final months and its aftermath; the latter which would constitute a study all of itself.

---

13 Szechi, *1715*, p. 143.

1

The Reasons Why

The Battle of Sheriffmuir resulted from actions taken by many individuals in the year before the fighting, and indeed years before that. There were three major reasons. Ostensibly it was a struggle over whether the branch of the Stuart monarchy exiled in 1688 should be restored or whether the newly established Hanoverian monarchy should prevail. Although the succession issue was a minority cause in itself, it crucially also gave other discontents a banner to rally behind. These were the religious and nationalistic discontent in Scotland, stemming from the religious settlement of 1690 and the Act of Union of 1707. Thirdly, to spark a light to these two issues there was the match in the shape of a Scottish politician with a grievance: John Erskine (1675–1732), 6th Earl of Mar. Without all three ingredients converging it is unlikely that there would have been a battle at Sheriffmuir or indeed anywhere else in Scotland in 1715. We will now take each of these three issues one by one.

In 1688 James VII of Scotland and II of England was deposed by his son-in-law, William of Orange, stadtholder of Holland. This was in part because he was Catholic in a largely Protestant country and wished to advance the interests of his co-religionists, and because William wanted British resources in his war with France. The invasion was precipitated by the birth of a legitimate son, James Francis Stuart (1688–1766) on 10 June 1688 and the prospect of a line of Catholic monarchs. This was much resented in most of mainland Britain (though not in Ireland) and led to a falling away of support for the incumbent King. James fled England but returned to Ireland in 1689 to carry on the fight against what he, and others, saw as the usurping William. James' supporters existed throughout the British Isles and were known as Jacobites, after the term *Jacobus*, Latin for James.[1]

William and Mary were offered the English throne in 1689. The question was which way would Scotland turn, and the Scottish Convention, now in charge of the country, was approached by both James and William. James' message to them was hectoring whilst William's was conciliatory. The Convention chose the latter. James had some supporters in Scotland and principally Colonel John Claverhouse who had

---

1   Lenman, *Jacobite Risings*, pp. 28–30.

1. Prince James Francis Edward Stuart, recognised by
the Jacobites as 'James VIII and III'. (Public domain)

served in his army to suppress the Presbyterians earlier in the decade. With a small
number of clans; including the MacDonalds, the Camerons and the MacLeans, they
faced a largely Scottish–Dutch army led by General Hugh Mackay at Killiecrankie on
27 July 1689. The Jacobites won but Claverhouse was killed and in the next month the
Jacobites were beaten at Dunkeld. There was more fighting, this time at Cromdale, in
the following year and once again the Jacobites lost. James' attempt to defeat William
in Ireland was halted at the Battle of the Boyne in 1690 and once defeated he fled,
never to return. The war in Ireland continued for another year until the Jacobites sued
for peace and many were exiled overseas.[2]

James himself was allowed by Louis XIV, King of France and foremost Catholic
monarch in Europe, to live at the chateau of St. Germain, near to Paris, as well as being
allotted a generous pension. Whilst absent from Britain, his autocratic policies which
he had pursued when in power could be forgotten whilst discontent against the new
status quo gathered. James died in 1701 and his son was immediately recognised by
Louis as the *de jure* monarch of Britain; James VIII and III. When William died in
1702, his sister-in-law Anne succeeded him. The War of the Spanish Succession then
began, with France, Bavaria and Spain at war with Britain, Holland, Austria and some

---

2   *Ibid.*, pp. 30–1.

of the German states. In 1708 there had been a French invasion attempt to Scotland to retake what James saw as rightfully his, where James had accompanied the fleet on its route to Scotland. Bad weather and the Royal Navy prevented the fleet from launching James, and the French troops at his back, onto Scottish soil. Yet, as a recent historian has argued, had the weather been kinder and had different decisions been made, resulting in a landing of James with French troops, support in Scotland could have been far stronger than in 1689, resulting in civil war and a perhaps a change in history. James' desire to regain what he saw as being rightly his remained, however.[3]

Some men who fought in the Jacobite armies were highly motivated by dynastic loyalty. Many were brought up in Jacobite households and thus imbided their Jacobitism at an early age and mixed with those of like minds. John Sinclair (1685–1750), son of Lord Sinclair, was one such, writing:

> I am of a Familie, who, at all times and upon all occasions, were attached to the Crown of Scotland … and that I was earlie instructed in the principles of an indispensable duty and fidelitie towards my Prince; and I must own from my infancie I had an innate zeale and affection for all the remains of the old Royal Familie of Scotland … I often lamented as well the past as the present misfortunes of that Illustrious Familie.[4]

Loyalty to the exiled Stuarts was not enough; only a minority of the Scots had been willing to fight for James II in 1689–1690. However, James Stuart did offer possible solutions to the problems that many in the British Isles faced. As with his father and uncle he was a supporter of episcopalianism and might well dissolve the Union. To do this, however, he would need to become King and after the fiasco of 1708, the eventual death of his half-sister would present another opportunity. There were genuine Jacobites, of course, but most were motivated by contemporary religion and political concerns, which will now be outlined.

In 1690, following the political turmoil of 1688–1689, the Presbyterian Church became Scotland's official Church. This was in part a culmination of the struggle between the Episcopalians and the Presbyterians which had taken place throughout the seventeenth century. After the Restoration of the monarchy in 1660 the Stuart Kings had supported the Episcopalian Church. When the Presbyterians rebelled, they were crushed at the Battle of Bothwell Bridge in 1679 and dealt with severely in the next decade, known to their historians as the 'Killing Times'. With the overthrow of the Stuart monarchy in the person of James in 1688, a new religious settlement was hammered out by the allies of the new monarchs. This saw a reversal of the previous decade's persecutions, as episcopacy was abolished and most of its ministers were hounded out of their parishes as they refused to swear allegiance to William and Mary. Between 1688–1716, 664 out of 926 lost their parishes. There was also a purge

---

3   *Ibid.*, pp. 77–8, 88–9; Szechi, *Britain's lost Revolution, Jacobite Scotland and French Grand Strategy, 1701–1708* (Manchester University Press, 2015), pp. 198–9.
4   Walter Scott (ed.), *Memoirs of the Insurrection in Scotland in 1715* (Edinburgh: Abbotsford Club, 1845), pp. 1–2.

of the universities, too, as men felt they could not go back on the oaths they had taken to King James on his accession in 1685. This created strong religious divisions in Scotland and some were pushed into the Jacobite camp because of it.[5]

One reason why Episcopalianism was so influential was that some of the deposed ministers became tutors and chaplains to influential Scottish families. Again, a restored Stuart monarch would, as James' uncle Charles II had in 1660, restore their branch of Protestantism, too. The Catholicism of a minority of clans, notably the MacDonalds, led them to support their exiled co-religionist monarch. Other resentments in Scotland included the Massacre of Glencoe of 1692, the years of famine of the 1690s, the fact that Scottish trade had suffered from the wars with France and many impoverished because of the Darien disaster, a failed colonial venture in which many in Scotland lost considerable sums.[6]

Just as importantly, there was the question of the union of the kingdoms. Although ever since the Union of the Crowns in the person of James VI and I in 1603, there had been talk of a union of the kingdoms, nothing had come of it except the forced Cromwellian union of 1654–1660. However in 1700 the matter became critical. This was because William III was now a widower and had no children. His hereditary successor was his sister-in-law, Anne. In that year the last of her children, the Duke of Gloucester, died. The English Parliament passed the Act of Settlement to ensure that the Crown passed after Anne's demise to the Electress Sophia Dorothea of Hanover (1630–1714), a northern German electorate which was crucially Protestant. She was a distant descendant of James VI; after her death the throne would pass to her heirs.[7]

The difficulty was that Scotland's Parliament had not been consulted on this critical matter, nor on the forthcoming war with France. Scotland's Parliament passed two acts in 1703 in direct opposition to those of England. One, that they could choose their next monarch and two that they could choose whether to participate in the war (Scotland being independent had its own army and its own fiscal powers; albeit both small in comparison to those of England).[8]

This exacerbated the conflict. With the possibility of James Stuart being proclaimed King in Scotland there was the real prospect of civil war and invasion following Anne's death. The English Parliament then passed the Alien Act in 1705 which was an ultimatum to the Scottish; either begin negotiations for union or be barred from English trade. Given that England was Scotland's main trading partner and the fact that a major recent Scottish colonial venture, the Darien expedition, had failed and lost considerable sums of money, Scotland had no choice.[9]

Scotland's MPs were divided into parties. Those in favour of union were led by John Campbell (1680–1743), the 2nd Duke of Argyle, leader of Scotland's biggest clan, staunchly supportive of the Hanoverian Succession and opposed to the Stuarts.

5   Rab Houston and William Knox, *The New Penguin History of Scotland* (London: Penguin, 2001), pp. 260–1.
6   Lenman, 'The Scottish Episcopal Clergy and the Ideology of Jacobitism', in Eveline Cruickshanks (ed.), *Ideology and Conspiracy* (Edinburgh: John Donald, 1982), pp. 36–48.
7   John and Julia Keay, *Encyclopedia of Scotland* (London: Harper Collins, 1994), pp. 955–6.
8   *Ibid.*
9   Houston and Knox, *New History*, pp. 317–8.

He and the 2nd Duke of Queensberry managed the Bill through Parliament on the English government's behalf. There was a great deal of propaganda written by both sides. One strong argument put out by the unionists was that it would lead to great economic growth for Scotland. Given Scotland's parlous economic position, this seemed a strong card to play. The opposition appealed to the sense of Scotland's history, citing their identity, with the wars of the Middle Ages and the Covenanting struggles of more recent times. There was also opposition among the crowds in Edinburgh, Glasgow, Dumfries and Stirling.[10]

Yet those opposing union were divided. They were also susceptible to financial incentives, or bribes, depending on viewpoint. If the Bill was passed, nearly £400,000 of English money would be given to compensate those who had lost money in the Darien disaster and to promote Scottish industry. Furthermore, Scotland's Church and legal system would be untouched by union. With this neutralisation of these two powerful interest groups, and the money offered, opposition receded. In the end, union was passed by 110 votes to 67. The union meant one monarch, one flag, one country, one army, one navy, one economic system. Scots merchants now had legal access to English colonial markets.[11] Great Britain had been created. Scotland now sent 45 MPs and 16 lords to sit in the Parliament in London.

The Union of 1707 was regretted by many Scots in years to come, and this was a very common theme among appeals to Scots recruits to the cause. Sinclair referred to the 'infamous surrender of our rights and liberties, or Union', which he stated had led to the loss of national independence as Scotland was reduced to a 'contemptible province to a neighbouring Nation'. Scotland was suffering from being in 'a degenerate state, groaning under a load of taxes, which accumulated on us every day' while those who were responsible grew rich out of it. Prominent among these new taxes were the Malt Tax, which provoked riots.[12] Other motivations were thought to have been materialistic. Sinclair wrote, 'The Highland men would rise out of hopes of plunder, and would do as they always had done'.[13]

Many in Scotland were still unhappy. The economic benefits of union, much trumpeted by propagandists such as Daniel Defoe, did not materialise as soon as anticipated. Yet these discontents were not in themselves enough. People complained, but they needed a mouthpiece and a method of resolving their grievances. One existed because of a disputed dynastic succession in 1714. Recent historians have referred to the 'proto-nationalism' of those Scots seeking to restore the Stuarts.[14]

In the early hours of the first day of August, 1714, the middle-aged Queen Anne (1665–1714) of the recently united kingdoms of Great Britain breathed her last. Sophia had predeceased Anne by a few weeks and so her son George (1660–1727) was now Elector of Hanover and King of Great Britain. James Fitzjames (1674–1734),

---

10   Houston and Knox, *History of Scotland*, pp. 263–5.
11   *Ibid.*
12   Scott, *Memoirs*, pp. 2–3.
13   *Ibid.*, p. 26.
14   Lenman, *Jacobite Risings*, pp. 105–6; Szechi, *1715*, p. 61.

Duke of Berwick, a Marshal of France and an illegitimate son of James VII and II, later claimed he urged the leading politicians in England to act to restore the exiled dynasty as the Queen was ailing.[15] His call went unheeded. Yet the Queen's death caught some on the back leg. Henry St John (1678–1751), 1st Viscount Bolingbroke, a senior politician, wrote 'The Queen's death was a very great surprise'.[16]

Anne's death should not have come like a bolt from the blue. The middle-aged Queen had been unwell for some time and from 29 July was obviously near death. Because it was felt that she was unlikely to recover, a meeting of her Council summoned all Privy Councillors in or near the capital to attend. Orders were sent to secure London by summoning the City Trained Bands and the militia to be in readiness, and for the ships of the Royal Navy to be likewise on the alert. Messages were sent abroad; firstly to the Hanoverian Court, to ensure George of their loyalty, but also to Holland to remind them of the Barrier Treaty signed between Holland and Britain which included a clause for the security of the Protestant Succession in Britain. Army officers in Britain were told to join their units and ensure that the peace was undisturbed.[17]

Whether such measures were needed is another question, for there was no sign of revolt popular or otherwise, in favour of James Stuart. It is worth noting that the government which supported the Hanoverian Succession was made up of Tories. Since the 1970s, historians have debated over whether the Tories were Jacobites or not. Clearly some were, the number depending on political circumstances. Yet the Tories in government in 1714 were the men who had summoned George as the new monarch.[18]

It should perhaps be worth mentioning that in the past decades a situation approaching two party politics had grown up in the English/British Parliament. These parties were the Tories and the Whigs, competing for power during elections held every three years, and following the death of a sovereign. In 1710 and 1713 the Tories had been victorious at both General Elections, in part because the patronage possessed by the monarch had been put at their disposal, as well as having some popularity in the constituencies. The Tories were strong defenders of the established Church of England and sympathetic towards Episcopalianism in Scotland, they had supported the British unilateral exit from the recent War of the Spanish Succession (1702–1713); whereas the Whigs favoured a measure of toleration for Protestant dissenters and had been wholeheartedly for the war. Perhaps of greatest significance in 1714 was that the Whigs were strongly supportive of the Hanoverian Succession and the Tories were divided between those who favoured it and the minority who were more doubtful and who had corresponded with the Jacobite court.[19]

---

15   *Memoirs of the Marshal Duke of Berwick*, II (London: T. Cadell, 1779), pp. 191–192.
16   Gilbert Parke (ed.), *Letters and Correspondence of Bolingbroke*, IV (London: G. G. and J. Robinson, 1798), p. 582.
17   Rae, *History*, pp. 57–8.
18   Lenman, *Jacobite Risings*, pp. 112–4.
19   William Speck, *Stability and Strife: England, 1714–1760* (London: Edward Arnold, 1977), pp. 147–152.

Yet in 1714 positive support for the Stuarts, even among the Tories, was low, and was absent from the party leadership. It has been recently estimated that there were 51 Tory MPs who were probable Jacobite with 15 possibles; among the peers there were 19 probables and three possibles. This antipathy was mainly on religious grounds. Anti-Catholicism was a very strong force in seventeenth and eighteenth century Britain and Catholicism was often equated with the perceived tyranny then allegedly in existence in Catholic states such as Spain and France. It was no little matter. Like his father, James was an ardent and open Catholic. Should he change religion, as the formerly Protestant Henry IV of France had done a little over a century ago, and for whom Paris was worth a mass? Charles II's restoration to the British thrones in 1660 had been in part because of his willingness to be flexible and compromise for the sake of power. James was not so cynical and stated 'if he should declare himself a Protestant, very few even of his friends would believe him, and his enemies would be sure to turn against him not only as a mean and dishonourable but danger dissimulation'. Instead he stated that he would give the Church of England all the protection he could and would defend all his subjects' rights and liberties. These were similar guarantees to those his father had given on his accession in 1685, though they had proved inadequate.[20] In 1688 seven members of the English elite wrote to William to invite him to invade; in 1714 no one wrote to James with an equivalent message.

With the absence of a monarch in Britain, the Lords Justices, loyal to King George, now formed a seven-man regency until George could arrive. A monarch was expected to rule as well as reign, and though in Britain his or her powers were not absolute, they were the principal figure in government and the role of monarchy was one of real authority. On 1 August the council caused George to be proclaimed as King throughout London. There were official celebrations; bonfires were lit, flags were flown, church bells were rung, houses were lit up and artillery fired salutes. As a contemporary observer noted, 'the Jacobite Faction being struck with this surprising turn of Providence, and not yet recovered from their Consternation, the whole Solemnity passed without any Disorder'.[21]

Yet for all the concern, real or imagined, about a possible Jacobite coup, the succession progressed peacefully. Bolingbroke wrote 'There never was yet so quiet a transition from one government to another … the present is likely to be, nay as the present already is, for we are of the moment in as perfect tranquillity as ever'.[22]

News of the proclamation of George as King were sent on 1 August to Archibald Campbell, Earl of Ilay (1682–1761), Lord Justice of Scotland. They arrived at Edinburgh on midnight of 4 August. Ilay, James Graham (1682–1742), 1st Duke of Montrose and numerous others of the Scottish nobility met together on the following morning along with the foremost soldier in the country, Major General Joseph Wightman (d.1722). They then met the City Council and armed with the

---

20   Szechi, *Jacobitism and Tory politics, 1701–1714* (Edinburgh: Donald, 1984), pp. 200–203; *Calendar of the Stuart Papers*, I (London: HMSO, 1902–1920), pp. 343–4.
21   Rae, *History*, pp. 59–61.
22   Parke, *Letters*, p. 583.

proclamation for announcing the accession of the new monarch, all signed it. The City Trained Bands lined the streets. The proclamation was then read out in public and there were the same demonstrations of support as had occurred in London. Everything seemed to be passing off smoothly.[23]

James, George's rival, was not without supporters in Scotland: in 1689–1690 there had been fighting in Scotland on his behalf and in 1708 the invasion force, had it landed in Scotland, its destination, would have been supported. After all, the Royal House of Stuart had reigned in Scotland since the Middle Ages, only taking the English Crown in 1603. Yet they were no less taken aback than their English counterparts. As the Rev. Peter Rae, a Dumfries clergyman, who was in Edinburgh on 5 August, observed:

> The Jacobite Party were so confounded at this surprisingly Turn of Providence, that they durst not move a Tongue against it in publick; some of them in their private Whisperings, advised others to Silence; telling them, that the Elector of Hanover being now proclaim'd King, it was Treason to speak a word against him: Others of them affirmed to those they thought fit to be fore with, that King James (as they called the Pretender) would land, with a foreign force, in the road of Leith, in a very short time: And some of them said plainly, that this being the only proper Season for him to appear, if he did not come then, they would look on him as an Imposter, ever after that. This was some of their private Jargon, at Edinburgh, that Night.'[24]

Rae was a supporter of the government and was writing in 1718. It was in his interests and those of his masters that there was an atmosphere of conspiracy surrounding the succession. Yet in Edinburgh, as in England, the news of the new king was greeted with the ringing of bells, illuminations and 'without the least Disorder or Disturbance'. Similar celebrations occurred elsewhere in Scotland; in Stirling, Lanark, Kinross and Coupar.[25] James II's accession in 1685 had been greeted likewise in both countries, yet he was deposed less than four years later.

Even so, General Wightman, in Scotland, did not take chances. The defences of Edinburgh Castle were strengthened and troops put on the alert. Other forces in Scotland were summoned to the camp near Edinburgh and arrived there in the next two days. George was announced King in Ireland and throughout the kingdoms. There was remarkably little opposition. Even Louis XIV made assurances that he would not support James, though he was not taken at his word and Portsmouth's defences were strengthened by military reinforcements.[26]

James Stuart went to Paris on receipt of the news of the death of the half-sister he had never seen. He discussed the matter with his allies there, including his mother, Mary of Modena. Apparently he was 'fully resolved to go over afterwards into the

---

23 Rae, *History*, pp. 61–3.
24 *Ibid.*, p. 63.
25 *Daily Courant*, 3996, 14 Aug. 1714; 4003, 23 Aug. 1714.
26 Rae, *History*, pp. 65–6.

island of Great Britain to lay claim to his right'. The French were unenthusiastic and the Marquis de Torcy, Jean-Baptiste Colbert (1665–1746) the Foreign Minister, was told to persuade James to return to Lorraine, where he had lived since 1713; if he did not go of his own free will he was to compel him to depart. Yet on 29 August at Plombieres James made a formal protest at the accession of George, but to no noticeable effect.[27]

In the following weeks, as George in Hanover was making preparations to journey to his new kingdom, there were murmurings of discontent among the Jacobites in Scotland. A letter from Edinburgh noted, 'The Highlands was the only part of this country from whence we apprehend any Disturbance'.[28] Their leaders were George Gordon (1643–1716), the 1st Duke of Gordon; Alexander Gordon (1678–1728), the 5th Marquess of Huntley, and James Drummond (c.1673–1720), 4th Earl of Drummond. Apparently they began to recover from their shock and disappointment at the Hanoverian succession becoming a reality. Some were seen bearing arms and marching men towards the Highlands. Yet after various meetings they concluded that they could do nothing immediately and so returned to their homes. There was a Jacobite gathering near Inverlochy, but it was rapidly dispersed. In some places, at night-time, James was proclaimed King. It was not only in the Highlands but also in the Lowlands where Jacobite gatherings were apparently taking place. The Scottish magistracy had some of these men seized.[29]

The States General of Holland pledged their support for the new British monarch, as they were treaty-bound to do so for their former ally in the recent war. By the end of the month, having made arrangements for his departure and for the government of Hanover in his absence, George and his family travelled to The Hague en route for England. There were a number of official receptions which had to be attended to along the way.[30]

King George finally arrived in England on 17 September, on the yacht *Peregrine*, captained by Commander William Sanderson, landing at Gravesend in the evening and thence to Greenwich on the following day. On his arrival at the latter, he was accompanied by 'most of the Nobility and great Numbers of the principal Gentry, through a vast Crowd of People, who repeated their joyful Acclamations; and the night concluded with Bonfire, Illuminations and all other Demonstrations of Joy'. Over the next few days, the King now installed at St. James' Palace in London, he undertook various oaths before the Privy Council, chiefly in agreeing to uphold the Protestant religion as by law established and received numerous foreign ambassadors.[31]

George I did not see eye to eye to the Tory ministers who met him at Greenwich and London. Some were initially not apparently averse to serving him. One politician who apparently desired to support the new monarch was Bolingbroke, writing, 'I

---

27   *Memoirs of Berwick*, II, pp. 193–194; *HMC Stuart Papers*, I, p. 333.
28   *The Post Boy*, 3029, 5–7 Oct. 1714.
29   Rae, *History*, p. 77.
30   *Ibid.*, pp. 79–84.
31   Rae, *History*, pp. 96–98; *The Post Boy*, 3022, 18–21 Sept. 1714.

will serve the King, if he employs me; and if he does not, I will discharge my duty honestly and contently in the country, and in the house of peers'.[32] Yet the Tories had unilaterally withdrawn British forces in the War of the Spanish Succession and so had deserted their allies which included George's electorate of Hanover. The Whigs, the rival party to the Tories, who had been out of government from 1710 to 1714, had denounced the Tory peace policy and thus were the new King's natural allies. This was to have decisive political effects, as we shall see.

There were, therefore, a number of changes made in the key personnel of the state once the Whigs were in the King's favour. James Butler (1665-1745), the 2nd Duke of Ormonde, was dismissed from being Captain General of the Army and was replaced by John Churchill (1650–1722), the 1st Duke of Marlborough. William Bromley (1663–1732) was replaced by James Stanhope (1673–1721) as being one of the two principal Secretaries of State. The Duke of Montrose replaced Mar as Secretary of State for Scotland. Argyle became commander-in-chief in Scotland. Sir Robert Walpole (1676–1745) became Paymaster General of the Forces. There were many other changes in lesser military and political offices in the kingdom.[33]

Basically, the new king and his government removed men with alleged dubious loyalties from official positions both at the centre and in the provinces, most of whom were identified as Tories, and replaced them with men seen as being politically reliable, mostly taken from the ranks of the Tories' rivals, the Whigs. This was far from being an entire purge (some Tories were offered new positions in government, though most refused) and was commonplace on the change of monarch and/or government. In doing so, they necessarily created enemies from those now out of office and who desired it. Admittedly, some of the Tories were Jacobites and sympathetic to his royal rival, though this action pushed more of the former into the latter's camp.[34] With one man, as we shall see, this was to prove critical.

Two and a half months after the death of Anne, James made a declaration, setting out his stall as prospective monarch of Great Britain:

> James the 8th by the Grace of God of Scotland, England, France and Ireland, King, Defender of the Faith, to all our loving subjects of what degree or quality whatsoever Greeting. As we are firmly resolved never to lose an Opportunity of asserting our undoubted Title to the Imperial Throne of these Realms, and of endeavouring to get the possession of the Right which is devolved upon us by the Laws of God and Man; so We must in justice to the Sentiments of our own Hearts, declare, That nothing in the World can give us so great Satisfaction as to owe to the endeavour of our Loyal Subjects both our own and their Restoration to the happy Settlement, which can alone deliver the Church and Nation from the Calamities which they at present lye under and this future Miseries which may be of the Consequences of the present Usurpation'.[35]

---

32 Parke, *Letters*, p. 584.
33 Rae, *History*, p. 99.
34 *Speck, Stability and Strife*, pp. 174–5.
35 Taylers, *1715*, p. 311.

He then went on to elaborate on these themes after praising the reign of his half-sister. First of all he denounced the foreign nature of the Hanoverians and the fact that they had put the government into the hands of the Whigs who would use their power corruptly to the detriment of the country. He alleged that a once mighty nation would be reduced to being a province of a small German state. He noted that the people were opening their eyes to their plight and that he was ready to come to Britain to restore it 'to its ancient free and independent state'. He referred to his ancestors being subjected to terrible abuses. Scotland would have its parliament restored, he promised. He looked forward to a restoration and urged all officials to publish the said declaration or incur his displeasure once he was King.[36] He also appealed to the newly politically dispossessed and to the xenophobic instincts of others in Britain.

Yet for all this, the practical effect of his manifesto was very limited. In Britain, the coronation of his rival took place on 20 October at Westminster Abbey. Lady Mary Cowper (1685–1724), wife of the new Lord Chancellor, who was herself a lady-in-waiting to the new Princess of Wales, wrote, 'One may easily conclude this was not a Day of real joy to the Jacobites. However, they were all there, looking as cheerful as they could, but very peevish'.[37] Many towns and cities throughout the realm sent addresses, assuring the King of their loyalty. There were officially sponsored celebrations in public. Scottish towns which celebrated included Dundee, Aberdeen, Kelso and Stirling. But all was not calm. There were a number of disturbances throughout many towns in the south of England; perhaps over 20. Coronation celebrations were under attack; bonfires were pulled down, houses which were lit up had their windows broken. Crowds gathered together with shouts such as those heard in Reading: 'Down with the Roundheads, God bless Dr Sacheverell, [a Jacobite preacher in Anne's reign] Sacheverell for ever, and down with the Whigs, no Hanover, no Cadogan; but Calvert and Clarges, no King William, nor Traytor; Sacheverell for ever; who dares disown the Pretender'. King George's supporters were attacked as well as being verbally abused. John McAllen, an Excise officer in Crieff, and a supporter of George, had his house broken into at night on 30 November and was seriously beaten up.[38]

Even though George had been crowned King, James did not give up his hopes. On 28 November, Berwick noted that:

> The King [i.e. James Stuart] is firmly resolved to goe himself in person to them as soon as he possibly can, and to carry me along with him … a little time must be allowed for getting together what is necessary, especially for raising of money, and for taking measures with friends in England, without which little good can be expected.

Yet his allies were to be kept initially in the dark, 'that for the better keeping the secret, the King's friends must to expect to know the precise time of his embarking'.[39]

---

36   *Ibid.*, pp. 312–5.
37   Spencer Cowper (ed.), *Diary of Lady Cowper* (London: John Murray, 1865), p. 5.
38   Rae, *History*, pp. 108–109, 115; *Daily Courant*, 4074, 13 Nov. 1714.
39   *HMC Stuart Papers*, I, pp. 336–7.

The political tempo remained high, for Parliament was dissolved on 5 January 1715, as it had to be on the death of a monarch, and a General Election called. In Scotland, some Parliamentary candidates called for a dissolution of the Union. One part of the war of words was the publication of two pamphlets; the *English Advice to the Freeholders of Great Britain*, a Jacobite piece which was soon denounced as libel, and the *British Advice to the Freeholders of Great Britain* which aimed to counter it. During the general election campaign, there was a great deal of animus shown towards the King personally, spread partly by some of the Anglican clergy. Many of the latter alleged that the Church of England was in danger from a King who wished to maintain the toleration of Protestant Dissenters and thus retain the official diversity of Protestant religious denominations.[40]

It was not only the clergy who attempted to sway the electorate. At Inverness, McKenzie of Preston Hall and Alastair Macdonell (d.1724), the Laird of Glengarry, came with a strong body of Highlanders to persuade them to vote for him rather than the lawyer, Duncan Forbes of Culloden (1685–1747), who supported the new government.[41]

Whigs were also concerned about a possible Jacobite insurrection in Scotland. Mungo Graeme wrote to Colonel Cornelius Kennedy (1674–1739) in London on 15 February that he believed that the Jacobites would take to the field prior to James' arrival as in 1708 they had not risen as promised, so that he would 'not stir now till they are out. This they are to do very soon, they say'.[42] Two weeks later, Graeme identified Mar who 'designs to set himself at the head of a party'.[43] This was not a view universally held and certainly not by anyone in a position of authority. It was, however, a prophetic remark, as we shall see.

Yet there was more alarming news in Scotland. Argyle, as commander in chief there, was in Edinburgh on 24 February. He heard that a ship carrying ammunition and arms had landed on the Isle of Skye. He was told by another source that the Jacobites were distributing money, arms and ammunition among their followers and that they daily expected James to come to Scotland to lead them. It was also said that James was to arrive with a French army and would be joined by 12,000 Highlanders and as many men again from England and Ireland. Against such a potential onslaught there were limited means of dealing with it, but Argyle met with Montrose and John Ker (*c*.1680–1741), Duke of Roxburghe, to discuss how best to use the few troops they had in Scotland. They decided to concentrate them. Forfar's infantry regiment was reviewed at Edinburgh. The detachments of dragoons at Jedburgh, Kelso and elsewhere were summoned to be encamped at Leith.[44]

More dangerous activity was occurring in the northern kingdom; activity that was potentially far more perilous for the new king and his allies. In Dumfriesshire, a Jacobite

---

40 Rae, *History*, pp. 115–6, 118.
41 *Ibid.*, p .122.
42 National Records of Scotland, GD3/24/1.
43 *Ibid.*, 5
44 Rae, *History*, p. 123.

peer and his allies were buying up horses, horse equipment and arms, yet nothing could be done because the justices of the peace in that county were sympathetic to his aims. Boxes of arms were also ordered, but the provost of Glasgow and the governor of Fort William were able to seize three of these.[45]

The Jacobites abroad had not given up hope. They had managed to amass 10,000 guns and 100,000 crowns in France. Father Callagahan, a Dominican, desired James go to England. James agreed and decided to travel to Le Havre and a vessel was prepared there.[46] Up to now little notice had been taken officially of James, save that on 15 September 1714, a reward of £100,000 had been put out for his arrest if he came to Britain.[47]

It is possible, though, that there was a more concrete danger to George I. The King and Argyle received news on 7 March of a deep laid conspiracy emanating from Scotland. This report stated that, though there had been little correspondence if any between James and his Scottish supporters before Anne's death, there had been a meeting at Castle Kilchurn between Cameron of Lochiel, the 4th Viscount Strathallan, William Drummond (1690–1746), the 1st Earl of Breadalbane, John Campbell (1636–1717), and Glendaroule. They sent William Mackintosh of Borlum the Younger (c.1657–1743) and Allan Cameron to see James at Bar le Duc to invite him to Britain. James accepted and promised cash. Mackintosh returned with £1,400 to buy targes (shields).[48]

The report continued, alleging that James and Berwick promised to be in Scotland in March or April 1715. They wanted the Jacobite clans to be formed into battalions of 500 men each to meet them on arrival. There were also those in London who were not thought to be Jacobite but in reality were. Sir John Forster arrived in the Highlands from Bar le Duc with £2,500 to be lodged at Drummond Castle. He was told that 45 Jacobite battalions would be raised by the Highlanders, John Murray (1660-1724), 1st Duke of Atholl – who was seen in 1714 by James as being the man in Scotland to lead the Jacobite restoration attempt – promising six, William Mackenzie (d.1740) 5th Earl of Seaforth, and Huntley four each. There was division over who should command, with James wanting Atholl under Berwick and the Scots wanting Drummond as commander-in-chief. Arms from France to the tune of 5,000 were sent for distribution but without much ammunition. Berwick allegedly told Mackintosh that he had permission from Louis XIV to join James in a French-backed expedition. How useful a general accustomed to leading regular troops would have been in leading irregulars is another question and one that must be forever unanswerable. Finally Drummond would provide a 24-gun frigate to carry James to Scotland.[49]

Whether such a story owed anything to reality is unclear. John Hay (1695–1762), 4th Marquess of Tweeddale contradicted it and so it was not given any further

---

45   *Ibid.*, pp. 138–9.
46   Berwick, *Memoirs*, p. 205.
47   Taylers, *1715*, p. 14.
48   National Library of Scotland, MS 489, f. 520.
49   *Ibid.*

credence. A report from Bar le Duc in May was that James would not stir unless war broke out between France and Britain.[50] Some credence is given to part of this in that another source stated that an agent from the Jacobite court attended a meeting at Inverness where Mackintosh was present, and that Lochiel and Glengarry had been attending secret meetings.[51]

Meanwhile, Parliament met on 17 March after the general election, in which a previous Tory majority had been converted into one favouring the new government. This was in part because unlike in the two previous elections, the influence of the court was behind the Whigs, but also because some of the electorate identified the Tories with the Jacobites and thus the Catholics.[52] The new Commons majority enabled the Whigs to investigate the activities of their enemies, who had brought about the Treaty of Utrecht in 1713, bringing the War of the Spanish Succession to an end, which had been denounced by the Whigs. The leading Tories – Bolingbroke, Robert Harley (1661–1724), the Earl of Oxford, and Ormonde – could therefore expect action to be taken against them for their role in this. Bolingbroke disguised himself as a servant and fled to France on 25 March, leaving behind a letter in which he explained that he feared judicial murder. He was later impeached for treason in his absence. Oxford was imprisoned in the Tower, but Ormonde fled the country on 21 July (later Berwick stated that Ormonde promised to raise a rebellion in England but failed to do so, though it is hard to see how he could have been successful without foreign support which Ormonde thought was critical).[53] Both he and Bolingbroke were soon reunited in Paris; Bolingbroke becoming James' Secretary of State.[54] Although Ormonde had briefly been Captain General from 1712–1714 he was described by a fellow Jacobite thus: 'a very brave officer, tho' he never had that of a very able one … irresolute and timorous … apt to lose good opportunities'.[55]

In their absence, the Jacobites' problem was that there was no one in Britain of sufficient standing to lead a rising against George I. One possible figurehead was the newly restored Captain General, Marlborough, who had been a devoted servant of James' father until 1688, when he had thrown in his lot with William of Orange, but despite that was in occasional contact with the Jacobite court. As head of the British army he would be a valuable acquisition and perhaps might play a similar role in 1715 as General Monk had in 1660 to effect a Stuart restoration. Yet Berwick was not hopeful (writing of him, 'I do not much reckon upon') and nor were others, believing his love of money and power would not leave him to desert George; James wrote, 'I hope little from him', though Marlborough did contribute £2,000 to the Jacobite war chest that summer, possibly as a form of political insurance if the Jacobite cause prevailed.[56]

50 NRS, GD38/2/2/37.
51 *Ibid.*, GD158/1269/1.
52 Speck, *Stability and Strife*, pp. 176–8.
53 Berwick, *Memoirs*, pp. 207–8, 197.
54 Rae, *History*, pp. 131–2, 146, 165.
55 James Keith, *A Fragment of a Memoir of Field Marshal James Keith 1714–1734* (Edinburgh: Spalding Club, 1843), p. 3.
56 *HMC Stuart Papers*, 1, pp. 338, 394–5, 407.

Anti-government, though not necessarily pro-Jacobite, sentiment certainly existed throughout England as well as in Scotland. It came out into the open and led others to believe that there was strong Jacobite support in England. During the spring of 1715 there were a number of riots throughout England; far more than there had been on Coronation Day in 1714. There was a riot in London on 23 April, the anniversary of Queen Anne's coronation. This seems to have been an isolated incident because the major spate of riots occurred on 28 and 29 May and 10 June. Each date was pregnant with political significance. The first was the birthday of King George, the second was the anniversary of the Stuart restoration of 1660 and the third was the birthday of James Stuart. These outbreaks of physical and verbal violence occurred in many towns and cities in England. There was also a rash of attacks on Dissenting chapels in June, especially in the Midlands and Lancashire, as well as in the south, for the Dissenters were thought to be in favour of the Hanoverian Succession and the new government as they guaranteed their religious rights. There were disturbances in Leeds, Manchester and Oxford to name but three of the affected towns.[57]

These attacks included shouting Jacobite and anti-government slogans, breaking the windows of their enemies and drinking toasts to the Jacobite leaders. James was often proclaimed as King. Whigs found themselves physically attacked, although no one was killed. Some Whigs believed that these riots had been part of a carefully laid and organised conspiracy by Jacobite leaders in Britain and elsewhere, with the aim of diverting troops. There is little evidence for such planning, however, though a letter from Bolingbroke referred to the need to 'keep up the spirit of the People, and to encourage the Riots and Tumults'. By the end of June these disorders were over, sometimes because, as in the case of Manchester, troops had been sent to maintain order and to arrest any of the culprits if they could be found. The rioting also led to the passing of the Riot Act, enabling justices of the peace to disperse riots. These disturbances not universal, however, for there were many towns and cities in which there were no disturbances whatsoever, such as Preston and Lancaster, and most of those in Yorkshire. There were none in Cumberland, Westmorland and Durham.[58]

The significance of these outbursts of popular hostility towards George I and his government have been debated by historians. Nicholas Rogers has concluded that it was a way of demonstrating social and political discontent among Tories and that 'Jacobitism was a familiar idiom of defiance', though not denying that some was genuine.[59] Paul Monod differs, in viewing these widespread riots as being supportive of the Church of England and that George I was not seen as a monarch who would uphold it, as his predecessor Anne had. As Head of the Church this was one of his key roles and if he would not do so, perhaps another, namely James, would.[60] However,

---

57   Rae, *History*, pp. 135, 140–1, 151.
58   *Ibid.* and pp. 149, 151.
59   Nicholas Rogers, 'Riot and Popular Jacobitism' in Cruickshanks, *Ideology and Conspiracy*, pp. 84, 81.
60   Paul Monod, *Jacobitism and the English People, 1688–1788* (Cambridge: Cambridge University Press, 1989), pp. 173–194.

James II had sworn to defend the Church of England and then, with his promotion of Catholicism, appeared to undermine it.

In Edinburgh Bailie Duncan recorded that George's birthday was celebrated in public, and 'everie bodie here seems joyfull and are hearty on having the occasione to solemnise this day'.[61] Yet, there were also similar outbreaks of Jacobitism in Scotland; albeit on a smaller scale, but then with so much support for James in Scotland anyway, there was less need to parade it. In Dundee on 27 May the magistrates decreed that the King's birthday not be celebrated on 28 May, but those loyal to him celebrated it outside their enemies' jurisdiction. Five of the Dundee magistrates had cursed the King on 20 January and they also publickly drank James' health on his birthday.[62]

On James' birthday, the Edinburgh City Guard were on the alert for any Jacobite activity there. All they could discover was 'some of the meanest sort of people were found walking up and down the streets crying hoasas' and 'a highland man being found … walking upon the streets with a drawn sword in his hand Crying he was for King James'.[63]

These riots may have encouraged Jacobites at home and abroad that their cause had mass popularity in Britain. Daniel Dearing wrote on 9 August, 'The Tories by their rebellious riots and their open and disrespects to the King had encouraged the Pretender to think of invading us'.[64] Tories hoped that they would return to power if James was crowned. Jacobites in Scotland were also encouraged; 'the mobs and broiles in England had rowzed the Scots Tories'.[65] Yet there is all the world of difference between rioting and the more risky pastime of rebellion, though the county which supported the Jacobite cause in England with the largest number of men was Lancashire, which had seen much Jacobite rioting earlier in the year; though Northumberland which had seen none provided the second highest number of recruits.

Rioting in England and conspiracies in Scotland were not in themselves sufficient. By the summer of 1715, the leading English Jacobites, Bolingbroke and Ormonde, had fled. Marlborough was not deemed reliable. There was no obvious leader in Scotland or England. Bolingbroke would not go to Britain and James was not ready. Popular history often states that 'the hour provides the man'. In this case it was the Earl of Mar. He is perhaps the most single important actor in the forthcoming drama and without him it is unlikely that there would have been a rising at this time. As Bruce Lenman has observed, 'In one sense the 1715 rebellion in Scotland was the result of a private decision taken by one man because of his personal circumstances. The man was John Erskine, the Earl of Mar'.[66]

61   William Kirk Dickson (ed.), 'Warrender Letters: Correspondence of Sir George Warrender, Bt., Lord Provost of Edinburgh, and Member of Parliament for the City, with Relative Papers, 1715' (Edinburgh: Scottish Historical Society, 1935), p. 35.
62   Rae, *History*, p. 141.
63   Dickson, 'Warrender Letters', p. 39.
64   British Library Additional Manuscripts 47028, f. 56r.
65   Scott, *Memoirs*, p. 66.
66   Lenman, *Jacobite Risings*, p. 126.

Mar's career prior to 1714 can be briefly summarised. He succeeded to his title on his father's death in 1689 and took his seat in the Scottish Parliament in 1696, becoming Privy Councillor in 1697, Keeper of Stirling Castle in 1699 and Keeper of the Thistle in 1706. He became a commissioner of the Union in that year in order to push through the Act of Union to unite Scotland with England. He was a Scottish representative peer in the House of Lords from 1707. His politics were clearly, in these years, anti-Jacobite. He became Secretary of State for Scotland from 1713–1714 as a Tory in Anne's last government. He was also a man of taste and culture, with a fine house and estate at Alloa, which he had cultivated and had extensive gardens laid out, though with an annual income of apparently £1,500, without lucrative government employment, lacked the means to support such a lifestyle. Although his first wife had died young, in 1714 he remarried: the lady was Frances Pierrepoint, from a Whig family. Yet like many in politics, he kept his options open by corresponding with the Stuart exiles, first tentatively in 1710, but then more so following the Hanoverian accession.[67]

Mar was not, as James was, a man of principle. On hearing of Anne's death he wrote 'I can make as good terms with the other side for myself as any of them, and I will not be made the fool of the play'.[68] Indeed, on the arrival of George I, one of the many of those congratulating him was Mar, who, along with many other nobility and gentry, had already signed his name on a document attesting to the validity of the Hanoverian succession. He also wrote a letter on 30 August and parts of it read as follows:

I beg leave by this to kiss your Majesty's Hand, and congratulate your Majesty's Happy Accession to the Throne … And since your Majesty's happy Accession to the Crown, I hope you will find that I have not been wanting in my Duty, in being instrumental in keeping Things quiet and peaceable in the Country to which I belong, and have some interest in. Your Majesty shall ever find me as faithful and dutiful a Subject and Servant, as ever any of my Family have been to the Crown … may your Majesty's Reign be long and prosperous.

He stressed his former loyalty to Anne and his role in bringing about the controversial Union of England and Scotland in 1707 and hoped that the new King would not listen to any of the 'misrepresentations' of his enemies.[69]

Yet Mar later stated that the above was not entirely sincere. Apparently he had been a Jacobite for some years, or so he later claimed:

When I found that we (in Scotland) [meaning the Scots] continued to be ill treated under the Union, I became as much for having it broke as ever I had been in earnest for having it made … I found the breaking of it impossible without an entire revolution by restoring our Natural King to who's family I had always had a hearts liking. This made

67   *Oxford Dictionary of National Biography*, 18 (Oxford: 2004), pp. 552–7.
68   *Report of the Manuscripts of the Earl of Mar and Kellie preserved in Alloa House* (London: HMSO, 1904), p. 505.
69   Rae, *History*, pp. 85–6.

me enter into a correspondence with the King about the same time of the change of the ministry, the last years of Queen Anne'.[70] Therefore, 'On the Queen's death, I entered into measures with those of England who favoured the Jacobite interest, and also some in Scotland.[71]

Mar was one of a number of disappointed politicians, having lost the office of Secretary of State for Scotland which he had held in the previous reign. Legitimate means of political advancement having failed him, he turned to Jacobitism as a necessary creed and tool. Although he told his son in the years after 1715 that Scottish independence was his main goal, he also admitted pecuniary motives, too. Mar had never received his £6,000 salary owed to him as Secretary of State for Scotland under Anne and with the change of ministry on her death he was unlikely to receive it any time soon.[72]

Mar was interested in power and the wealth that went with it. In order to regain these he needed there to be a new monarch who would be grateful to Mar for his services and would suitably reward him. George I and the new Whig government seemed strongly entrenched in power and only a major political upheaval would remove them. Mar was determined to be the catalyst to upset the new status quo and he had a discontented constituency who would support him for the cause he now represented. Resort to arms was not his first recourse, needless to say; he had attempted to mobilise his fellow Scottish peers in 1714–1715 in an attempt to dissolve the union, but in this had been unsuccessful.[73]

It should be noted that there were many who had a strong interest, politically and religiously in upholding the new status quo. In Scotland Clan Campbell and the Presbyterians were staunch enemies of any attempt to restore the Stuarts. By espousing the claim of James Stuart, the forces of anti-Catholicism were unleashed and as noted in the previous century, these should not be underestimated, both in England and Scotland. Furthermore, all those who had been given positions of power and profit by the new dynasty and government were unwilling to lose them without a fight. Mar had unleashed forces both for and against his cause. It was a gamble played for the highest of stakes.

---

70 Tayler, *1715*, pp. 197–8.
71 Mrs Grant (ed.), 'Mrs Warriston's Diary; Mar's Legacies to his son, 1639–1746', Scottish Historical Society, 26 (Edinburgh: T. and A. Constable, 1896), p. 163.
72 Grant, 'Mar's Legacies', p. 176.
73 Szechi, *1715*, pp. 41–42.

2

Countdown to the Rising, July–August 1715

It had been a politically tense summer following the end of the rioting in England and rumours of conspiracy in Scotland. For the government, there was variable intelligence from France. That an invasion was being planned, though, was almost common knowledge. Bolingbroke told James:

> I soon found a general expectation gone abroad that your Majesty was to undertake somewhat immediately; and I was not a little concerned to hear, in two or three places, and among women over their tea, that arms were provided and ships got ready … I beg your Majesty to depend upon, that the factor of Lawrence [George I] knew of the little armament, and sent advices of it home.[1]

Mar was in London in the summer of 1715; unlike Bolingbroke and Ormonde he does not seem to have come under the government's radar as a possible Jacobite plotter, possibly because they had been politically senior to him and perhaps because he was of a dissembling nature. It is not known exactly what he did at this time nor who he conspired with; understandably enough: conspirators do not keep incriminating diaries nor write letters. Apparently he was in the receipt of money from abroad, allegedly to the tune of £100,000, and a commission from James himself, appointing him as lieutenant general of the Jacobite forces (the latter was untrue). According to the Rev. Robert Patten, 'he concerted Measures with the Jacobites and Papists to form a Rebellion and by force of Arms to make way for the Pretender, as well as to bring him in'.[2] Apparently the English Jacobites argued that Mar should go to Scotland and raise the Scottish, and then they would assist him and gave him £7,000.[3]

Mar had given the restoration attempt some thought when in London and contacted the Stuart court with his thoughts on it. On 16 July 1715, he wrote a memorandum and it is worth quoting at length:

---

1   Dickson, 'Warrender Letters', p. 69n.
2   Robert Patten, *History of the Rebellion* (London: J. Baker and T. Warner, 1745), p. 128; Rae, *History*, p. 187.
3   Keith, *Fragment*, p. 9.

There is no hope of succeeding in it without the assistance of a regular force, or without a general rising of the people, in all parts of England, immediately upon the King's landing, and that the latter of these depends very much on the former. For though the generality of the people are extremely averse to the Court and Ministry, (whom they hate and despise) and well inclined to the restoration; yet it is not to be expected that they should declare themselves all at once, unless they see the King attended with such a force as will give some reputation to his undertaking, and encourage the country to come in to him.

Without such a support even the well affected in these parts of the kingdom, which are distant from the places where the King shall land, will not venture to make any attempt in his favour, the lieutenancy and shrievalty of the several counties being now lodged in confiding hands, will be a good check on the inclinations of the people everywhere, these, who are only enemies to the set of men now in power and not thoroughly engaged for the King (which is the case of many in the Tory Party) will either stand and gaze, and expect the event, or join with the present government, as thinking that way out of danger, whichever side prevails.[4]

In order to tap this latent support, James would need to land in Britain with about 3,000–4,000 regular troops, as Ormonde also acknowledged. The difficulty was that France would not supply them, despite lobbying by Ormonde and Berwick. According to the latter, this was because the French lacked the money, due to declining trade and population, caused by the recent War of the Spanish Succession. France, as with other European states, needed peace, not war. Therefore, Berwick thought that a restoration attempt would be doomed, 'without the assistance of 4,000 men at least, and a quantity of arms, and of a considerable sum of money, it would be rash and even impossible to commence an Insurrection'. An unarmed mob or even a semi-disciplined and variously armed force as Monmouth's rebels had been in 1685 risked defeat by regular troops.[5] As in 1688, a nucleus of regular troops adding to the forces of internal discord, though, could be decisive in bringing about a new regime at Westminster.

The assistance of regular troops would augment the Jacobite military position greatly. As shall be noted in chapter seven, the Jacobite army was weak in artillery, cavalry and specialist troops crucial for siege warfare. Regular troops could provide this deficiency. Lacking such, money was a good second best for that would enable the Jacobite army to purchase military equipment and help with paying and equipping the troops.

Because of the perceived necessity for regular troops from abroad, throughout the year the Stuart court discussed their need of allies among the Continental powers. Some historians, though, have discounted foreign support.[6] Others stress the importance of the international aspect of Jacobitism. Both Smith and Szechi discuss the diplomatic efforts made in France, Spain and Sweden on James' behalf. These countries were

---

4   *HMC Stuart Papers*, I, p. 520.
5   Berwick, *Memoirs*, pp. 197, 200, 202.
6   Reid, *Sheriffmuir*, p. 10.

antagonistic towards George I's Britain, but Jacobite representatives did not enjoy plain sailing. Yet, though they eventually did succeed in securing monetary aid, these supplies were to be too slow in arriving.[7]

There were three possibilities canvassed: France, Spain and Sweden. Mar stated, 'it was necessary that the King should act in concert with some ffroreigne power or Prince, by whose assistance he might be thus more easily restored. France was the power most proper for this'.[8] This was so because until 1713 she had given James shelter, and was Catholic as well as being Britain's principal foe in the late war. In 1708 French troops had sailed in French ships to restore James.

Bolingbroke talked to de Torcy about French support and by 18 August James believed that ships and arms would be provided. Apparently Louis would assist 'in every thing that did not fly openly in the face of the Treaty of Utrecht' and suggested that Irish troops in French pay, the 'Wild Geese', if not in formed units, could support the Jacobite war effort. James had hopes for these men too, and sent a circular letter to their officers to encourage them. Yet Bolingbroke believed French support depended on Louis XIV, but he was elderly and in poor health; as the former wrote, 'as long as that is precarious no dependence can be had on anything from him'.[9]

French help would, at best, be circumspect, however. A request for £200,000 was turned down. Louis 'pleaded poverty' and Mary of Modena, James' mother, wrote that he was 'neither in a condition nor a disposition of giving any' yet nor would he flatly refuse all overtures.[10]

There was sympathy from the French court but only limited aid would be forthcoming as Bolingbroke noted that there was:

> No want of good inclination either in His Most Christian Majesty or in those who have the honour to serve him. But such are the present circumstances of affairs here … that the utmost help which the King can expect from hence is a supply of 10,000 arms, which allied to those already provided will make 20,000 and vessels to transport them … No troops, no money, no officers, no appearance which may not be disavowed on the part of France.[11]

On 21 August 1715 (Old Style) Louis XIV, ruler of France for over half a century, finally died. James Keith (1696–1758), a junior Jacobite officer, wrote that this 'mightily discouraged many of our party'.[12] Bolingbroke agreed: 'If the French King had lived we should have obtained some assistance directly, much more indirectly and yet many

7   Lawrence Bartlam Smith, 'Spain and the Jacobites, 1715–1716' in Cruickshanks, *Ideology and Conspiracy*, pp. 159–171; Szechi, 'Towards an Analytical Model', pp. 295–300.
8   Grant, 'Mar's Legacies', p. 167.
9   *HMC Stuart Papers*, I, pp. 381, 387, 395.
10   *Ibid.*, pp. 368, 385; Keith, *Fragment*, p. 8
11   *HMC Stuart Papers*, I, p. 529.
12   Keith, *Fragment*, p. 13.

facilities by contrivance … But the case is altered'.[13] John Percivall agreed, writing that the death of the Sun King was 'a more than ordinary Providence has ordered it so' and that the French regent would find it 'worth his while to cultivate friendship with us'.[14] James Stewart did not entirely agree, writing, 'The news of ye French King's death gives a great damp to ye Jacobites here', but he thought that they would appear in arms anyway and believed that this would occur even if James did not appear in person. He rightly believed that Mar's presence in the Highlands would lead to a rising of the Jacobite clans.[15]

On Louis' death, his five-year-old great-grandson Louis XV (1710–1774) became king with his uncle Phillipe (1674–1723), duc d'Orleans, as regent. The latter was not enthusiastic for an aggressive foreign policy and realised France needed peace. This was because the government was close to bankruptcy due to debts accumulated in the War of the Spanish Succession. In 1715 France's royal debt stood at between 1.8 to 2.3 billion livres, between 35 and 40 times the state's annual revenue. The French financial system was unable to handle long term debt which could not be paid off. With a royal minority there was apprehension of internal disorder and so Orleans needed peace in order to address these pressing domestic concerns. Berwick wrote, 'France, however well intentioned she might be, was not in a condition to risk a war to support the interests of the young Pretender' (the term 'Pretender' was the hostile name given by his enemies to James; historians often refer to James as the Old Pretender in contrast to his eldest son, Charles, the Young Pretender. It is worth remembering that in 1715 James was a young man). The Jacobites could not, therefore, rely on any explicit French aid; unofficial support, however, might be another matter as we will see and as Mar noted, Orleans 'received it [the Jacobites' proposal] very graciously'.[16]

The Jacobites still expected seaborne aid, even though Louis XIV was dead. A few days after the King's death, James Murray arrived in Scotland. He had been with James Stuart and brought with him from France seemingly important news: a verbal assurance of a strong force from France of both arms and men. Rae later observed, 'if the Pretender's affairs abroad had continued in the same flourishing Condition as when Mr Murray left the Court of St. Germain's, 'tis probable the Rebels here might quickly have seen the Performance of these Assurances'.[17] Mar was convinced that Orleans 'would push that affair with more vigour than the old King'.[18] Likewise Berwick reported a government source claiming, 'the Duke of Orleans having refused to hinder the Pretender'.[19]

---

13   Lord Mahon, *History of England from the Peace of Utrecht to the Peace of Versailles*, I, Appendix, p. xxi (London: John Murray, 1858).

14   British Library Add. MSS. 42078, f. 63r.

15   The National Archives, SP54/7/71B.

16   Guy Rowlands, *The Financial Decline of a Great Power* (Oxford: Oxford University, 2001), p. 236; Parke, *Memoirs*, p. 193; *HMC Stuart Papers*, I, p. 419; Grant, 'Mar's Legacies', p. 167.

17   Rae, *History*, p. 221.

18   Scott, *Memoirs*, p. 32.

19   *HMC Stuart Papers*, I p. 419.

The Jacobites on the Continent had indeed been both active and lavish, with funds from various sources: including minor Catholic princes, the papacy and British supporters, amounting to about £64,000. Their efforts were to be disappointed. Twelve large warships and a number of frigates were being loaded with a significant amount of military stores; namely 12,000 muskets with bayonets and cartouches, 2,000 carbines, 2,000 small muskets, 6,000 cartouches and bayonets for those who already had guns, 18,000 swords, 2,000 halberds and half pikes, 12 brass cannon with carriages, 16 large brass cannon, 40 iron cannon, with all necessary accoutrements, 4,000 barrels of gunpowder and 300 tonnes of lead, iron ball and shells. There were 1,861 volunteer officers and soldiers and 120 artillerymen from the French Army. These were assembled at Havre de Grace, St. Malo and Dieppe.[20]

Naturally, these preparations could not go unnoticed. John Dalrymple (1673–1747), the Earl of Stair, George I's representative at Versailles, told his master about these and he also spoke to Orleans. He reminded the latter that for him to allow such preparations to take place on French soil ran contrary to the provisions of the Treaty of Utrecht. Therefore, to breach the recently signed treaty could be construed as an act of war against Britain. British warships under Admiral Sir George Byng (1663–1733) sailed off the northern French coast, to back up Stair's words. Orleans claimed he had no knowledge of such warlike activities and promised that he would have them cease, which he did. France was greatly in debt and so could not afford the monetary price of further conflict, however much her rulers might have liked to see their recent foe discomfited by prolonged rebellion or even civil war. The Intendants of Marine Affairs were sent to inspect the said ships and to seize their contents.[21]

The Jacobite cause in France was hindered in other ways, too. Berwick wrote, 'Stair never failed paying his court assiduously … he pressed the regent strongly to prevent the Pretender from passing through France'. Orleans claimed he was not pursuing a formal alliance with France's recent enemies, Britain and Holland, and Stair told him that if this were so, then he must take steps against James. The regent did not want open war and so could not turn the blind eye that he had done previously.[22]

Berwick was more optimistic over aid from Charles XII of Sweden (1680–1718), 'whose interests seemed entirely opposite to those of King George', for the two (George as Elector of Hanover) were in competition for possession of the north German ports of Bremen and Verden.[23] Approaches had been made to Sweden in March 1715, offering financial aid. And, unlike Louis, Charles was a Protestant and so more acceptable to the majority of the British. Berwick wrote 'We have good reason to hope this gentleman will be glad of the proposal'. At the end of June he had spoken to a Swedish agent and he 'makes no doubt but his master will put it into execution immediately by sending an army straight to England' and a letter was sent to the King.[24] Yet Charles XII was not

---

20   Rae, *History*, pp. 221–2; Lawrence Bartlam Smith, *Spain and Britain, 1715–1719: The Jacobite Issue* (New York/London: Garland, 1987), pp. 23–4.
21   *Ibid.*, p. 222.
22   Berwick, *Memoirs*, pp. 227–8; TNA, SP84/253, ff. 43v, 44v, 140r.
23   Berwick, *Memoirs*, p. 210.
24   *HMC Stuart Papers*, I, pp. 372–4.

quick to respond to such overtures, and in any case, was already at war with Denmark and Russia.[25] In late August, though, there was discussion of 12 battalions of Swedish troops and 50,000 crowns being provided from Sweden.[26]

When Charles XII replied at long last, his answer was 'both reasonable and unanswerable'. It was negative. This could have been over differences in religion: the Protestant Sweden not been in favour of assisting a Catholic restoration of one of Europe's foremost Protestant powers. According to Berwick, 'The King of Sweden missed a glorious opportunity'. Yet Sweden had so many enemies that adding to them was not a wise move. James claimed he never expected much help from this source anyway. James still believed, though, that Bolingbroke could 'do the most good in France'. Yet he was not optimistic, 'I must confess my affairs have a very melancholy prospect ... all hope of the best foreign help are extinguished'.[27]

There was also negotiation with Spain, now ruled by Louis XIV's grandson, Philip V (1683–1746), whose accession had been opposed by Britain and her allies up to 1713. Furthermore, there were differences of opinion between Britain and Spain over trading agreements and Spain's former possessions in Italy; a Stuart on the British throne would alter such positions to Spain's liking. In March the Jacobite Sir John Forrester was sent to Spain. Ormonde asked for a loan of a million livres and this was agreed to. Although its despatch was tardy, this raised Jacobite morale: 'This encouragement which the Jacobites received abroad gave great life to their party at home'.[28] In August 1715 Louis had asked his grandson to give the Jacobites 400,000 crowns and the Spanish ambassador promised a total of twice that being provided by the Spanish treasury.[29] This decision was unknown to James for another four months, however.[30]

Bolingbroke was most despondent about support from these three countries, writing on 20 September:

> The whole coast from Jutland to Spain is against us ... The troops we hoped for from Sweden are refused us, and the bills which were given for their embarkation are returned. The money we expected from Spain, is in my opinion, still in the clouds and was it actually in our hands we should be at a loss to get it on board. Instead of having the arms which were promised us by the late King it is become doubtful whether we shall have it in our power to carry off those which we have of our own.[31]

None of these three states wanted to be seen as openly backing the Jacobite cause. They did not want to be in open conflict with Britain. On the other hand, they would not object to a more friendly (and in the case of Spain and France, Catholic) ruler on the throne of Britain who would be duty-bound to support their interests. They had to

---

25   *Ibid.*, pp. 370, 387.
26   *Ibid.*, p. 413.
27   *HMC Stuart Papers*, I, pp. 425, 430, 433; Smith, *Spain and Britain*, pp. 25–6.
28   Keith, *Fragment*, p. 8.
29   *HMC Stuart Papers*, I, p. 413.
30   Smith, *Spain and Britain*, p. 63.
31   Mahon, *History*, I, Appendix, p. xxiii.

walk the tightrope between outright support and surreptitious aid. This had potential benefits for the Jacobites but also meant that these allies were of limited value as their prime interests were their own and so they wanted to back the winner in the Hanover versus Stuart conflict.

James' presence in Britain was clearly crucial in order to garner support. Men needed to know the man they were fighting for and to see and hear him and know that he was, to an extent, sharing their dangers. He was certainly eager for the venture, writing on 23 August, 'I think it is more than ever Now or Never!'[32] The question was where he should land. Northumberland was suggested as one possible location, for the many Catholic nobility and gentry there should be sympathetic. The difficulty with arriving in England was that 'The whole country of England is ill provided with arms and particularly those parts which are best affected'. James would need about 10,000 arms and artillery with him and additional arms in those locations where there was thought to be sympathisers to his cause; Cornwall, Devon, Lancashire and Wales. Much money would also be needed both before his arrival and on it. A force of 500 army officers and their servants should also come with James, too.[33]

The other advantage of landing in Northumberland, especially near to Berwick-upon-Tweed, was because of 'his friends in Scotland', for if they had advance notice of his arriving, 'they may march with all expedition towards him'. The best places for James to arrive in Scotland were thought to be in Angus or Mearns, or to the south of Aberdeen, 'these counties being well affected and near the Highlands'. As to James' Scottish supporters:

> About 8,000 Highlanders well armed in about a month's time may be had from Scotland, but they must be regularly paid … Few more Foot can be expected soon from Scotland, because they must be raised and modelled as new troops are. Though therefore they may be of use in Scotland towards keeping that part of the country in the King's interest, yet they will be of little service upon so sudden an occasion in England.[34]

Mar wanted Berwick to arrive in Scotland with officers, arms and ammunition, because 'his reputation is great in that country and his presence there would animate the King's friends exceedingly'. If Berwick could not go, then Mar thought that the Duke of Atholl (who stood aloof from the Jacobite cause in 1715) be appointed general and that he 'act and give commissions and do everything else by the advice and consent of the Earls of Mar and Marischal or any two persons of quality and authority that His Majesty shall think proper'.[35]

Another option canvassed by Bolingbroke was to land in the West Country, where Monmouth had arrived in 1685 and, successfully, William of Orange in 1688. He wrote, 'The seizing of Exeter, of Bristol, of Plymouth, or some place of equal

---

32   *Ibid.*, p. xx.
33   *HMC Stuart Papers*, I, p. 522.
34   *Ibid.*
35   *Ibid.*, p. 525.

consequence should be proposed to him as his first attempt on account of the spirit and resolution which will arise from such a beginning'. French aid would be able to arrive more easily if the Jacobites opened their campaign in southern England.[36]

For the rising to begin in Scotland, Mar needed to be at liberty and to be with his supporters there, as well as being where he lived for part of each year when not in London. It is alleged that he had attended various meetings in London that summer with a number of Jacobite lords and gentry including Ormonde's brother. Following the arrests of leading Jacobites in England (see chapter four), there was no safety in the capital. Mar was concerned that he might be arrested ('I found that I could continue noe longer at London with my Liberty for I had certain information that I was one of those to be very quickly taken up' though he claimed he was innocent), for he had formerly sworn allegiance to George in the previous year, and left London in secret with only Major General George Hamilton and two servants. For all the government's much vaunted intelligence service which led to the arrest of leading conspirators, this was an instance in which it failed. They took a boat in the Thames on the evening of 1 August (ironically exactly to a year of George becoming King) and arrived at Newcastle two or three days later (possibly having met Newcastle Jacobites there, such as Sir William Blackett (1690–1728), a Tory MP). They hired another vessel there, belonging to John Spence of Leith, aiming to reach St. Andrews, but could not do so, arriving at Elie instead, where they crossed the River Crail and entered Fifeshire. He went under the name of Mr Maule and at first went to Bethun of Balfour's house, who was Hamilton's son-in-law. He assured them that he was merely the forerunner and that Berwick and James would arrive thereafter, with great stores and supplies and thought that Louis XIV would provide substantial aid.[37] This promise, born out of a politician's optimism rather than any knowledge of James' timetable, would be repeated frequently in the weeks and months to come. Lord John Drummond advised Mar to be cautious. He claimed that James advised, they 'lie quiet if possible, till his arrival'.[38]

The Lord Justice Clerk, Adam Cockburn (1656–1735), the principal civil magistrate of Scotland, knew of Mar's arrival and was apprehensive, stating that it 'gives just ground of suspicion and will raise the spirits of ye Jacobites'. Mar met Sir Alexander Areskine, Lord Lyon, King of Arms, and other allies in Fife and told them what his plans were. He stayed at Kinnoull on 17 August and passed the Tay on the following day. He spent the night with Thomas Rattray of Craighall and told him of his plans. On the 19th he sent letters to summon all Jacobites in the neighbourhood, inviting them to meet him in Braemar in Aberdeenshire; he arrived there on the 20th. This was no last minute plan but quite possibly the result of medium-term planning before he had left London. On 6 August his Edinburgh friends knew of his imminent arrival and on the following day John Dalzell had thrown up his army commission and told his brother Robert Dalzell (c.1687–1737), the 5th Earl of Carnwath, who in turn

---

36   *Ibid.*, p. 528.
37   *Ibid.*, p. 528; Edward Gregg, 'The Jacobite Career of the Earl of Mar', in Cruickshanks, *Ideology and Conspiracy*, pp. 181–2.
38   Keith, *Fragment*, p. 10.

contacted other Lowland nobility, such as William Maxwell (1676–1744), the 5th Earl of Nithsdale, and William Gordon (d.1716), 6th Viscount Kenmure. These men travelled northwards, alleging that they were to attend a hunt, which was the term used by other Jacobite nobility and gentry who were on their way to meet Mar.[39]

Although Mar was to declare on 20 August to his younger brother, James Erskine (1679–1754), Lord Grange, that on his arrival in Scotland he found the country, 'very quiet and peaceable', this was not the case. Jacobite supporters had been gathering in the Highlands prior to Mar's arrival. On 6 August there had been a report of Lochiel and Glengarry meeting. Arms, ammunition, tents and horses were being gathered together. The Duke of Gordon's men were said to be exercising with arms and drinking James' health. Seaforth was 'much employed of late in warlike preparations', having 1,500 men he could call upon. Huntley was buying up horses for cavalry and George Keith (c.1692–1778) the 10th Earl Marischal was putting together a magazine of arms and ammunition, making uniforms and tents. Regular meetings were taking place between these men. Others openly carried weapons in Angus.[40]

The auspices for Mar bringing them together was described thus by Patten:

> He made, for a pretence, a great Hunting. This proclaiming a Hunting, is a custom among the Lords and Chiefs of Families in the Highlands, and on which Occasions they invite their Neighbouring Gentlemen and Vassals to a general Rendezvous, to hunt or chase deer upon the Mountains, of which they have there great plenty. The Usage on these Occasions is, that all the People round the Country, being well arm'd, assemble on the day appointed, and after the Diversion is over, the Persons of Note are invited to an Entertainment.[41]

According to Patten, 'Several Noblemen, Gentlemen, and others in Scotland, being prepared by the Management and Influence of the Earl of Mar, began to draw together their Servants and Dependents in all Places where they had Interest, making divers reasons for so doing, but not for some time discovering the real Design; till at length Things ripening upon them, and Notice being given them … they boldly drew together'.[42] Sir George Warrender, MP and Provost of Edinburgh, was convinced of the danger, writing on 26 August, 'Nothing less than a sudden insurrection is intended'.[43]

Another Whig commentator observed about Jacobite activity in the Highlands in August:

> They are much animated since they heard of the Pretender's Design to invade us, and the Gentry of that sort are said to have been very busy of late in conveying their Estates to their Friends, which looks as if they had an Ill Design in their Heads, We hear that the Jacobite Highlanders are much better furnish'd with Arms, Money and Horses than they us'd to be.[44]

39   Rae, *History*, pp. 415–7; TNA, SP54/7/63.
40   TNA, SP54/7/62; Rae, *History*, p. 188.
41   Patten, *History*, p. 128.
42   *Ibid.*, p. 3.
43   Dickson, 'Warrender Letters', p. 79.
44   *Flying Post*, 3682, 9–11 Aug. 1715.

Jacobite aid from abroad was greatly dreaded in August among Scottish Whigs. James, it was feared, would bring former Scottish, English and Irish officers with him. Furthermore, Ormonde was also seen as a major danger, for he was deemed 'very popular and that there is a very powerful disaffected party … so what will be the result God only knows, only one thing is certain that if there is an invasion there is like to be great bloodshed and a severe civil war'.[45] John Aik predicted 'bloody confusion this summer' and 'misery … upon this poor country'.[46] On 24 August James Ogilvie (1663–1730), 4th Earl of Findlater, reported that 'accounts that the preparations for the invasion are going on, and it is thought that it will come on speedily'.[47] Hugh Rose thought differently: 'I cannot allow myself to believe that men will venture to make disturbance as this time'. [48]

It was known that Mar was arranging a conference, though a letter to Thomas Kennedy on 25 August stated 'I suppose little credit can be given to these reports'.[49] Kennedy was wrong. On 26 August there was, then, at Braemar, 'a great Number of Gentlemen, of the best Quality and interest of all his Party'; perhaps 800 were gathered together. They included some of Scotland's most prominent men, such as Huntley, earls, viscounts, lords and gentlemen; this was to be a rising very much more different to the doomed lower-class revolt led by Monmouth in 1685 or the even more limited one led by an earlier Earl of Argyle in the same year, or even the briefly successful rising of 1689, and so, to the government, far more dangerous. Mar addressed them in a speech 'full of Invectives against the Protestant Succession in general, and against King George in particular'. He also had to justify his seeming political volte-face:

That tho' he had been instrumental in forwarding the Union of the two Kingdoms, in the Reign of Queen Anne, yet now his eyes were open'd, and he could see his Error, and would therefore do what lay in his power to make them again a free people, and that they should enjoy their ancient Liberties, which were by that cursed Union delivered up into the hands of the English, whose power to enslave them further, was far too great: and their design to do it daily visible, by the Measures that were taken, especially by the Prince of Hanover, who ever since he ascended the Throne, regarded not the Welfare of his People, nor their Religion, but solely left it to a set of Men, who whilst they push'd his particular Interest to secure his Government, made such alterations in Church and State, as they thought fit and that they had already begun to encroach upon the Liberties of both; which he assured them, had already given occasion to some to consult their own safety, and who were actually resolved vigorously to defend their Liberties and Properties, against the said new Courtiers, and their Innovations, and to establish upon the Throne of these Realms, the Chevalier St. George who he said, had the only undoubted Right to the Crown, had promis'd to hear their Grievances, and would redress their Wrongs. And hereupon excited them all to take Arms for the said Chevalier, who he stil'd King James VIII and told them, that for

---

45   NRS, GD248/561/53/23.
46   *Ibid.*, GD30/1724.
47   *Ibid.*, GD248/561/53/53.
48   *Ibid.*, GD27/6/14.
49   NRS, GD27/6/13.

his own part he was resolved to set up his Standard, and to summon all the fencible men of his own Tenants, and with them to hazard his life in the Cause. He encouraged them likewise by giving them assurance, that there would be a general Rising in England, on the same account: That they should certainly have a powerful Assistance from France, and from other Parts, from whence their King, had already large supplies, and Promises of more; that Thousands were in League and Covenant with him and with one another to rise and depose King George, and establish the said Chevalier.[50]

Mar was a good speaker, he had 'a popular insinuating air' and he also showed those assembled letters from the Stuart court bearing promises that James would come over to lead them and in the meantime would provide arms, ammunition, military stores and officers. There is no reason to believe that Mar was insincere in any of this. However he was deceitful in other ways. Mar himself showed a commission allegedly from James to act as lieutenant general (this was a fraudulent claim; the Stuart court had no advance knowledge of Mar's enterprise) and told them that he had enough money to pay and feed the men so that no one need be out of pocket by joining the Jacobite cause. Mar was successful in persuading many of them to join with him and asked that they bring their dependants and friends. They took an oath that day at Braemar to stand by one another.[51] However, some were suspicious of Mar, believing him to be an agent of the government sent to ensnare them.[52] Keith believed that it was an ill omen having an architect of the Union as leader of the insurrection to break it.[53]

Mar also spoke of Hamilton and himself as leading an army southward in order to dissolve the Union and redress the country's grievances. He resorted to scaremongering, adding that the present government planned to introduce new taxes on farm animals and birds, large and small, and also crops, 'and this was no mean reason for him to take up arms, since otherwise in a very short time the nation should sink under such burdens'. Unsurprisingly, 'This took extreamly with the common people and animated them to take up arms'.[54]

Mar emphasised that the Scots would not be rising alone. James and Berwick would soon arrive and bring large quantities of arms from France. England was also all for James, and the army was on their side. Troops would arrive from abroad, too.[55]

Even with such a strong constituency, Mar had had to overcome some natural grounds for concern, as he later noted:

> It was not without Difficulty that we could allay their first Heat. But the Chevalier not going into England, nor the Duke of Berwick coming to Scotland, as was generally expected, abated very much of that Forwardness … it was not without Difficulty that he could persuade some to join with him, they apprehending great Uncertainty of

---

50   Rae, *History*, pp. 189–190.
51   *Ibid.*, p. 190; Patten, *History*, p. 131.
52   Patten, *History*, p. 128.
53   Keith, *Fragment*, p. 11.
54   Taylers, *1715*, p. 190.
55   Scott, *Memoirs*, p. 20.

the Success of the Affair, by no Account being come of the Chevalier, or the Duke of Berwick's Arrival, nor of Money, Arms and Ammunition, or Officers, tho' others were all along very forward.[56]

It should be noted that Mar had no authority from James to lead his cause in Scotland. James Murray (1690–1770), second son of Viscount Stormont, wrote on 23 August that Mar was 'under great uneasiness that there is no authority to act in that country'.[57] Four days later James wrote a commission appointing Mar as commander-in-chief in Scotland and empowering him to appoint officers under him.[58] The commission read, 'Wee, reposing especial trust and confidence in your loyalty, courage, experience, capacity and good conduct, do by these presents constitute and appoint you to be our General and Commander in chief of all our forces … in Scotland'.[59] James had never met Mar, but those around him such as Ormonde and Bolingbroke, presumably as a matter of necessity, advised him to grant Mar the initial command in Scotland.

It should be noted that James had initially envisaged someone quite different as leading the restoration attempt in Scotland on his behalf. In 1714, 'the person proposed by my friends to be at the head of my affairs till my arrivall' was the Duke of Atholl, a leading anti-unionist in 1707 as well as being one of the most eminent noblemen in Scotland. A commission to act in such a manner had been made out to him in October 1714. As matters transpired, James had to accept the situation as it stood in reality: Atholl never took part in the campaign.[60]

Years later, Mar justified his taking command as he had to his son, writing:

I thought myself enough authorised to make the first step, since this project was the only way that appeared wch would bring the Duke of Orleans to quit his conjunction with King George and had His majesty come in time and those of England ansuered their engagements, both wch was so reasonable to be expected that I could not doubt of.[61]

The Jacobite nobles, gentry and Highland chiefs went back to their estates in order to gather in their men. Mar remained at Braemar with but a few attendants, and this led Cockburn to believe on 28 August, that 'we find that the encampment does not appear yet to be so formidable as it was at first thought'. From 5,000 men there were now only 300 with Mar. As Sinclair wrote, 'what was so hastlie promised was slowlie perform'd and all of them cooled after returning home'.[62]

Findlater downplayed the likelihood of Mar being at the head of a rising, writing on 3 September, 'We hear that the Earl of Mar is at Braemar and is very confidently said that he is convening the Highlanders to disturbance but I hope his proposals will be

56 Patten, *History*, p. 210.
57 *HMC Stuart Papers*, I, p. 415.
58 *Ibid.*, p. 415.
59 *HMC Mar and Kellie*, p. 445.
60 British Library Add. MSS. 38851, f. 62r.
61 Grant, 'Mar' Legacies', p. 168.
62 TNA, SP54/7/87; Scott, *Memoirs*, p. 22.

disappointed and I cannot believe he will be so foolish'.[63] Some government supporters had a low opinion of Mar, but were fearful of his cause. William Murray (d.1726), 2nd Baron of Nairn, wrote of him on 29 August, 'That little great man who makes sutch a noise in Britain nor does ev'en make the government folks think there must be more in it then they imagine that one of his parts, character and caution has made sutch a step'. A deeper plot than that which appeared on the surface was feared.[64]

Mar called another meeting, this time at Aboyne in Aberdeenshire on 3 September in order to concert measures for the Jacobites all appearing together in arms. At the Aboyne meeting were Huntley, William Murray (d.1746), Marquess of Tullibardine, Southesk and several clan chiefs or their representatives. Mar showed them a picture of James, which he kissed, 'frequentlie with the appearance of more than ane ordinarie affection'. Sinclair suggested that this gave him credit amongst them and was highly persuasive in their believing that Mar was an honest man.[65]

Not all Jacobites were impressed by Mar. Sinclair was one of Mar's most virulent critics and he thought, at least in retrospect, that the enterprise was foolish, as he saw it as being too dependent on English support. According to him, 'I could see no reason why we should be made use of as the Cats foot by a Nation who, we knew, wither Whig or Tory, was uppermost, would oppress us' and that the rebellion would 'run my countrie into certaine ruine'. He also considered that there was a lack of horses and arms.[66]

Mar's motivations seem to have been to further his political and financial ends, but he was able to tap into existing Jacobite sympathy and discontents among the Scottish nobility and gentry. He was addressing an aggrieved constituency (due to discontent over the religious settlement of 1690 and the Union as well as a preference for a Stuart monarch than a Hanoverian one) which was seeking a leader for immediate action. In the absence of James, Mar provided that deficiency. He was also fortunate that the government's military position in Scotland was relatively weak.

We should also question the timing of the onset of the uprising. Military campaigns conventionally began in the spring; Marlborough's Blenheim campaign began in the April of 1704, for instance, and ended in November. This meant that armies could march and fight in the most clement season of the year and had six months to do so, which made movement and supply easier. It meant longer days and so more time for action. However both the Fifteen and the Forty Five began towards the end of the conventional campaigning season; Mar was no soldier, however, and he began the campaign, as noted, to suit his own immediate needs. It meant he needed a quick victory before winter set in, however.

Mar also believed that the attempt should take place when it did because he believed that George and his government would become more and more unpopular and thus the 'public ferment will probably be at the highest, when the credit of this parliament shall be sunk to the lowest pitch'. The government would also be divided

---

63   NRS, GD248/561/53/10.
64   NRS, GD38/2/2/40.
65   Scott, *Memoirs*, pp. 19–20.
66   *Ibid.*, pp. 27, 18.

as well as unpopular if it acted against its internal opponents. George's allies on the Continent might become embroiled in conflict in the near future and so be unable to support him, whilst Sweden might be able to disentangle itself from war and so be in a position to aid the Jacobites.[67]

After all the preparations and build-up in the previous weeks, the Jacobites threw down the proverbial gauntlet on 6 September by holding a public gathering to proclaim their cause. This took place in the Highlands at Braemar. The Jacobite standard was raised and unfurled; James was pronounced as rightful King – of Scotland, England, France and Ireland. It is not known how many were present at the ceremony, possibly as many as 600, but it seems it was marked by the following incident: 'when the standard was first erected, the Ball on the Top of it fell off, which the superstitious Highlanders were very much concern'd at, taking it as an Omen of the bad success of the cause for which they were then appearing'.[68]

The Jacobites had finally declared their aims on British soil and now had to make good their strength in order to deal with the forces that would be assembled against them. Yet some already believed, and without the benefit of hindsight, that the rising was facing insurmountable difficulties. Apart from The absence of foreign support, Bolingbroke was both convinced of the strength of George I's position and the uncertainty of support for James in Britain. He concluded:

> I must therefore be of opinion, that a more fatal conjuncture can never happen, and that the attempt can probably end in nothing but the ruin of our cause forever … But if our friends are not in a condition to wait, without submitting and giving up the cause entirely and forever, desperate as I think the attempt is, it must be made; and dying for dying, it is better to die warm, and at once, of a fever, than to pine away with a consumption.

On the following day he added, 'The more I think, the more I hear, and the more I struggle forward in this business, the more impracticable it appears to me'.[69]

Yet though James did not deny this, replying to Bolingbroke thus, 'I confess my affairs have a very melancholy prospect; every post almost brings me some ill news or other, all hopes of the least foreign help are extinguished' but continued 'this is so far from discouraging me, that it does but confirm me in my opinion of a present undertaking' as matters would become even worse by further delays.[70]

For better or worse, the die was now cast.

67 *HMC Stuart Papers*, I, pp. 523–4.
68 Rae, *History*, p. 191; Taylers, *1715*, p. 41.
69 Mahon, *History*, pp. xxiv–xxv.
70 *Ibid.*, p. xxix.

3

Raising the Men and the Money

Once the restoration attempt had officially begun and its aims stated, the key question was how was the Jacobite aim of a Stuart restoration to be achieved. The emphasis on domestic support in the summer had initially been on the English Jacobites rising but by September the focus was on Scotland and the Highlands in particular, principally because of Mar and because the government's military position was weaker in Scotland than in England. The means to a restoration was to raise men and create an army strong enough not only to take over the civil government of Scotland, but to be able to defeat the British army and advance into England to final victory. Szechi, in his discussion of the military model of effectiveness discusses this in his second of four points. He concludes that the Jacobites' assumptions crucial for success were flawed, in part due to failures of intelligence, and an unrealistic reliance on English and Irish support.[1]

Despite the numerous grievances held by many in Britain, the Jacobites' task was a difficult one; namely to convert grievance into the all or nothing risk posed by participation in armed rebellion with all its possible consequences in the event of failure. Since the fifteenth century the English state had only been overthrown once by rebels relying on domestic support alone, and that during the Civil Wars of 1642–1646. This had only been possible because the then King lacked a standing army – constituted on a permanent footing only in 1660 – with which to quickly crush his enemies' fledging forces. There had been numerous rebellions during the Tudor era. All failed. Scottish attempts to restore the Stuarts in 1648 and 1651 resulted in swift defeat, as had Royalist insurrections against the Commonwealth in the 1650s. Monmouth's and Argyle's rebellions in 1685 also came to speedy ends. James II was only overthrown in 1688 due to a foreign invasion; widespread domestic discontent was not enough. Even so, the French-backed civil war in Ireland in 1688–1691 met with eventual defeat.

That there was a great deal of domestic support was undoubted, though was exaggerated. In 1685 it was stated that the rebellion in Scotland would receive a great deal of support but in the event very little was forthcoming; insurgents need to be

---

1   Szechi, 'Towards an Analytical Model', pp. 300–304.

optimistic but in being so can delude themselves and others. In 1685 a supporter of the rebellious Earl of Argyle noted that 'all Protestaints in both keingdoms ... as one man [will] joyne us'. In 1689 the Jacobites claimed 'three partes of four' in Scotland would rally to their cause as well as many in northern England. In neither case did the hoped for support emerge.[2]

Berwick was convinced that there was a high level of support for the cause in Britain, writing, 'Ormond, Mar &c assured us that the people had never been so well disposed, that there was 9 out of 10 against George', though this was a very optimistic assessment of the situation. This sympathy existed in both Scotland and England. The former, were already deemed to be armed and only wanted a signal before rising and the country, 'ever since the Revolution has always shewn itself attached to the Prince's Family'. It could supply about 8,000 armed men, though this proved to be a considerable underestimate.[3]

The more populous England, it was thought, could supply more men, perhaps 10,000, but there were difficulties there. They would need arms and money. Hatred of Hanover, loss of offices and concerns for both the security of their liberties and the Anglican Church provided apparent incentives for support for the Jacobite cause, especially among the Tories. As with Mar, Berwick thought that Britain was ripe for a change of dynasty, claiming, 'The majority of the English Nation is so well affected, that we may venture to say, 5 out of 6 are for the Prince ... numbers of noblemen, clergy and gentlemen have given assurances of their good intentions. Many persons of the greatest consideration, interest and abilities have assembled to concert the means of restoring the King'.[4]

Yet support from England was limited. In part this was because of the steps taken by the government against possible Jacobite supporters in England; for which see chapter four. Leadership was thus lacking. Then there was the indecision about where the English rising should begin; as seen Northumberland was first proposed and then the South West. Bolingbroke was not optimistic, writing 'We do not know, which is a most uncomfortable consideration, what our friends in England will resolve to do'.[5] Support in northern England, despite the strongholds of Catholicism in Northumberland and Lancashire was relatively limited. There was brief cause for Jacobitism optimism at the end of October 1715 when a small English rising was underway in the north of England; Lord Forfar, a Scottish officer in the British Army, wrote 'this begins now in good earnest to alarm people'.[6] Mar agreed, having received a letter on 29 October from Thomas Forster, MP, leader of the English Jacobite army, about the southern Jacobite army's imminent advance into England where they had been assured of great

2   Tim Harris, *Revolution: The Great Crisis of the British Monarchy, 1685–1720* (London: Allen Lane, 2006), pp. 75, 409–10.
3   Berwick, *Memoirs*, pp. 195–196, 200–201.
4   *Ibid.*, pp. 201–202.
5   Mahon, *History*, Appendix I, p. xxii.
6   NRS, GD3/20/5.

many supporters joining them. Mar told Lord Strowan 'I am mightily well pleased with this'.[7] Yet as we shall see, this came to naught.

Elsewhere, prospects for the Jacobite cause were not favourable despite Mar being upbeat at Ormonde's departure for England, believing James was to follow.[8] This latter was not to be successful. In October Ormonde embarked from Cherbourg with a ship loaded with arms and ammunition and arrived off Torbay. He had three cannon fired as a signal to the Jacobites onshore, whom he believed were ready to receive him. On hearing no response, he returned to France.[9] Berwick was critical of Ormonde, writing later that the scheme needed a hero, 'and that is what Ormonde was not ... he had few of the talents necessary for such an enterprise, and very little knowledge of the art of wear'.[10] Ormonde had not been wrong to believe there were Jacobite sympathisers in the South-West. In October the government seized a cache of muskets, cannon and swords, 200 horses and a number of suspects in and around Bath, and it was believed that others escaped before the soldiers arrived. In the same month, James was proclaimed King at St. Columb.[11] The stationing of troops in the West Country must have discouraged most potential Jacobite supporters there.

The dependence on the South-Western Jacobites was such that it delayed James' presence in Britain. Mar wrote to his master, constantly imploring his arrival throughout October and November, to which James had replied, 'I have not words to express to you the satisfaction I have of your sagacious and prudent conduct ... The accounts he gave have increased the desire you know I have long had of coming to you which nothing but cross winds do now hinder'. James had been waiting for Ormonde and some of the Irish troops in French service who would, he hoped, assist his cause. Mar was also told about other developments abroad. Bolingbroke was in discussion with the French as to arms to be sent. Talks with Spain and the French regency over financial support dragged on, without much obvious sense of urgency. Ormonde could report to James a private audience he had had with Orleans, promising supplies and 'great profession of his concerne and friendship for you'. He was also in talks with the Dutch, demanding their neutrality in return for the promise of an alliance with Britain once he was restored. There was, then, no hope for immediate succour for Mar, though James elevated him from Earl to Duke.[12]

Support from Ireland was apparently of great potential given the great predominance of Catholics and the fact that many in Ireland had supported James II in 1689–1691. There does not seem to have been any attempt made to gather support in Ireland, however, though rumours abounded and some security precautions were taken there.[13]

It was important that James arrived in Britain to reclaim his throne in person. On 5 July Berwick declared that the Jacobites in England and Scotland expected that of

7   NLS, Adv Ms 13.1.8.42.
8   *Ibid.*
9   Rae, *History*, p. 293n.
10   Berwick, *Memoirs*, p. 209.
11   Rae, *History*, pp. 216–217.
12   *HMC Stuart Papers*, I, pp. 437, 442, 445.
13   *Ibid.*, p. 375.

him as 'his friends will give over the game if they think him to be backward'.[14] By the end of the next month James was eager to go, writing of England, 'All seems ripe in that country, the dangers of delay are great, proposals of foreign help are uncertain and tedious'.[15] They also looked forward to seeing James, as a memorial noted: 'his friends in Scotland are in the best condition to receive him and in the greatest want of his presence ... wherever he goes the rising must be general in all parts of these islands; so as to distract the forces of the enemy'.[16]

As well as James' arrival, as to military leadership, Berwick was seen as the man to lead the Jacobite army. He had been given James' commission to act as Captain General in Scotland. He was an experienced and successful soldier (having defeated the allies at Alamanza in 1707) and so could well have been very useful. Writing in July, James had high hopes of him, writing, 'You know what you owe to me, what you owe to your own reputation and honour, what you have promised to the Scotch and to me, of what vast consequence you accompanying of me is'.

But by late October he declined, after having consulted with others. He later told Mar, 'as a Marshal of France he could not desert like a trooper'. In his memoirs, Berwick explained his refusal:

As I caused myself to be a naturalised Frenchman ... was consequently become a subject of His Most Christian Majesty ... an officer of the Crown of France, engaged by several oaths, not to go out of this kingdom. Without leave in writing, which was far from being given to me ... I did not think myself at liberty either in honour or in conscience to obey the order I had received.[17]

Scotland, then, would be where the rising was to begin. Some Scots had fought for James' father in 1689–1690 and rather more had anticipated helping his son in 1708. Berwick added, 'We were sure of the Scots, who had already provided themselves with arms and waited only for the signal to rise'.[18]

As well as suiting his own needs, Mar believed there were great possibilities there:

The body of Highlanders which, on the first occasion cou'd be drawn together, and if well commanded were able to have made themselves masters of the whole kingdom of Scotland, and secondly, on account of the many sea ports they were masters of, by which succours might come from abroad.[19]

Following the news of the death of Louis XIV, the Jacobite Highland chiefs held a meeting as to whether they should disperse until James arrived, because of this, or whether they should persist. They decided to put their trust in their as yet undeclared

---

14 Rae, *History*, pp. 341–350.
15 *HMC Stuart Papers*, I, p. 410.
16 *Ibid.*, p. 421.
17 Taylers, *1715*, p. 16n; *HMC Stuart Papers*, I, pp. 376, 451; Berwick, *Memoirs*, p. 242.
18 Berwick, *Memoirs*, p. 196.
19 *HMC Stuart Papers*, I, pp. 349, 425, 367.

allies in England and carry on. According to Sinclair, 'the greatest part thought they were strong enough to doe the work themselves'.[20]

After 6 September, Mar's main concern was to raise the men, money and equipment he needed to create an army capable of forwarding his political aims. It had to have the potential to fight. Mar had already begun to gather men around him, with various accounts giving both 60 and 2,000 prior to the rising.[21] He wrote to John Gordon of Glenbucket (*c.*1673–1750) on 1 September, asking him to summon his master's tenants, 'to require and empower you to raise such of the Marquess of Huntley's men and following as he shall direct you'.[22] Glenbucket was to gather the men of Strathdon, Glenlivet and Badenoch and Mar expected to see them gathered together on 12 September at Atholl.[23] Stewart thought that Mar had 300 horse and 200 infantry, just his own men as a bodyguard.[24]

Mar also directed Glenbucket to additional tasks:

To raise such of the Marquis of Huntley's men and following as he shall direct that you with their best arms and accoutrements, and to obey his lordship's order in your marching of them to join the Kings forces, who will be on their march through Perth towards Stirling. You are likewise empowered to secure what arms and ammunition in the hands of suspected persons in the neighbourhood of the said Marquis' countries.[25]

Mar also penned a declaration of his own, addressed to the gentlemen of Kildrummy. He announced that James was expected to arrive and in the meantime he was their leader, stating that 'Our Rightful and Natural King … having been pleased to entrust us with the Direction of his Affairs, and the Command of his Forces in this his ancient Kingdom of Scotland'. He said that a number of Scottish nobility and gentry had, with him, appeared in arms in order to further the restoration. He urged them to join him at Braemar, 'Now is the time for all good men to shew their Zeal for His Majesty's Service … In so honourable, good and Just a Cause, we cannot doubt of the Assistance, Direction and Blessing of Almighty God, who has so often rescued the House of Stuart, and our Country, from sinking under Oppression'.[26]

Methods used varied from gentle persuasion to naked threats. The former included a letter from Huntley, to the lairds of Achloyne and Knockespack on 28 September:

The present expedition being undertaken by a great number of honest and brave men who have for motive their Loyalty to the King; their love to their Country, and the good of their posterity I cannot doubt but that you will cheerfully contribute your best endeavours in so good a cause. I doe therefor recommend to you to raise your men and provide them

20   Rae, *History*, p. 192; Scott, *Memoirs*, p. 21.
21   Rae, *History*, pp. 190–1.
22   Taylers, *1715*, p. 201.
23   *HMC Stuart Papers*, I, p. 419.
24   TNA, SP54/8/18.
25   *HMC Stuart Papers*, I, p. 417.
26   Taylers, *1715*, pp. 192–3; Patten, *History*, p. 137.

with arms … for nine days, to join Me in My March I intend to begin in a few days, if your present circumstances doe necessarily hinder your coming in persone, I recommend the raiseing and leading of the Men to Tillefour I expect your chearfull compliance in this matter.[27]

Mar's demand for manpower, addressed to his Baillie at Kildrummy on 9 September, was rather more aggressive:

I have used gentle Means too long, and so I shall be forced to put other Orders I have in Execution … you are immediately to intimate to all my vassals; if they give ready Obedience it will make some amends, and if not, ye may tell them from me, that it will not be in my power to save them … from being treated as Enemies … if they come not forth with their best Arms, that I will send a Party immediately to burn what they shall miss taking from them … this [is] not only a threat, but by all that's sacred, I'll put it in Execution.[28]

There were others, too, who had to be coerced into enlistment. In the following year, when some Jacobites were on trial, the Scots amongst them claimed, 'that they were forced into that service by a Cross-stick, commonly called a firey cross, with Blood on one end and Fire on the other, the person that carried it from House to House, assuring them, that unless they repaired immediately to Mar's camp, that was to be their fate'.[29]

William Adamson related that he 'being under the Marquis of Huntley [he] was forced to come out in the month of September 1715'. Sir Thomas Calder was another of Huntley's tenants and said that whilst obliged to attend his master, he refused a commission. James Gardiner, a surgeon, claimed he was bound to assist Sir Donald MacDonald (d.1718), 4th baronet, as he was in his employ. John Robertson and 12 others of Strathairdle only joined 'under pain of fire and sword'. A party of Jacobites had arrived at the village and the inhabitants 'did conclude that it was to execute Mar's threatening by burning and slaying, and under terror and apprehensions of this fear' they enlisted.[30]

If Mar had to bend the truth to encourage potential supporters, he was not afraid to do so, as a letter of his indicates:

I had a messenger from the King last night. He himself with the Duke of Berwick is coming at once. Ormonde and Bolingbroke are going to England. All friends are to rise and wait for nothing. How soon my friends joyn me, I am to begin my march to Dunkeld. I hope to be joined by Seaforth, also by Huntley and yourself before I get to Perth.[31]

---

27 Dickinson, 'Warrender Letters', pp. 99–100.
28 Rae, *History*, pp. 193–4.
29 *Ibid.*, p. 192n.
30 NLS, MS 902, 20, 22–23, 38, 44.
31 Taylers, *1715*, p. 50.

Mar also delegated recruiting. Marischal contacted Sir Alexander Burnett of Leys, on 25 September, informing him that in James' name and 'by virtue of a Power given me by ye Earle of Mar', to 'requyre you with your best horses and armes and what men ye can rayse, to meet me at Stonehyve on Saturday next'.[32]

Similarly, Huntley acted on Mar's behalf, contacting potential supporters. As with Mar, he was not shy of putting the best possible gloss on the level of support the Jacobite cause could hope for. Writing from Gordon Castle on 30 September, he gave 'ashurances of his [James] own and the Duke of Berwick in the north of England or Scotland and the Duke Ormond and L. Bullenbruck's landing in the west'. Huntley wanted only 'franke young fellos volunteers'. Other reluctant Jacobites were reassured that if they supplied arms and horses for the cause, they would have them returned in six months time.[33] Huntley himself set an example to any waverers. His men were to gather in bodies at Strathbogie and then towards Perth, arriving there with 500 cavalry and 2,000 infantry on 5 October.[34]

Attempts by their opponents to stem Jacobite recruitment in Scotland were largely ineffectual. General Whetham's continued attempts to arrest suspects were clearly too late. On 7 September he instructed William Grant to try to take Mar and Hamilton. Needless to say, these instructions were impossible to carry out given the weakness of the state compared to the strength of its opponents.[35]

Mar was glad of the actual support he was beginning to accrue, writing on 19 September, 'The Athole people have behaved nobley in spite of the Duke, and Ld Tullibardine has done the King real and effectual service'. He was eager for Huntley's men and had written to him again to hurry them up, for he expressed 'surprise and concern' about it. He looked forward to Glenbucket arriving but feared that Huntley's delay was a sign that he might not come after all.[36]

According to Sinclair, Jacobite numbers were exaggerated among Whig circles. Tales of 'the noise of the great numbers that had joined Mar' were passed to Argyle, along with daily messages from the Jacobites in Perth. Sinclair wrote, 'For, could he doubt of what those of his own partie, of the best credite of that place, assured him of'. Seeing numbers of men together, in 'a countrie like ours, who were not used to war', they 'imagined everie hundred men to be a thousand'.[37] Concerns about these numbers extended to he majority of those in the government's service, such as Argyle.

It is uncertain how strong Mar was at Perth by the end of September. One report listed only 800 infantry and 200 cavalry at Perth on 23 September, but with many more men expected. Huntley was at Strathbogie with 1,500 infantry and 200 cavalry; Seaforth at Badenoch with 2,500 infantry and 200 cavalry; with another 2,000 infantry and 100 cavalry at Angus.[38] However, an informer stated on 1 October that

---

32   *Ibid.*, p. 222.
33   *Ibid.*, pp. 201–3.
34   *Ibid.*, pp. 201, 204–5.
35   TNA, SP54/8/25.
36   Taylers, *1715*, p. 239.
37   Scott, *Memoirs*, p. 41.
38   TNA, SP54/8, 88.

the numbers at Perth were as follows: Earl of Linlithgow's cavalry (60 men), Panmure's battalion of infantry (400), the Perthshire Horse (60), Mar's first battalion (400 men) and Mar's second battalion (300 men), the Dunkeld and Glaenarren regiments (300 men each), the Fife Horse (100 men), Angus Horse (70 men), Strathmore's and Strowan's Foot (300 men in each), Granthilly's and Knentty's men (250) and another 210 men on detachment. The total was 2,550 infantry and 500 cavalrymen and this figure was reported in the press in early October.[39] Yet Cockburn had a report that the Jacobites had between 3,000 and 4,000 infantry and 500 cavalry.[40] More men were being called up; on 24 September James Ogilvie had orders to summon all the men of the Forest of Boyn and to select those fit to serve King James.[41] Mar gave Tullibardine orders to have the men of Strathgowrie and the clans to march to Perth.[42]

There were also hopes about additional forces reaching Perth. Yet loyalist forces in the north and west of the Highlands and the garrison of regular troops at Fort William had deterred Jacobites from these parts of Scotland from reaching Mar. Clanranald told Major General Alexander Gordon (1669–1751) that people were terrified that the garrison would destroy all the countryside if they left to join Mar.[43] The MacDonalds and Camerons were some of those clans reluctant to march, though this may be more of an excuse rather than a reason given the weakness of the garrison. Gordon was becoming exasperated with their delays. Others did arrive at Perth: Marischal's 300 cavalry arrived on 8 October and Huntley on the 10th with 500 more, but the latter had to be initially quartered at Coupar due to lack of accommodation nearer to Perth. Seaforth was asked to hurry to Perth and wrote 'I have called in all our Party every where'. Gordon, who was at Achalader, was given a similar request, to march to Monteith. By the end of October, the clans had been gathered and were encamped in and around Auchterarder. Mar had ordered Rob Roy to Perth, but by 4 November was complaining of his failure to arrive.[44]

An estimate of Jacobite strength in mid to late October states they had 13 battalions of infantry: Lord Strathallan's, Drummond of Logie's, Indernetty's, Tullibardine's, Strathmore's, Mar's, Southesk's, Panmure's, Huntley's and Mackintosh's, though their strength is unstated. Mar's and Huntley's men were divided each into three battalions. There were six units of cavalry: Huntley's, Marischal's, Perthshire, Fife, Stirlingshire and Angus, with Huntley's divided into six troops and Perthshire's into three. The cavalry numbered 1,200 men. There were six cannons guarded by 100 men, with 200 men at Drummond Castle and 400 in Fife. The document noted that MacIntosh and 1,000 men were in England. They were expecting 2,500 clansmen.[45]

On the whole, the Jacobites were successful in maintaining their forces to the point of battle. Although Mar, on 3 October, could state that he had a 'powerful and numerous

---

39 TNA, SP54/9/2D; *St. James Evening Post*, 56, 6–8 Oct. 1715.
40 *Ibid.*, 9/3a.
41 NRS, GD248/561/53/3.
42 Patten, *History*, p. 211.
43 NRS, GD1/616/12.
44 Rae, *History*, pp. 433, 434, 436, 445–446, 459, 466.
45 British Library Stowe, 228, f. 161r.

confluence of noblemen, gentlemen and soldiers' who were 'all cheerfully resolved to venture their lives and fortunes' for the Jacobite cause, there were difficulties. Apart from men, the Jacobites needed to raise money to pay them and to obtain supplies to feed them. The campaign was proving expensive, for his men were 'but indifferently provided in money to defray the necessary charges'. Sinclair wrote, 'Some of our gentlemen, who had thought that they had taken monie enough with them to doe their business, or who came out in such haste that they had no time to provide, were goeing daylie home to get new supplies'.[46]

Sinclair stated that there was even a mutiny, presumably by the rank and file, over the lack of pay, 'it had been supposed they could liv'd without it, as well as fight without pouder and armes'. As an emergency measure, Southesk and Panmure gave £500 each to settle the pressing claims. Some of the Jacobite gentry had 'already very cheerfully lent their money towards supporting so good a cause ... All the security they demand is my bond for it either in my own name or the publick or both'. So Mar contacted potential supporters for cash: writing to Lady Ruthdon and Baillie David Maxwell of Dundee, a merchant. He was wanting sums of £500 or £1,000 or even more, 'which I hope will not straiten you much'. All this of course was in the way of a loan to be repaid by James once he was King.[47]

A council of finance was formed and it levied funds from the surrounding districts. Taking tax revenues, namely customs and excise money, from tax collectors was the easiest step, because this money had already been extracted from the populace. Furthermore there would be no popular animosity against the Jacobites and it would also serve to deprive the government from revenue they needed. On 4 October Mar issued a proclamation which decreed that each landowner who was actively supporting the Jacobite cause pay 5 percent of the annual income from their lands; those who were not sending men to support it were charged double.[48] This was the cess tax, a major form of revenue in Scotland and was the equivalent to the land tax in England, being a tax on landowners. John Forbes was collector of the cess tax for the county of Aberdeen and was a Jacobite, so he naturally offered his professional services to Mar, which were accepted. He therefore put the machinery into operation and had his deputy collectors begin the process of assessment and collection. He ordered this to be done on 4 October, but it was a lengthy process to collect from all 97 parishes in the county. It was not until 21 November that £1,210 was paid to the Jacobites' Finance Committee at Stirling.[49]

Mar's steps to have a proper supply of money came to fruition. Sinclair noted, 'Monie came in apace, in greater plenty than we had a notice of'. Food for the increasing Jacobite army was also critical. A committee was formed to oversee the provision of food and forage. Sinclair noted, 'Nothing favoured us so much as that

46 Rae, *History*, p. 429, Scott, *Memoirs*, p. 52.
47 Scott, *Memoirs*, p. 72.
48 Patten, *History*, pp. 143–144.
49 Alastair and Henrietta Tayler (eds.), *The Jacobite Cess Roll for the County of Aberdeen in 1715* (Aberdeen: Spalding Club, 1932), pp. xxi, 1–28.

year's plentifull crop, for nobodie remembered they had ever seen such aboundance of corn in Scotland'. Yet gathering it in and storing it for distribution to the troops was another matter; 'we could never contrive it to have provisions in store, even with the help of a navigable river … yet we were always from hand to mouth, and often in want, and when meale was got could never fall on methods of backing bread to serve the whole'.[50] Sinclair took this as a sign that Mar's sloth was all pervasive and the men had to live by a hand to mouth existence.[51] Yet on 4 October, Mar stated that questions of pay and supply had been dealt with; the men receiving three pence per day each as well as three loaves or the equivalent of meal, each day.[52]

Mar also ordered those towns under Jacobite control to supply money and equipment. Although Aberdeen had initially supported the government, there had been a coup on 28 September and a council composed of Jacobites had taken over. So, on 17 October Mar could confidently ask the council to supply his army with 300 Lochaber axes and for a sum of £500 taken as payment for the cess tax ten days later. The city also provided a printing press for the propagation of propaganda.[53]

Throughout the next few weeks, Mar focused on keeping his men supplied with food, arms and ammunition, sending out many letters to encourage/order the civil magistrates to supply him with these. Much was expected of the town council of Montrose; on 6 October, Mar demanded £56 17s 3d payable to the town clerk on 10 October. On the 11th he demanded a loan of £500.[54] As well as money, arms were also demanded. Montrose was also asked for 150 Lochaber axes on 14 October, and was expected to be 'punctual and speedy … as you will answer at your peril.[55]

Orders for gunpowder and lead were made on 23–24 October. More direct methods were the searches of Auchterarder, Tullibardine, Dunning, Crieff and Muthill for leather and for shoes on 31 October. Colin Simpson of Whitehills was appointed Commissary of stores on 19 October. He was to deal with the administration of meal and bread for the army, sending, for example, 129 bolls of meal for distribution at Auchterarder on 29 October, and 20 bolls to Logierate two days later.[56]

On 28 October, William Duff of Braco was ordered to give £500 to George Gordon for the collection of supply for the county of Bamff. Six months of cess tax was required from the said county and if it were not forthcoming by 15 November double the amount assessed would be wanted. Troops would be quartered on the county if these monies were not paid.[57]

Not all were so co-operative. Sinclair was ordered to make a progress through Fife and to stop at each town on the way. He was to instruct the customs and excise men to

---

50 Scott, *Memoirs*, pp. 73, 84.
51 *Ibid.*, pp. 72, 84.
52 Rae, *History*, p. 431.
53 James Allardyce, *Historical Papers relating to the Jacobite period*, I (Aberdeen: New Spalding Club, 1895), pp. 432, 439.
54 Rae, *History*, pp. 443–4.
55 *Ibid.*
56 *Ibid.*, pp. 452, 459, 462–3.
57 NRS, RH9/18/1/24/24 (5 and 6).

deliver their collected monies to him. Arms and ammunition were to be seized, as were horses belonging to the Jacobites' enemies. Magistrates could be taken as hostages if need be. Finally, as if to emphasise the legality of all this, James was to be proclaimed King.[58] Similarly, on 20 October, Seaforth told Ranald MacDonald to take 200 men to Loch Ness and drive all cattle and horses and to take all meal 'as falls your way'.[59] Huntley and his men, however, seem to have given receipts for money levied, so gave the pretence of legality.[60]

Expeditions by Jacobite troops were made to collect money and supplies. Not all these trips met with success. In early October, Sinclair was concerned that Argyle's superior cavalry might threaten him on his return trip. Mar told him he could supply infantry to assist him, but what Sinclair really needed was cavalry patrols to give him warning of any movements of British troops. Sinclair set off on the expedition with much trepidation. He arrived first at Coupar and then at Dundee the next day, and then at other towns in their itinerary. Yet although James was proclaimed with ceremony in all these places, the main purpose of the journey was frustrated. Virtually nothing was found; at Coupar and at Dundee there were 'onlie a few broken rustie muskets', likewise at Crail and nothing at Kilrenney, Anstruther and Pittenweem, except some bars of lead. It was a dispirited band who returned to Perth.[61]

These raids, however futile to their supporters, disconcerted their opponents. Forfar wrote on 10 October, that the Jacobites 'doe what they please with all the country that lyes on the north side of the Forth which they are entire masters of'. They were well aware that the Jacobites were extracting money from towns, villages and private individuals, 'it is rally a dismal thing to see the country ruin'd when soe small a body of troops might have prevented it'.[62]

A well known expedition to gather arms took place, following intelligence being procured that Argyle was sending arms from Edinburgh to the Earl of Sutherland in the north of Scotland. Apparently this was the result of a merchant, who was an old friend of Sinclair, riding through the night to let him know the news; apparently there were about 3,000 muskets there or more. These supplies were put on board James Watt's ship, *Helen*, at Leith, but because of an inclement wind, the ship had to drop anchor at Burntisland and Watt went into the town to see his family. This put his cargo within range of the Jacobite forces. Sinclair approached Mar with the story but there was no immediate decision. Eventually he agreed, though it was taking a risk that Argyle did not learn of the proposed raid and send dragoons from Stirling to intercept the Jacobites. There was also discussion as to how the arms be transported; baggage carts were ruled out because the time needed to find them would allow Argyle to learn what they were planning.[63] However, Mar was not averse to what are now termed 'forward operations' as part of the petite guerre, as Sinclair implied. He had written

58   Scott, *Memoirs*, p. 107.
59   NRS, GD46/6/98.
60   *Ibid.*, GD44/57/500/8.
61   Scott, *Memoirs*, pp. 95–7.
62   Taylers, 'Lord Forfar and the '15', *Journal of the Society for Army Historical Research* 15 (1936), pp. 132–3.
63   Tayler, *1715*, pp. 63–4; Scott, *Memoirs*, pp. 97–9.

to the Earl of Struan on 21 September thus: 'If they be no apprehensions of us or our parties we shall loose some of our reputation' and had sent men to Castle Campbell to deter the enemy.[64]

Sinclair left Perth at five in the morning of 2 October with a party of 80 Jacobite horsemen and a detachment of Highlanders. They took care to avoid riding near any settlements where news of their movements might be passed to Argyle. However, just three miles out of Burntisland, Thomas Hepburn told Sinclair that the ship with arms had left the harbour. Major Balfour, who was with Sinclair, was still hopeful, so they rode a further two miles forward. Hepburn then took a dozen men who knew the district to approach the town to prevent boats from leaving and to locate the skipper of the ship they wanted. Once in the town, local men were obliged to join with Sinclair's men to bring the ship in. Whilst this was going on some of Sinclair's men were 'bussie drinking, contrarie to my express orders'.[65]

The ship was eventually brought in and Sinclair waded into the water to personally receive the weapons stored there. However, 'to my great grief', the haul was far less than anticipated: 299 muskets, a bag of flints, two barrels of musket balls and two or three barrels of gunpowder, weighing about a hundred pounds each. Another ship yielded 25 muskets, the armoury of the town guard another 30, and another barrel of gunpowder was taken. It was then that Sinclair learnt that 500 Highlanders were at Auchertool, only four miles away. He returned an order for them to remain there, whilst he prepared to leave Burntisland. It was now between three and four in the morning, and Sinclair was 'faint and sick with that confusion and running up and doun working'.

It was impossible to keep his little command together as they left, for some went to visit a minister they knew. When they arrived in Auchertool, they found that only 40 Highlanders remained; the others were 'spread up and doun the countrie, plundering'. The men who were there would not obey the now increasingly exasperated Sinclair. He and his horsemen eventually left for Perth, but not before telling the Highlanders that Argyle was within three miles of them. That lie brought them along with Sinclair more quickly than anything else could. They eventually arrived back in Perth that evening. He and Balfour reported to Mar and complained incessantly about the indiscipline of the Highlanders.[66]

They had been unmolested because they had had the town surrounded during the operation and so no one could leave with news of their arrival to Argyle, who only heard about it on the 3rd and by then they had already returned to Perth. This exploit was of great morale to the Jacobite cause, as Patten wrote, 'The Success the Rebels found at Brunt Island mightily encouraged them and their Friends' and it led to additional forays in Fife in search of arms. It had been a risky business, but they had

---

64   NLS, Adv.Ms.13.1.8./40.
65   Scott, *Memoirs*, pp. 98–9.
66   TNA, SP54/8/127; 9/2c.

covered 40 miles in 24 hours.[67] It had not, however, produced much of a concrete result in terms of muskets gained.

Irregular methods were also noted as being used. Macintosh was reported as having 'carried of some of the tenants' cattle and rifled their houses', taken plunder from a ship and having threatened to burn the Grants' country. The Duke of Atholl's hay was taken for the horses' forage. On other occasions, food and drink were taken and arms were gathered from Montrose's tenants by the MacGregors and Glengyles.[68]

One of the Jacobite weaknesses was intelligence. This was despite the fact that a committee of intelligence had been summoned into being. Sinclair wrote of it thus: 'All they did was to seem usefull in buseing themselves in scribbling to engage some poor gentlemen with lyes … or keeping correspondence with some woman, or poor tool, who returned them some of Mar's idle stories'.[69]

The following is an example of the lack of Mar's knowledge of events much removed from Perth. On the 21 October, he wrote two letters, one to Kenmure and the other to Thomas Forster (the two leaders of the Jacobite force then in northern England). Mar asked each of them for news. His problem was that the 'passage over the Forth is now so extremely difficult'. Boats coming over with messages had failed to deliver them. As Mar observed, 'I know so very little of our friends on that side, and less of you, which is no small loss to me'. He even suggested that Forster could help him by supplying newspapers from England, whose news was inevitably dated as it was printed and published in London. He was unable to advise Forster as to what his next step should be.[70]

This lack of intelligence may be due to a lack of agents and sympathisers being available and willing to provide Mar with information about the position of his enemies. Or it may have been because none were sent out. There seems to have been similar lack of knowledge among the Jacobite army in England about the whereabouts and strength of their enemy. Or possibly information was gathered but was not being efficiently processed. Certainly Mar's ignorance was to handicap his movements and made coordination of far flung forces impossible.

He may have been capable of forwarding disinformation, however. Mar sent John MacLean to Argyle's camp on 1 November. His main purpose was to send a request from Mar about his private property near Stirling. Mar was concerned that his house and gardens at Alloa might be damaged by Argyle's forces, and hoped that Argyle 'being a lover of Gardens, encourage me to it'. He received the assurances that no harm would come to them. Whilst awaiting this answer, MacLean, either on his own initiative or because he had been ordered to do, gave disinformation. The captain of the guards asked him about the strength of the Jacobite army, its pay, its reinforcements, and when it was expected to leave Perth. MacLean did not mention any of its officers, but stated that there were over 15,000 infantry and that they were paid four and a half

67   Scott, *Memoirs*, pp. 101–102.
68   Rae, *History*, p. 234; Patten, *History*, p. 134.
69   Scott, *Memoirs*, p. 248.
70   Patten, *History*, pp. 58–63.

pence per day, plus bread. Nearby were an additional 4,000 infantry and 2,500 cavalry; all these figures were gross exaggerations. Their plan was to immediately march to Stirling and surround Argyle, forcing him to surrender. MacLean was released after he had his answer from Argyle.[71]

Mar has often been accused of being too accustomed to the pen to the detriment of the sword. Yet the former is equally important to any commander-in-chief. Mar had Robert Freebairn set up his printing press at Perth, in order that propaganda be issued from there, to encourage his followers and to persuade others to join. Amongst the fiction issued was that Newcastle had fallen and that King George had fled the country. Mar also claimed he had lawyers to advise him on wording his documents.[72] As well as such news sheets, Mar also issued orders for raising money on 21 October.[73]

He also indulged in countering some of his enemies' actions in print. This was explicitly meant to counter Argyle's second proclamation to promote recruitment for his army. After asserting James' right to the throne, he prohibited anyone from executing Argyle's instructions to them concerning recruitment. Clergy were banned from praying for the Hanoverian monarchy; any who did could be arrested. Again, the efficacy of this step is uncertain.[74]

In the space of eight weeks a Jacobite army was in the process of being formed at Perth. Men were arriving. The necessary sinews of war were being provided for its maintenance. However, it was to an extent acting in the dark without much real knowledge of what was happening elsewhere. It also lacked the presence of James Stuart as a figurehead leader, or a general such as the Duke of Berwick. But for all that, it was in existence and could not be easily knocked out.

---

71   Rae, *History*, pp. 460–1.
72   *Ibid.*, pp. 297, 442.
73   *Ibid.*, p. 295.
74   Patten, *History*, pp. 147–8.

4

The Government Strikes Back

We now turn our attention to the role played by the government and its supporters, in particular the armed forces, to ascertain how, when and where they responded to the danger posed by the Jacobites. In theory the government should have been in a relatively strong position if it came to a passage of arms. They had the advantage of possessing a standing army, trained, armed, equipped and already in being and the Jacobites, barring assistance from abroad, had none. Yet there were difficulties; principally because it was not clear where the danger they had to face was coming from and that it might well be multi-pronged: from England, Scotland and overseas. This meant that it would be difficult to possess superior forces in several places at once. Yet if an outbreak of Jacobitism was not quickly dealt with, or worse, defeated a government force, then that would only encourage others to rise. Furthermore, the army was relatively small, being on a peacetime footing with merely internal policing duties. That a challenge was imminent there was no doubt, however.

On 20 July the Houses of Parliament were informed of the intelligence garnered by Stair, 'That he had certain Advices, that Attempts were preparing by the Pretender from abroad and are carrying on at home, by a restless Party in his Favour'. It was uncertain where the danger would manifest itself, 'There is no account where the landing is to be, but it is generally believed to be in Scotland'.[1] The assembled members swore their utmost loyalty to George I. They also issued a number of directions for practical measures to be taken against the Jacobites. Firstly, for a period of six months, habeas corpus was suspended so that suspects could be detained without trial. In Scotland the equivalent Act of 1701 to prevent wrongful imprisonment and undue delays in trials, was also suspended. Horses valued at £5 or over belonging to suspects could be seized for a period of six weeks, as could weapons. Suspects in Scotland were to present themselves at Edinburgh to be bailed for good behaviour.[2]

Civilian forces also had a role to play in basic security roles. In Edinburgh the constables were assigned a number of police duties. A list of all strangers in the city was to be made. All lodging house keepers were to make a return each night of any

---

1   Rae, *History*, p. 169; NRS, GD248/561/53/27.
2   Rae, *History*, pp. 170–1.

new guests. Horses worth above £5 were to be noted. This was undertaken on 25 July and 'wee find nothing extraordiner in either'. Their masters, the city magistrates, were encouraged to preserve the public peace in the area under their jurisdiction.[3]

Justices of the Peace were required to confiscate the horses and arms of those suspected of Jacobitism in order that they not be used against the government. There was a great deal of delay in implementation however. Eventually, as Sinclair noted, 'I found them very hot upon seizing horses and arms' but was able to retain his by procrastination. However, some Jacobites were less concerned about this, believing that supplies would arrive from France.[4]

Scottish magistrates began to share information about the Jacobites with one another. John Aird, Provost of Glasgow, along with his counterparts in Stirling and in other towns, began to do so in late July and would also collaborate with those in Edinburgh. Aird wrote, 'it is all our Concern that Joynt measures may be taken for the preservation of our Common interest and peace of the country'.[5] Robert Stewart, Provost of Aberdeen, was very proactive in this regard, writing on 3 August, 'I have sent severall spies towards the hillands ... I shall not faill to acquaint you of anything extraorinar occurs and shall expect ye same from you'.[6]

Another step by the government was to order the arrest of those nobility and gentry suspected to have Jacobite sympathies, with an order being sent to Whetham on 12 August and on 18 August a further one for taking Mar and Hamilton was despatched. A few were caught: George Lockhart of Carnwath (1681–1731) Alexander (d.1720), 7th Earl of Home, the Earl of Wigtoun, George Hay (1689–1758), 8th Earl of Kinnoull, and Lord Deskford. They were conveyed to Edinburgh as prisoners. But most escaped the net. Then there was the Act for encouraging loyalty in Scotland passed on 30 August. It stipulated that anyone corresponding or assisting the Jacobites was guilty of high treason and liable to have their lands forfeited to the Crown. Tenants whose masters joined the Jacobites would, provided they continued to live in peace, be allowed to hold on to their lands. Any Jacobite who had assigned their lands to anyone else since 1 August 1714, in order to avoid any subsequent seizure, would find that that assignment would be null and void. Finally, there was a list of noblemen (21) and gentry (42) who were suspected of being Jacobite. They were ordered to go to Edinburgh and find bail for their good behaviour. The list included most of the Jacobite notables, including Mar and also Rob Roy MacGregor (1671–1734). Only two men did as they were bid: Sir Alexander Erskine and Sir Patrick Murray on 17 and 20 September, who were then housed in Edinburgh Castle. The others were denounced as rebels.[7] Sinclair believed the measure was counterproductive ('it must be owned that the Government contributed most to Mar's project'), and Keith suggested this led to the Jacobites taking up arms immediately.[8]

---

3 Dickson, 'Warrender Letters', pp. 62–3, 65, 66.
4 Scott, *Memoirs*, pp. 14–5, 17.
5 Dickson, 'Warrender Letters', p. 66.
6 *Ibid.*, p. 73.
7 Rae, *History*, pp. 208–211; TNA, SP55/3/81, 87.
8 Scott, *Memoirs*, p. 36; Keith, *Fragment*, p. 10.

There would need to be more than this to tackle what would be, as in 1689–1690 and potentially in 1708, a major military threat. However, the British state was not in an immediate state of military preparedness. Marlborough's magnificent war-making machine had been largely dismantled following, indeed before, the Treaty of Utrecht of 1713. At the beginning of 1715 the British military establishment was composed of six troops of Household Cavalry, two regiments of horse, 19 regiments of dragoons, three regiments of Foot Guards, 25 battalions of infantry and 16 companies of invalids, totalling 8,164 cavalry and 24,490 infantry, though a report of July 1715 listed eight regiments of horse, six of dragoons and 32 of infantry.[9] However, in addition there was the separate Irish establishment, which consisted of five regiments of Horse, two of dragoons and 13 of infantry – of which at least seven were eventually sent to England and Scotland.[10] However, as with all counterinsurgency wars, most regular troops are needed in garrisons and only a small proportion are available for a field army, as had occurred during the Monmouth rebellion of 1685 and was to occur in the War of American Independence.

The number of regular troops in Scotland (other than those in garrisons at Stirling and Edinburgh castle and at Fort William) was small, amounting to a battalion of infantry and two regiments of dragoons. They were initially concentrated near Edinburgh in the summer. Government supporters there began to raise the militia and, in towns and cities, augmented the numbers in the existing Trained Bands. In Edinburgh, 400 men were raised. In Glasgow a militia regiment was also raised for service, to the strength of 500 men. They were to have first use of any arms and ammunition made by the city gunsmiths and armourers. Other towns in the west of Scotland and in the Lowlands followed suit, though on a smaller scale. In Dumfries seven companies were formed, totalling about 300 men, and underwent training in military drill and exercise. Yet, by the end of July it could be reported, in Edinburgh, that 'all being for the time in peace and quietness'. Likewise, in Perth, rather closer to the Highlands, the provost wrote, 'there are no appearances of any motions in the Highlands in so far as I can learn'. In the Lowlands and north of England, there were reports of Jacobites on the move in small bodies but these were thought to be men fearful of arrest rather than those about to rebel.[11]

Meanwhile the government was already taking military steps to counter the Jacobites. These were directed by the two Secretaries of State, the aforementioned James Stanhope, a former soldier, and Charles, 2nd Viscount Townshend (1674–1738), brother-in-law to Sir Robert Walpole. They were among the leading politicians at Westminster and their remit included the direction of internal security. As early as 21 July Wightman had been warned by Townshend to be on his guard. On the day before, there were orders sent for three battalions of infantry to be sent over from Ireland, Forfar's (246 men plus officers), Orrery's and Hill's. They arrived at Edinburgh on 24 August. Wightman ordered them to march to Stirling in order to prevent the

9   *Political State of Great Britain*, XIII (1717), pp. 606–10; TNA, SP41/5, f. 26.
10   British Library Add. MSS. 61636, f. 216r.
11   Rae, *History*, pp. 180–3; Dickson, 'Warrender Letters', pp. 67, 69–71.

Jacobites passing from the Highlands to the Lowlands of Scotland (and thus becoming masters of that kingdom) as well as preserving the castle there. Portmore's and Stair's dragoons were also sent there on 29 August. Two cannons and six wagon loads of ammunition were also despatched on the next day. Shannon's battalion of infantry (328 men and officers) was also marched there, leaving Edinburgh bereft of troops save for the garrison in the castle, though the forces at Stirling were, it was hoped, enough to prevent Mar from marching into the Scottish capital.[12]

These battalions of infantry and two dragoon regiments numbered 1,365 men (1,038 infantry and 327 dragoons) and officers.[13] These were the only troops available to form a field army (there were also troops in garrisons at Fort William – three companies of infantry from Forfar's, Montague's and Orrery's – and those in the castles at Edinburgh and Stirling but these were unavailable for action). Money was also provided: on 28 July £6,000 was allocated for the troops in Scotland, this being for 'the extra charge of providing forage or other necessary contingents for securing the public peace and quiet'.[14]

Extra troops were forthcoming. On 19 August, officers of 100 men of Grant's infantry were given marching orders from London to Edinburgh.[15] Additional forces were marching slowly northwards. On 15 August Carpenter's regiment of dragoons had been ordered from Wolverhampton, Leeds and Manchester to Berwick and thence to Scotland.[16] Cockburn complained on the 28th that this regiment had not arrived yet. Nor were there any orders to augment weak units nor to employ half-pay officers who were available for service.[17] Clearly Carpenter's men had not moved at all, for on 31 August William Pulteney (1684–1764), Secretary at War, ordered both them and Kerr's dragoons be put in readiness to march from England to Scotland as soon as possible. Three days later they were given their orders to march there.[18]

This was a reasonably sized concentration of force, though not all were fit for immediate service. It was said of Portmore's Dragoons, who had marched from Shrewsbury to travel to Scotland, 'the route directed proving so very long and almost impassable by horses, several horses died and many were disabled for our service'.[19] Their principal enemy, Mar, was also unimpressed, writing, 'They are so weak at Stirling, and so ill payed, that they scarce know what to do, in so much that their general, Whetham is gone for London, to represent it, and is it not a thousand pittys that we should loose so luckie an opportunitie?'[20] So much for Mar's alleged and oft-cited lack of aggressive spirit.

---

12 Rae, *History*, pp. 206–7.
13 British Library Stowe MSS. 228, f. 125r.
14 William and Slingsby Shaw, FH (eds.), *Calendar of Treasury Books*, XXIX, Part II, 1714–1715 (London: HMSO, 1957), p. 657.
15 TNA, WO5/20, p. 88.
16 *Ibid.*, pp. 85–6.
17 *Ibid.*, SP54/7, 87.
18 *Ibid.*, WO4/17, pp. 179, 181.
19 *Calendar*, 1714–5, pp. 351–2.
20 *HMC Stuart Papers*, I, p. 420.

The most senior soldier in Scotland, Major General Thomas Whetham (d.1741), spent money in order to make initial preparations. Robert Campbell was sent to provide intelligence for the government at the cost of £20; Gilbert Moor was contracted to provide forage for the dragoon horses, costing £161 5s and Campbell was also paid £21 10s towards the cost of forming a train of artillery for field service.[21]

Stirling was a strong place, as the journalist, Daniel Defoe (c.1661–1731), observed:

> The castle is not so very difficult of access as Edinburgh; but it is esteemed equally strong, and particularly the works are capable to mount more cannon, and these cannon are better pointed; particularly there is a battery which commands, or may command the bridge, the command of which is of the utmost importance; nay, it is the main end and purpose for which, as we are told, the castle was built.[22]

Yet this concentration of force at Stirling was not pleasing to all loyalists. Warrender (as provost and MP for Edinburgh) naturally wanted one regiment to remain in the capital for 'it will not only very much animat the minds of his Maties good friends, But will also much discourage those of his enemies'. After all, Edinburgh was 'the metropolis of No.[rth] Britain where are all the seats of Judicaturs, besyds the money of the nation in the Exchequer, excyse, Custome house and Bank'.[23] His wish, though, was not granted, but his fears were not ill-founded as we shall see in the next chapter.

Scotland was not the government's only security concern. The garrison at Portsmouth was reinforced by two battalions of infantry. The three regiments of Foot Guards and four troops of Horse Guards along with artillery, were to be encamped at Hyde Park under Major General William Cadogan (1671–1726). The Militia of Westminster and the Trained Bands of the City of London were reviewed and put on the alert to suppress any riots. Catholics in the capital were ordered to leave the city and could be deprived of their horses and arms. As for the army, politically unreliable officers were purged. Commissions were issued for the raising of 13 new regiments of dragoons and eight regiments of infantry and these were all deployed in England. More men were to be enlisted for the Guards battalions, too, and for the Royal Navy, for the duration of the crisis.[24]

Allies from overseas were also sought. It was not uncommon for the English state to employ troops from abroad to quell domestic disturbances. Tudor governments had employed German troops to defeat rebels. In the next century, Charles II negotiated with Louis XIV for assistance in dealing with potential internal enemies, though none were ever used. William of Orange offered military aid to his father-in-law to deal with Monmouth's rebels in 1685, though again this was declined. Dutch troops were in battle in the British Isles at Killiecrankie in 1689 and, successfully, at the Boyne in 1690.

---

21   *Journal of the House of Commons*, 18, p. 554.
22   Pat Rogers (ed.), *Daniel Defoe's Tour of the Whole Island* (Harmondsworth: Penguin, 1971), p. 612.
23   Dickson, 'Warrender Letters', p. 86.
24   Rae, *History*, pp. 170–2.

In the summer the States General of Holland were reminded of their treaty obligations to supply 6,000 troops and also warships if needed. They agreed to do so and entered into negotiations to discuss how this would be implemented. A representative of the Austrian Emperor (an ally of George in previous wars on the Continent) in London asked if Imperial troops were needed, but this was declined for it was thought that sufficient foreign forces would be supplied by the Dutch. However, the British battalions now in Flanders were recalled home and their place supplied by an equivalent number of Imperial troops.[25] Dutch forces were available because of the First Treaty of Barrier and Succession, made between Britain and Holland in 1709. It provided for the security of Holland but also that they would provide armed assistance if required to uphold the Protestant succession in Britain, too. This was reinforced by a second Barrier Treaty as part of the settlement at Utrecht four years later, which promised 6,000 soldiers. However, access to such support was not immediate.[26] As a friendly gesture, though, on 20 August, they detained two ships at Ostend which were being equipped for Scotland.[27]

It was not entirely plain sailing. Holland had employed 130,000 soldiers by the end of the War of the Spanish Succession, but by 1715 this number had fallen to 40,000. Most of these were Dutch, Swiss and Scottish (during the war many had been from German Protestant states) and most were employed in Holland's frontier fortresses as garrison troops. Military expenditure had plummeted and the country was in debt to the tune of 128 million guilders.[28]

Letters were sent to Holland to bring the 6,000 Dutch troops over. Two battalions marched from Maestricht to Ypres by 30 August. However when the French assured the Dutch that they were not about to assist the Jacobites and thus break the Treaty of Utrecht's stipulations, the Dutch halted these troop movements towards Britain.[29] The Jacobites were initially relieved about this delay. Bolingbroke had certainly written on 8 August that any Dutch aid would not be forthcoming and later in that month a similar hope was expressed, 'It is to be hoped with reason that the States of Holland will not be able to be very ready to engage in this war'.[30]

Townshend sent Horatio Walpole, younger brother to Robert, the Chancellor of the Exchequer and soon First Lord of the Treasury, and Cadogan, to The Hague to ensure the troops were sent. Walpole met the Pensionary, the deputies of the States General and the Council for Foreign Affairs and entered into negotiation; Argyle could only hope he would be both successful and speedy.[31]

---

25   *Ibid.*, pp. 172–3.
26   Geoffrey Holmes and Daniel Szechi, *Making of a Great Power, 1660–1722* (London: Longman, 1993), pp. 436–7.
27   *Manuscripts of the Marquess of Townshend* (London: HMSO, 1887), p. 159.
28   Jonathan Israel, *The Dutch Republic: Its Rise, Greatness and Fall, 1477–1806* (Oxford: Clarendon Press, 1995), pp. 985–6.
29   Rae, *History*, pp. 207–8
30   *HMC Stuart Papers*, I, p. 414.
31   *Political State of Great Britain*, X (1715), pp. 411–2.

Negotiations were progressing favourably. Cadogan, who was well versed in diplomacy, and Walpole at The Hague and Antwerp, dealt with the Pensionary, the States General and councils of deputies to remind them of their obligations as to the fourteenth article of the Treaty, the resolution was passed. On 7 October the States General ordered that the 6,000 troops be sent to Britain with all expedition and shipping arranged forthwith.[32]

Stanhope imparted this news to Argyle in a letter of 11 October, 'We have this day received the good news from Holland that the States have agreed to send over six thousand men immediately'.[33] Of course, they could not be despatched as quickly as Stanhope optimistically expected. Nine days later he wrote to Stair in relation to their being sent to Britain, 'tis certainly prudent to make every thing sure and you may depend upon it that no vigour will be wanting here'.[34]

Dutch troops began to gather at Ostend in late October. Transport ships and provisions arrived next and their planned departure was on 4 November. This, however, depended on the winds. It was not until 7 November that the first detachment of five battalions sailed to the Humber. On the 9th the remainder sailed for the Thames.[35] They would, however, arrive too late for the clash of arms that would decide the campaign. Yet this is to use the benefit of hindsight, for a victory for the Jacobites would have rendered their use imperative and in any case, as we shall see, they bolstered the government's position immeasurably in Scotland during the final stages of the campaign.

Effective defence entails extraordinary public expenditure. Britain's financial status, as with all the other great powers who had participated in the recently ended War of the Spanish Succession, was hardly robust. Annual average expenditure during the war had been an enormous £7.06m and of this, 72 percent had been on the armed forces (135,646 men in all). This had led by 1714 to a national debt of £40.4m and 44 percent of government income went to servicing that debt alone when income from taxation per year was a little over £5m.[36]

In order to help pay for the defence of the realm, offers were made by a number of key financial institutions. The Lord Mayor and City of London offered, on 20 July, to lend £1 million. The Bank of England and the South Sea Company also offered similar sums. By 26 July, the East India Company had also offered money. In all this amounted to about £4 million, almost the same as the annual tax yields, in order to 'Equip a fleet and raise an armie suitable for the occasione'. They clearly had confidence in the permanence of the new dynasty for if it fell, its successor would not honour its debts.[37]

Yet these institutions were not giving money; expecting repayment in the short term. For instance, on 29 July Robert Walpole borrowed £51,000 from the Bank on a deposit of £57,000 based on tallies and malt duties, repayable in two months at 5

32   Rae, *History*, p. 298; *London Gazette*, 5373, 11–18 Oct. 1715.
33   TNA, SP78/160, 136.
34   Leeds University Library Special Collections, *Despatches of Viscount Townshend*, f. 24v.
35   *London Gazette*, 5377, 25–29 Oct., 5378, 1–5 Nov., 5381, 12–15 Nov. 1715.
36   Holmes and Szechi, *Making of a Great Power*, pp. 432–3, 439.
37   Dickson, 'Warrender Letters', pp. 59, 66.

percent interest. Four weeks later he borrowed £38,007 14s 4d; again to be repaid in two months at 5 percent.[38]

On 22 July the Lords of the Treasury sent Pulteney a letter to prepare warrants, to be signed by the King, to have the Paymaster of the Forces ready to pay 'all such sums of money as shall be directed at the Treasury and put into his hands for any extraordinary or contingent uses of the Forces' as had occurred in the past.[39]

In August, it was announced that £10,000 be provided for the army 'to enable the officers to buy horses, tents and other necessaries for putting them in a condition for service'. Some of this money had to be borrowed as this expenditure had not been anticipated earlier in the year. Walpole borrowed £16,098 17s 8d for the army from the Bank of England on a deposit of tallies and orders on Malt Duties for 1715.[40]

It was not certain when and where the Jacobite thrust was to take place; not surprisingly so because the Jacobites were equally uncertain, as noted in the previous chapter. Warrender believed that James was to land in Britain with a large army in early August. He thought that London was their target, but that there might be a 'stir and Commotion in Scotland as well'.[41]

Although there was concern among government supporters about a potential Jacobite challenge in Scotland, at first this was limited and there were hopes that there would be no military danger from the Highlands whatsoever. On 2 August, the sheriff of Dumbartonshire told Montrose that he hoped Mar's vassals would be 'far from doing anything against the government, but on the contrary exert themselves withal the vigour in their power for and in conjunction with the government'. Likewise, Cockburn reported that in Ross and Douglas, 'all is quiet'. A week later it was written that in the Highlands, according to yet another correspondent, there was 'not the least stir'.[42]

Yet others were worried about what they saw and heard. Rumours abounded that Berwick had arrived or that James' landing was imminent.[43] There were reports of arms and ammunition being landed in Fifeshire for the Jacobite cause. Even before Mar's arrival in Scotland, Jacobite activity appears to have become known, as the provost of Aberdeen wrote on the third of August, 'all the disaffected hillands are in readiness to gather together in armes upon 6 hours'.[44]

Jacobite activity at Braemar under Mar's direction was certainly not unknown to their enemies. On the same day as Mar's first meeting with his confederates, Warrender wrote to Stanhope, telling him that although he and his colleagues would do all they could do to defend Edinburgh, they were 'in great consternation being threatened by the enemies of the government and alltogither in a defenceless condition'. Because of their vulnerable position in regard to the Jacobite Highlanders, 'it is earnestly intreated your Lo[rdshi]

38 Bank of England Archive, G4/9, pp. 118, 120.
39 *Calendar of Treasury Books*, 29, 1714–1715, p. 126.
40 *Ibid.*, pp. 138–140.
41 Dickson, 'Warrender Letters', p. 58.
42 TNA, SP54/7, 11, 12, 19.
43 *Ibid.*, 67, 23.
44 Dickson, 'Warrender Letters', p. 73.

p. Will be pleased seriously to recommend our caice to his Majestie and send us such a number of standing forces as may secure us from being overrun by the enemie'.[45]

It was believed that James was on board a ship to Scotland in late August 1715. Warrender informed Stanhope of this belief on 23 August. As there was only one Royal Navy warship in Scottish waters, Captain Haddock's ship the *Portmahon*, Warrender ordered it to patrol the seas off Aberdeenshire.[46] What was needed were more ships, 'it is the generall oppinion of everie bodie here that our coast is left too much naked and exposed to the eneimie for want of ships of war which if possible I wish the Lords Commissioners will please prevent by ordering such cruisers here as they shall think convenient'.[47] A week later, Warrender was informed by the Admiralty that two frigates were being sent to the Scottish waters.[48] Sir William Gordon, lieutenant governor of Fort William, was concerned that 'if the Pretender should come in Person amongst them, they were certainly resolved to join him'.[49]

Scottish loyalists were beginning to become fearful by the end of August. Warrender wrote on the 26th, 'The well affected in thes pairts are in a great consternation being threatened by the enemies of the Government and alltogither in a defenceless conditione ... in caice ther happen ane incursion from the Highland Clans or others in the north it is to be feared that we shall not be able to stand our ground'.[50] There were complaints about the lack of arms for loyalist volunteers.[51]

Steps that could be taken against the Jacobites were thought to be limited because of the lack of regular troops in the country to enforce directives. On 16 August, seeing a need to arrest suspected Jacobites from the Highlands, Whetham informed his superiors, 'I feare the few Troops we have here will not be sufficient to performe this service'.[52] Warrender agreed as to the lack of troops, writing to the government on 26 August, 'send us such a number of standing forces as may secure the south part of Scotland from being overrun by the eneimie'.[53] Several horses belonging to James Maule (1658–1723), the 4th Earl of Panmure, were seized at the cost of £8 4s 8d.[54] The soldiers that were despatched managed to take up Hume and Lockhart, but three other men who were sought heard of the plans to arrest them (it was not only the Jacobites who had intelligence leaks) and fled from their usual homes. There were other such failures, but Whetham was nothing if not persistent and vowed that he and his men would be more diligent in future. Yet there was another issue to be concerned with: 'The forces we have here are so few tis very dangerous the dispersing of them after all the persons named many being at a great distance from one another'.[55] After all he

45   *Ibid.*, p.79.
46   TNA, SP54/7, 80.
47   Dickson, 'Warrender Letters', p. 77.
48   *Ibid.*, p. 80.
49   *HMC Mar and Kellie*, p. 508.
50   Dickson, 'Warrender letters', p. 79.
51   TNA, SP54/7, 80.
52   *Ibid.*, 46.
53   Dickson, 'Warrender Letters', p. 79.
54   *Journal*, p. 551.
55   TNA, SP54/7, 61, 65.

only had two regiments of dragoons and three battalions of infantry at his immediate disposal. Yet as late as 1 September, he did not think an insurrection was imminent, that it would only occur when James arrived personally, as had been planned in 1708. He noted, 'I cannot find that the villains are up in arms'.[56] Sir William Gordon wrote on 29 August, 'the country is certainly as quiet as ever I knew it' and he had received a letter signed by Lochiel and Glengarry for him to assure the 'government of there dutifull and hearty resolutions to serve His Majesty King George'.[57]

Although there were concerns about Scotland, there was, however, the belief that there would be only a limited challenge from the Jacobites from overseas. On 28 July Stanhope told Stair, 'We shall I doubt not be very soon in a condition to withstand any attempt from abroad'. At the onset of September, Stair wrote that 'ye pretender has not lay'd aside his design of invading ye kingdom this season, but they seem to be at a stead at present'. Orleans seemed to appear sympathetic to the government, as Stair wrote, 'He is mightily obliging and offers me an audience every time I see him' and was 'importing his most earnest desire and resolution to live in perfect friendship and good understanding with our master'.[58]

However, neither Whetham nor Wightman were destined to be in command of the government's forces in Scotland for long. The commander-in-chief for that country was Argyle and his post was no sinecure. On 1 September he was told by Townshend that the arms and ammunition stored at Edinburgh Castle were to be used by the field army. On 8 September, he was given £1,000 of the £1,500 arrears of pay he was awaiting.[59] Furthermore, the government was to lodge £10,000 with the Barons of the Exchequer of Scotland from the Lord Commissioners of the Treasury for military use.[60] He was received by the King on the 8th and began travelling to Scotland on the following day. He was apparently chosen because of his family's and his own loyalty to the Hanoverian Succession and his own influence in Scotland as leader of the important Clan Campbell (the largest in Scotland).[61]

Argyle made his way to Scotland, having left London on 9 September. His orders, given at court on the previous day, were eightfold. These were to provide directions to the lieutenancy as needed, to maintain military discipline in his army with the units to be as complete as possible and for the officers to be at their posts. He was to do his best to prevent the Jacobites from being supplied and also to seek out intelligence from their ranks He was to assure penitent Jacobites of mercy and to assist in the disarming of Catholics and other suspected persons. He was to promise rewards to soldiers and others who distinguished themselves. Finally he was to appoint courts martial if necessary.[62] On the 12th he was at Boroughbridge in the North Riding of Yorkshire. It was here that he made his first of many requests to Townshend for additional troops:

---

56   *Ibid.*, 8/7.
57   *HMC Mar and Kellie*, p. 509.
58   TNA, SP78/160, 94v–r, 109r–110v.
59   *Calendar*, 1714–5, pp. 725–727.
60   LUL, Townshend, f.1r.
61   Rae, *History*, p. 218.
62   TNA, SP57/29, pp. 220–233.

I hope my Lord these confirmations of the strength and intentions of the enemy in Scotland will prevail with your lordship and everyone of His Majesty's council to advise him to reinforce his army in such a manner at least as that there may be a possibility of defending that country...if the enemy think fit to act with the vigour that men of common sense would in these circumstances, the handful of troops now in Scotland may be beat out of the country before my small reinforcement can joyn them.[63]

Townshend wrote back immediately, but failed to address Argyle's prime concern, instead remarking on the failure of the Jacobites to take Edinburgh Castle (see following chapter) and the success of Stair's diplomacy in France.[64] One issue that they could both agree on was the slow movement of Carpenter's and Kerr's regiments of dragoons which were trudging towards Stirling. Argyle commented on it and Townshend wrote that the King was unhappy about it.[65] Those nearer to the perceived danger naturally sided with Argyle. That more forces were needed was agreed with by a correspondent in Edinburgh who wrote on 14 September, 'nothing can more effectually prevent the Highlanders from invading this country than to have two to three regiments shipt in transports or men of war wch may land near their country'.[66]

Argyle arrived in Edinburgh on 14 September. He requested that the Glasgow magistrates send their 500 volunteers to Stirling and asked them to persuade others in the west of Scotland to send their forces there, too. Tweeddale was asked to send about 300–400 men to Linlithgow with 40 days' provisions and that Argyle would supply arms and ammunition if needed. John Hamilton (?–1721), 3rd Baron Belhaven, and Thomas Hamilton (1680–1735), the 6th Earl of Haddington, were already with Argyle. He discovered that the five regiments of regulars at Stirling totalled about 1,400 and even with the arrival of Carpenter's and Kerr's dragoons he would still only have a field army of 1,750 men. He wrote to his political masters: 'I am to oppose as everybody here tells me at least 10,000, armed and I am afraid to say, not very much worse disciplined ... declining or indeed delaying to reinforce this army be not exposing this country to ye most eminent danger'.

As we have seen in the previous chapter, Argyle's estimate of the number of his enemies at this time was vastly exaggerated. He had suggestions of his own to make to remedy the imbalance: that the three dragoon regiments in the north of England, Cobham's, Molesworth's and Churchill's, 130 miles away, and Evans' regiment (then in Ireland), be sent to Stirling; he also wanted Edinburgh's Castle's deputy governor replacing and feared that if the Jacobites beat him they could make a great impression on their allies in England.[67] Cockburn agreed with Argyle's need for additional troops, for if they were there, Argyle would be able to attack the Jacobites.[68] Dudley Ryder

---

63 *Ibid.*, 54/8/49.
64 LUL, Townshend, f. 5r.
65 *Ibid.*
66 TNA, SP54/8/59.
67 *Ibid.*, 68; NLS MS 7104, 109–110.
68 *Ibid.*, 72a.

(1691–1756), a London law student, agreed, stating on 22 September that Argyle 'has not men enough to make a stand against the rebels … they have but few men there yet'.[69]

On the 15th, Argyle inspected Edinburgh castle, perhaps mindful of the recent attempt to seize it. He reviewed the fortifications, the garrison and the magazines. He appointed Brigadier General Alexander Grant (c.1674–1719) as commander there, until Brigadier George Preston (1660–1748) arrived to replace the unfortunate Colonel Stewart as Deputy Governor.[70]

Argyle reached his army at Stirling by the 17th. Supply was now his major concern. He reported that the dragoons could not forage and there was insufficient money to pay for the feed that the horses needed. Bread prices were high and he could not expect the men to buy their own food. He stressed, however, that he would be careful with the money that he had already received. For once he did not complain about troop shortages, but noted that 70 of the Glasgow Militia had reached Stirling and the others were expected on Tuesday. Yet he was unimpressed by them, 'they are many of them so badly armed & having no bayonets, that I cannot possibly pretend to make any other use of them than to make them serve as a Garrison to the Town and Castle of Stirling'. Their very presence was at least 'so strong a demonstration of the hearty zeal of those honest people' in Glasgow and he suggested that the government send their official thanks to the provost. Argyle had at least, arms sufficient to deliver 1,000 for the use of the Argyllshire militia, to be distributed by his cousin, Colonel Campbell.[71]

Argyle was not short of advice. Daniel Stewart, chamberlain to the Duke of Atholl, suggested that Argyle secure Blair Atholl Castle and that his master would send men there to assist him. Apparently Argyle declined the offer and suggested that Atholl hold the castle with his own men. Presumably Argyle was concerned that he lacked the manpower to send anyone to a relatively forward position.[72]

Once ensconced at Stirling, Argyle stated that 'this country is in the extreamest Danger' and that he needed 'a considerable reinforcement'. According to him he had but 1,600 men and could not stop 8,000–10,000 with what he had. This estimate of Jacobite numbers was a wild exaggeration and in any case they were widely dispersed throughout northern Scotland. Argyle's intelligence reports were clearly very faulty at this stage in the campaign. He told the ministers on 21 September, 'I am extremely surprised that notwithstanding the alarms you have had from hence, we have heard nothing either from Lord Townsend nor you … His Majesty's ministers still persist in thinking the matter a jest, and that we are in a condition to put a stop to it'.[73] At least Argyle was joined by half-pay officers from Pocock's, Mark Kerr's, and Hamilton's regiments, who could assist in training the militia and volunteers.[74]

In fact, Argyle soon had another matter to deal with. He heard that Mar planned to march to Alloa, his country seat, about four miles east from Stirling, with a force

---

69 William Matthews (ed.), *Diary of Dudley Ryder, 1715–1716* (London: Methuen, 1939), p. 103.
70 Rae, *History*, p. 218.
71 TNA, SP54/8, 74a.
72 NRS, GD241/380/16A.
73 TNA, SP54/8, 80a.
74 *London Gazette*, 5367, 21–24 Sept. 1715.

of 6,000 men. Argyle ordered out picquets of both cavalry and infantry, and had the remainder of his troops to be ready to march in their support, had it been necessary to do so. However, the information received was false; no Jacobite forces were seen.[75]

The numerical strength of each side was a key concern for both commanders. Sarah (1660–1744), Duchess of Marlborough, wrote of Argyle's plight on 1 October:

> I don't find that the News from Scotland is so bad as some reported, and I am apt to believe the Duke of Argyle aggravated that Matter a good deal: for at the same time that a very terrible Account came from His Grace, I saw a letter from the Postmaster of Scotland, which said our Enemies there were not above 2,600, and there is no Certainty of any Numbers that have joined them since.[76]

Townshend, writing on 24 September, tried to reassure Argyle that the King was 'entirely satisfied with your Grace's conduct' and that George had ordered Evans' regiment to march to Stirling. He added that he would reply regularly to Argyle's correspondence. But as to the question of large scale reinforcements:

> You may have soon, such a body of Troops with you, as to give us a good account of your enemies. The situation of our affairs here, is such as makes it impracticable to spare anymore Regular Troops from hence, without apparent danger and hazard to the whole, the security & preservation of which, your Grace will agree with me, ought to be our main and chief business.[77]

The reason why Argyle was in receipt of less troops than he wanted was because of the perceived Jacobite threat in England. The government believed that that there would be an insurrection in England as well as in Scotland, and this was envisaged as being far more important than that which Mar had begun north of the border, a perception shared by the exiled Jacobite court, of course. The West Country from Bath and Bristol in the west to Exeter and Oxford in the east was seen as being as hotbed of Jacobitism, in part because of the rioting there earlier in the year. Arms, ammunition and horses were believed to have been stockpiled in these places, ready for use.[78] A report from Paris read, 'The revolt of the Scotch makes much noise here, and the adherents of the Pretender say out loud that there is a considerable one in England which must break out shortly'.[79]

Stanhope outlined the government's thinking thus:

> Every advice from home and abroad ... make it evident that a general insurrection is intended to be begun at the same time in several counties of England. They reckon

75   Rae, *History*, p. 234.
76   Cowper, *Diary*, pp. 183–4.
77   LUL, Townshend, f. 7r-8v.
78   Rae, *History*, pp. 211–212.
79   *HMC Townshend*, p. 163.

themselves sure of all the west, of Wales, of Staffordshire, Worcestershire, Derbyshire, Lancashire … [they] represent their hopes of success to be grounded upon the prospect they have that a great number of forces would be sent to Scotland … I submit it to your Grace whether the King's ministers will not be justified before God and Man, if they advise the King, to keep this nation in some posture of defence, and give me leave, my Lord, to offer you truly in my poor opinion, that nothing will so much dishearten the rebels in Scotland, as to find themselves disappointed of the hopes which had been given them from hence'.[80]

Captain Robert Parker (c.1665–c.1718), suggested that the distribution of military resources had been the work of the Captain General himself, 'the Duke of Marlborough had made such dispositions of the Troops in England, that in 48 hours, 2 or 3,000 of them might be drawn together to any part of the kingdom'.[81] It was his only known military act of the campaign.

Henry Liddell (d.1717), a London merchant, pointed out the plots that were envisaged there, to be led by various MPs:

This [Edward] Harvey was to have seiz'd St. James', [Sir William] Wyndham Bristoll, [Sir John] Packington was to have raised his men att Worcester and join'd [Corbet] Kynaston in Shropshire, your neighbour [Thomas Forster] was to have secured the town [Newcastle] and Tinm[outh] castle. Some others were to have attempted the Tower and Bank.[82]

For the government, control of England and, in particular, London, was seen as being paramount. Argyle, facing the bulk of the Jacobite army with modest numbers himself could not have been expected to sympathise with this point of view as it denuded him of troops. Yet there were precedents for such. In 1685 James II, when faced with a rebellion in the West Country, sent but a fraction of his army there, keeping more troops in and around the capital. He was doubtless aware that his father had lost the capital from the outset of the 'Great Rebellion' in 1642 and had gone on to lose the war, his throne and his head. This was because London was the administrative, financial and commercial centre of the kingdom. To lose London was, in the long run, to lose all. Scotland, was, in the short term, relatively expendable.[83]

Not all in government shared these views that there was a major Jacobite threat in England. Lord John Carteret (1690–1763) wrote to Spencer Compton (c.1674–1743) on 30 September, with the following views:

I still persist in my opinion that there will be no troubles in the West; notwithstanding there are many people in very ill humour, the design being so happily discover'd, that

---

80 *Ibid.*, pp. 174–5.
81 Robert Parker, *Memoirs of the most remarkable Military Transactions from the Year 1683 to 1718* (London: S. Austen, 1747), p. 263.
82 Joyce Ellis (ed.), 'Liddlell-Cotesworth correspondence' (Durham: Surtees Society, 1985), p. 180.
83 Peter Earle, *Monmouth's Rebels: The Road to Sedgemoor* (London: Weidenfeld & Nicolson, 1977), pp. 38, 9.

disaffected persons are so rapt that they rather strive to smother their own contrivances than to bring it to bear...the discontented people are rather cold to the present government, than dispos'd to venture any thing against it.

Yet even he added, 'If any insurrection shou'd be in this country, we are in a bad posture of defence'.[84]

The military strategic situation was seen differently by the Lord Chancellor, William the Earl of Cowper (1665–1723), and he outlined his thoughts in a letter to the King, regrettably undated, but presumably in mid to late September:

But what seems to me to be the more important and natural Consideration on the News from Scotland is, whether the Forces now in Scotland, or going thither, are probably sufficient to stop the March of the Rebels, and if not, whether the Consequences of that are not bad enough to require some Augmentations wherever it can be had, without exposing too much this Part of the Kingdom.

As to the first, I think your General or the Secretary-at-War should state plainly before your Majesty in the Cabinet, what Number of effective Men are now or will be in a short Time of your Forces in the Field; and then, by comparing that Number with what the Rebels will probably march, or your Majesty, by the next Advices, may hear that they have got together, a Judgement may be formed on that Point.

If your Majesty's Forces are found insufficient to stop the Rebels, I humbly think your Troops there should be immediately augmented, by all means consistent with the not leaving this Part of the Kingdom so unguarded as to invite an Insurrection or Invasion to be made here.

For it seems certain that if any Disgrace befall your Majesty's Troops in Scotland, Insurrections will immediately follow in England in many Places, and probably the Pretender will be encouraged to land here too.

On the other Hand, if the Rebels get no Advantage in Scotland, my Conjecture is, there will be no considerable Rising in England, and I take it to be much easier to prevent Commotions in England, by securing the Rebels shall make no Progress in Scotland, that it will be when any Success of the Rebels in Scotland, shall have made many Insurrections to break out in England, to find Means to suppress them.

The Scotch magnify their Danger something, and perhaps press for more Assistance than can be reasonably spared from hence. But I beg Leave to assure you I cannot but observe the prevailing Inclination here is to supply the Forces there but too sparingly, and as on the one Hand it would be extremely wrong to draw the Bulk of your Majesty's Forces to that end of the Kingdom, so on the other the not asking the Duke of Argyle strong enough to secure himself against a Defeat, or a Necessity of retreating, or of letting them go by him towards the South, will thoroughly involve England in a Civil War, of which None can answer for the Consequences, and therefore I humbly advise that this

---

84   *HMC Townshend*, pp. 162–3.

great Point should be thoroughly stated and considered by all such as have the Honour at any Time to advise your Majesty'.[85]

Steps had been taken in England to nullify this danger in addition to the arrests already noted. On 14 September, the Duke of Powis, a Catholic nobleman, was sent to the Tower. A week later, orders were sent out for the arrest of three noblemen; the Earl of Jersey and the Lords Dupplin and Lansdowne. They were all soon taken up. The MPs mentioned by Liddell were ordered to be arrested. Harvey and John Antis were in London and so were apprehended immediately (the former tried unsuccessfully to commit suicide). Packington was brought up for questioning from his house in Worcestershire, but was found to be innocent. Kynaston tried to avoid arrest but later gave himself up. Wyndham fled from the King's Messenger and the officer sent to Somersetshire to arrest him, but incriminating papers were found and a reward of £1,000 offered for him. He eventually surrendered, was questioned and confined in the Tower. The government's success in taking up would be conspirators was noted by Bolingbroke, who wrote, 'it grieves me to find they have singled out just the persons we depended upon ... it is to be fear'd they are got deeper into the secrets of our friends on that side than those friends apprehended'. The only Jacobite MP to escape was Thomas Forster, and of him more in the next chapter.[86]

On 22 September, the government sent instructions for the lords lieutenant in the English counties to give orders for the county militia to be raised. They also ordered that all Catholics and other Jacobite suspects be taken into custody and that their horses and arms be taken for the duration. London was seen as being particularly a place where there was a need to be vigilant.[87]

It was in the west of England that the danger was also being seen as being of critical significance and that the insurrection in Scotland was merely a diversion. Lumley's Horse, Stanwix's and Pocock's Foot were sent to Bristol. The Earl of Berkeley, Lord Lieutenant of Somerset, also went there to supervise civil defence. Chudleigh's Foot arrived at the beginning of October. Bath was also garrisoned by Major General George Wade (1673–1748), who had Windsor's Horse and Rich's dragoons with him.[88]

Oxford was seen as a hotbed of Jacobite activity. Thomas Hearne (1678–1735), an Oxford Jacobite, wrote unguarded comments of glee in his diary on hearing the news of an open Jacobite rising:

Things being now as it seems, full Ripe for an Invasion, we hear that the Highlanders, are up in Arms in Scotland, under ye Earl of Mar, & that they carry almost every thing before them ... This hath caused a great Consternation at Court, & divers persons are continually seized, the like insurrection being expected in England.[89]

---

85 Cowper, *Diary*, pp. 181–2.
86 *HMC Stuart Papers*, I, p. 391; Rae, *History*, pp. 213–4.
87 *Ibid.*, pp. 214–5.
88 *Ibid.*, pp. 215–6.
89 David Walter Rannie, (ed.), 'Hearne's Collections', Vol. V, 1714–1716 (Oxford Historical Society, XLII, 1901), p. 121.

On 5 October, Pepper's regiment of dragoons launched a raid at daybreak at Oxford to take a number of Jacobites there by surprise. In this they were largely successful, arresting 15 men and finding treasonable correspondence on them, and taking them to London. This did not damp down Jacobite ardour at Oxford, with James proclaimed as King there one night.[90]

Despite this myriad of anxieties in England, Townshend did, however, find that additional troops could be spared for Argyle, albeit from the Irish establishment. Those promised were Clayton's and Wightman's battalions of infantry and Evans' regiment of dragoons. Doubtless Argyle awaited these forces with great impatience, for they would take time to arrive.[91]

Argyle could do little with the few troops he had had in these weeks. The only instance of any positive action was when the John Leslie (1679–1722), the 9th Earl of Rothes, heard that a Jacobite party was to proclaim James as King at Kinross on 26 September. He took a party of Portmore's Dragoons and they arrived in the town, swords drawn, dispersed the Jacobites and put them to flight, without any fatalities.[92]

Argyle was concerned about the numbers and quality of his opponents in Scotland. On 24 September he wrote that well armed gentry were joining Mar on a daily basis and that in the Highlands there were 100 Jacobites to every one loyalist, 'our few friends in the north'. The Highlanders were 'all extremely well armed' and were 'the people in the world the best armed for their kind of fighting'. Even where there were Scots willing to fight for King George – and these were chiefly Argyle's own vassals in the western Highlands – 'they often lacked bayonets or in some cases, were too fearful'.[93]

All this meant, as ever, that 'The danger of His Majesty's affairs are increasing hourly'. He noted that Townshend and Stanhope had announced that they recently were 'out of all apprehensions of any attempt upon England', meaning, presumably, that they no longer feared an invasion from France or Sweden or any other substantial help for the Jacobites from either nation. So in response to this, Argyle concluded, 'I should humbly think is an irresistible argument for sending such a number of Troops to this country as might be sure of reducing this rebellion'. Argyle pointed out that it was beyond anyone's wit to stop thousands with his small force. Only if there had been a pass in which the small number could hold up the large would this be possible, but such a geographical feature was not to be conveniently had.[94]

Ilay backed up Argyle in a letter to Townshend, 'My brother will, I believe, do his duty with the few men he has. That is, he will defend the ground where he shall be, but he cannot be everywhere'.[95] Argyle later pointed out that there were 42 squadrons of cavalry and 22 battalions in infantry in England, and there was no enemy facing them. Yet in Scotland, with an open rebellion, there were only six battalions of infantry and

90   Rae, *History*, pp. 216–7.
91   *Ibid.*, p. 207.
92   *Ibid.*, p. 232.
93   TNA, SP54/8, 89.
94   *Political State of Great Britain*, X (1715), pp. 411–412.
95   Taylers, *1715*, pp. 60–61n.

eight squadrons of cavalry, all of whom were under strength.[96] It is not known whether Mar was aware of Argyle's numbers, however; his intelligence seems unimpressive, so perhaps not.

Yet Townshend was quick to point out that he still believed the real danger was not in Scotland. On 26 September, he told Argyle, 'I wish it were as easy to send you more Troops', but that the information he had received led him to believe that the main Jacobite threat was in England. Jacobites taken had said that 'there is to be a rebellion in England' and that a body of English cavalry would assist the Scots. A successful Jacobite rebellion in England could occur if 'a great number of forces would be sent to Scotland', and this was why the majority of the regular troops were to remain in England. Cockburn agreed about the danger to the government in England, writing that 'The Rebels in ye north depend more on a party from England yn on a foreign force' and that the English only awaited James' arrival. However, Townshend did give Argyle tactical independence of London, 'None of the lords here think it practicable, at such a distance, to give orders to a general, how he should act'.[97]

It was only by the end of September that Kerr's and Carpenter's dragoon regiments arrived at Stirling. The last of Kerr's left Edinburgh on 21 September and Carpenter's were expected soon. However, three junior half-pay officers of Kerr's deserted to Mar as did several privates and drummers from Montague's regiment.[98]

On 28 September, Argyle was stating that he no longer wanted his present command, referring to the time when 'these matters are put into the hands of others'. He was concerned for not only his numerical strength but also over his lack of both money and artillery.[99]

Unit	Sergeants	Drummers	Sick	Total
Forfar's†	18	9	4	268
Montague's	18	11	16	216
Orrery's	18	10	4	291
Shannon's	11	8	15	338
Grant's*	18	9	5	278
Portmore's	6	6	1	162
Carpenter's	6	6	0	168
Stair's†	6	6	6	155
Kerr's	6	6	0	157
* 6 deserted † 1 dead[100]				

Argyle's strength (excluding officers) on 1 October 1715

96   TNA, SP54/8/105.
97   LUL, Townshend, 11r–12r; TNA, SP54/8/99.
98   *Flying Post*, 3703, 27–29 Sept. 1715.
99   TNA, SP54/8/111.
100 *Ibid.*

On 1 October Argyle had four regiments of dragoons (Portmore's, Carpenter's, Stair's and Kerr's), totalling 642 rank and file. He also had five battalions of infantry (Forfar's, Montague's, Shannon's, Orrery's and Grant's), totalling 1,391 rank and file. Assuming a full complement of officers (three per infantry company and three per cavalry troop), it would seem that there were about 2,255 men.[101] Argyle had fewer men than Mar, but the margin was not considerable; certainly Argyle's fears of the numerical disparity he faced were exaggerated. Mar, though, was not in an immediate position to push southwards with a fair chance of success. The difficulty was that Argyle did not know when and by how much he would be reinforced, whereas Mar could expect far more men far more quickly (as he was: on 5 October, Mackintosh brought his 500 men to Perth).

Whilst Townshend could not supply all Argyle's needs, he wrote to try and reassure him a little. He told him that the King was ordering more battalions from Ireland to Scotland and then gave some moral support: 'His Majesty relies entirely upon your Conduct, and you doing everything that shall be most for his service, and does not think it is practicable at this distance to give positive Directions how to act against an enemy whose circumstances may alter every day'.[102] It is unlikely that these words would have given much comfort to the commander-in-chief in Scotland.

There was another contemporary suggestion as to why Argyle was allocated so few troops. Lady Cowper, wife of the Lord Chancellor, after referring to the animosity between him and Marlborough commented:

> Lord Townshend, Baron Bernstorff, Mr Walpole and Lord Sunderland, were all afraid of the Duke of Argyle, whose Favour with the Prince [of Wales] made them fear that one Day he would get the Better of them; so to lessen his Reputation, he had been sent to Scotland with very Few Troops, and even those that were to go to him, by the secret Orders of the Duke of Marlborough, were so long a coming that the Earl of Mar had time to strengthen himself. That made the Duke of Argyle fly out prodigiously. He complained loudly of the Ministry.[103]

Argyle acknowledged that the discovery of the conspiracy in England was good news and added that he had heard of a planned insurrection in the north of England. He noted 'the weight both my Lord Townshend and you [Stanhope] lay upon continuing all the troops in England'. His major concerns were of being surrounded by enemies both north and south of the Forth, and desired that the Dutch reinforcements should be sent to Scotland not England. Meanwhile, with the Bank of Scotland being closed he needed specie to pay the troops.[104]

Townshend acknowledged that the Bank was closed, but Argyle was told to use the funds he had already been given. It seems that Argyle was provided with money on a

---

101 *Ibid.*
102 LUL, Townshend, f. 13r.
103 Cowper, *Diary*, pp. 58–9.
104 TNA, SP54/9/2A.

monthly basis. On 1 October, the Receiver Generals of the Excise, Customs and Land Tax were to provide him with £10,000. The army's paymaster general would then draw bills. The Barons of the Exchequer in Scotland were to put all their money into the hands of the receivers and collectors for army needs. To put this into perspective, the cost for one month of three battalions of infantry was a total of £1,656 18s – from 25 September to 24 October in the case of Windsor's, Sabine's and Preston's battalions, all of which were now in England. Dragoon regiments cost more for there was a horse as well as a man to consider. In the same period, Kerr's and Carpenter's dragoons cost a total of £1,365.[105]

On the subject of manpower, Townshend stated that Argyle had been given 'a full proportion of the Troops has been ordered for your parts', presumably meaning that Scotland was a far less populated country compared to England and so (in theory) there were proportionately fewer enemies there. There was also an attempt to sympathise with Argyle's situation, 'all here are very sensible of the great Difficulties your Grace has to struggle with, but we still hope your Grace will be able to overcome them'. He could also stress one advantage Argyle had over his foe, 'the superiority of your cavalry in goodness over the Enimie'.[106] This was a good point but in any action the onus for victory or defeat rests with the numerically stronger infantry.

Argyle was not the only Scot to offer the government a gloomy prognosis of affairs there. The most powerful civilian in Scotland, Cockburn, was concerned that the campaign might lengthen, 'when so many of the nobility and gentry of North Britain have unhappily suffered ymselves to be misled & ruined into a rebellion, the melancholy consequence of a civil war must be astounding to think of'. Far more men were opposed to the Crown in Scotland than there had been in 1689. He suggested that there might be a way to reduce the fighting strength of the Jacobites. This was to follow the policy eventually instigated by William III in 1691, in giving a general pardon, which had 'broke ye party among themselves'. Cockburn admitted that this was not without difficulties:

How far such a Measure is adviseable in this Juncture, I confess has its own Difficulties and the objections to it are very weighty, yet on the other hand should a power be lodged with the Duke of that whoever acts in such a time shall lay down yr arms and submit to His Majesty's government shall have been a gracious pardon … may be of great use.

Cockburn stated he would not necessarily advise such a policy, but such was the danger, 'no cure is to be left unessayed'.[107] This issue was to be raised again in late November.

Correspondence to Montrose at this time was full of despondency as to the threat posed by the Jacobites, stemming from fear of military weakness. One of the letters, of 30 September noted, 'I do indeed believe that the little army we have shall not be

---

105 *Calendar of Treasury Books*, 29, Part 2, 1714–1715, pp. 90, 784, 811.
106 LUL, Townshend, f. 18r–19r
107 TNA, SP54/8/99

sufficient to stop their progress' and a week later, 'We should have a good body of foreign troops to be depended on here'. Jacobite strength was perceived as being great, 'Their never was so universal ane insurrection in the country at no time'.[108]

Apart from the land-based forces, there were also the maritime forces of the Crown to consider, and here the Crown enjoyed a clear superiority as there was no Jacobite navy. On 22 July ships of the Royal Navy under Sir George Byng were to rendezvous in the Channel, eventually numbering 22. A month later, he instructed Captain Charles Poole of HMS *Pearl* to cruise off the east coast of Scotland and especially in the Firth of Moray. He was to seek intelligence of any Jacobite activity and was to have command of HMS *Port Mahon*. They were to search any suspect vessels sailing between France and Scotland and to seize their contents if need be. By the end of the month there were five ships patrolling the Scottish waters, though Byng considered there should be more.[109]

The naval vessels off the east coast of Scotland were instructed to search 'all ships vessels and boats that may happen to arrive in any port harbour or crick whatsoever and to secure all armes that may be found on boord and passengers until they give accompt of them selffs'. Intelligence sharing was also encouraged.[110]

Warrender was also concerned with the several hundred vessels which lay on the north side of the Firth of Forth, that they might be used by the Jacobites to ferry men across (perhaps up to 3,000 and in a few hours' time) and perhaps to menace Edinburgh. He corresponded with the captains of the naval vessels, hoping that they might be able to seize or disable such boats. Captain Haddock told him that there would be some difficulty because these boats were in harbours controlled by the Jacobites. By 4 October, Warrender thought that there was an immediate Jacobite plan to seize the boats between Burntisland and Fife Ness to transport men across and attack Edinburgh. He ordered the Baillie of Leith, William Jeffrey, to disable all ferry boats at Leith Harbour by removing their masts, rudders and sails and asked the naval officers to do likewise on the north side.[111]

By 19 October, Argyle had cause to be pleased with the news that he would be reinforced by three battalions from Ireland, but he was still gloomy. Militia expected from Tweeddale failed to materialise at Edinburgh to aid in its defence, preferring to remain at home, and Argyle wrote, 'I am sorry to see by your lordship's letter you find the militia so backward and in so bad a condition'.[112] He did not know where Evans' regiment was and had heard nothing more about the Dutch auxiliaries. He downplayed the dangers posed by the English Jacobites, writing, 'I do still think there is nothing to be apprehended from the people of England who never had Arms in their hands'. Another concern was the increasingly worsening weather 'which the Highlanders

108 NRS, GD220/5/816/12, 16A.
109 TNA, SP42/14 f. 194; Ninian Hill, 'A Side light on the 1715', *Scottish Historical Review*, XVII (1919–1920), p. 225.
110 Dickson, 'Warrender Letters', p. 87.
111 *Ibid.*, pp. 101–105.
112 NLS, 7104, 114.

every body knows can bear and our own Troops cannot'.[113] Argyle's concerns as to his numerical inferiority were shared by Douglas Archibald (1692–1715), 2nd Earl of Forfar, who wrote that he was fearful the Jacobites would attack before the Dutch and the troops from Ireland would arrive, 'which gives us reason to be much surpris'd at ye slow procedures of some', which was presumably a criticism of the government.[114] Edinburgh was also more secure in case there was another attempt to take it. Grant's newly raised battalion at Stirling was not thought fit to take to the field, and so was sent to Edinburgh, arriving there on 22 October. The city magistrates had 20 cannon sited on the city walls.[115]

A letter from George (1683–1760), Prince of Wales, written on 7 October to Argyle and which never reached its intended recipient, gives an insight into government thinking about Argyle's situation and endorsed a defensive stance at this juncture:

> The King remits himself entirely to your judgement, and to your conduct. All that I can say to you is not to hazard an action without a probable appearance of carrying it, or rather to share an engagement and to yield them the ground, than to expose the affairs of the King to such ill consequences as would follow from a defeat.[116]

Unit	Sergeants	Drummers	Sick	Total
Portmore's	6	6	3	174
Carpenter's*	6	6	1	171
Stair's	6	6	10	161
Kerr's	6	6	3	166
Forfar's*†	18	18	9	309
Montague's†	18	12	10	238
Wightman's	20	10	3	258
Fusiliers*	22	18	13	369
Shannon's†	20	10	8	337
* 3/9/4 men deserted[117] † 1 company detached at Fort William				

Argyle's Army at Stirling (excluding officers) on 27 October

Closer to home, four regiments were eventually sent from Ireland for Scotland: Evans' Dragoons (who arrived on 25 October), as well as Egerton's, Clayton's and Morrison's battalions of infantry. Evans' were quartered at Falkirk, Egerton's at Kilsyth,

113 TNA, SP54/9/55.
114 Tayler, 'Forfar', p. 136.
115 *Daily Courant*, 4373, 29 Oct. 1715.
116 Katherine Thomson, *Memoirs of the Jacobites*, I (London: 1845), p. 96.
117 TNA, SP54/9/92

and the latter two quartered at Glasgow by 3 November.[118] Argyle was not wholly impressed, writing that Clayton's and Egerton's men were 'so ragged that they are fitter to serve in a warm climate than here'.[119] Without the three battalions of infantry just named, Argyle's little army amounted to 848 dragoons and officers and 1,677 infantry and officers; perhaps a 'grand' total of 2,525.[120] With the other three infantry battalions it was estimated Argyle had about 3,000 men.[121] Cockburn wrote, 'the Foot he has are good but too few thereof'.[122] Rothes was confident though, thinking that even with fewer men, Argyle would hold back the Jacobite army.[123]

Argyle, of course, was still despondent, and with good reason, for even with these reinforcements, he was still outnumbered, believing that Mar had 5,000 men under his immediate command. He was amazed that he had not been seriously threatened, telling Stanhope on 31 October, 'it is not more wonderful that we have not been beat out of Scotland'. Although he admitted that he was unable to attack the Jacobites, because of the lack of troops and supplies, and because of the poor terrain north of the Forth, he was resolved to go on the offensive in the case of a Jacobite advance around Stirling, 'every thing was to be risqué rather than prevent the eneimies main body to get between us and England'.[124] Yet he stated to Marlborough that the weather precluded any offensive action, 'it is impossible for us to drive them out of Perth at this time of year', but was confident he could stop an advance.[125]

Perhaps in one way, matters were becoming administratively better organised for Argyle. Pulteney decreed that William Burroughs was needed as Commissary and he was appointed as commissary of stores and provisions on 28 October.[126]

Argyle wrote that on this basis and on the contents of a letter from Mar bemoaning the state of the Jacobite army, 'is to prove that nothing is so easy as for to march straight to Perth and make an end to the rebellion at once'.[127] An anonymous correspondent believed on 21 October, once the reinforcements from Ireland had arrived, 'I mistake it much, if those with what are come and expected from Ireland won't put an end to this matter effectually'.[128]

Argyle, of course, smiled at such an assessment, writing, 'I wish from the bottom of my heart that it was true'. Although he had now 3,300 men compared to 1,300 in September, the Jacobites, in early November, had 7,000 and possibly more. The terrain towards Perth was hilly and the city defended by entrenchments. The climate was cold (conventionally armies rarely campaigned once the summer months were over), there were impassable fords and perhaps most of all, supply would be difficult. Argyle's

118 Rae, *History*, p. 297; TNA, SP54/9/85, 92, 10/8.
119 TNA, SP54/10/18A.
120 *Ibid.*, 9/92.
121 *Ibid.*, 9/8.
122 *Ibid.*, 10/98.
123 *Ibid.*, 10/2.
124 *Ibid.*, 9/101B.
125 British Library Add. MSS. 61136, f. 173v.
126 *Calendar*, 1714–1715, pp. 813, 304.
127 TNA, SP54/10, 18a.
128 NRS, GD220/5/816/28.

forces were supplied from Edinburgh and Glasgow and so to march north would stretch supply lines, making them vulnerable and less reliable. Without adequate supplies a campaign could grind to a halt.[129]

Yet at least Argyle felt strong enough to stand on the defensive against an offensive. He wrote, 'We are now strong enough to prevent the rebels from ever passing this river'. He considered that it was not possible to advance unless at least half of the Dutch troops arrived, though this would surely have exacerbated the supply difficulties inherent in an advance in winter time. Although the men's camps were dry and there was plenty of coal, they preferred being in town in winter. He concluded, reasonably enough, 'I see no other reasonable prospect at this time of the year when it is not in nature to keep in any time in the fields'.[130] By 11 November, due to the poor weather, the men were unable to lie in the fields but the infantry were billeted in houses in Stirling and the dragoons billeted in adjacent villages.[131]

However by this time, this lack of offensive spirit did not please his political masters in London, and there was even talk about replacing Argyle as commander. George I found Argyle's assessment of the military situation 'indeed most mortifying' and that 'he was not a little surprised at some expressions in them' when the letter was translated for him from English into French. Although Argyle claimed that he had served the King 'faithfully and zealously' he found the plan to supersede him 'most agreeable'. He stressed, though, that all his officers agreed with him that an advance on Perth was impracticable.[132]

Townshend told him that it 'seems very reasonable' to attack Mar if he marched to Dunblane, or if he tried to cross the Firth or encircle Argyle. The latter, if it occurred, would be 'of too great consequence, not to be prevented, if it can be done'.[133]

Colonel Kennedy in London noted additional criticism of Argyle then prevalent in London on 10 November, which was largely based on ignorance:

Folks that ask me what you have been doeing there severall weeks that you did not goe and attack Lord Mar at Perth before the clans and Seaforth join'd him for they say you were much stronger than he was, and why have you let him fortifie Perth without gieving him the least disturbance … nobody can be persuaded that those men Mar has with him can be better than your militia'.[134] George Bubb, British representative in Spain, and so comfortably distant, was also dismissive of the Jacobite threat, referring to them as 'a handful of Rebels in a barren Mountain.[135]

The government certainly seemed confident of ultimate success. Stanhope wrote to Stair to state that he did not possibly think a rebellion could start afresh in England

129 TNA, SP54/10/18A.
130 *Ibid.*
131 NRS, GD220/5/817/4.
132 TNA, SP54/10, 30, LUL, Townshend, 27r.
133 LUL, Townshend, 34v.
134 Tayler, 'Forfar', p. 141.
135 TNA, SP94/84, 11 November 1715.

and last very long. Having intercepted Mar's mail he noted that there were great expectations of James landing but Stanhope believed that it was only in Scotland where he would be safe if he did and then did not believe he could do so until the spring. He believed that 'upon the whole the more one thinks of the more one is amazed at the folly and wickedness of his abettors here'. Abroad, he believed that Orleans was being wooed by 'the frenzy of madness' if he did not pursue his own interests, which were, believed Stanhope, identical to that of Britain.[136]

Argyle also received some ill tidings. The Dutch forces, of whom Stanhope had told him would be arriving very soon, then learnt that the 3,000 which were to have sailed to the Firth with a month's subsistence, were now (8 November) ordered not to sail there, but to the Humber and only then would a decision be made as to their ultimate destination (the danger of the Anglo-Scottish Jacobite army then in northern England under Forster was seen as being critical). As ever, the government viewed the Jacobite threat in England as the more pressing. All this meant, at the very least, additional delay. Townshend told Argyle on 8 November, 'this march of the rebels into a county [Lancashire] full of papists and disaffected persons by whom they will probably be joined has occasioned some confusion here, & has had a bad effect upon the publick credit and it will be some time before Mr Wills, who commands in those parts, can have a sufficient Body together for reducing them, and can be joined by Carpenter'. Jacobite forces had brushed aside those civilian bodies in the north western counties and only regular troops could deal with them. Argyle was also told that there were rumours of Jacobite landings in England and Ireland, assisted by France.[137]

By the beginning of November, Argyle's forces had slowly increased in number compared to their state two months previously. They were still relatively small and Argyle was far from confident that they were strong enough for the task which he had been set.

---

136 *Ibid.*, SP78/160, 131r–132v.
137 LUL, Townshend, 31r 35v.

5

The Campaign of the Fifteen, 6 September–8 November 1715

Having seen the build-up of forces on either side, we now turn to the narrative of that campaign which was ongoing simultaneously. The campaign of the Fifteen in its first two months did not provide any battles or indeed much fighting. However, despite minimal bloodshed, there were a number of important manoeuvres which took place, as each side grappled for advantage. These will now be outlined.

Shortly after Mar had raised the Stuart banner in public, he and his following then went to Kirkmichael, arriving on 9 September. Once again they proclaimed James as King, summoning all the inhabitants there to this public declaration. The Jacobites stayed there briefly.[1] They then went to Moulin, in Perthshire, again proclaiming James there. Here they were joined by other Jacobites, considerably enlarging their numbers and then went to Logierait. According to Patten, Mar now had 1,000 well-armed followers. They then came to Dunkeld. Here they were joined by Tullibardine, the Earl of Breadalbane's men and others, allegedly to the tune of a further 2,000.[2]

Yet there was also debate as to whether the rising should be put on hold, given the news of the death of Louis XIV and the fact that James had not arrived yet. In 1708 the Jacobites had not formally risen, waiting for the French invasion fleet to land with James. Mar did not listen to such cautious voices, but 'pressed with much forwardness, that the severall clans should rendezvous on the 8th September … and march to Braemar, then to Perth southwards, then to England' and force George I to abdicate. An immediate march southwards was also advocated. The rising was to continue but the march to England was not begun.[3]

Elsewhere in the Highlands, similar events were taking place and James was being announced as King throughout the Highlands of Scotland by Marischal (Aberdeen), Tullibardine (Dunkeld), Huntley (Castle Gordon), Panmure (Brechin), the Earl of Southesk (Montrose), Viscount Dundee (Dundee) and by Mackintosh of Borlum as he occupied the ungarrisoned Inverness. Borlum had simply walked into Inverness with 500 men early one morning. He placed guards at the houses of the magistrates

---

1   Rae, *History*, p. 191.
2   Patten, *History*, pp. 3–4.
3   TNA, SP54/8/30.

2. Edinburgh Castle, a forbidding sight to a would-be attacker. The Jacobites made a failed attempt to capture it in September 1715. (Author's photo)

and ministers in order to prevent their communicating with the outside world. He took £38 from the collectors of the Customs and Excise. From the Customs House and merchants he took flints and lead, as well as all the letters he could find.[4] From Dundee to Cromarty, the ports on eastern Scotland were in Jacobite hands; James was proclaimed there and the Whig magistrates had been evicted and replaced by Jacobite ones. An agent arriving at Aberdeen for the government was arrested and so by these manoeuvres the Jacobites had prevented their enemies from learning anything from government supporters in these places.[5] A bloodless revolution was taking place throughout the country, but only because there were no troops there to oppose them.

Not all Jacobite initiatives in early September led to success, however. There had been an attempt to take Edinburgh Castle by a *coup de main* on the night of 8 September. In fact, the city authorities had 'a surmise of ane insurrection in this place on the 5th instant'. Warrender had met Whetham that day and 'earnestly entreated' that he leave Shannon's battalion behind in the city as the other units marched to Stirling. Whetham merely replied he 'hade express orders from the Government for their removeall', though Townshend later claimed that this was not the case and Whetham was using the discretion in command that he had been allowed.[6]

---

4   Rae, *History*, p. 191.
5   Dickson, 'Warrender Letters', pp. 100–101.
6   *Ibid.*, pp. 88, 91.

Edinburgh castle was an important place to hold and it would be difficult to quickly retake with the few troops available. It had held out for some months in 1689 for James VII, after all. There was a substantial amount of both money and arms there.[7] As Warrender noted, if the castle were taken, 'we hade then been reduced to the extreemest danger, and by this Government of the City taken out of our hands and lodged in the hands of our enemies who very soon would have made them selfs masters of all the Castle stores, moneys in the Exceise and Custome house and bank, and thereby been able to strengthen them self against the Government'.[8] The strength of the castle garrison was not substantial either, as Ilay observed, 'only of 100 men and 20 wanting – all in rags, no proper clothing and never more than one day's provisions'.[9]

The plan was directed by Lord Drummond, though Charles Forbes, 'a little brokne merchant' was in charge on the spot. A key member of his team was Thomas Arthur, who had been an ensign in General Stewart's battalion from 1712–1714. Arthur contacted a soldier of the castle garrison, one sergeant William Ainsley, on 6 September and promised him promotion to lieutenant and 100 guineas if he would assist them, and he agreed. On 7 September, Privates James Thomson and John Holland were brought into the scheme, and were given eight and four guineas respectively, with the promise of more money on its success. Drummond had about 80–90 men with him, half of whom were Highlanders, the others being Edinburgh apprentices and lawyers' clerks. The plan was for the two sentries to let down a thread with lead attached and then pull up a grappling iron with an attached ladder and let the insurgents over the walls.[10] Once the three soldiers had let them inside, Drummond would become the castle's governor and they would fire three cannons from the castle to let their allies know, and by a number of bonfires from Edinburgh northwards, to alert Mar of their success.[11]

They were initially able to keep their plan secret, but on the day before the scheme was to take place, Arthur spoke about it to his brother, an Edinburgh doctor. On the day that the attempt was to be made, the doctor could not conceal from his wife the fact that he was keeping a secret. She found out what this was and then reported it by sending a servant with an anonymous letter to Cockburn.[12]

Cockburn had heard of the plan at 10:00 p.m. that evening and told Warrender this news. They had the Town Guard doubled.[13] He also sent a messenger with the news to the deputy governor of the castle, Lieutenant Colonel James Stewart. It was at about 11:00 that the message arrived. He posted guards to the north and south flanks and the fore wall of the Low Guard. After he had doubled the guards 'it seems that he either went to Bed, or otherwise fail'd of his Duty, and acted not vigorously enough upon this occasion, or suitably to the Danger'.[14]

---

7   TNA, SP54/8, 37d.
8   Dickson, 'Warrender Letters', p. 90.
9   Taylers, *1715*, p. 60n.
10 TNA, SP54/8/35; Scott, *Memoirs*, p. 29.
11 Rae, *History*, pp. 198–9.
12 *Ibid.*, p. 199.
13 TNA, SP54/8, 37d.
14 Rae, *History*, p. 199.

The plan was that when the Jacobites were standing at the foot of the wall, at West Kirk, Thomson and Holland would be waiting to assist them from above at 9:00 p.m. They were delayed by a number of them enjoying premature, and loud, celebrations in city hostelries and did not leave until 10:00. It took time for them to gather together, armed with pistols and swords. At 11:15 the two sentries called down to check whether Arthur and his fellows were there, concerned that they would soon be relieved from sentry duty, the latter replying 'wee are not yet ready', but would let them know when they were. Haste was needed because another sentry round might soon be upon them and the two could not stand guard there much longer. They let down the rope ladder and began to pull it up to let the others up. However, Lieutenant Francis Lindsey of Orkney's battalion led a party of soldiers towards the sally port. On seeing them, Holland and Thomson threw the ropes over the battlements and the ladder fell to the ground outside. One of them cried out, 'God damn you all! You have ruined both yourselves and me! Here comes the round I have been telling you of this hour. I can serve you no longer!' and fired and the Jacobites fled.[15] However, according to Patten, the rope ladder, though it could enable several men to climb up at once, was not long enough.[16]

Meanwhile, outside the walls, the City Guards were vigilant, but not fast enough to catch many of their foes. James Aikman, once major in General Preston's battalion of infantry, 'a gentleman known to be well affected to the Government' took some of the City Guard and marched to the west port of the castle and then to the sally port. There they found a rope ladder with an anchor at one end of it. His men were then reinforced by their compatriots under three more captains of the guard. They arrested four of the plotters. They also found a quantity of arms and ammunition: muskets and pistols double-balled and allegedly all poisoned too, with some bayonets and swords, left by the Jacobites in their speedy departure from the scene. Despite a search by the constables for horses and arms, most of the plotters had fled that same night. The City Guard patrolled around the base of the castle walls until six on the following morning.[17]

The four Jacobites were questioned before the magistrates on the following morning. Statements were taken from those arrested. Suspecting a more widespread plot, perhaps because of the lack of any regular troops nearby, the magistrates ordered a virtual curfew that afternoon and the constables made a renewed hunt for the conspirators, but found that the latter had fled long ago. Warrender told Townshend that the magistrates would be as vigilant as possible but what they wanted him to do was to 'order some regular forces for the security of the Government'.[18] Few loyalists thought themselves safe, one writing to Montrose on 15 September, 'Providence, I must say, has wonderfully saved us hitherto, but we ought not to tempt Providence either'.[19]

---

15   Scott, *Memoirs*, p. 31, Rae, *History*, p. 200.
16   Patten, *History*, p. 135.
17   Dickson, 'Warrender Letters', pp. 88–89; TNA, SP54/8, 37d.
18   Dickson, 'Warrender, Letters', p. 89.
19   NRS, GD220/5/816/4.

Perhaps it was bolting the stable door once the horse had bolted, but the castle's defences were strengthened following this incident. From 1 August 1715 to 12 March 1716, £1,206 16s was expended on additional officers and men. A further £674 19s 11 ½d was spent on the repair of guns and bayonets in the castle.[20]

The security of the city was somewhat strengthened a few days later when Townshend gave permission to raise another 200 men for the City Guard and promised that the government would foot the bill. The seizure of Perth by the Jacobites (which will be explained shortly) gave the City magistrates a further impetus to do so, and Jacobite prisoners were transferred from the City Gaol, the Tolbooth, to the castle. By the end of September, Edinburgh was defended by an additional 240 men of the City Guard and had about 400 gentlemen and volunteers who supplemented the role of the former.[21] James Bailey, an Edinburgh writer, supplied 185 guns with bayonets and cartridge boxes to the city's defenders and was later reimbursed £94 7s 6d.[22]

Other measures were taken for the city's security. All saddlers, gunsmiths and sword cutlers were to report to the magistrates on 27 September. They were to list their stock, list to whom they had sold it to in the last seven months and to state the details of any current orders. The eight city ministers were told to make lists of all strangers and lodgers, and to mark whether any were Catholic. Intelligence gathering and sharing with John Sibbitt, the mayor of Berwick, and William Cotesworth of Gateshead (1673–1725) was also undertaken. Sibbitt noted, 'I do assure you it will be a good service done to the Government and no use but a very Right one made of it'.[23] Polwarth noted the prevention of the coup at the castle but wondered 'whether the defeating the design … will be a stop to their march southward I doe not know'. George Drummond expected a second attack on the castle.[24] Likewise, at the end of the month, Montrose's correspondent was far from convinced that the danger was over: 'We here in this town [Edinburgh] under very great apprehensions of having some desperate attempt made by the disaffected people from without supported by those within.[25]

Yet, despite this setback, in the wider scheme of matters in Scotland, the Jacobites were progressing well. Their designs centred around Perth, an important city and gateway to the Highlands. Defoe wrote of it, 'The chief business of this town is the linen manufacture; and it so considerable here, all the neighbouring country being employed in it, that it is a wealth to the whole place. The Tay is navigable up to the town for ships of good burthen: and they ship off here so great a quantity of linen (all for England) that all the rest of Scotland is said not to ship off so much more'.[26]

Atholl realised the danger the city was in on 7 September and wrote, 'It seems most proper that the forces in Scotland march immediately to Perth … Perth is the most

---

20   *Journal*, pp. 552, 554.
21   Dickson, 'Warrender Letters', pp. 91–2.
22   *Journal*, 18, p. 551.
23   Dickson, 'Warrender Letters', pp. 96–9.
24   *HMC 14th Report*, Appendix III, p. 163.
25   NRS, GD220/5/816, 12.
26   Rogers, *Daniel Defoe's Tour*, p. 645.

proper place to stop the passage of the Tay. When the general comes there I shall concert measures with him, to assist with all my men in Atholl'.[27]

Apparently if the Jacobites gained possession of the city, they could be joined by their allies and then force King George to abdicate when James arrived.[28] To prevent this, Atholl wrote on 10 September to suggest that Whetham should march to Perth where Atholl would support him.[29] However, Whetham stated that he had no forces to spare and in any case was waiting for Argyle's instructions before taking any action.[30] At this time Argyle was riding northwards from London.

A letter from a loyalist in Perth on 11 September painted a despondent picture of the state of affairs in Scotland. There was news that Mar had 2,500 men and expected another 10,000 who would soon march on Perth, and Whetham told him that he could do nothing until Argyle arrived. There was little prospect of help, for 'The government seems to abandon us, but we must trust in God for his mercy in a good cause'.[31] The magistrates were also told on this day about the gathering of Jacobite forces and that 'they fear no forces and are to go straight about Stirling and to Edinburgh'.[32]

The Jacobites were expected at Perth to the tune of 500 horsemen on the 13th, in order to proclaim James as King. To counter this, Rothes armed his followers in Fife and aimed to ride to Perth by the 15th.[33] However, according to Sinclair, few gentry supported Rothes and the common people only did so after having been harangued from the pulpits, and later deserted for fear of the ferocious Highlanders.[34]

Whigs despaired of the consequences which would flow from a Jacobite seizure of Perth. Cockburn wrote, 'This town of Perth is of great advantage to ye Enimie, it secures ym the shire of Angus & all be north it, tis the entry into Fifeshire, by which they have plenty of provisions'.[35] Their fears were soon to be realised. On the morning of 14 September, the Jacobite John Hay of Kinnoull (1691–1740) with a number of horsemen, variously stated as 40 and 200, entered Perth, assisted by some of its inhabitants. Possibly he had been sent by Mar who had heard of Rothes' intention to secure the town for the government and so wanted to beat them to it. Atholl had sent 140 men to defend the town and these had arrived before Hay.[36]

Measures were being taken in the town itself. Provost Austin and the former provost, Robertson, had 300–400 loyalist inhabitants, armed and assembled in the market place. Yet they were threatened, not only by Kinnoull's men, but by those sent by Atholl as well as Jacobite sympathisers in the city. At the critical moment, the magistrates did not give the order to fire; the provost apparently shouting 'No blood, no blood'.[37]

27 TNA, SP54/8/26.
28 *Ibid.*, 30.
29 *Ibid.*, 41.
30 *Ibid.*, 47.
31 *HMC 14th Report*, Appendix III, 1894, p. 163.
32 NRS, GD158/2880.
33 TNA, SP54/8/60, 67.
34 Scott, *Memoirs*, pp. 38–9.
35 TNA, SP54/8/72A.
36 *Ibid.*, 74a; Patten, *History*, p. 4.
37 TNA, SP54/8/74c.

Some loyalists fled to Stirling, spreading panic-stricken stories of thousands of Highlanders being at Perth. Others surrendered, because, though armed, they 'durst not stir, for fear of the Highlandmen'. James was proclaimed by the town's magistrates, who were now apparently prisoners, though one source stated, that apart from the provost, they 'played all ym ye jade' and proved useless. Bells rang, there was cheering 'No Hanover, no popery, no Union', despite the fact that James was Catholic. The Jacobites seized what arms and ammunition they could find, as well as taking any tax money in the collectors' hands.[38]

However, it had been a fortunate victory. Had Rothes arrived, even though he had with him but 'his Fife mob', he might have been able to have deterred an attack. This was even though the place was deemed defenceless. The Highlanders had no gunpowder for their few firearms, so would have been unable to mount a serious attack until their numbers had grown considerably.[39]

Patten enumerated why the taking of this city was a significant victory for the Jacobites. Firstly it gave Mar command of the county of Fife, one of the wealthier parts of Scotland and gave him a sea port. Secondly, 'it gave a great Reputation as well to his Conduct as to his Party'. It provided him a headquarters to which other Jacobites could rally, which was what happened in subsequent weeks.[40] A correspondent of Montrose's gave the Whig perspective: 'I am sorry for the news we have had today of Perth's falling into the Enemies' Hands. I can see a world of bad consequences for that unluckie affair that I wish with all my heart had been prevented'.[41]

Sinclair remarked that the possession of Perth was crucial for the success of the Jacobite campaign, otherwise, the 'whole designe must have proven abortive, for there was no other place where ane armie could have been formed'.[42] It was not all plain sailing for Mar knew it needed reinforcing as soon as possible for a troop of horse alone could not hold it, these men being 'uneasie', and 'That place is of such great importance to us that we must not by any means lose it'.[43] This was proved soon enough. On the 16th, Mar was writing that Tullibardine, Lord George Murray (1694–1760) and their men had arrived, and with all the additional Jacobites that he expected; 300 of Atholl's men and Lord Huntley's followers. On 1 October, Panmure's 203 men arrived. At the beginning of October, about 500 Mackintoshes under Borlum appeared there.[44]

The Jacobite occupation of Perth was not necessarily a burden to the merchants there, as Defoe later observed. They enriched themselves by their presence and public and private buildings were erected in the town shortly afterwards. This was because, 'the Pretender and his troops lay near, or in this place a considerable time; now the bare consumption of victuals and drink, is a very considerable advantage in Scotland,

38   *Ibid.*, 74c, 77; Rae, *History*, p. 220; Scott, *Memoirs*, p. 39.
39   Scott, *Memoirs*, p. 40.
40   Patten, *History*, pp. 4, 133.
41   NRS, GD220/5/816/8.
42   Scott, *Memoirs*, p. 40.
43   NLS, MS Adv.Ms, 13.1.8/39.
44   Taylers, *1715*, pp. 47–8.

and therefore 'tis frequent in Scotland for towns to petition the government to have regiments of soldiers quartered upon them'.[45]

Yet Mar was in no hurry to advance from Perth, where he was accumulating men, so the prospect of immediate action was limited. This inaction attracted criticism, in retrospect, from his own followers. A suggestion to seize the weakly defended Rothes in order to take the arms stored there was considered but not undertaken.[46] Sinclair made a damning indictment, 'Mar, after comeing into Perth, did nothing all this while but write', making little effort to procure essential military supplies.[47] Berwick thought so too, writing that 'Marr, in the meantime, amused himself with forming his army and settling all his affairs; as if he was assured of having all the time he wanted … his little skill in military affairs made him lose this opportunity … After he had drawn the sword, he did not know in what manner to proceed'.[48] There was the suggestion that the Jacobites, having seized Perth, would attack Argyle before Carpenter's and Kerr's Dragoons could arrive. Yet the same informant felt this was unlikely because they would need more men before they could act so aggressively.[49]

However these assessments of Mar (echoed by a myriad of writers in the last three centuries) are harsh and must be countered by two points. Firstly, Mar was awaiting additional reinforcements to strengthen his still relatively small army. Secondly, those men that he did have were in need of training and arms; to attack prematurely could well have been disastrous and any debacle would have led to strong criticism towards Mar.

Yet if the Jacobite army at Perth was relatively, though understandably inactive, affairs in England were not so. The government had long feared that an insurrection would break out in England and that time came on 6 October. Only it occurred in Northumberland, not the heavily garrisoned London nor the south-west, also scarcely bereft of troops, which made it potentially all the more dangerous given the potential for English and Scots Jacobites to merge their strength against their outnumbered and disparate foes. There were no regular troops in Northumberland except for a small garrison at Berwick. Furthermore, there was also a small revolt in the Scottish Lowlands. This had even more dire prospects for Argyle and his relatively small command at Stirling, who were noted for their inactivity by one loyalist writing on 8 October.[50] Loyalists in Edinburgh also felt beleaguered.

The rising in England already referred to had come out into the open in Northumberland. Following an order on 22 September to have the Catholic James Radcliffe (1689–1716), the 3rd Earl of Derwentwater, and one of the county MPs, Thomas Forster (c.1675–1738), a High Tory, taken into preventative custody, both men fled their pursuers. Realising that they could not do so indefinitely, they persuaded some of their relatives, friends and tenants to rise in arms, at Greenriggs on the Northumberland moors on 6 October, before arriving at the coastal Warkworth

45   Rogers, *Defoe*, p. 645.
46   Scott, *Memoirs*, pp. 52–3.
47   *Ibid.*, pp. 92–3.
48   Berwick, *Memoirs*, pp. 231–232.
49   TNA, SP54/8, 78.
50   NRS, GD220/5/816/21a.

on the following day, where they stayed for a few days, possibly in the expectation of support from overseas. Forster was nominated as leader, for political, social and religious reasons, though as with Mar, he was no soldier. He wrote to Mar to tell him of the need for reinforcements from his army in Scotland.[51] Elsewhere the impact in England of Mar's rising was limited to Jacobite rhetoric being overheard by soldiers in Leicester and other verbal murmurings of discontent.[52]

News of the English rising was soon common knowledge among those in the know in government circles in Scotland. Cockburn was aware of it on 7 October and was very concerned about its potential. He wrote 'that all the disaffected people on this side of the Forth and in the south of Scotland shall one way or another joyn those in the north of England and may some way fall on this town [Edinburgh] in concert with the rebels from Fife or may assist Mar in passing it'. He added, pessimistically, 'I am afraid that if once our rebels pass the Forth, they shall be able too soon to reach England'.[53] William Cockburn, his brother, added similarly, 'The situation of our affairs appears every day more and more to threaten trouble and confusion'.[54] Argyle was, characteristically, downbeat, writing to Marlborough on the 7th, 'I confess I should humbly have hop'd that I should not have been pitch'd upon to act ye disagreeable part of commanding a detachment which was only to serve to keep the enemy in play. Had these troops my lord which are now order'd from Ireland been sent over a month agoe I think I could not well have fail'd of doing His Majesty some service'.[55]

Their worst fears were not, however, immediately realised. The English Jacobites had high hopes of support in the wealthy and strategically important town of Newcastle. Yet it barred its gates to them, raised militia and volunteers and was soon reinforced by units of the British army. The Jacobites made no attempt to force the issue. Although support from England was initially limited to about 300 men, they were soon to link up with a small force of Lowland Scots. On 12 October Kenmure raised the Jacobite standard at Moffat in Annandale, having been urged to do so by Mar and others for some time previously. He had about 150–200 horsemen. On the following day they hoped to march to Dumfries, but the loyalists there, having been forewarned, were able to thwart them by the previous arrival in that town of the Marquess of Annandale and the militia. On the following day they were at Lochmaben, then marched to Ecclefechan. At Hawick on 15 October, they had a message from Forster, who was now at Hexham, suggesting they meet at Rothbury. En route, at Jedburgh, they heard that Mackintosh's command had crossed the Firth.[56]

We now turn to Mackintosh's movements. Mar had control of all the towns on the northern side of the Firth up to its mouth, as well as the county of Fife. There were no bodies of loyalists there; Rothes and his command having been forced to

51 Patten, *History*, pp. 16–20.
52 Peter Drake, *Amiable Renegade: The Memoirs of Captain Peter Drake, 1671–1753* (Stanford: Stanford University Press, 1955), p. 334.
53 TNA, SP54/9, 18a.
54 *Ibid.*, 26a.
55 British Library Add. MSS. 61136, f. 170r.
56 Patten, *History*, pp. 26–28.

withdraw to Stirling. Mar decided to reinforce the risings in Northumberland and the Lowlands by detaching part of his army there. This meant weakening his own strength but presumably thought that this might encourage additional English and even foreign support, both anticipated as being crucial to the venture. The plan was that a strong body of troops would take boats to cross the Firth, land at Lothian and join their allies nearby. It would mean that Argyle would be encircled, or as Mar put it, 'we shall have our Enemies in a Hose-net'.[57] However, Sinclair claims that Macintosh had not been given instructions as to what he should do.[58]

This was, perhaps, the highpoint of the campaign for the Jacobites. Optimism was rife. In Bar le Duc, James was writing enthusiastically about Mar's achievements, 'Lord Mar's behaviour on this present occasion is such that I thought I could not too soon give him marks of my favour' and made him a Duke in the Jacobite peerage. He also thought 'he should alone have the honour of ending alone what he has so successfully begun'.[59]

The decision had been taken by Mar by the 8 October. He planned that over 2,000 men would cross from Burntisland to Leith, arriving at the former by the evening of the 8th and reaching the latter by the end of the following day. Mackintosh of Borlum's command consisted of his own regiment, and those of Logie Drummond's, Strathmore's, Lord Nairn's, Mar's and that of Lord Charles Murray (1691–1720). It may have numbered between 2,200 and 2,500 infantry in all.[60]

Mar believed that their crossing would be unopposed due to a lack of warships on the Firth. Meanwhile, as a diversion to deceive Argyle, Mar would lead the main army from Perth towards Stirling on the morning of 9 October. He was sure that Argyle would soon learn of his southward march and that would distract him from Jacobite movements elsewhere.[61]

To undertake this venture boats were needed. Malcome of Grange, who had knowledge of the coastline, suggested they be found from Wemyss to Crail. One suggestion was that the boats be concentrated at Burntisland, where the Jacobites had a garrison in the castle. Yet this would be brought to Argyle's attention, as well as to the warships which were in the Firth, contrary to Mar's belief; another failure of Jacobite intelligence.[62]

Mar, believing that the warships were nowhere to be seen, ignored this advice and had, on 7 October, ordered boats to be brought to Burntisland with the aim that the troops be embarked on the following day. Henry Crauford had been active in ensuring that the transports were prepared, but that they could not all be ready until the 10th.[63]

In fact, Mar did not leave Perth until 10 October. Once they had marched three miles southward, he learnt that Argyle's forces remained inactive, though apparently a

---

57   Patten, *History*, p. 5; Rae, *History*, p. 435; Scott, *Memoirs*, pp. 129, 142.
58   Scott, *Memoirs*, p. 142.
59   *HMC Stuart Papers*, I, p. 443.
60   Patten, *History*, pp. 120–2, 5; Scott, *Memoirs*, p. 104.
61   Rae, *History*, p. 435.
62   Scott, *Memoirs*, pp. 104–6.
63   *Ibid.*, pp. 117–118.

party of them had marched to Dunfermline and on the 7th this had led Mackintosh to believe he was to be attacked by Argyle, despite having superior forces to the latter. The Jacobites halted, formed up in two lines and their leader gave them a speech. He read his commission to them, they cheered and shouted 'God save the King', before being marched back to Perth later that day. A few days later, a letter from his English allies advised him to move against Argyle before he could be reinforced by troops from Ireland, but Mar merely wrote 'I wish heartily to do, but that must be as things happen'.[64]

Mar's other concern at this time was the arrival of his master. He was not sure where this would be, so sent troops to both Angus and Banff to await his presence there. He was in correspondence with allies in France and a letter was sent to Orleans. He hoped that James would not be in France when the letter arrived.[65]

Mackintosh's force marched to various points on the coast, including Crail and Anstruther, covered by horsemen led by Sir John Areskine, Sir James Sharp and Sinclair. Despite this, Argyle learnt of their march and put 300 dragoons and some mounted infantry in readiness to advance against them, but did not move them. Apparently, he also heard some potentially alarming news that transpired to be false yet could hardly be initially discounted: that Ireland was in arms for James and that all the north of England was in arms for the Jacobite cause. He was, though, dismissive about a Jacobite plan to cross to Lothian, 'which I think a very odd project and one would think it would not be easy for them to find boats'.[66] Boats on the north side had already been gathered together by order to transport them over the water. There were ships of the Royal Navy on the Firth whose goal was to intercept their passage. The latter had orders to search all ships passing from one side to the other and any refusing risked being taken or sunk. However, their task was made all the more difficult because the Jacobites marched from one place to another. The attempt to cross was finally made on the nights of 11 and 12 October. Most crossed without incident, in part by some of the Jacobite vessels distracting their enemy by making it appear that a crossing was intended from Burntisland, by having another body of troops march openly in daylight there, board boats and make it appear that they would sail. Warrender's intelligence was that they were to leave from there. The Jacobites also had a battery of guns placed at that spot. The Royal Navy frigates, the *Royal Ann* galley on the north side and the *Pearl* on the south, and several customs vessels, exchanged fire with the Jacobite artillery in Burntisland Castle, without causing any damage to either side. The wind was also blowing against the government's forces.[67]

Mackintosh's men had lain concealed elsewhere: Pittenweem, Crail and Elie. All did not go to plan, despite the advantages numerated above. About 1,000 men were unable to cross, including Strathmore himself and many of his men; likewise most of Drummond's failed to reach the south shore (these returned to Perth on 14 October). Strathmore and 300 of his men were forced ashore at the Island of Moy and had to

64   Rae, *History*, pp. 438, 441.
65   *Ibid.*, pp. 435–9.
66   TNA, SP54/9/24.
67   Rae, *History*, pp. 258–9; Patten, *History*, pp. 6–7; Dickson, 'Warrender Letters', pp. 106–107.

remain there for several days, managing to deter an attack from the Royal Navy vessels. Some men of Mar's and Nairn's regiments also had to turn back. One boatload of 40 men was captured; the officers were sent to Edinburgh and the men to Leith, though the latter were soon released by their compatriots.[68]

Those who arrived quartered themselves at Haddington and Tranent. According to Patten, 'This was a bold, and to give them their due, a brave Attempt, for Men in open Boats to cross an Arm of the Sea sixteen or seventeen miles broad, and indeed in Defiance of three Men of War, whom they fell in among, but received no Damage from them'. The lights of the enemy vessels had actually guided the Jacobites' boats towards their destination. By the morning of the 12th, however, there were Jacobite forces at North Berwick and Aberlady.[69]

There had been attempts to stop the Jacobite advance by the civil authorities. The Edinburgh magistrates, following instructions from Argyle, had given orders to take all the boats on the north side of the Firth to Leith, using the three customs vessels as well as the two naval ships. Yet these boats were in Jacobite hands and so could not be taken.[70]

Just before this exploit was taking place, Mar's main force began to make a feint southwards towards Stirling, via Dunblane.[71] At daybreak on the 9th the army was drawn up outside Perth and stood to for three hours. Then came the news that Bristol, Newcastle and Berwick were in the hands of the English Jacobites; 'which occasion'd great rejoicings and huzzas', though this information was not true. Mar summoned all chiefs, noblemen and colonels, and behind closed doors told them that Mackintosh was beset by Argyle's force at Leith and that his end might be near. According to Sinclair, 'My Lord Mar said, He have him over for lost, and did not see what we could help him in the least, except by making a feint towards Stirveling, to bring the Duke of Argyle back'. Hamilton backed the proposal and no one else said anything. Yet they did not move towards Stirling for another week.[72]

Mackintosh had received no information from Jacobites in the Lowlands or England whom Mar wished him to reinforce. The Jacobites with him rested for a night at Haddington in one body. On the 14th they marched westwards towards Edinburgh, which, save for the garrison in the castle, was without any regular troops to defend it. The question was, how would Edinburgh react towards the Jacobites. Could Mackintosh have been joined by sympathisers within? Some did exist, as had been seen in the attempt on the castle in the previous month. As we have seen, the magistrates were firmly supportive of the government against the Jacobites. John Campbell, the new provost, knew of the Jacobites being at Haddington on the 13th, so wrote to Argyle on the morning of the next day, at the same time as Mackintosh began to move against the city. The magistrates also attempted to suppress any internal threat

68   Patten, *History*, pp. 6–7; Rae, *History*, pp. 439, 259.
69   Patten, *History*, p. 6.
70   *Ibid.*, p. 7.
71   Scott, *Memoirs*, p. 131.
72   Patten, *History*, pp. 7–8, Rae, *History*, pp. 260–1, 262n.

by summoning all city men who were loyal to the government to form a defensive association. Protestant clergymen even armed themselves with muskets and bayonets to encourage their congregations to follow their example.[73]

The militia forces in the city were composed of 600 infantry and 300 cavalry and were led by Tweeddale. The infantry were divided into eight companies under Aikman, whilst the cavalry were made up of gentlemen and lawyers under one Mr Boyde, the Earl of Kilmarnock's brother. When reviewed in the previous month they were apparently found to be in good order. Yet they lacked bayonets. David Dalrymple (c.1665–1721) was very concerned: 'This town has made all the Dispositions possible to resist for a Day or two and that is all they can do in an open defenceless place'.[74] Apart from the militia, raised following an order of 26 August, there was also the City Guard of about 120 men.[75] Cockburn had little confidence about the militia or the volunteers, either, stating them to be 'so little to be depended on'.[76]

Argyle was of the same mind as Cockburn, for he informed Townshend shortly afterwards:

> Our well affected people cannot be persuaded to defend themselves against the very smallest numbers of the rebels till they had arms and ammunition, from all corners of the country, they assured me they would do wonders. Now they have them whenever the smallest numbers of rebels approaches, they say nothing can be done without regular troops. The faintheartedness of the small number of loyal subjects, excepting a few noblemen and gentlemen is beyond all sort of imagination.[77]

There was certainly a degree of panic within the city. A run on the Bank of Scotland resulted in the temporary suspension of payments.[78] Forfar wrote that when his troops arrived, 'Never were people in such consternation as the inhabitants who thought of every thing but the defence of their town'.[79] There was no council meeting in the city on the 12th 'in respect of the appearance of the rebels approaching the Citie'.[80] On the 14th orders were sent for the parishes in Edinburgh to send their militia to Grassmarket in the City with horses, arms and pay for 10 days and five days later most had arrived, though by then the immediate danger had passed.[81]

Writing a few days later, Mar expressed his concern that Mackintosh had moved against the Scottish capital, referring to it as being 'an unlucky mistake'. He had

---

73   Rae, *History*, pp. 260–1, 267.
74   TNA, SP54/9, 38-9; *Flying Post*, 3715, 25–27 Oct. 1715; *Daily Courant*, 4329, 8 Sept. 1715.
75   Helen Armet (ed.), *Extracts from the Records of the Burgh of Edinburgh, 1702–1718* (Edinburgh, 1968), pp. 272, 296.
76   TNA, SP54/9, 45.
77   *Ibid.*, 9, 53.
78   *New Statistical Account of Scotland*, I (1845), p. 658.
79   Taylers, 'Lord Forfar and the '15'', p. 137.
80   Armet, *Extracts*, p. 299.
81   NRS, GD18/4142, 4144.

wanted the force to link up immediately with those in the Lowlands of Scotland, but Mackintosh was being insubordinate, perhaps for reasons of prestige and plunder.[82]

Mackintosh marched his force to within sight of the city, about a mile from the palace of Holyrood, but finding no one to welcome him in, as well as hearing news that there were civilian defenders to be reinforced by regulars, held a council of war. As with the Jacobites in Northumberland (or Monmouth before Bristol in 1685), he was reluctant to take a place by force. To date this had been a bloodless military campaign. The small size of his force, perhaps about 1,400 infantry and with no artillery, was another key reason for holding back. To take Leith seemed a safer option. That undefended town was occupied that afternoon. There, they marched over the bridge and took possession of the old Cromwellian fort. This they improved as best they could in the short time available, chiefly by removing cannon from ships in the harbour, together with shot and powder, and then mounting the guns on the walls. The entrances were barricaded with wood and stone. Food and drink was also acquired from the ships.[83]

Meanwhile, Argyle received Campbell's express on the noon of the same day as its being sent. He later stated that the arrival in Lothian of the Jacobites had 'put the Town of Edinburgh into a very great alarm', adding, 'I received a letter in the most pressing terms from the magistrates'. It put Argyle on the horns of a dilemma, 'This … put me under very great difficulties'. Either he reinforce Edinburgh, but that would seriously weaken the forces at Stirling facing Mar's at Perth, only 32 miles away, or he abandon the Scottish capital to its fate. There were insufficient men to adequately do both, as he later reminded Townshend, 'if you had been here this moment, you would wish from the bottom of your heart that the representations that I had made some time ago had been so unfortunate as to have been attended with more success'. The first option was clearly the least dangerous. So he marched off and arrived in Edinburgh late on that same day, with 300–400 cavalry (taken from Portmore's, Carpenter's and Stair's Dragoons) and 200 infantry (taken from Shannon's, Forfar's and Orrery's battalions) mounted on horseback for speed. The distance between Stirling and Edinburgh being but nine miles. He had little faith in the effectiveness of the militia, writing a few days previously, 'a lamb is not more afraid of a lyon, than these low country people are of the Highlanders'.[84]

Along with 400 men taken from the Edinburgh militia and 200 men of the City Guard, Argyle marched out on the morning of the 15th towards Leith. However, when, by midday Argyle and Generals Evans and Wightman examined the defences before them, they saw that the Jacobites were well entrenched and that without artillery it made no sense to attack them there. When they made a formal demand that the Jacobites surrender, a Highlander called Kinackin retorted, 'That as to surrendering they laughed at it; and as to bringing cannon and assaulting them, they were ready for him, that they would neither take nor give any Quarter with him, and if he thought

82   Patten, *History*, p. 58.
83   *Ibid.*, p. 8.
84   TNA, SP54/9/24, 53.

he was able to force them, he might try his hand'. Argyle reconnoitred the place to within 200 paces and risked being killed by some cannon fire directed against him. The Jacobites outnumbered their opponents, had artillery and were strongly entrenched. Argyle could not hope to defeat them and avoid taking heavy losses. Forfar wrote, 'I was very glad when I saw the place that we had not attack'd it … it was impracticable ever to have taken it without cannon and to a demonstration my whole detachment must have been cut in pieces'. Some volunteers seemed eager for action but when told that they would suffer heavy casualties, became more cautious. Therefore Argyle returned to Edinburgh at two in the afternoon, but gave orders that preparations for an assault be commenced.[85]

Furthermore, a defeat for Argyle would have probably entailed the loss of Edinburgh which had only just been saved on the previous day. Those, chiefly from afar, who criticised Argyle for his caution would have been even more aggrieved had he been defeated.[86] Stanhope was one who believed that aggressive action should have been taken and would have been successful, writing to Stair on 20 October that 'we hourly expect to hear they are taken or destroyed'. Generally speaking he was confident that the Jacobites would soon be defeated, in part because he thought that they were unable to subsist their army and that the detachment of Mackintosh's men was proof of this. Stair, too, believed it would soon be over as Stanhope wrote to him, 'Your lordship's notion of ending this Highland war in the winter is certainly right and that will be put in execution'.[87] An anonymous correspondent from Glasgow was also confident of immediate victory, writing on 16 October, 'We are impatient here to have a good account of the Duke of Argyle's success with the detachment he has marched to Edinburgh'.[88] Such optimism was unwarranted.

Mackintosh expected to receive reinforcements from Edinburgh, who, he hoped, would be encouraged by the strong position he had established himself in. A few gentlemen sympathisers visited him and told him that nobody had risen to help him and if they had, would have been opposed by the forces of the city authorities. They also told Mackintosh that he could expect to be attacked by Argyle later that day. Averse to a fight, Mackintosh had a message sent to Mar to inform him of their progress. This was sent by a messenger in a boat; to make the naval vessels think this was a boat containing allies, he had a cannon fire at it as it departed northwards. This tactic worked and the letter got through.[89]

It was rapidly answered. Robert Douglas arrived from Mar that night and told Mackintosh that Mar did not want him to advance further westwards than Dunbar or North Berwick. Mackintosh did not think it safe to stay at Leith as he feared being attacked and decided to join Kenmure. Douglas was sent to Kenmure to tell him of this. That night the Jacobite force left Leith in near silence and waded across a branch

85   Patten, *History*, pp. 8–9, 59, Rae, *History*, pp. 261–263; Tayler, 'Forfar', p. 135.
86   Tayler, 'Forfar', pp. 137–8.
87   TNA, SP78/160, 136.
88   NRS, GD220/5/816/25.
89   Patten, *History*, p. 9.

of the river at low tide to Seaton House. About 40 men were left behind because they had become incapacitated after drinking the brandy seized from the Leith custom house. The night march was not an unalloyed success, either. Near Musselburgh they were fired upon by some townsmen, and though no one was killed, it did create confusion among the Jacobites.[90]

Later that night there was a confrontation between a Highlander and a Jacobite Lowlander who was on horseback, one Alexander Maloch of Mutree Shields. Maloch was challenged by the Highlander, but not understanding Gaelic was unable to answer him and so was shot dead; probably the first fatality of a campaign that had begun over a month previously. He was left unburied and Mackintosh took the 60 guineas Maloch had on his person. Later, at the other side of Musselburgh, the Jacobites were alarmed by the sound of gunfire. Mistaking a party of their own men as enemies, they exchanged fire. A sergeant and private from Mar's battalion were killed. As Patten noted, 'The Night proved so very dark, that they could not distinguish Friends from Enemies; which was their happiness one way; as it prevented their being discovered and pursued; but their great Mischief another way, as it made them liable to such false Alarms, and made them kill their own friends instead of Enemies'.[91]

They arrived at Seaton House, home to the absentee Kenmure, at two in the morning. Here they were joined by a few stragglers who had crossed the Firth at the most eastern point and had hitherto been unable to meet up with them. They told Mackintosh that Strathmore and others who had tried to cross had been forced ashore at the Isle of Moy and then had to return to Perth. Whilst at Seaton House, after daybreak, the Jacobites were alarmed by news that some of the regular troops and loyalists from Edinburgh, had marched towards them, reaching Prestonpans. Some of the Jacobites marched out to meet them, but both sides halted and withdrew.[92]

Meanwhile, on the evening of 15 October, Argyle was in Edinburgh, planning how to attack the Jacobites at Leith. On the following morning, he learnt that they had left and were at Seaton House. With a mind to attack them there, he ordered six artillerymen from Stirling to be sent to him, and ordered that two cannon and two mortars be ready from Edinburgh Castle for his use. Before he could move, Whetham, who had been left behind in Stirling with about 1,700 men, wrote on the 16th and 17th that Mar was finally on the move with 10,000 men and that the vanguard of 4,000 were expected at Dunblane on the 17th. As ever, he was being as alarmist as Argyle in grossly exaggerating the number of his opponents who were probably nearer 4,000 in total. Argyle took the hint, and noting Edinburgh was no longer in critical danger, left the city, taking 200 dragoons and 150 infantry, leaving at noon on 17 October and arriving back at Stirling late that evening.[93] He had done his job and on 17 October

90   *Ibid.*, p. 10; NRS, SP13/212.
91   Patten, *History*, pp. 10–11.
92   *Ibid.*, p. 11.
93   Rae, *History*, pp. 264–265.

the city council sent him 'their heartie thanks and humble acknowledgement of the seasonable relief'.[94]

A move was made against the Jacobites on the 16th when Rothes and James Sandilands (d.1753), 7th Baron of Torphichen (lieutenant colonel of Kerr's Dragoons) took 300 gentlemen volunteers and the 200 dragoons from Argyle's command to within sight of Seaton House. This was a strongly defended castle, and it seemed, as with the fort at Leith on the previous day, too difficult to attempt an assault without the benefit of artillery. The defenders were encouraged by their opponents' reluctance to attack and they advanced from behind the walls as if to charge. There was an exchange of musketry, albeit at long range and without any casualties on either side. Rothes withdrew his men to Edinburgh.[95]

Meanwhile, the Jacobites at Seaton House had scoured the countryside for supplies and brought in cows, sheep and meal to feed themselves. They announced that they would make Seaton House their base and as a centre for Jacobites in the Scottish Lowlands and north of England.[96]

Meanwhile, the Jacobites' main body had finally marched from Perth on 16 October. Their strength at this point was not agreed upon by contemporaries. There were six units of cavalry: Huntley's (400–500), Marischal's (180–300), Perthshire (70), Stirlingshire (77), Angusshire (100) and Fifeshire (90 men). Then there was the infantry, 1,200–2,000 led by Huntley, 230 by Lord George Murray, 415 by Panmure, 351 by Ogilvie, 203 by Strowan (over 400 according to Mar) and 267 by John Stewart of Invernytie.[97] It was in no way the strength as reported by Whetham, but perhaps he felt he needed to exaggerate in order to induce Argyle to return as soon as possible, for he had little over 1,500 troops plus the potentially unreliable militia. Or possibly he was in the receipt of poor intelligence, for there was a tendency for Jacobite numbers to be inflated.

The Jacobites reached Auchterarder by nightfall and planned to move to Dunblane on the following day. Mar urged his allies in the west and elsewhere to join him as soon as possible. On the 17th the infantry reached Ardoch and the cavalry were at Dunblane, four miles north of Stirling. At Dunblane, all was in confusion, sentries were not posted and the cavalry were thus in a potentially vulnerable state. Sinclair later wrote, 'I lookt on that night as the last of our affairs' for he was sure that their enemies must know of their location and state and move to take advantage of it. Marischal was convinced there would be no attack as Argyle had gone to Leith and had probably not given Whetham any orders to attack in his absence but Sinclair was unconvinced. Late that night, Glengarry's exhausted infantry joined them.[98]

When, on the 18th, Mar knew that Argyle was returning to Stirling and he had a regiment from Ireland about to arrive (three were actually en route), he became

94 Armet, *Extracts*, p. 300.
95 Patten, *History*, pp. 11–12.
96 *Ibid.*, pp. 12–13.
97 *HMC Mar and Kellie*, p. 511; Robert Campbell, *The Life of the most illustrious Prince John Duke of Argyle and Greenwich* (Belfast: F. Joy, 1745), p. 164; NLS, ACV MS 13.1.8.42.
98 Scott, *Memoirs*, pp. 133–136.

disheartened. Furthermore, they had advanced without any provisions being ready and found that the district around Stirling had been denuded of any surplus by Argyle. It is possible that this had only been a feint anyway or perhaps there was a lack of supply waggons. There was no news from General Gordon, expected to reinforce Mar from the west with the clans from there. Having managed to remove Argyle's threat to Mackintosh, Mar decided that he had now done all he could do and returned to Auchterarder, which took place on the 19th.[99]

Once back, Mar heard news that Mackintosh had retreated to Seaton House and let it be known he was pleased by the success of this manoeuvre for giving the Jacobites a good reputation, though privately he was less happy. Sinclair later insinuated that the only reason why Mackintosh was despatched with so many men was to make it impossible for Mar to have acted aggressively towards Argyle.[100]

Mackintosh did not remain long at Seaton House. Whilst there, a boat from the north side of the Firth, despite being fired upon by the naval vessels there, arrived safely at Leith. It was the same boat that had been sent across the river from the south side a few days previously. As before, it carried a message. This gave news about Jacobite activity at Perth and also orders to march into England and meet the Jacobites who had risen in Northumberland. On the 18th news reached them from other sources about a rising in the Lowlands and there was a message from Forster, advising them to rendezvous with his force at Kelso. Therefore on 19 October they marched southwards, leaving some of their supplies behind, reaching Longformacus after a 17 mile march, and suffering a few desertions en route. These latter were captured by a party of both regulars (100 dragoons and 150 infantry), militia and 300 volunteers sent from Edinburgh on 17 October led by Wightman and Rothes. Seaton House was then garrisoned by 50 infantrymen.[101]

Meanwhile, and unknown to Mar, the Lowlanders and English Jacobites had met at Kelso on 22 October, to be joined later that day by Mackintosh's men, 'they made a very indifferent figure; for the Rain and Long Marches had extremely fatigu'd them'. Patten estimated that the strength of the force; consisting of six Scottish infantry battalions, five Lowland troops of cavalry and five English troops of cavalry, at a total of 1,400 men, but this was probably an underestimate unless we can conceive that Mackintosh who began on the south side of the Firth with 1,500 men could have lost about 500 already; losses there had been but probably not on that scale.[102] Sibbitt gave an estimate of 2,000 in total and that seems more accurate.[103] At Kelso, Forster told Douglas to tell Mar that the Scots did not want to march into England but that Newcastle should be easy to take as there were sympathisers within the gates and that money and arms could be secured there.[104] Yet to date, on 25 October, it was noted

99   Patten, *History*, pp. 60–1; Rae, *History*, pp. 450.
100 Scott, *Memoirs*, pp. 143–4.
101 Patten, *History*, pp. 12–13
102 *Ibid.*, pp. 30–51.
103 TNA, SP54/9/60.
104 NRS, SP13/212.

that 'all is quiet in England not any appearance of insurrection known or heard of in London except Northumberland'.[105]

Facing the Anglo-Scottish force at Kelso was General George Carpenter's (1657–1732) three regiments of dragoons and one battalion of infantry at Newcastle. Argyle feared that the former force might march to Scotland. If this were to happen, he asked Wightman to order Carpenter to pursue.[106] It seems Carpenter would have done so, writing, 'I am impatient to follow him'.[107]

On the 27 October the Jacobites had the prospect of attacking Carpenter's force from Newcastle, but as on previous instances in the campaign, discretion was thought best and the Jacobites marched along the Borders to Jedburgh. An alternative idea, made by George Seton (c.1679–1749), 5th Earl of Wintoun, and Mackintosh, had been to march further into Scotland. Two days later there was a similar suggestion made. Wintoun suggested marching to join the clans in western Scotland, or crossing the Firth or informing Mar that they could fall on Argyle's rear if he advanced southwards. None of his colleagues agreed. Two days later, there was the suggestion that Dumfries be taken. This was a wealthy town, unfortified and defended only by militia. It could have reaped rich rewards, strategic as well as material, for it opened up the prospect of reaching Glasgow and receiving assistance from abroad. Argyle was, perhaps, hardly in a position to harm them, with Mar's forces at Perth. But the English Jacobites insisted on a march to Lancashire where they were adamant that substantial support awaited them. This plan was adopted.[108] The southern threat to Argyle was now gone, along with 1,500 of Mar's troops, which served to weaken Mar, though the venture had provided Argyle with worrying moments.

At this time, there were three Jacobite forces in being, one to the north of Argyle, at Perth, one to the north west in the Highlands, and one to the south, and this gave them potential for success. Mar later wrote:

Now, had the Scots and English Horse, who were then in the south of Scotland, come and join'd the 1,500 Foot [Mackintosh's forces], as was expected; had the Highland Clans perform'd as they promised the Service they were sent upon in Argyleshire, and march'd towards Glasgow as the Earl of Mar march'd towards Stirling, he had then given a good account of the Government's Army, the Troops from Ireland not having yet join'd them, nor could they have join'd them afterwards.[109]

Yet co-ordination was impossible because of inadequate communications and therefore such a scenario was highly unlikely.

Meanwhile, the Royal Navy had some little success at this time. Captain Eaton of HMS *Chester* attempted to persuade the owners of boats on the north side of the Firth

105 *Ibid.*, GD28/2300.
106 TNA, SP54/9/83.
107 *Ibid.*, 63a.
108 Patten, *History*, pp. 51–6.
109 TNA, GD241/380/21

to surrender them to prevent the Jacobites using them, but his orders were ignored. He then had his guns fire on St. Mennins and Petervennes again, before sending 50 men on shore to take or destroy boats found there. Thirty were sunk and another 33 were promised to be sent across the Firth but only eight reached there. Some food supplies were also confiscated. By 8 November there were six ships to patrol the Firth and the coast from St. Abb's Head to Buchanness; another five were sailing off the Western Isles. A further nine were in English waters and another nine off France. The Navy also used its ships to convoy arms to the northern Highlands for John Sutherland (1661–1723), 16th Earl of Sutherland's, loyalists and to protect the Dutch transport vessels when they eventually sailed.[110]

Although the loyalists were on the strategic defensive in Scotland, they were able to occasionally make attacks on the Jacobites. The dash to Edinburgh and back excepted, the British army mostly lay inactive at Stirling, despite schemes laid to adopt a more aggressive stance. Many parties were apparently ordered to march from there, but few actually did so. Rothes led one and in another, 20 dragoons were sent to Fife to reconnoitre. Perhaps the most ambitious was when Lieutenant Colonel Charles Cathcart (1685–1740) of Portmore's Dragoons took 140 dragoons to seize Mar, reputedly at Alloa, but as Forfar bitterly wrote, he was not there, 'yt expedition only serv'd to shew how good our intelligence was'. Forfar was uncertain as to news as he told his friend in London. This defensive mentality was undoubtedly due to the lack of troops; 'It is odd wee should be sacrificed for want of a few troops' and the belief that they were outnumbered by the Jacobites fourfold.[111]

Parties of cavalry and infantry mounted on horses were regularly sent out on patrol to intercept any small groups of Jacobites in the vicinity of Stirling. The last known one occurred on 24 October, reacting to a finance-gathering expedition organised by Hamilton. His initial plan was to march to Kinross and then to march by night so as to evade any troops sent out by Argyle. Mar decided to ignore this suggestion and made his own dispositions, giving Major Thomas Graham the command.[112]

Graham took 80 cavalry and 300 Highland infantry on 23 October. They did not march directly, but marched to Dunning in order to pass by Castle Campbell, six miles from Stirling. This was only held by militia so posed no obvious threat, and they could be insulted by the Jacobites with apparent safety. Once the party arrived at Dunfermline, the officers went to the taverns and inns before retiring for the night. Graham placed a sentry at the Abbey and one on the bridge on the Stirling road, since if the enemy were to arrive it was probable that they would do so by that way. Graham and James Malcom sat down with a 'heartie bottle' when a deputation of three officers arrived. They suggested that rather more sentries be deployed and other precautions be taken. Graham assured him that there was no danger, for his cronies knew the country

110 Dickson, 'Warrender Letters', pp. 110–112.
111 Tayler, 'Forfar', pp. 132, 133, 135.
112 Scott, Memoirs, pp. 167–8.

better than they did, dismissed the interlopers and returned to the more pleasurable task of drinking.[113]

They did not know that on the previous day, Argyle had learnt of their intentions. Cathcart was sent against them with a detachment of 150–200 dragoons, possibly Portmore's. Cathcart had arrived near the town discreetly by marching through the night and arriving at five in the morning. Spies were sent into the town to discover the Jacobite dispositions. He then dismounted some of the dragoons and placed them in the churchyard lest the Jacobite infantry attempted to leave the Abbey. Captain Augustus Duquerry of Stair's Dragoons was in command of a reserve at the end of the town to cover the retreat, whilst Cathcart and 40 of the cavalry attacked and went straight for the cross. The Jacobite sentry on the bridge was slain, though only after he had had the chance to discharge his pistols. The Jacobite captain Forbes fired at them and then drew his sword, but was then killed, as was the other sentry. Other Jacobites, more alert – or sober – than their fellows, ran out into the street and were taken prisoner.[114]

Most of the Jacobites, though, remained in the Abbey where they had slept, thinking themselves outnumbered and perhaps in imminent danger of being attacked themselves. Others ran in all directions throughout the town. After killing and wounding a few, the dragoons made 17 prisoners, most of whom were gentlemen, and took them, and 15 horses, back to Stirling. They had no desire to remain in the town and made no attempt to molest anyone who was indoors. One dragoon was wounded in the cheek and one of the horses was hurt, though Mar later insisted that many had been wounded. Mar was shocked, though, stating, 'That it was a shame to see so may run away from two hundred of the enemie', yet when Graham returned, Mar did not blame him but those under his command.[115] This little encounter was a fillip to the morale of the British soldiers, with Forfar noting 'soe that the order have had the honour of drawing the first blood'.[116] This had been the first clash between the British Army and the Jacobite forces of the entire campaign.

On another occasion, the Earl of Hay and some troops intercepted 400 of Breadalbane's men who were travelling towards Perth, surrounded them and forced them to return home.[117] Concerned that Forster's Jacobites might march northwards to join Mar, Argyle posted 40 dragoons and a battalion of infantry at Kilsyth and a further 200 men at Falkirk to prevent such an eventuality, which was never to occur.[118] Argyle was also the recipient of advice. Daniel Stewart had advised him to attack Mar at Perth on 15 October, just after he had returned to Stirling and was now bereft of Mackintosh's command and before he could be reinforced, for he only had between

---

113 *Ibid.*, pp. 168–9; NRS, GD220/5/489/3/91.
114 *Ibid.*, pp. 169–170.
115 TNA, SP54/9/101A.
116 Tayler, 'Forfar', p. 136.
117 NRS, GD241/380/16A.
118 Rae, *History*, p. 297.

3,000 and 4,000 men and Argyle would be aided by the impossible figure of 7,000–8,000 men of Atholl's at Tullibardine. Argyle did not take this suggestion on board.[119]

Uncertainty was commonplace. A letter to Montrose on 19 October reported 'Their was never a time we had more news, and yet I never had greater difficulty in writing then we have so many storys going this hour and contradicted the next, that one knows not what to say or think'.[120] Much was uncertain and little known for sure. Rumours abounded. A letter of 23 October reported inaccurately that either Berwick or James had arrived in the north of Scotland with 'a considerable force'.[121]

The campaign was certainly not a case of 'war to the knife' and in some aspects was most gentlemanly. Mar was concerned that the Jacobites taken at Dunfermline were being 'very ill used at Stirling, that they are stript of their cloathing and ly on the bare boards in the common guard rooms'. He informed Argyle of this and he promised that they would be well treated in future and that he would allow them to receive money from Mar. Those few prisoners in Mar's hands, were apparently 'well used'. Mar wrote, 'I have no doubt of your doing all you can to prevent the disorders and inconveniencies of a civil war as much as may be'. He added that 'no difference of opinion or being of different sides shall lessen my respect and esteem for your Grace'. Very civilised behaviour indeed, but both men were Scottish noblemen who were acquainted and had a great deal in common. These attitudes would ensure that the conflict would be kept in reasonable bounds and bloodshed kept to a minimum.[122] Yet for all this, a battle could not be infinitely postponed.

---

119 NRS, GD241/380/16a.
120 *Ibid.*, GD220/5/816/26.
121 *Ibid.*, GD28/2296.
122 TNA, SP54/9/101A

6

March to Battle, 9–12 November 1715

In popular and general histories, Mar is condemned for having raised about 10,000 men in September and then having sat inactive at Perth for two months before marching south. Sinclair, Mar's chief detractor, wrote that his commander had:

> A strong inclination, when in his warm snug room at Perth, to doe very bold things; who, if he had been as bold in the field as he was at home, and weighed every thing as cautiouslie at home as he did in the field, and at a distance as he did when present, might have come nearer to the character of the great general he so much affected.[1]

Nothing could be further from this travesty of the truth, though it is often repeated. As we have seen, Mar needed to wait for support, often reluctantly, to arrive, as well as training the men in and around Perth.

Mar was well aware of the need for action. Before all these reinforcements could arrive, Mar felt that he was obliged to sit on the defensive at Perth. On 24 October, he wrote, 'It is impossible to move from Perth under Seaforth and General Gordon join the army. They are expected in two or three days'. He was concerned that Argyle, reinforced by the battalions he knew were arriving from Ireland, would march to Perth before Seaforth and Gordon could reach him. If this should happen, 'those at Perth have nothing to do but defend the town the best they can, and retire to the north side of the Tay, when they can defend it no longer'.[2]

Defensive preparations were made at Perth. Colonel Urchard was concerned that Argyle might attack the place. Part of the town wall, which was still very high, could have been lowered and the stone used to make parapets for firing from. New gates were made in the gateways, but modern suburbs had been built near the old walls, easing the task of any attacker. Part of the town lacked any wall, and though there was a water-filled ditch there, this could be made passable. Defences were needed here, but when Sinclair raised the matter with Colonel Hay, it was dismissed out of hand.[3]

---

1   Scott, *Memoirs*, p. 166.
2   *HMC Mar and Kellie*, pp. 512–3.
3   Scott, *Memoirs*, pp. 44–6.

However, some measures were taken. Fourteen cannon were brought from Dundee and Dunottar Castle. Parties were sent out from Perth to find what weapons and ammunition they could and were generally successful.[4]

At the beginning of November, Hamilton asked Sinclair about the possibility of erecting defences around Perth. This had been raised hitherto but nothing had come of it. Some little work was carried on, with the making of *flèches*, but the Frenchman who supervised it 'made the strangest line that ever was made, which served for no other use but the least of the enemies' armie'.[5]

It seemed that Mar claimed to want to take the offensive, writing of his 'regret' of 'keeping me so much the longer from joining you' and 'I hope my Stay here will be very short, and you may depend upon its being no longer than it necessarily must'.[6] He was awaiting Gordon and so 'it was resolved not to stir from Perth till they had joined us'.[7] On 30 October, Mar had written that 'There has been orders these two days for the Armies' marching but for some reasons I have put it always off, tho' I shall not I hope long'.[8] A letter on the 14 November, though, claimed 'Tis said this march was against his opinion, but Seaforth and the clans said they must come now to action, else they would leave him'.[9] Some of these delays may have been because of desertions, as on 25 October it was observed, 'ye know, they have no great disposition for fighting and pretty indifferent (at best) who is King'.[10] Sinclair believed that without a battle, the Highlanders would go home, noting that they were those 'who were already deserting daylie'. He added, 'We had no other chance for our Countriue, our Lives and honours, but attacking him wherever we could'.[11]

Some support from the Jacobite cause was draining away in early November. Several hundred of Mackintosh's men had deserted the army as it was about to march through the north-west of England. Country people seized about 200 Highlanders and locked them into a church. Edinburgh castle held a further 200 prisoners and was becoming overcrowded with the attendant fears of sickness resulting from it. Another 250 Jacobites were taken near Biggar, having lain down their arms and surrendered on learning troops were nearby and let themselves be taken to gaol in Glasgow. This gave the government's supporters the problem of how to deal with 'such a multitude of prisoners'. There was other evidence of the lack of warlike zeal among other of the erstwhile Jacobites. Ilay intercepted Breadalbane's men at Lorne and they dispersed without a fight, 'all declaring they had been forced to rise and some of them very ill treated for refusing'.[12]

---

4   Rae, *History*, p. 223.
5   Scott, *Memoirs*, pp. 196–199.
6   Patten, *History*, p. 61.
7   Keith, *Fragment*, p. 13.
8   NLS, Adv.13.1.8.42.
9   NRS, GD220/5/817/5.
10   *Ibid.*, 816/29a.
11   Scott, *Memoirs*, pp. 210–1.
12   TNA, SP54/10, 18A, 11/20.

By early November, though, Mar had gathered about him a numerically significant force. A detailed list of the Jacobite army in and around Perth on 5 November 1715 gives the following units and their strengths:

Horse
Marquis of Huntley, 264
Marquis of Seaforth, 50
Earl Marischal, 120
Earl of Linlithgow, 108
Earl of Southesque, 74
Lord Rollo, 70
Master of Sinclair, 80
              Total, 766

Foot
Huntley
    Gordon of Glenbucket, 330
    Leith, 303
    Innes, 322
    Cluny McPherson, 207
Tullibardine
    Lord Nairn gone to the south
    Lord Charles Murray south
    Lord George Murray, 343
Seaforth
    Aplecross, 350
    Fairbairn, 400
    Ballmackie and McKeddin, 350
    Frazerdale and Chisholm, 500
    Sir Donald MacDonald, 650
Marquis of Drummond
    Lord Strathallan, 257
    Logie Almond, 366
    Enveys, 240
    Strathmore's, 144
    Panmures, 475
    Lord Ogilvies, 352
    McIntosh in the south
    Strouan Robertson, 223
    Innernyties, 397
              Total, 6,209

Clans
Lochiel, 611

Breadalbane, 253
Glengarie, 461
McLean, 327
Appin, 263
Clanranald, 528
Glencoe, 105

        Total, 2,548

        Total Horse, 766
        Total of the Foot, 8,757

        Total, 9,523

Not yet come up
Three battalions of Breadalbane's (400 men) and the MacGregors.[13]

The term 'south' here means that those forces were now part of Forster's command in northern England. But, despite this, it was an impressively numerous force and far larger than any other raised in Scotland since 1651. More importantly it far outnumbered that of his opponent. And as will be noted in the following chapter, it was not merely a large mob.

Mar could now act. He had also had the time for his other forces in Perth to be trained and disciplined in the arts of war. With winter approaching and the prospect of Argyle being reinforced, it was a time for action. Campaigning as late in the season as this meant that it would be difficult to even exploit a victory, but if there was no advance then nothing else could have been realistically accomplished that season; it was a case of now or never.

Mar began to stir on 9 November. Cockburn believed that this was because otherwise he would 'find difficultie in keeping a Highland Army together all winter so has a mind to undertake something before the Dutch Troops arrive our troops desire nothing more than a fair meeting with the Rebels'. They thought that Mar risked desertions by inaction so had to fight.[14] Forfar shared Cockburn's view, writing at the end of October, 'it is impossible soe great a body can subsist this long soe that he either must attempt something in a few days or of necessity he must disperse his army'.[15] Not for the first or last time in military history have questions of supply influenced an army's strategy.

Yet it was surely also because of the numbers of Jacobite troops in or near Perth. By now the forces of Seaforth, Sir Donald MacDonald, Gordon and the western clans, had all arrived.[16] Gordon was at Castle Drummond. Yet it was not obvious to all

---

13   NLS, MS 1498, ff. 1r, v.
14   TNA, SP54/10, 41.
15   Tayler, 'Forfar' p. 140.
16   Patten, *History*, p. 151.

their enemies that there was any immediate urge to go on the offensive. Lord Provost Campbell remarked on 8 November:

> We must admire since Lord Mar has been joined by the Clans from the West and North that he has not made any motions, but as they tell us, justifying himself, and as his friends give out, is in great expectation of receiving the Pretender at Perth. In my opinion he waits to know the fate of his detachment with Borlum in the South.[17]

The Jacobite plan, as devised at a meeting of a council of war held at Perth on 9 November, was to march to the south west, to cross the Forth and then to march south to join the Jacobite army in Lancashire. It was an ambitious plan, for it was a lengthy march, needing considerable supplies to maintain a steady rate of march. Some men, perhaps 3,000, were to stay to garrison Dundee, Burntisland and elsewhere along the Fife coast. The majority were to march to Dunblane straightaway, and then to send out three detachments of 1,000 men in each. They were to make diversionary attacks to distract Argyle's small force. One of these was to attack the end of the long causeway towards Stirling Bridge, taking care to avoid the cannon fire from the castle. The second force was to approach Abbey Ford, a mile below the bridge and the third was to threaten Drip Coble, a mile and half above the bridge. These feints were to force Argyle to remain at Stirling and not to be able to molest the main body of the Jacobite army. Should he attack the main party once they had crossed the Forth, these three parties were to take Stirling or harass Argyle in the rear.[18] Yet Sinclair thought this scheme for crossing the river by ford was impossible because Rob Roy McGregor was the only man who knew how and he was deemed untrustworthy. Furthermore, he assumed that Argyle would not have neglected to make these fords impassable or would have them properly defended on the other side.[19]

The other drawback to this plan was that as with the march towards Stirling in the previous month, the Jacobites did not have the supplies and logistics to be able to feed their men for more than a few days. Such a sizeable army would consume a large amount of food and fodder and would need sufficient wagons to transport these. Insufficient attention seems to have been given to this, and it is odd that it had not, given the previous experience of exactly the same difficulty which had led to a retreat in the previous month. The Jacobite plan also relied on Argyle not moving his force northwards to intercept them. So far, of course, he had never ventured northwards. Mar seems to have been completely in the dark about Argyle's intentions; either he lacked spies or those he had were ineffective.

Taking their baggage wagons, their artillery and enough bread for several days only, the Jacobite army moved towards Dunblane on 10 November. Sinclair had argued with Mar about the advisability of taking the artillery with them, presumably on grounds of speed, but Mar ignored him. They arrived at Auchterarder, nine miles

---

17 TNA SP54/10/33.
18 Rae, *History*, p. 299.
19 Scott, *Memoirs*, p. 201.

away, by the evening. The infantry cantoned in and around the village; the cavalry at Dunning. That night there were numerous desertions. The Frasers went home, hearing that their new chief (Simon Fraser, 11th Lord Lovat (1667–1747)) had arrived there; 200 of Huntley's men deserted on the grounds that they had had to do more than their fair share of sentry duty hitherto. However, the army was then allegedly joined by the Camerons of Lochiel, though the list cited above suggested they were already with Mar. On the 11th Mar reviewed the troops at daybreak. This exhibition led to 'squabbles about the posts of our squadrons and we were never do constant in any thing as our being disorderlie'. Marischal was apparently particularly unhappy. They were then allegedly met by the clans from the west, possibly 100 cavalry and 3,000 infantry; another powerful reinforcement. Nothing else happened on that day, though the order of battle and march was settled.[20]

Throughout the campaign, a great deal of effort and money was spent by the government's supporters of procuring intelligence of the enemy's movements, numbers and intentions, though as noted the Jacobite numbers were often exaggerated. In September, Atholl spent £400 on such. Many ordinary Scots provided information to the army; a payment of £280 18s 6d was given 'to inferior people employed for intelligence'. Some agents were caught. Neil Campbell procured information at Weem but was captured; as was a gentleman by the name of Donevan. These funds were, however, about to pay dividends.[21]

Argyle was aware of Mar's marching on the evening of 9 November; not long after the decision to march had been made. It gave him time to prepare. On the next day he ordered that his forces quartered at Glasgow and Kilsyth would march to Stirling, to arrive there at noon on 11 November. Wightman and a train of artillery from Edinburgh were also summoned; arriving on the next day. Wightman later wrote that Argyle was glad to see him. Argyle wrote 'so if I have time I design to pass the river and meet them' as he had outlined to his political masters a few days previously. If he found the Jacobite army at Dunblane, he would 'attack them, if impossible to do so, will head them off at the head of the river when find the first tolerable ground'. He sounded more aggressive than usual, writing that on, 'the first tolerable ground we can find them in, they shall be attacked'. He was also acting contrary to what the Jacobites believed and so their plan would now be null and void. The weather dismayed him, for on the 10th he saw the first sign of frost on the ground; clearly the winter was coming with a vengeance. This would mean that his men would have to sleep in the open without tents. He ordered that carriages filled with bread be sent from Edinburgh to feed his men. If there was one sight that encouraged him, it was Evans' regiment, 'the very best without exception that ever I saw in my life and their cloathing and accoutrements in perfection'.[22] Colonel Charles Dubourgay took an advance guard of 30 cavalrymen forward that morning.[23]

---

20   Rae, *History*, p. 301; Scott, *Memoirs*, pp. 202–3.
21   *Journal*, pp. 551–2.
22   TNA, SP54/10/39.
23   NRS, GD220/5/787/A.

Argyle had previously no hurry for battle, given the disparity of forces. Yet Mar's actions had forced his hand. Colonel Thomas Harrison, Argyle's ADC, summed up the dilemma:

> He was obliged either to engage them on the Grounds near Dunblain, or to decamp and wait their coming to the Head of Forth. He chose the first on many Accounts, and amongst others, that the Grounds near Dunblain were much more advantageous for his Horse, than those at the Head of the River; and besides this, by the Frost then beginning, the Forth might become passable in several Places, which the small Number of his Troops did not enable him to guard sufficiently.[24]

Some of his fellow officers looked forward to the fight with confidence. One such was Forfar, writing, 'I doubt not, if we have the good fortune to meet them, wee shall give a very good account of them and put an end to this disagreeable campaign'. This is a particularly significant comment, for as noted, Forfar had been as despondent as his general in October. Another commentator observed, that the troops 'desire nothing more than a fair meeting with the rebels'.[25]

Having made preparations, the force was in a state of readiness to march on the evening of the 11th. David Erskine (d.1745), 9th Earl of Buchan and Lord Lieutenant of the county of Stirling, was left with the county militia and the 500-strong Glasgow militia, at Stirling. It had been envisaged that the latter could have accompanied Argyle, but they lacked tents and it was thought that the men would be unable to withstand the cold of a November night in the open. On the morning of Saturday the 12th, Argyle marched his army northwards, with the knowledge that the Jacobites were at Auchterarder and planned to arrive at Dunblane.[26] It was a leisurely and brief march of but four miles.

The Jacobites had waited at Auchterarder for two days for two battalions from Fife who never arrived. Eventually, on the 12 November, Mar instructed Gordon and Brigadier Ogilvie to take the clans and the cavalry in order to move ahead to take Dunblane. The remainder of the army was drawn up on Tullibardine Moor early that morning, with orders to march after Gordon. Gordon's forces were the MacDonalds, the Camerons, the Appin Stewarts and the remainder of Huntley's. Sinclair's troop accompanied them. Mar went to Castle Drummond to consult Breadalbane, leaving Hamilton in charge of the main body of troops.[27]

Sinclair had his horsemen at the front of the force, and had an advance guard scouting ahead. This part of the army was now only three miles from Dunblane by three in the afternoon. It was at that time that the quartermasters, who had gone ahead to secure food and accommodation for the army, came back with a young servant of Lady Kippendavie, wife of the leading landowner in Dunblane. He had the shocking

24 Patten, *History*, pp. 151–2.
25 Tayler, 'Forfar', p. 140; TNA, SP54/10/41.
26 Rae, *History*, pp. 300–302.
27 *Ibid.*, pp. 301–302, Scott, *Memoirs*, p. 204; Keith, *Fragment*, p. 16.

news that Argyle's entire force was marching through Dunblane towards them. Hitherto they had believed that Argyle would not advance. Sinclair went to Gordon, who was at the head of the clans, and they discussed what they should do. Sinclair was undecided, believing that it would be odd for a body of soldiers to halt because of such a unsupported story but on the other hand, if they continued and ran into the enemy, 'I did not think it was our business to engage with them, since the gross of our armie was so far behind'. It was estimated that Argyle had not more than 3,000 infantry and 1,200 cavalry and as we shall note, this was to be a slight overestimate.[28]

Sinclair sent six of his horsemen to uncover the truth of the situation and Gordon passed word to Mar. The bulk of the Jacobite force halted and were formed up. Their youthful informant maintained the truth of his statements. Peter Smith, who was the army's quartermaster, announced that Mar's orders were that Gordon was to quarter at Dunblane and that 'it was a shame to halt'. Sinclair, who always thought that Smith was an 'ignorant noisaei fellow', was 'stunned at his impudence … to pretend to speak to a Generall after that manner'. Gordon heeded Smith's reminder, however, despite the possibility that the situation before them had altered.[29]

As the army marched on, they met numerous country people who told them that the boy's story was true and that Argyle was on the east side of Dunblane. Furthermore, it was becoming dark and after a mile the army halted. Sinclair told Gordon 'That it would be of very bad consequence at any time to stumble in our marche, in the dark, on the Duke of Argyle's whole armie' especially as the British were probably formed up on a strong position and that much of the Jacobite army was far away. Of course the Jacobites' intelligence might be incorrect, but to ignore it would be taking a huge risk and that caution would be wiser.[30]

Gordon agreed and the army stopped and drew itself up on rising ground. The men sent out to reconnoitre returned, telling that they had heard the enemy but given the darkness, had not seen them and had dared not approach closer for fear of being captured. The Jacobites then considered standing at arms that night on high ground and awaiting Mar's instructions. This was at Kinbuck, two miles north of Dunblane and on the east side of the River Allan. Their enemy was only two miles distant. There was also the question of lack of forage for the horses who would otherwise be worthless on the next day. They were sheltered in farm buildings. The Jacobite force itself was not well ordered, Sinclair writing, 'it can't be properlie said we had front or rear, more than it can be said of a barrel of herrings'.[31]

Southesk arrived with the Angus troop of cavalry. He reported that Mar was following with the rest of the army. Mar himself arrived at 9:00 p.m. He asked them what intelligence they had, but apparently did not treat it seriously. He called for Gordon, who came with Huntley. Gordon told Mar the same as Sinclair had. Fresh information confirmed what had already been said. After that Sinclair slept with two other officers

---

28   Scott, *Memoirs*, pp. 204–205; Keith, *Fragment*, p. 16.
29   Scott, *Memoirs*, p. 205.
30   *Ibid.*, pp. 205–6.
31   *Ibid.*, pp. 206–7.

on the straw.[32] It cannot have been a pleasant night, as Keith wrote, 'The want of tents and the coldness of the weather rendering it impossible for us to incamp'.[33]

The army slept within a very small space of ground. Sinclair wrote 'I believe eight thousand men … were never packt up so close together since the invention of pouder'. It was potentially very vulnerable 'a place fit for the destruction of me, without being in the least capable to help themselves'. An attack by three regiments of dragoons would have been fatal to them. However, they were not molested.[34] Night attacks were usually frowned upon by regular forces; the ultimately disastrous example of Monmouth's rebels at Sedgemoor 30 years ago was not one to be emulated.

The Jacobite plan to outflank Argyle's force at Stirling had failed. This was due to a complete lack of information about Argyle's movements. It was also due to a failure to send cavalry sufficiently ahead of the army in order to ascertain the location of their enemies until the last minute. Yet they were now being presented with an opportunity to destroy their outnumbered enemy and so become masters of Scotland. Argyle was about to have the battle he sought; his strategy was working and now his tactical skill would be put to a severe test.

A map held at the National Library of Scotland is the only contemporary map of the battlefield and though incomplete is still of value. It shows that the Jacobites had crossed the River Allan before encamping and that they spent the night on the south side of the river; that is on the same side as Argyle's men had they but known it. They were arrayed between the hamlet of Gate Side and the right side of the muir of Kinbuck, with some lying near fields. Lying in the open after wading through cold water on a November night would not have made for a pleasant night.[35]

Argyle had won the race to Dunblane and even heard the signal of the three Jacobite guns. That evening the left of his force was encamped at Dunblane and the right towards the open moor of Sheriffmuir. The enemy were clearly close by but neither side could hear one another because of the hills which lay in between them. Argyle was concerned that an attack might be imminent and may have remembered that the regular army at Sedgemoor had almost been surprised by a night attack 30 years previously. Despite the inclement weather he ordered that no tents be pitched that night and that applied to officers as well as soldiers. The army therefore lay in their battalions or regiments in battle formation. Such preparedness, known as 'standing on their arms' was commonplace and had occurred on the night before the Battle of Oudenarde in 1708, though that had been in the summer. It was an ordeal for the men. Private Walter Gibbons of Montague's battalion, aged 24, who had seven years of service in the army, lost the use of his limbs by lying 'on the ground in a lamentable condition' and was discharged with a pension in 1718.[36] Argyle himself may have slept in a sheep cote on straw at the foot of the hill, to the army's right, though another

---

32 Rae, *History*, p. 302; Scott, *Memoirs*, p. 207.
33 Keith, *Fragment*, p. 16.
34 Scott, *Memoirs*, p. 208.
35 <www.nls.uk/exhibition/jacobites/1715/sheriffmuir>.
36 Parker, *Memoirs*, p. 151; TNA, WO116/1.

source claims that he and his fellow peers spent the night in 'a smoking country house'. There he wrote a letter to be sent to Stirling, advising them to be alert for a column of 600–700 Jacobites apparently making their way to Gargimouth. His men stood in position, lying with their weapons ready. At midnight, Argyle received a message, informing him where the Jacobites were and what their order of battle was. He ordered his artillery commander, who was clearly in charge of the ammunition for the infantry as well, to ensure that each infantryman had 30 musket balls by two that morning.[37] It was believed that the two armies were in cannon shot of each other.[38]

A battle was imminent and its outcome would be crucial in deciding the fate of the whole campaign. The decision to fight a pitched battle was a highly risky one and generals knew that its outcome was partly dependent on factors outside their control. It risked their army, their reputation, their life and those of their men. They were therefore relatively rare. In this case, the outnumbered Argyle would appear to have been at a disadvantage, but numbers are not the only deciding element in warfare and we shall now spend the next chapters discussing the strengths and weaknesses of the officers and men in the opposing armies.

37   Rae, *History*, p. 302; NRS, GD220/5/817/5.
38   Keith, *Fragment*, p. 17.

7

The Jacobite Army

It is important, when considering a military action, to discuss the quality of the forces opposed to one another. We will examine both armies, beginning with the commander-in-chief, his immediate subordinates, then the regimental and junior officers, before studying the men under their commands. Experience, arms and tactics will also be explored. Although there has been much discussion about the armies involved in the 1745 Jacobite campaign that of its predecessors in 1715 has only been considered in three studies.

The foremost author on the topic, Szechi, had applied a model of twentieth century military effectiveness to the Jacobite military machine in Scotland in 1715. Under the heading 'Building Infrastructure', Szechi discusses the remarkable achievement of the Jacobites in the autumn of 1715 in managing to build up a sizeable force from scratch, able to take on a professional, though smaller, army in the field, unaided by foreign support. It was paid, trained and armed.[1]

Szechi then goes on to discuss the fourth element of military effectiveness, by focussing on the battleworthiness of the Jacobite army. Again, the author considers this to have been largely successful. He stresses the efficiency of the Highland troops, but only when led by their own leaders, which was not always the case. Lowland units, though, were less successful in fighting British troops on their own terms. The Scots forces were not always used to their full potential, however.[2]

Two years after Szechi's article, there was a more descriptive account of the forces at Sheriffmuir. The Jacobite army and the British Army in Scotland were described in general by Reid, focussing on their history, tactics, uniforms and equipment, and listing known officers. There is also a study of both sides in the campaign in the north of England in 1715.[3]

The army was led by Mar. Traditionally he – as with Thomas Forster, in charge of the Jacobite army in England – has been held responsible for the unsuccessful campaign. This is not surprising, for it is commonplace for the leader of a defeated

---

1   Szechi, 'Building Military Effectiveness', pp. 304–309.
2   *Ibid.*, pp. 309–314.
3   Reid, *Sheriffmuir*, pp. 23–33, 155–167; Oates, *Last Battle*, pp. 97–122.

army to incur the responsibility for failure, just as it is for a victorious general to claim the credit, though in both instances this may not be justified when other points are taken into consideration.

Sir Charles Petrie, a leading Jacobite historian in the mid twentieth century, was scathing, writing that Mar:

> Was essentially a weak man ... of an inactive disposition ... He gives the impression of a man, who, almost unwittingly, had let loose a tempest which he had not the faintest idea how to control, and a more ineffective insurgent than Mar never plunged two kingdoms into civil strife ... had there been no opposition at all, it is doubtful whether Mar could have achieved anything.[4]

Contemporary to Petrie, the Taylers thought likewise, noting that for a leader in a military enterprise, 'The Earl of Mar was the worst possible choice ... no soldier and never knew what to do, or if he did, never had the strength of mind to carry it out'.[5]

More recent historians have not been kind to him either. Lenman, stating that Mar was a politician, used to the ways of patronage to manipulate men, but not a warrior, being 'in the last analysis, a self centred, monstrously incompetent poltroon. He deserves all the contempt history has traditionally showered on him'.[6] Szechi is also scathing about the Jacobite leadership generally: 'Mar and Forster were both unsuitable as military commanders and urgently needed good firm professional advice. Neither got it. General Hamilton was a competent logistician rather than a field commander and had no understanding of how best to use the main Jacobite army's prime military asset, the Highlanders'.[7]

The only defence that has been made of Mar comes from Baynes. He notes Mar's unpopularity among historians, but believes that he was a good staff officer, an able organiser and a man of initiative. According to him:

> Mar was not the incompetent fool of the history books, but rather a man who had a position thrust upon him which he had neither the stature nor the military knowledge to carry out. Had his duty been merely that of raising the army, and then perhaps handing over to Berwick, he would have succeeded admirably. His energy and political skill would have made him an excellent chief of staff: he lacked the extra qualities demanded of a successful Commander in Chief.[8]

Contemporaries were no more favourable than most historians. As has been seen, Sinclair was vitriolic throughout, but was not alone. Patten was hostile towards Mar, citing George Lockhart, 'He was not a Man of good coram vobis, and was a very

---

4   Charles Petrie, *The Jacobite Movement* (London: Eyre and Spottiswoode, 1932), pp. 128–129.
5   Taylers, 1715, p. 16.
6   Lenman, *The Jacobite Risings*, p. 154.
7   Szechi, *1715*, p. 195.
8   Baynes, *Jacobite Rising*, pp. 24, 204.

bad, tho' frequent Speaker in parliament; but his great talent lay in the cunning Management of his Designs and Projects, in which it was hard to find him out when he aim'd to be incognito; and this he shew'd himself to be a Man of good Sense, but bad Morals'.[9] Mar was essentially an aristocratic politician. As Keith wrote, he had been 'bred up to the pen'. A mixed assessment comes from Robert Campbell, thus, 'an able statesman, and wanted not personal Courage; but was entirely Ignorant of the art of war'.[10]

His military experience prior to 1715 was certainly nil. This might not have mattered had he been able to give operational command to a man who did have that experience and sufficient ability, especially one who could lead irregular troops. Mar's principal general was George Hamilton, once a regular soldier, who had served in the Dutch and British armies for three decades, including being at Malplaquet alongside two of the generals he would now be facing in battle: Argyle and Evans. His strengths and weaknesses were outlined by Keith:

> Who, tho' an old officer, was not in the least equal to the affair he was to undertake, for tho' he had served long and with very good reputation in the Dutch troops, yet being a man whom only experience, not natural genius, had made an officer, he did not know how to make use of his new troops, who are of a disposition as hot and quick as the Dutch are slow and phlegmatick.[11]

Parker added that he was 'reputed a brave and good officer', though he had been dismissed from the Dutch service. Sinclair claimed that his authority was eventually usurped by Mar. Another senior officer was Gordon who had served in the French and Russian armies from 1686–1711, being described as 'a very good officer of long experience and great bravery'.[12]

Most of the lower-ranking Jacobite officers were men chosen (sometimes by themselves) because of their birth, family connections and political affiliations. Very few had ever served in any role in warfare. Panmure had supported the abortive 1708 rising and led a regiment at Sheriffmuir.[13] Seaforth was another Jacobite officer who had no previous military experience.[14] Huntley's father had been a Jacobite conspirator in 1708 and was another senior Jacobite officer at Sheriffmuir.[15] William Drummond led the cavalry at Sheriffmuir. His credentials were that his father had been a supporter of James II, he was a Catholic and had been a plotter of 1708.[16] Of the lieutenants and

---

9 Patten, *History*, p. 43.
10 Keith, *Fragment*, p. 3; Taylers, *1715*, p. 193.
11 Keith, *Fragment*, p. 10; Charles Dalton, *English Army Lists and Commission Registers*, VI, 1707–1714 (London: Eyre and Spottiswoode, 1904), p. 302n.
12 Parker, *Memoirs*, p. 262; Scott, *Memoirs*, p. 83; Taylers, *1715*, pp. 231–5.
13 ODNB, 37, p. 431.
14 *Ibid.*, 35, p. 620.
15 *Ibid.*, 22, pp. 850–1.
16 *Ibid.*, 16, pp. 992–3.

ensigns in Panmure's regiment (listed in appendix III), five were sons of noblemen and two were brothers of peers. One was son of a late sheriff depute.[17]

Yet this was a hierarchical society. Men expected to be led by noblemen and gentry especially those they knew as landowners and landlords. These members of the elite were born to give orders and would have been accustomed to do so. This would have been seen as perfectly natural. Whether it was militarily sound was another question, but should not be dismissed out of hand.

Clansmen certainly expected to be led by their own leaders. To try to do otherwise was to court failure. Sinclair noted, 'detachments of different clans were not to be so easily managed as a whole clan, with their chief at their head; and if his lordship designed doing good with Highland men that was the onlie way, which was a rule he followed ever after'.[18]

Yet some officers had seen military service, though often years ago. Even so, they formed a minority of the whole. William Clephame had been a lieutenant colonel in Grant's regiment from 1712–1714. Mar later wrote of him thus 'good, honest, colonel Clepham … I was in great want of those who understands, as he does, the business of a souldier. He did very good service'.[19] Thomas Bruce, son to Lord Kincardine, 'was formerlie Muster Comissarie in King William's and Queen Anne's reignes' but his skill lay in conspiracy. Better were Harry Balfour, appointed as a colonel: 'He had been an Officer and Major to the Grey Dragoons in King William's war in Flanders and had not so intirelie forgot his trade'. Harry Bruce and Thomas Graham had been officers in the army when James II had been king. The latter was said to be 'one of the best horse officers in Europe'.[20]

Other officers had military experience. James Wood was 56 in 1715 and had seen service as a cadet in the Scots Dragoons under Charles II and later as an ensign in the same regiment. He had later been in Colonel Wauchope's infantry battalion and in Oxburgh's Foot in Ireland, serving at Aughrim. In 1715 he was given a commission in Pitsligo's Horse.[21] One Charles Chalmers had been an ensign in the 3rd Regiment of Foot Guards from 1703–1714 and served as a major in Mar's regiment.[22]

Some of the junior officers had seen active service. Most famous was Sinclair, who had been a captain lieutenant in the recent war, up until his forced exit from the army over duelling in 1708.[23] Likewise, Lord George Murray had been appointed as an ensign in the Royals in 1711, though he had seen no actual battle service.[24] John Hay (1691–1740), had been briefly a captain in the Foot Guards in 1714, but as Mar's political agent, he was made a major general in the following year.[25] According to

17 NRS, GD45/1/201.
18 Scott, *Memoirs*, pp. 102–3.
19 Grant, 'Mar's Legacies', p. 174; NRS, SP13/215.
20 Scott, *Memoirs*, pp. 166–7, 137, 170–1.
21 *HMC Stuart*, VII, p. 333.
22 Rae, *History*, p. 310.
23 ODNB, 50, pp. 756–7.
24 *Ibid.*, 39, pp. 897–901.
25 *Ibid.*, 25, pp. 1016–7.

Sinclair, he 'was a young lad, who stood much in need of advice, being latelie come from the schoole'.[26]

Marischal had served in Flanders in 1708–1711 and ended as a captain in the Horse Guards in 1714, resigning in 1715. He commanded two squadrons of Horse at Sheriffmuir.[27] William Murray (1689–1746) had served in the Royal Navy from 1708–1711 and led three battalions of Atholl men at Sheriffmuir.[28] Bartholomew Gibson, once a volunteer in Orkney's regiment and later a customs official, became a lieutenant in Drummond's regiment.[29]

At least 22 officers from the British Army (including Hamilton who had been a lieutenant general, two lieutenant colonels, a major, six captains and the remainder junior officers) deserted to the Jacobites and some are known to have held ranks in the Jacobite army.[30] Only six, though, were reported by name by Argyle to Pulteney on 9 November. They were Captain Hepburne and Ensign Patrick Smith from Dubourgay's battalion and ensigns Wedderburne, Fleming, Calderwood and Chambers from Lauder's.[31] A list of these men, their ranks and their units appears in appendix II.

At least three officers had served in the Jacobite campaign of 1689 and had fought at Killiecrankie and Dunkeld in 1689. These men were Allan MacDonald of Clanranald, Alexander Robertson of Struan, both aged 42 in 1689 and John Cameron of Lochiel, eldest son of his elderly father, the clan chief, Sir Ewan.[32]

The selection of officers was often controversial. Sinclair complained that in his regiment, 'It was no easie task to get everie bodie to agree to be commanded by the same officers ... for we had nobodie who had served, and a great manie aspired to a greater or lesser command ... those who deserved least, or were good for least, pusht hardest for it'. Once officers were chosen, 'tho', I can't say, to everie bodies satisfaction'. Yet it was worse elsewhere: 'we seemed to agree in it rather better than the other regiments ... but no bodie consented to be Corporalls, because it was honour, not fatigue, they wanted'. Some men were unhappy that they were not made officers. Mr Carstairs of Kinucher, 'never having been a sojer' successfully lobbied Tullibardine to be made major in his regiment.[33] Sometimes men were chosen as officers because they were friends with the regiment's colonel, as in the case of Robert Douglas, a writer of Edinburgh, who went to Perth in mid September. He approached the Earl of Strathmore and 'having been acquainted before, and in very good friendship together' was given a lieutenant's commission.[34]

As to the rank and file, many men, whether clansmen or not, were forced out or came under some form of compulsion, as noted in chapter three. One report claimed

---

26 Scott, *Memoirs*, p. 45.
27 ODNB, 31, pp. 66–8.
28 *Ibid.*, 39, pp. 991–2.
29 NRS, GD241/380/23.
30 NRS, SP13/215.
31 TNA, WO4/17, p. 266.
32 Rev. Alexander Murdoch (ed.), 'The Grameid: an heroic poem on the Campaign of 1689', Scottish History Society, I, vol. 3 (1888), pp. 125n, 195n, 133n.
33 Scott, *Memoirs*, pp. 77–8.
34 NRS, SP13/212.

that some men were 'carried along in the rebellion … the original motive of their coming into the rebellion … being the fear of a force which they were unable to resist'. There were 'children in the family with their parents who came out and menial servants'. Boys aged 14–21 were in the ranks because of the alleged 'error of their near relations before they came to that maturity of judgement'.[35]

Yet the officers, amateur or professional, sought to build up a rapport with those under them – often, of course, men whom they knew through kinship. Both the following examples are taken from Highland units operating in England in 1715 but there is no reason to suppose that their counterparts in Scotland operated any differently. Lord Charles Nairn, for example, 'took a great deal of pains to encourage the Highlanders, by his own Experience, in their hard Marches, and always went with them on Foot through the worst and deepest Ways, and in Highland dress'.[36]

Likewise, Lord Charles Murray, 'Upon all Marches, he could never be prevailed with to ride, but kept at the Head of his Regiment on foot, in his Highland dress without Breeches: He would scarce accept of a horse to cross the Rivers, which his Men in that season of the Year forded above mid-thigh deep in Water. This powerfully gained him the Affection of his Men; besides his Courage and Behaviour'.[37]

The rank and file of the Jacobite army at Sheriffmuir are all but hidden from history. There are no regimental lists made by the Jacobites though lengthy rolls of prisoners were made by the victors at Preston. However, they may have been similar in origin and occupation to those Scots taken prisoner at the Battle of Preston. In any case, two of the units which were sent south with Mackintosh left many men from the same unit with Mar. These details from the southern army have been recorded.

The men in these units were far more geographically homogenous than those in the British army, indicative that men were recruited on a territorial basis. For example, of the 123 men recorded from Murray's battalion, all but three were from Perthshire; likewise from Mar's, 28 out of 29 men were from Aberdeenshire and 91 out of 92 from Lord Nairn's were from Perthshire. Although the men came from a multitude of parishes within these Scottish counties, there were some parishes from which a disproportionate amount of men hailed. More than half of Murray's came from just two parishes; 35 (29 percent) from both Loggie Reale and Forlichell. A further 19 came from the parish of Dull. Over a third of Mar's contingent (10 out of 29) came from Kildrummy. For Nairn's, 29 (31 percent) came from Moulin and 16 (18 percent) from Blair. Mackintosh's battalion mainly hailed from the county of Inverness and from the parishes of Dunlichity (48), Dellerish (43), Moy (32), in particular. Yet those from Strathmore's battalion were from seven counties and 47 parishes; but even here, nearly one third of the men were from Glamis (36) with another 14 from both Forfar and Kilmuir; all three parishes being in Angus.[38] Many of the men from each unit

---

35   *Ibid.*, GD205/38/8/2/1.
36   Patten, *History*, p. 44.
37   *Ibid.*
38   TNA, KB8/66.

therefore had known one another for many years, which was an aid to unit cohesion, and so they might fight well together or alternatively leave as a group.

The occupations from which these men were drawn were also more homogenous than those men serving with Argyle. Of Mar's 29 men, 23 (80 percent) were labourers; from Nairn's, 61 (63 percent) were labourers and from Murray's, 103 (80 percent) were labourers. The next most common occupation from Murray's and Nairn's were gentlemen, 13 (11 percent) and 8 (9 percent) respectively. Mackintosh's regiment was dominated by yeomen (167 men; over 50 percent) and 44 gentlemen (nearly 20 percent) and 29 labourers (10 percent). Strathmore's battalion included 55 men described as labourers (46 percent) and 13 gentlemen (about 10 percent). This in itself is a reflection of the overwhelmingly agricultural and rural societies that most Scots lived in.[39]

It is often stated that the units in the Jacobite army were over-officered. According to Patten, this was because there was a need for the colonel to oblige as many gentlemen as he could with officers' commissions. The ratio of officers to men in the five units that we know of certainly suggest this – 108 to 712 – almost one in eight men being an officer. Yet we must also recall that the numbers that we know of are the men who surrendered; many had deserted already and it is likely that there could have been a disproportionate numbers of rank and file compared to officers deserting as the latter were probably more highly motivated.[40]

Organising the men was a major issue for Mar. He seems to have left it to others, though, and not imposed his authority. Possibly he was wise not to do so as he had no knowledge or experience of such and as this was a largely irregular force lacking conventional discipline.

There are numerous myths about the Jacobite armies, often coloured by literature and propaganda. Not all were made up of Highland clans; many were the tenants and dependants of Highland lords such as Seaforth and Huntley. Furthermore, recent research has shown that the Highlanders, who made up the bulk of Mar's armies, were not a warrior people, where every man had training and use of weapons. Clan warfare was in the past and the majority of the men in the ranks were peasant conscripts. There was great potential, of course, for the Scots have a long tradition of fighting overseas; 2–3 percent of the Scots in the early seventeenth century did so.[41] We should also distinguish between the men who fought in their clans, the MacDonalds, Camerons and Frasers for example, and those who fought in non-clan Highland regiments, brought into the field by magnates such as Huntley and Seaforth. The latter appear to have been formed into more or less regular units and to fight in such a manner.

When the Jacobites began to gather at Perth 'they were in all a great many men, but no such thing as order … there would be no doeing till all that mob was regimented'. An army had to be created. Sinclair claimed 'I did what I could to persuade those who

---

39   *Ibid.*
40   Patten, *History*, pp. 120–2.
41   Charles Singleton, *Famous By My Sword: The Age of Montrose and the Military Revolution* (Solihull: Helion & Company, 2015), pp. 23, 15.

commanded them to pick out such as had served, to make officers and serjeants, and where they were wanting, to take some of the activest of their folks to supplie'.[42]

Sinclair also complained about the indiscipline of the Highlanders after having witnessed them in the operation to secure arms at Burntisland: 'It was needless to complain to those who commanded them, who said it was not in their power to help it … the Highlandmen would not by any means, and run together in troops of nine or ten, without taking the least notice of what was desired, except a very few'.[43] According to Mar, the Highlanders were 'the people who can be of the greatest use for relieving the country when an opportunity offers'.[44]

Non-clan units of the Jacobite army was organised into battalions and squadrons just as any conventional army of the time was. If Panmure's battalion is a representative sample, for which records survive, this would seem to have been the case. It was divided into 12 companies, one of which was termed the grenadier company. Each had a captain and a lieutenant, though the grenadiers had two lieutenants. Ten of the 12 companies had an ensign, too. Each had two sergeants and two corporals. The colonel's company had one musician (either a piper or a drummer) and the grenadiers had two but none of the others had any. There were between 29 and 44 privates in each company. There was also a quartermaster, a surgeon and an adjutant.[45] These men are listed in appendix III. They certainly looked convincingly military. All apart from Strathmore's regiment (described by Robert Douglas as 'modell'd into a regiment') wore Highland garb. They had drummers, bagpipers and carried standards.[46]

This was the case with other units, too. Mackintosh's battalion consisted of 13 companies of about 50 men in each prior to the desertions at Langholm. There was a colonel, a lieutenant a colonel, a major and ten captains (each had charge of a company of men, as with regular armies); 15 lieutenants (two of whom were ADCs), an adjutant, a paymaster, a quartermaster and another ADC. Only part of Strathmore's battalion crossed the Firth: about four companies; four captains and four lieutenants, five ensigns and a quartermaster. Lord Drummond's regiment included three captains, a lieutenant and three other officers. There were three companies of Mar's battalion; a major, three captains and three lieutenants. Lord Nairn's regiment was commanded by himself as colonel and included five companies and Lord Charles Murray's regiment was similarly composed. This seems to have applied to clan regiments as well as non-clan regiments: Clanranald's had a colonel, lieutenant colonel, a major, nine captains, 15 lieutenants, 22 sergeants, 12 corporals and 506 men.[47]

Although Mar had a great deal of raw material at his disposal, training seems to have been very variable. Sinclair reported, 'nobodie engaged in that affair gave the half of the application to their dutie, or disciplining their regiments as my Lord Strathmore and Panmure; for the others seemed to doe nothings for their humour, or rather did

42   Scott, *Memoirs*, pp. 50–1.
43   *Ibid.*, p. 101.
44   Grant, 'Mar's Legacies', p. 172.
45   NRS, GD220/45/1/201.
46   *Ibid.*; NRS, SP13/212.
47   Patten, *History*, pp. 120–2; *HMC Stuart*, I, p. 472.

nothing at all'. He added, 'Tho' orders were given out to form regiments, everie one did as they pleased'. Drummond had 600 men but formed them into three battalions whereas most thought they should make but one.[48]

The Jacobite army also had to be paid. According to Mar, the men received three pence and three loaves of bread per day; presumably this was for the infantrymen.[49] The weekly total pay of a sample of units in early November 1715 was as follows: Clanranald, £70 3s 6d; Appin Stuarts, £33 6s 7d; MacLeans, £38 1s 3d; Glengarry's, £54 18s 10d; McDougals, £3 8s.[50]

The average Jacobite fighting man is often depicted as one with sword, shield, musket and pistol, but very few except the social elite carried such a complement of weaponry. Rather, in some ways, the Jacobites utilised the same type of weapons as their opponents; muskets for the infantry and broadswords for the cavalry, as well as artillery. Some had Lochaber axes, but they were a minority, which would have struck a discordant note with those punctilious about conventional warfare. Yet arms were lacking at the beginning of the campaign; certainly among some units. Sinclair wrote that in one case, the gentry and their servants were 'without carbines, who could be no use in the defence of the place', the Lowlanders 'with old rustie muskets, who had never fired one in their lives, and without pouder and flints', whereas the Highlanders were 'no better accoutred'. In September, the Highlanders had 'not one graine of pouder' he claimed. He made similar allegations that the Jacobites were badly armed, having only old weaponry and lacked powder. Mar promised that supplies from France would solve this deficiency. When the clans joined the rest of the Jacobite army, Sinclair thought they were 'no better armed than we'.[51]

Yet not all agreed with Sinclair's pessimistic comments. Sibbitt reported in October that Mackintosh's Highlanders 'arrived with musquet, sword and target (shield) according to the Highland manner', but 'they have neither ammunition nor provisions but what each man carries himself'.[52] The Rev. John Anderson concurred, writing, 'The clans here have graly muskets, but few swords, which are the arms they mostly depend upon'.[53] Two reports in late September referred to the infantry being 'in Highland habits, with swords, pistols and targets and some had forelocks … dirks but no Bayonets', but another stated 'a good dale of them want firelocks'.[54] Gunpowder to the extent of 3,681 pound weight had been secured from Aberdeen.[55]

It is not certain how well the Jacobite army was eventually armed. Extensive attempts were made to acquire both muskets and melee weapons, as noted from Sinclair's semi-successful raid on Burntisland in September 1715 and Mar's orders to towns to supply weaponry. The figures for the wounded among the British army at Sheriffmuir suggest

48 Scott, *Memoirs*, pp. 52, 75.
49 Rae, *History*, p. 431.
50 *HMC Stuart Papers*, I, p. 472.
51 Scott, *Memoirs*, pp. 45, 40, 17, 189.
52 TNA, SP54/9/47.
53 A. W. Anderson (ed.), *The Papers of the Rev. John Anderson* (Dumbarton: Bennett and Thomson, 1914), p. 35.
54 TNA, SP54/8/127, 9/2d.
55 Allardyce, *Historical Papers*, pp. 40–41.

that about a quarter were injured by musket balls but over half by cutting weapons, including broadswords and Lochaber axes. This does not suggest a lack of arms, but rather a preponderance of melee weapons over guns or perhaps the fact that more casualties were caused in the melee and pursuit than in exchanges of fire.[56] However, a list of 76 Highlanders who surrendered arms in 1716 states that 18 handed in guns (almost 25 percent) and seven gave up swords (about 10 percent), suggesting that the Jacobites were more commonly armed with guns rather than swords; research covering the Jacobite army of 1745–1746 also suggests that this was the case then too.[57]

Where the Jacobite army was different to regular forces was in their appearance and tactics. Contemporaries did not record much about the appearance of the Jacobite army in 1715. Patten writes that the Scots battalions sent from Mar were mostly in 'Highland dress', though he does not trouble to explain what this was, his very use of the term indicates that their costumes were distinctive, even alien, in comparison to English clothing.[58]

James Maxwell, a Jacobite officer in 1745, explained why the Highlanders were so much different from the English and Lowland Scots:

Their language is originally the same with the Irish, which has no affinity with the English, but their dress is peculiar to themselves. Light, clever, and easy, and adapted to their country and manner of living, they are not encumbered with breeches, instead of which they wear a kind of petticoat or shirt, which reaches from their middle to their knees. Their plaid is the most useful part of their dress; it is a piece of woollen stuff from a yard to 1 ½ yard in breadth, and six yards in length, when folded; this they wear in sundry shapes as a kind of cloak, and wrap themselves up in when they lye down to rest.[59]

This garb was seen as being unconventional to their foes. This had an effect on their enemies, as the Rev. John Home explained, 'As to their dress, or Highland garb … which, like every thing unusual in war, had an effect of terror in the last rebellion [that of 1715]'.[60]

Another point which made the Jacobite army distinctive was that it was partly made up of some of the Highland clans. The clansmen in the Jacobite army were men who had been summoned into battle by their clan chieftains. Clansmen had the same surname and were all allegedly descended from the chief of the clan's family. Although laws had been passed to subvert the power of the chief, these had had limited effect in the Highlands due to their remoteness and the pull of tradition. The hereditary jurisdiction of the chief and his relatives was still what mattered the most to the clan. Yet as well as this authority from top down, 'the principal source of it is a real attachment of the people to the persons of their chief. Each clan looks upon

56   *Ibid.*, WO116/1–3.
57   NRS, GD44/51/167/4.
58   Patten, *History*, p. 42.
59   James Maxwell (ed.), *Narrative of Charles Prince of Wales' Expedition to Scotland in the Year 1745* (Edinburgh: T. Constable, 1844), pp. 25–6.
60   John Home, *History of the Rebellion* (London: T. Cadell jun. and W. Davies, 1802), p. 11.

itself as one family, and the chief is the common father'. Clanship served as a strong bond between members of clan regiments, which 'gives them that Espirit de Corps, so remarkable in some old regiments, that have, generally speaking, behaved well'.[61] Sinclair wrote, 'its taken for granted, that the best half of the Highlandman's courage consists of his love for his chief or master, and him he will not easlie desert'.[62]

The clan chief acted as chief magistrate, judge and general for his people. From him there was no further court of appeal and to seek justice elsewhere was regarded as treason against the clan. A chieftain would be usually accompanied by a number of his clan when he was away from home. He cultivated hospitality, martial exercise and masculine activity. His lands were divided among his nearest relations and let on easy terms in order to create a strong bond between them. In military terms, the clan chief would be the colonel of his clan regiment, the eldest son the lieutenant colonel, the next would be the major and so on. According to Home:

> The most sacred oath to a Highlander, was to swear by the hand of his chief. The constant exclamation, upon any sudden accident, was May God be with the Chief, or may the Chief be uppermost. Ready at all times to die for the head of the kindred, Highlanders have been known to interpose their bodies between the pointed musket, and their chief, and to receive the shot which was aimed at him.[63]

Recruitment for the Jacobite clan units was thus of men obliged to serve his landlord or chief; many probably were willing to do so. Others went by informal force of conformism and some by the threat of force against them, their family and property. Some may have been hired out by employers as substitutes. Others volunteered.[64] Yet the clan regiments were not wholly or even mostly manned by men of the same surname. The Mackintosh battalion, 295 strong, only numbered 37 men of that surname; little over 10 percent, and a disproportionate number of these were officers.[65] Only 13 out of 33 officers in the Mackintosh regiment bore that surname.[66] During the Forty Five the Mackintoshes also only had a minority of the men in the unit of this name.[67]

The clan in battle reflected the social order of the clan. Home wrote:

> Order and regularity, acquired by discipline they had little or none; but the spirit of clanship, in some measure, supplied the want of discipline, and brought them on together; for when a Clan advanced to charge an enemy, the head of the kindred, the chief, was in his place, and every officer at his post, supported by his nearest relations, and most immediate dependants. The private men were also marshalled according to consanguinity: the father,

---

61   Maxwell, *Narrative*, pp. 26–27.
62   Scott, *Memoirs*, p. 231.
63   Home, *History*, pp. 9–10.
64   Jean Gordon Arnot and Bruce Gordon Seton, 'Prisoners of the '45', Scottish Historical Society, 3rd series, 13 (1928) pp. 269–274.
65   TNA, KB8/66.
66   Patten, *History*, pp. 120–121.
67   Arnot and Seton, 'Prisoners', I, p. 281.

the son, and the brother, stood next each other. This order of nature was the sum of their tactic, the whole of their art of war.[68]

The Highland attack has often been seen as the Highland charge, which originated in 1641 in Ireland. It was not primarily based on musketry but rather than on shock tactics, but often the equipment was lacking for it to work in practice.[69] Major General Hugh Mackay (d.1692), who had fought the Jacobites at Killiecrankie in 1689, described the Highland method of battle:

> They attack bare footed, without any cloathing but their shirts and a little Highland doublet, whereby they are certain to outrun my foot and will not readily engage where horse can follow the chase any distance … They come on slowly till they be within distance of firing, which, because they keep no rank or file, doth ordinarily little harm. When their fire is over, they throw away their firelocks, and every one drawing a long broad sword, with his targe (such as have them) on his left hand, they fall a running towards the enemy, who, if he stands firm, they never fail of running with much more speed back again towards the hills.[70]

The Jacobite technique in battle was devastatingly simple. David Wemys, Lord Elcho (1721–1787), described what happened when the Jacobite army met their enemy at Prestonpans in 1745:

> They sett up a hideous noise and run in as fast as they Could … The Prince's first line closed again, and Continued running in, when they Came near enough; the right & left firr'd upon ther Dragoons … the Centre firr'd upon the Foot & … Continued to run in upon them sword in hand (for After firing they threw away their Guns).

In another battle, 'Most part of the highlanders as usual Threw down their Guns and advance very quick sword in hand … & beat & putt them to flight'.[71] Jacobite musketry should not be dismissed out of hand. Patten wrote that the Highlanders 'are extremely good Marksmen'.[72] They were able to hold their fire and discharge a volley at devastatingly short range as occurred at Falkirk in 1746 when threatened by three regiments of mounted dragoons. Infantry volleys at Preston in 1715 also caused their attackers much loss.[73] In 1688 Highland soldiers fired at one another in battle for an hour before resorting to melee.[74]

---

68   Home, *History*, pp. 11–2.
69   Singleton, *Famous By My Sword*, pp. 30–1.
70   Hugh MacKay, *Memoirs of the war in Scotland and Ireland, 1689–1691* (Edinburgh: Bannantyne Club, 1833), p. 51.
71   Lord Elcho, *Short Account of the Affairs of Scotland, 1744–1746* (Edinburgh: John Douglas Publishers, 1907) pp. 271–272, 375–376.
72   Patten, *History*, p. 68.
73   Walter Biggar Blaikie (ed.), 'Origins of the '45', SHS, 2nd series, 2, 1916, p. 195.
74   Scott, *Memoirs*, p. 130.

Yet not all had a high opinion of this method of warfare. Sinclair admitted that:

No man of the partie has so bad ane opinion of Highlandmen as I; and that what they are capable of doeing, in a plain field, against regular troops, depends on accident, or the irregularitie of the troops and that they never will be brought to attack anie who have the least cover, nor will the wit of man bring them to stand cannon, which has an astonishing influence over them.[75]

The non-clan troops, who made up the majority of the army, were rather different. They had been drilled and trained to a degree when at Perth. It is not known how efficient they were but they impressed onlookers. Wightman wrote of them at Sheriffmuir, 'I never saw Regular Troops more exactly drawn up in Line of Battle, and that in a moment.[76] As to firing, a commentator wrote, 'They fired in rancks each rank reteering and not in platoons'.[77]

Jacobite cavalry and artillery were relatively few in number and the least effective of the three arms of the army. James Johnstone, a Jacobite officer in 1745, later wrote of the guns: 'The importance commonly attached to artillery, their supposed utility, or rather the absolute necessity for them on all occasions, are greatly over-rated'.[78]

Artillery needed skilled men to handle it; had there been French troops or volunteers within the Jacobite ranks, as in 1746, they could have been usefully employed here. Sailors were often used to handle guns, as occurred with the British army at Prestonpans and with the Jacobite army at Preston in 1715. In neither instance were there happy results. In 1715 Patten noted the six guns employed by the Jacobites at Preston, 'the Rebels ... did not much use them, except at first only; in short they knew not how, having no Engineers amongst them, and a Seaman who pretended Judgement; and upon his own Offer took the Management of the Cannon ... acted so madly, whether it was he had too little Judgement, or too much Ale'.[79] It seems that the guns were loaded with a form of canister, but when fired hit the sides of houses 'so that no execution was done thereby'. Roundshot was also used, and though the first shot only demolished a chimney pot, the other caused some damage 'execution, and oblig'd the regiment to halt'. We know that one soldier later claiming a pension alleged that he had 'lost a piece of his right shoulder by cannon ball'.[80]

At Sheriffmuir, the Jacobites had 11 cannons, six brass and five iron, 'which we had pickt up in severall places' (some of which came from Dundee and Dunottar Castle). However they lacked powder and ball with which to make them effective. Nor was there any one who knew how to operate them. Highlanders would not use them. According to Sinclair, they merely took up horses that could be used to carry supplies,

75   Donald MacBane, *The Expert Sword-Man's Companion* (Fallen Book Publishing, 2015), p. 77.
76   Patten, *History*, p. 161.
77   Archibald Francis Steuart, *News Letters of 1715* (Edinburgh: W. and R. Chambers, 1910), p. 70.
78   James Johnstone, *A Memoir of the Forty Five* (Oxford: Alden Press, 1970), p. 81.
79   Patten, *History*, p. 90.
80   *Ibid.*, p. 90; TNA, WO116/1.

but Mar believed 'many cannon would give us a name and strick terror'.[81] It seems that they were brought along for their symbolic value and for prestige on the lines that regular armies had cannon but armed mobs did not and the Jacobite army wished to be classed as the former, not the latter.

Action taken by Jacobite cavalry tends to be little mentioned by contemporaries, apart from on roles were mobility not combat was required. Sinclair referred to these, and mentions a rearguard role. In a landed society, horse riding was part and parcel of aristocratic and gentry life both in the hunt and in the everyday business of travel. There was dissension among the cavalry units as to whom should have precedence and have the honour of bearing the royal standard of the Stuarts. Linlithgow's Stirlingshire squadron had that honour as they were the first to be formed, but Sinclair claimed they were the weakest and their leader was boastful. To add insult to injury, the other squadrons had to supply some of their horses to Linlithgow in exchange for some of their worst ones.[82]

There were attempts to train the cavalry's horses and there are a number of references to 'using them to the drum and to bide fire'. Some of the horses were coach horses and mares. Southesk's cavalry were stated as being '60 well managed horses, that might pass in any Troop with saleable furniture'. Some, though, 'would endure neither Drum nor Pipe'. If the horses were a mixed bag, the arms carried by the cavalry were also a mixture. One report referred to them being equipped with holsters and side pistols, with some armed with firelocks (perhaps carbines are meant). Another report refers to the same armament but that some had broadswords.[83] Their effectiveness was thus limited and they were never able to engage their opposite number.

The Achilles heel of the Jacobite army was its likelihood of considerable desertion when not on the field of Mars; whether defeat or victory resulted. The latter had happened to Montrose in 1645 when his successful army suffered severely from desertion after a string of victories. After the setback at Dunkeld in 1689 the Jacobite clans had not remained together as a fighting force. So although often effective on the battlefield, as at Killiecrankie in 1689, they were difficult to hold together for any long period of time. Sinclair noted:

> The Highland men would rise out of hopes of plunder, and would doe as they had always done, which the historie of Montrose and since that, of my Lord Dundee, was enoughe to convince anie bodie of, which is, they certainlie desert on three events; first, they'd wearie and goe home, if they could not come to action soon; the second if they fight and get the victorie, plunder following on that, they'd be sure to goe home with it; the third is, if they are beat, they run straight home.[84]

Yet properly used in a plan which needed courage but little technical finesse, they could be deadly.

---

81   Scott, *Memoirs*, pp. 200, 202.
82   *Ibid.*, pp. 75, 136.
83   TNA, SP54/7/40b, 8/127, 9/2d.
84   Scott, *Memoirs*, p. 26.

8

The British Army

If there has been relatively little attention paid to the Jacobite army of 1715, there has been even less study of the British army that fought at Sheriffmuir. This is quite typical of writings on the Jacobites and the Jacobite rebellions, which focus almost entirely on the Jacobites rather than their opponents. Writings on Marlborough's forces and on those troops who fought the Jacobites in 1745 are fairly strong on the ground, but Argyle's forces have not been sufficiently analysed hitherto. Reid's account is a fairly general overview of the British army at the time; focussing on tactics and organisation and listing officers but not men who served in each unit.[1]

Where historians have commented upon Argyle's performance, they, unlike the case with Mar, have been positive. Baynes states, 'Argyle's handling of his command deserves high praise on many scores ... he showed remarkable skill in the handling of small forces to the best advantage ... he won the day against numerically superior forces ... his deeds speak for himself'.[2] Szechi is equally admiring, writing, 'He was, by and large, a soldiers' general, in the sense that he essentially sought to keep his men well paid, well drilled, well fed and well armed and expected to lead them – from the front – to the enemy ... fighting nearly two and a half times his own number to a standstill in a sprawling encounter battle was no small credit to him'.[3] Both attest to his loss of control of his troops during the Battle of Sheriffmuir, however.

Unlike Mar, Argyle was a soldier. He had been commissioned as colonel of his father's regiment when aged only 14, and was made colonel of the 10th Foot in 1702, then of the Horse Guards. In 1696 he was a major general and saw active service in the War of the Spanish Succession, rising to lieutenant general by 1709. At Malplaquet he 'at the head of troops made the last brave and successful attack' against the French entrenchments.[4] Yet he gained Marlborough's displeasure, the latter stating, 'I cannot

---

1   David Chandler, *Marlborough as Military Commander* (London: Batsford, 1984); Michael Barthorp, *Marlborough's Army, 1702–1711* (London: Osprey Publishing, 1980); Christopher Duffy, *The '45* (London: Cassell, 2003); Stuart Reid, *Culloden* (Barnsley: Pen and Sword, 2005); Jonathan Oates, *The Jacobite Campaigns* (London: Pickering and Chatto, 2011); Reid, Sheriffmuir, pp. 12–22.
2   Baynes, *Jacobite Rising*, p. 203.
3   Szechi, *1715*, p. 196.
4   Drake, Amiable Renegade, p. 164.

have a worse opinion of anybody than I have of the Duke of Argyle'. As with Mar, he used his political influence in Scotland to support the Union, but was critical of it thereafter and stated he was no longer in favour of it. He was dismissed from military offices in 1714 but restored to them on the onset of the Hanoverian Succession.[5] Sinclair complimented him thus, 'tho' a young man, full of fire, [he] acted, in my private opinion, the part of ane old wary Generall'.[6]

Yet some London-based contemporaries, more sympathetic to Marlborough and the court, were critical of him. Dudley Ryder wrote:

> He is of a proud, hasty, insolent temper and very covetous and debauched, and it is said was endeavouring to change the present ministers … He is said to have been very much the cause of the mercy which the Government has shown the rebels, which he did in order to make himself popular. It is thought also that he favoured the Pretender's cause in Scotland and gave them advantages on purpose.

On a later occasion Ryder wrote that he was 'a strange, restless, troublesome man and so as he may but govern, be at the head of affairs, does not care how he disturbs and perplexes the King and Parliament'. Argyle was very much a friend of the Prince of Wales and so was at loggerheads with the Prince's father, the King, and his government, which was headed by Stanhope and Townshend.[7] The Princess of Wales claimed 'he had a great many good Qualities, but some Faults that covered them'.[8] He was also a significant figure in Scottish politics, as head of the powerful Clan Campbell, so was 'a man of interest in Scotland'.[9]

There has been no discussion hitherto on Argyle's immediate subordinates, who were all experienced career soldiers. Thomas Whetham had been commissioned as an infantry ensign in 1685, was a captain lieutenant in Leslie's Foot in 1694 and a full captain later that year. He rose in rank steadily in the first decade of the eighteenth century; major of the 11th Foot by 1700; colonel of the 27th in 1702; brigadier general in 1707, major general in 1710 and commander in chief in Scotland in 1712. Unlike many of his peers he had served in Canada. He had also campaigned in Scotland, the West Indies and Spain.[10]

Then there was Joseph Wightman. As with Whetham he had seen much military service in the last quarter century. He was commissioned into the Foot Guards in 1690, becoming lieutenant and captain in 1693, then captain and lieutenant colonel in 1696. He had served in Sir Matthew Bridge's regiment in Flanders in the War of the League of Augsburg. He became a lieutenant colonel in 1702 and was promoted to brevet Colonel on Marlborough's recommendation and he deemed Wightman 'a very careful, diligent officer'. He was a colonel in 1707 and major general in 1710. In

5   ODNB, 9, pp. 814–816.
6   Scott, *Memoirs*, p. 94.
7   Matthews, *Diary*, pp. 267, 373.
8   Cowper, *Diary*, p. 68.
9   Parker, *Memoirs*, p. 263.
10 Romney Sedgwick, *History of Parliament: The Commons*, II (London: HMSO, 1970), p. 533.

1712 he was appointed deputy commander in Scotland in 1712, though Argyle's first choice was William Breton.[11]

Finally there was Major General William Evans (died 1740). Commissioned in the First Foot Guards in 1690, he had served at the siege of Namur, being wounded twice and then promoted to captain lieutenant in 1695. He became colonel of a regiment of Foot in 1703, was a brigadier in 1707 and became a major general three years later. He and Argyle had served together at Malplaquet.[12]

Of Argyle's brigadiers, Forfar was the youngest. He had a modicum of military experience, being made colonel of infantry in 1713 and then brigadier in 1715. His regiment was at the Battle of Sheriffmuir.[13] Jasper Clayton (1670–1743) was the second of Argyle's brigadiers and his regiment was also with the army. He had served at Alamanza in Spain and had become colonel of his regiment as recently as 1710. Finally there was Grant who had served in his father's infantry regiment in 1700, becoming colonel of Mar's Foot in 1706 and was then with the regiment in Flanders from 1708–1711, seeing action at two sieges but mostly in garrison duties. A close colleague of Argyle and a staunch Whig, he was removed from his post in 1711 following the Tory purge of the officer corps, but was reinstated in 1714.[14]

Leading the battalions and regiments were the lieutenant colonels, also men of military experience. Henry Hawley (c.1685–1759), in charge of Evans' Dragoons, was one such experienced officer. Commissioned as an ensign in 1694, he saw service as an aide in the campaign in the Low Countries. He rose through the ranks in the War of the Spanish Succession from lieutenant to colonel, fighting at Alamanza in 1707 and in the Cherbourg expedition in 1708. He was known as both a disciplinarian and a capable cavalry officer.[15]

The other regimental and battalion commanders had similar experience. James Campbell (?–1745) led Portmore's Dragoons and had done since 1706. He had been captain of the Royal Scots Fusiliers in 1702, rising to the rank of lieutenant colonel of dragoons in 1706 and was brevet colonel in 1711. He had seen action at Blenheim, Oudenarde and Malplaquet. Fellow cavalry commander was Halifax-born Joseph Guest, a rare example of a man who had risen through the ranks to senior level (and was to finish his career as a major general). His first commissioned rank was at the relatively elderly age of 44, as a cornet, but he was a captain in 1707 and lieutenant colonel of Carpenter's Dragoons in 1713, a rank he held at Sheriffmuir. He had been at the Battle of Alamanza, too.[16]

Most of the other lieutenant colonels had served in the army for the previous decade or two. Only one is known to have been wholly inexperienced: Alexander Ross, appointed lieutenant colonel of Forfar's Foot earlier in 1715. John Grace, in charge of Shannon's Foot at Sheriffmuir, was appointed as a cornet in 1694 and rose through

---

11   ODNB, 58, p. 850.
12   Charles Dalton, *Army of George I*, I (London: Eyre and Spottiswoode, 1930), p. 331.
13   ODNB, 16, p. 627.
14   *Ibid.*, 23, pp. 278–279.
15   *Ibid.*, 25, pp. 966–8.
16   Dalton, *Army*, I, pp. 107, 109.

the ranks to be lieutenant colonel in 1712.[17] Cathcart had served throughout the War of the Spanish Succession, first as captain, then as a major in Portmore's Dragoons in 1709 and finally as a colonel.[18]

Their captains were also mostly seasoned soldiers with similar levels of experience. John La Farey had been a 2nd lieutenant in Holt's Marines in 1705, then a captain in Hill's in 1707 and a captain in his present regiment, Montague's Foot. Captain Sir Robert Hay had been a captain in the Scots Fusiliers in 1704, before transferring to Portmore's Dragoons in 1706 and briefly being a brevet major in 1711. He had fought at Ramillies and Oudenarde. Patrick Robinson, a captain in Portmore's had been soldiering since 1692. One of Wightman's captains had been at Namur and another two at Alamanza. Of the other captains that we know about in these units some were probably battle tested; one had been appointed in 1702 and another in 1705; two in 1707, six were appointed in 1708, one in 1710 and three in 1711. Yet some had more limited experience of soldiering; two had been appointed in 1712, six in 1714 and eight as recently as 1715, though it is worth noting that all these men would have been lieutenants and ensigns prior to having obtained their captaincies.[19]

Naturally the junior officers – the lieutenants, ensigns and cornets – had least experience as they were the youngest men among the officers. But even here there was a variety in their lengths of service. Some of the lieutenants had received their commissions over a decade ago; one was in 1696, another in 1699, and another in 1703. Most were relative newcomers, though, with three being commissioned in 1704, two in 1705, four in 1706, five in 1707, three in 1708, eleven in 1709, six in 1710, three in 1711, four in 1712, four were appointed in 1713; five in 1714 and eight in 1715. Of the cornets, 19 had been appointed during the War of the Spanish Succession and 18 from 1712–1715; the latter would have had no experience of warfare whatsoever.[20]

Men wishing to become army officers had to buy their commissions in this period, thus ensuring that most officers would be men of social standing and/or wealth. At least two were aristocratic: Lieutenant Colonel James Campbell was the son of the 2nd Earl of Loudoun and the lieutenant colonel of Kerr's Dragoons was Lord Torphichen; Cornet James Agnew was the son of Sir Andrew Agnew, a baronet. Lieutenant Colonel William Murray was a brother of Sir James Murray of Clermont. Not all were from the social elite, however. Captain Lieutenant George Carpenter served in his father's own dragoon regiment. Charles Kendal, lieutenant colonel of Clayton's, was a merchant's son. Major James Montresor was the son of Jacques de Tresor, a Huguenot refugee, and at least five other officers at Sheriffmuir were of French extraction (probably descendants of Huguenot refugees, forced into exile by Louis XIV and thus anti-Catholic). Guest had been a humble ostler when enlisting and was now a commissioned officer.[21]

---

17   *Ibid.*, pp. 223, 308.
18   ODNB, 10, pp. 538–9.
19   Dalton, *Army*, I, pp. 109–111, 138–139, 148–149, 307, 331, 339–340, 341–342, 345–346.
20   *Ibid.*
21   *Ibid.*, pp. 109, 339–340, 345–346.

To progress through the ranks meant waiting for a vacancy of the next rank, caused by death or retirement, and then purchasing that commission, always at a higher tariff than the lower rank which was then in turn sold to another. Yet a commission had first to be offered in order of seniority and had to be approved. There was a table of fees for commissions. During wartime, promotion was accelerated as officers were killed and in these cases commissions were 'free'. An important part of the system was that those wanting a commission in the first place needed friends who could recommend them to the regiment's colonel. For example, John Kynaston, arriving in London in 1704 in search of a military career, later wrote, 'I apply'd myself to my friends in order to get a commission I was recommended by two members of Parliament to James Craggs and he was pleased to use his interest to the Duke of Marlborough and got me colours in the Regiment of Foot'. Officers received no formal training but learnt the trade of soldiering on the job.[22]

On the whole the officers that commanded the regular army at Sheriffmuir were veterans of the European conflicts of the past decade and in many cases the previous 20 years. A few of the junior officers had been appointed with the coming of the peace, though almost all of these were to be found among the cornets and ensigns. However not all officers were with their units on the day of the battle 'to the great Detriment of His Majesty's service' as noted in correspondence between Argyle and Pulteney after the battle, but unfortunately no numbers or names are given (in September, 31 officers from seven units were absent, about one man in every seven, some of whom were recruiting, or sick).[23] We shall now examine the men under their command, of whom rather more is known about than it is for their Jacobite counterparts because of the existence of their pension records.

The men in the ranks tended to come from a different social stratum from their superiors. In war time bounties were offered to encourage enlistment. Sometimes men in prison joined the army. John Watson, a debtor in a gaol in London was discharged because he 'has enlisted in the regiment of Colonel Thomas Handiside'.[24] Civil magistrates and parish officers were also offered cash incentives to encourage men in their counties/parishes to enlist. Yet the army did not want to have gaolbirds, but young, fit men who were preferably Protestant. Each unit would send out recruiting parties to places where such men could be found: markets, fairs and taverns. Economic motives could play their part for men deciding to join, as well as to evade family responsibilities. Donald MacBane, a 23-year-old apprentice, who enlisted in 1687 (and who was later at the Battle of Preston in 1715) later wrote, 'My mistress began to lessen my Dish which I could not endure, I being a Raw young fellow would have eaten two days' meat in one day – so I went and listed myself a soldier'.[25] Although soldiers' pay was low, it was at least guaranteed, and often soldiers could participate

22   Anon, *The Case of John Kynaston* (London, 1716), p. 3.
23   TNA, WO4/17, p. 322; SP54/8/74B.
24   William John Hardy (ed.), *Calendar of the Middlesex Sessions, 1689–1709* (London: Sir Richard Nicholson, 1905), p. 269.
25   MacBane, *The Expert Sword-Man's Companion*, p. 75.

in other forms of paid employment, too. Unlike the officers, the men had to undergo training in the form of drill and musketry. A man's service was theoretically for life but wounds, illness and being 'worn out' often meant retirement with a pension on reaching middle age. A man might serve in more than one unit throughout his career.[26]

The lists of soldiers given disability pensions from 1716–1745 give some details about soldiers who fought at Sheriffmuir and who survived, and those who served in the battalions that fought there at the relevant time.

Of these, they came from a diverse range of both parishes and occupations, but they only tend to be routinely recorded from the 1730s (listed in appendix I). Of the 139 who gave parish of origin, 73 came from England (52 percent), 33 from Ireland (24 percent), 27 from Scotland (20 percent), three from Wales (2 percent) and three from elsewhere; one came from Frankfurt and two from either Africa or the West Indies. These proportions roughly reflect the population composition of the British Isles, though the Scots were significantly over-represented (making up 11 percent of the population but almost twice that proportion of the army). This should not be too surprising for in the previous century about a fifth of the country's young men volunteered to fight abroad; in part this was probably due to the relative poverty in Scotland and the lack of other economic opportunities. They came from a very disparate array of parishes. Cities, perhaps not surprisingly, produced more, with five men from Dublin and three from Glasgow. Four men came from Nottingham, but for most parishes only one man is recorded.[27] Most though were from numerous small rural parishes.

The sample of 92 men whose occupations were recorded (listed in appendix I) show that the rank and file were made up of a number of different skilled working men. Whether they had become tired of their work, had become unemployed or had domestic troubles is unknown. Twelve were husbandmen, there were 11 weavers, 10 shoemakers, eight labourers, six tailors and five servants, and men from another 33 occupations.[28]

The ages and length of service of rather more men were also recorded (again, see appendix I). Of the 130 known about, their ages ranged from 19 to 58, with a 63-year-old from the Edinburgh Independent Company also claiming service at the battle. The mean average age was 34 and a half, with the vast majority being in the 19–48 age range (only 11 were aged 49–63). The most common age of the men in the ranks was 29.[29]

Years of service was often recorded, too, for 120 men. Their length of service ranged from new recruits to one man with 33 years of service at the time of the battle; this man having enlisted in the reign of Charles II and possibly having fought during the wars of both William III and Anne. The mean average service length was just over nine and a half years. Given that British involvement in the War of the Spanish

26   Oates, *Jacobite Campaigns*, pp. 12–17.
27   TNA, WO116/3–4; Holmes and Szechi, *The Age of Oligarchy: Pre-Industrial Britain, 1722–1783* (London: Longman, 1993) pp. 345, 350.
28   TNA, WO116/3–4.
29   *Ibid.*

Succession ended in 1712, then of these 120, 34, or just over a quarter would have seen no active service in a shooting war, and 18 of these men were newly recruited. However, nearly three quarters had seen service in battle overseas in recent years. The average soldier in Argyle's forces, then, was aged in his mid thirties with nearly 10 years of military experience behind him. Yet it is worth noting that the majority of this experience would have been against regular soldiers in the armies of Spain, Bavaria and France, who fought primarily with musket volleys and cannon fire, supported by cavalry. Infantry charges with sword and other weapons were uncommon in this conventional warfare. Their opponents in 1715 were not men who all fought in the way of Continental adversaries.[30]

There are also descriptions of those who served in the regiments at Sheriffmuir, and though they are not noted as having been injured there, their service periods overlap with those of the battle so it is reasonable to assume they were present. They serve to illuminate the rank and file. One man in Morrison's battalion is described as a tall man; one in Shannon's as being 'an undersiz'd man with a perriwig'. Thomas Hallicott of Egerton's was 'a short old man', Robert Steel of Kerr's, 'a little man, says he was never wounded' and John Graves of Clayton's was 'a low thin man with a grey beard'. John Mitchael of Kerr's was 'a little pale black man', presumably a negro, as was Edward Ingleish of Wightman's, 'a thin black man', and perhaps most surprisingly was Christian Welch (1667–1739) of Stair's, 'a fat jolly woman, in the habit of a man, received several wounds'. She had served in the army on and off since the 1690s and became somewhat of a celebrity.[31]

For some of these men, injuries received at battles from 1689–1710 are noted. Walter Mclaughlin of Stair's, was cut by a sword at Killiecrankie, the first battle in the Jacobite campaigns in 1689. A few had seen service in the War of the League of Augsburg: Andrew Read of Kerr's had been wounded by a bomb shell at Namur and two of Clayton's had also been injured there. More, though, had soldiered in the War of the Spanish Succession. James Mitchell had sustained a wound in the shoulder at Ramillies. In all, of the men who fought at Sheriffmuir, 19 had been wounded at Alamanza, four at Ramillies and three at Malplaquet.[32] However, not all men were veterans. A contemporary account states that 400 of Argyle's men at Sheriffmuir, or just over 10 percent, were newly recruited men.[33]

It is not known who made up the artillerymen present at Sheriffmuir. Coming under the direction of the Master of the Ordnance they were not strictly speaking answerable to Argyle. It is likely that they were taken from the garrison at Edinburgh Castle. In 1715 these gunners were composed of Captain John Slezer and Captain Theodore Dury, an engineer. They had a lieutenant, two commissaries, a corporal, nine paid gunners, six practitoners, six bombardiers, a petardier and two miners. Yet it is unlikely that the castle was wholly denuded of artillerymen and so probably only a

30 Ibid.
31 Ibid., WO116/1.
32 Ibid., 1–4.
33 The Annals of King George the second Year (A. Bell: London, 1717), p. 89.

handful of these men were at Sheriffmuir. Some may have been too elderly or infirm to have been used on active service as opposed to garrison duties.[34]

However, of these men, it was deemed that the captain and lieutenant of the Train were able to serve in the field because of their age. The others who could do so were paid an additional £46 15s. They were with the field army from 27 August 1715 until 1 March 1716. From 15 September until 9 January they were joined by a carpenter, smith, collar maker and servants, each man being paid a generous nine shillings per day (totalling £157 19s). They also had the services of a number of horses to pull the guns and ammunition, costing almost £300.[35]

None of the units in the army was up to its full strength. Sickness and desertion thinned the ranks even before any actual fighting. On 27 October, Pulteney urged Argyle to vigorously recruit to make the companies in each battalion up to 50 men. He had certainly tried; by adding two companies to each battalion of infantry, or an additional 100 men. He asked that civil magistrates and landowners be encouraging recruitment. Each recruit would receive a bounty of 40 shillings and was only obliged to serve a short time in the army. As noted above, about 400 men were new recruits. It was also noted that not all the officers (the deficient numbers not known) were actually with their men. This was commonplace in peacetime and less crucial, but on active service it was another matter. However, Argyle reported to Pulteney that there were good reasons for this: possibly age and bad health might account for some of those missing.[36]

The British Army was a relatively new phenomenon as a standing army – and was also politically controversial and often unpopular. There had been no permanent armed forces in the British kingdoms before the civil wars of 1642–1651. The Cromwellian army had been mostly disbanded at the restoration of the monarchy in 1660, but part of it together with Charles II's guards formed the nucleus of a standing army of 'guards and garrisons', chiefly used for guarding Britain's few colonies, fortresses in Britain and for policing duties at home. There were, in fact, until 1707, three different establishments: in England, Scotland and Ireland as the Crown's three kingdoms were not yet united. After the Union with Scotland, the Scottish forces and the English ones came under one single establishment, alongside the garrison forces in Ireland, who remained a separate establishment until 1800. The army was expanded during wartime and also to meet serious domestic rebellions, such as that of Monmouth's in 1685. During the 1690s the new armies were blooded in Ireland and in the Low Countries, and though they, alongside Dutch and German allies, had fought Louis XIV's French forces to a standstill in the latter, they had not been spectacularly successful either. Yet under the command of the Duke of Marlborough during the War of the Spanish Succession of 1702–1713 they had won great victories at Blenheim, Ramillies, Oudenarde and Malplaquet, though they had fared less well in Spain at Alamanza. They had been part of a formidable fighting machine under a great

---

34   Dalton, *Army*, p. 237.
35   *Journal*, pp. 552–553.
36   TNA, WO4/17, pp. 249, 266; Patten, *History*, pp. 145–147.

leader, equal to any. With the coming of peace in 1713, most of the battalions raised were disbanded, leaving a small nucleus sufficient for internal security and policing at home as well as garrisoning Britain's increased number of colonial possessions overseas (including Gibraltar, Minorca and the West Indies). It was capable of expansion during wartime. The army was administered by the Secretary at War, but armament was the responsibility of the Master of the Ordnance.[37]

The army was composed of horse, dragoons, infantry (often termed 'foot') and artillery. Regiments and battalions were known by the name of their colonel. He was the man given the commission to raise the unit, to choose the officers and to recruit the men. Since only one regiment of horse saw active service in 1715 and that in England, this arm of the service need not be considered here.

Argyle's five regiments of dragoons had all been founded between 1681–1690. Carpenter's and Evans' were raised in 1685 to deal with the Monmouth rebellion of that year. Stair's was an Irish regiment raised in 1689 and Kerr's were raised in 1690 in Scotland. The oldest of the dragoon regiments at the battle were Portmore's, raised in Scotland in 1681. All had served in the recent war of the Spanish Succession. These were Carpenter's, who had been in Spain in 1702 and 1706–1707; Kerr's, who had served in Flanders 1711–1712 and Stair's, who had fought in Flanders from 1702–1712 and fought at all of Marlborough's four great victories: Blenheim, Ramillies, Oudenarde and Malplaquet. Portmore's and Evans' had likewise served in that war. They could also fight on foot, with carbines and bayonets, as at Schellenberg in 1704 and at Preston in 1715. Each regiment was divided into six troops, each led by a captain.[38]

Dragoons were cavalry; originally mounted infantry in the civil wars, but by now the mainstay of the cavalry. A Military Dictionary in 1702 decreed that they were 'Musketeers mounted, who serve sometimes a-foot and sometimes a-horse-back, being always ready upon anything that requires expedition, as being able to keep pace with the horse, and do the service of the foot'. Their task was to undertake reconnaissance work before the battle and on campaign. On the battlefield their task was to engage the enemy cavalry and other troops with the sword as shock troops. They could often turn a retreating enemy army into a routing one, with shockingly high casualties for the would-be escapers. Yet they were more expensive than infantry to maintain as both horse and man needed feeding and paying.[39] Dragoon regiments were smaller than battalions of foot and were made up of two squadrons each, subdivided into three troops each.

Cavalry were at their most deadly when pursuing a fleeing foe over level terrain, as Jacobite Colonel John O'Sullivan (c.1700–1751) explained occurred during the Jacobite rout at Culloden in 1746: 'The Dragoons & horse yt follow'd the MccDonels, MccIntoshes & another Clans … what slattor they made of them, & if it was not for the Parks & inclosiers of Castle Hill, where the horse cou'd not follow them, not a soul

---

37   Barthorp, *The Jacobite Risings*, pp. 22–4.
38   Reid, *Sheriffmuir*, pp. 170–5.
39   Barthorp, *Marlborough's Army*, pp. 21–22, 10–11.

wou'd escape'.[40] According to Sinclair, Portmore's Dragoons were most feared by the Jacobites, 'tho' not 200 men, they were a greater terror than all the others'.[41]

Infantry were the most numerous of troops on the battlefield because they were the cheapest and the quickest to train. They were an essential part of any army and victory depended on them holding firm. Each battalion was divided into 10 companies (seven commanded by a captain; one by each of the battalion's three field officers; below them were the lieutenants and ensigns) with the elite company being known as the grenadier company, made up of the battalion's best and steadiest men. Each battalion carried two flags: the King's colour and the regimental colour. Officers and sergeants were armed with swords, spontoons and halberds. The infantryman was armed with a flintlock musket and socket bayonet, which meant one could fire with the bayonet affixed, as had not been the case at Killiecrankie in 1689. It was a heavy and long weapon: five feet without the bayonet. At least powder and ball were pre-packaged into cartridges. The British infantry had a reputation for their firepower. Usually two shots per minute were possible, with an effective range of 60 yards and a maximum one of 250. They were also armed with short swords or hangers.[42]

Musketry was where the regulars scored over the Jacobites as Sinclair noted, 'I had no great expectation of the Highlanders standing the fire of regular troops … tho' we had more men, they had more fire arms in a condition to fire'.[43] When volleys of musketry were steady, they were lethal. O'Sullivan stated that at Culloden, the British infantry fired thus: 'the enemys musqueterary begins, & continues as regular as nurrished a fire as any troops cou'd. Our men advances but slolly, & really it is not possible yt any troops yt cant answer such a fire as the enemy kept can do otherwise'.[44] Yet inexperienced troops could be defeated. Maxwell noted that at Prestonpans, 'The foot gave one good fire from right to left; but before they could give a second, the Highlanders were upon them, sword in hand'.[45]

Fire was by platoon: that is to say a section of each battalion would fire, then another section and then another, the theory being that men reloaded whilst their comrades fired and so the enemy was presented with a continuous barrage of fire. Conventionally battalions in other armies fired by battalion en masse. Robert Parker, a grenadier captain of this period, recalled how this worked and gave proof of its effectiveness. In an encounter between a French and a British battalion, the former fired first and killed or wounded 10 of their enemy. When the British returned fire, their battalion inflicted nearly 40 casualties on the French.[46]

It was not only the impact of the little lead ball through flesh and bone that was lethal, but also the fact that that ball would carry with it part of the victim's clothing

---

40   Alastair and Henrietta Tayler (eds.), *1745 and After* (London: Thomas Nelson & Sons, 1938), p. 165.
41   Scott, *Memoirs*, p. 85.
42   Barthorp, *Marlborough's Army*, p. 12.
43   Scott, *Memoirs*, p. 211.
44   Tayler, *1745*, p. 164.
45   Maxwell, *Narrative*, p. 41.
46   Parker, *Memoirs*, p. 165.

and with it bacteria that had accumulated there, meaning that the target might well die slowly and painfully of the wound after the battle.[47]

A recent study of British infantry firepower in this period argues that platoon fire began in the early 1690s in Ireland and within the Scottish army. As one platoon would fire the next would reload and so the effectiveness of fire was doubled. The system was further developed in Ghent in 1706–1707 and by 1713 each platoon equated to a company of the battalion. However, platoon fire was inadequate against a fast moving enemy intent on melee. British infantry could also be ferocious in melee as well as with their firepower. At Schellenburg in 1704 and at Malplaquet in 1709 they used their musket butts and bayonets to deadly affect, as they were to do at Culloden in 1746, too.[48]

Of the infantry under Argyle's command at Sheriffmuir, all were veteran units. Forfar's dated back to 1665; whilst Clayton's, Montagu's and Morrison's were all raised in 1685 due to the Monmouth rebellion. Wightman's was raised in 1688 and Egerton's in 1701. Shannon's and Orrery's were both raised in Scotland in 1689 and 1678 respectively. Orrery's had fought in the four Marlburian victories, and in Flanders from 1703–1712. Wightman's served in Flanders from 1701–1702 and then in Spain from 1703–1710. Although another five had also served abroad in that war, Clayton's had only recent experience of garrison duty in Ireland.[49]

Last and certainly least were the men of the Train of Artillery (the Royal Artillery was not founded until 1716). Unlike the infantry and cavalry they were administered by the Board of Ordnance, not the War Office, but as with the infantry and cavalry, they wore red jackets. The most senior were the gunners, who charged, laid and fired the guns. Then there were the matrosses, who assisted them with tasks around the guns. The drivers and waggoners who moved the guns were civilians. Heavy guns were restricted for siege use, both in attack and defence, where they would be relatively stationary, because they were too cumbersome to pull at any speed along the road network, such as it was, or to manoeuvre on the faster-moving field of battle.[50]

Rather, small calibre guns, such as three-pounders (this being the weight of the cannon ball fired) were often employed in the support of infantry in the field. Artillery used solid ball (stone or iron) at between 300–450 paces which was its effective range and at close range would switch to canister – a bag of small balls, and lethal, as a Jacobite officer once noted in 1746, 'when they [the Jacobites] Came pretty near they charged [the guns] with grape shott, and as they were well pointed they did great execution'. Marlborough used about 100 guns in each of his major battles, about 1.34 guns per 1,000 men, though Argyle was to have six at Sheriffmuir.[51]

Conventional land warfare in western Europe at this time dictated that an army would march into battle in columns and deploy several hundred yards away from the

47   Anthony Pollard and Neil Oliver, *Two Men in a Trench*, II (London: Michael Joseph, 2003), p. 212.
48   David Blackmore, *Destructive and Formidable: British Infantry Firepower, 1642–1765* (Barnsley, Pen and Sword, 2014), pp. 168–170, 111, 94, 75, 80.
49   Reid, *Sheriffmuir*, pp. 176–82.
50   Barthorp, *Marlborough's Army*, pp. 14, 38.
51   *Ibid.*, pp. 14–15; Elcho, *Short History*, p. 431.

enemy at long range for artillery. Each army would form into two lines. There might also be a reserve third line if numbers permitted. The post of honour was on the right wing where the commander might be found. Cavalry were often arrayed at the flanks, and certainly this was the French preference, but Marlborough had his cavalry as a central reserve to deliver a final crushing blow. Putting an army into such an array could take hours, depending on the size of the force, for the Allies needed nine hours to form up their 50,000 men at Blenheim.[52]

When both sides commenced battle, artillery would fire and infantry advanced or stood firm. It all began in a leisurely manner. Conflict was basically attritional as each side tried to wear the other down by firepower. Battles could often be inconclusive, with one side choosing to retire as night fell, leaving the victor in charge of the field, but without having being able to achieve a killer blow. Marlborough always attempted to use his three arms together for maximum effect and he fought his battles in an aggressive manner, which was relatively unconventional. Infantry firepower was maximised by having the troops fire in ranks of three, often with close artillery support as guns were sited with battalions rather than being in grand batteries.[53]

There were concerns among some that the army might be politically unreliable. Bolingbroke told James that he had been reliably informed of 'the dissatisfaction of the people and the soldiers, both in the old regiments and in the new levies'.[54] After all, some of its officers probably had Tory sympathies, some having been appointed when Ormonde was Captain General in 1710–1714. We have already noted in the previous chapter that over a score of army officers went over to the Jacobites, including six from Kerr's Dragoons and one from Forfar's. It was not only some officers who were suspect. In the summer of 1715, Dudley Ryder reported that a friend considered 'we cannot depend upon our English troops, the common people are so poisoned with Jacobitism and so much set against the present government'.[55]

Some instances of this unreliability can be certainly found. Colonel Joshua Paul of the Foot Guards had been arrested for attempting to enlist men for the Jacobite cause.[56] In September, a sergeant and nine men of a newly raised regiment were sent from Chelmsford to London on suspicion of treasonable practices.[57] At the onset of the Battle of Preston, the Jacobite Earl of Derwentwater was convinced that the British troops advancing on the town were in sympathy with the Jacobites.[58] Ironically, among Shannon's Foot was one Arthur Elphinstone (1688–1746), a Jacobite and Scottish nationalist who later claimed that fighting for George I was 'against his conscience'.[59] However, by the eve of the battle, all those who were to desert had long done so already. Desertion among the rank and file seems to have been about one

---

52   Chandler, *Marlborough as Military Commander*, pp. 86–87.
53   *Ibid.*, pp. 88–93.
54   Mahon, *History*, I, Appendix, p. xxx.
55   Matthews, *Diary*, pp. 61–62.
56   British Library Add. MSS. 47028, f. 67r.
57   *The Flying Post*, 3694, 6–8 Sept. 1715.
58   Tyne and Wear Archive Service, CP3/22.
59   ODNB, 18, p. 309.

percent at most; on 1 October, nine out of 2,053 had left; four weeks later it was 15 out of 1,511.[60]

Many soldiers were well motivated by factors other than money. A recent study of Scottish soldiers opposed to the Jacobites suggests that anti-Catholicism was a key spur to recruitment. Religion, not patriotism was essential. The martyr mythology of the bad old days of the later Stuarts in Scotland where the Presbyterian Covenanters had been persecuted by the forces of the (Stuart) Crown was of importance; so, too, was the example of friends and neighbours and perhaps a desire for a military career (always significant in less economically developed states).[61]

Apart from the regular troops, there were also volunteers at Sheriffmuir, under Rothes. As with their leader, those that we know about were Scottish gentry who were in favour of the Union as well as being supporters of the current government, and included John Ker, Duke of Roxburghe, a Scottish representative peer and other noblemen: Loudoun, Belhaven, Lauderdale and Haddington. As with their Jacobite counterparts they lacked military experience but were strongly politically and ideologically motivated. As well as these noblemen there were also Scottish gentry and their servants, too. It is not known how they were armed, but presumably with swords and pistols.[62]

In short, most of Argyle's forces were the product of what late twentieth century historians have called 'The Military Revolution'. This was an increasingly professional army, well organised and administered, with a new military culture of career officers and soldiers, with a strong community identity and emerging traditions of its own. The Jacobite army was, in some ways, a traditional one, but it was not static, with some officers having seen service abroad, for example. It relied more on cold steel – or its threat – than on musketry, cannon fire and cavalry charges as did Argyle's men. In this it was not alone: Charles XII's highly effective Swedish army had a contempt for firepower and with its sword as well as musket and bayonet-armed infantry, played down the role of firepower as a deciding factor in battle. Musketry could still be slow and unreliable, especially in damp weather.[63]

It should not be thought that a more 'backward' army would necessarily be defeated by a more 'advanced' one. At the Battle of Fraustadt in 1706 the Saxon infantry fired by platoon as did the British, before a charging Swedish foe. In theory the Saxons should have been able to loose off five or six volleys before their enemy crashed into them, but only managed one or two and were defeated. Likewise at Killiecrankie in 1689 a numerically weaker Jacobite Highland army relying on shock routed a larger Scottish–Dutch army, whose dependence was on firepower.[64]

Although this was the last set piece battle in which Jacobite Highlanders had faced regular troops, a replay after 26 years was not inevitable. Firstly William's forces in

60 TNA, SP54/9, 2E, 9/92; NRS, SP13/215.
61 Victoria Henshaw, *Scotland and the British Army, 1700–1750: Defending the Union* (University of Birmingham, 2014), pp. 60, 116.
62 ODNB, pp. 31, pp. 383–4, 902–3; *Daily Courant*, 4391, 19 Nov. 1715.
63 Robert Frost, *The Northern Wars, 1558–1721* (Pearson: London, 2000), pp. 309, 274.
64 Ibid., p. 275.

1689 were at a very low ebb indeed, morale wise, having virtually collapsed at the end of the previous year during the revolution of 1688. That of 1715 had a fine experience and tradition of victory behind it. Secondly they were no longer armed with muskets which could not be fired with fixed bayonets. Thirdly the Jacobites lacked an aggressive and experienced military leader of the calibre of Viscount Dundee.

Mackay, who had led regulars against Jacobite Highlanders in 1689–1690, had the following remarks to make: 'All our officers and souldiers were strangers to the Highlanders' way of fighting and embattailling, which mainly occasioned the consternation many of them were in … if a battalion keep up his fire till they be near enough to make sure of them, they are upon it before our men can come to their second defence, which is the bayonet in the muzzle of the musket'.[65]

There were many differences, but also some similarities, between the two opposing armies. Argyle's had the edge with its largely more professional and experienced officers and men, many of whom had seen active service on the Continent in recent warfare. The Jacobite army had been transformed from being a semi-armed mob in September to something resembling an organised force; its officers were very variable in quality and discipline, but did have the valuable asset of superiority of numbers.

---

65   MacKay, *Memoirs*, p. 52.

9

The Battle of Sheriffmuir: Opening Phases

What happened on a battlefield is often difficult to ascertain, for both participants and historians. The greater the number of accounts, the greater the potential for confusion. This is because of the inherent chaos associated with any rapid, violent actions, but also because of the diverse recording of it in the aftermath, tailoring their accounts to the perceived needs of their audiences. Memories of dramatic events tend to shift and merge with others that the author has been told or has read.

An anonymous Jacobite in 1715, remarked a few days after the Battle of Sheriffmuir: 'There being various and different Reports industriously spread abroad, to cover the Victory obtained by the King's Army over the Enemy; the best way to set it in a clear light, is to narrate the true Matter of Fact, and leave it to the World to judge impartially thereof'.[1]

Or as Tobias Martine wrote after the battle, 'We have had the most comfortable news of an intire victory … but we are at a great loss for want of the particulars thereof'.[2]

Lord George Murray wrote the following in his memoirs of the Jacobite campaign of 1745:

> It is not an easy task to describe a battle. Springs and motions escape the eye, and most officers are necessarily taken up with what is immediately near themselves; so that it is next to impossible for one to observe the whole: add to this, the confusion, the noise, the concern that the people are in, whilst in the heat of action. The smallest oversights and the most minute incidents are often the cause of the loss or gain of the day; an opportunity once missed, cannot be recalled; and when a commanding officer commits a mistake it may perhaps not be perceived but by very few, if by any and yet prove fatal.[3]

In order to understand the battle as well as we can, we shall first examine the numbers of each army.

---

1   Patten, *History*, p. 164.
2   Anderson, *Papers*, pp. 38–39.
3   James Forbes (ed.), *Jacobite Memoirs* (Edinburgh: William and Robert Chambers, 1834), p. 82.

Strength of the opposing armies

The Battle of Sheriffmuir was fought by small armies by Continental standards (under 15,000 men); there had been 108,000 combatants at Blenheim and 165,000 at Oudenarde. Yet these armies were made up of troops from several nations. By the standards of battles in Britain, those numbers fighting at Sheriffmuir were significantly higher: 7,000 fought at Sedgemoor in 1685, 6,500 at Killiecrankie in 1689, about 5,000 at Preston in 1715, and under 4,000 at Glenshiel in 1719.[4]

British Army

It is agreed that Argyle's forces were outnumbered by their opponents, but the figures are stated variously. Historians and contemporaries differ widely. The Taylers quote several contemporary figures and seem to conclude with about 3,500, of which 1,200 were dragoons.[5] The most detailed breakdown of figures was given by Baynes: 900 dragoons and 2,200 infantry. Barthorp duly repeats these.[6] Reid does likewise, but has the cavalry as numbering 960 (probably by including the figure of 60 for the volunteer cavalry as noted by Rae). As with Baynes and Reid, Barthorp gives suspiciously rounded figures for each unit (180 men per dragoon regiment and 240–340 per infantry battalion), which are based on the figures in Rae's *History*.[7] Sinclair-Stevenson gives a total of 'some 3,000'.[8] Szechi does not enumerate Argyle's numbers, but has him being outnumbered by two and half times his own strength, and, because he notes the Jacobites as being 9,000, that would put him at about 3,600 men.[9] Inglis gives no figure. Historians, then, list Argyle having 3,000–3,600 men under his command.

Contemporaries also differed. Wightman put the army at not above 1,000 cavalry and about 2,500 infantry.[10] Colonel John Blackader (1664–1729) thought the total was 3,400.[11] The best method is to examine the figures given in the Scottish State Papers of 1715 compiled by the army for the government's benefit. These figures below are those for 29 October (for the first five battalions, then stationed at Stirling) and for 24–31 December 1715 (for those who did not arrive until after that time) and so are those nearest the date of the battle. Casualties taken at Sheriffmuir, based on newspaper reports, which may be incorrect, have been added to the last three battalions.

---

4   Chandler, *Marlborough*, pp. 334–335; Pollard and Oliver, *Two men in a Trench*, II, p. 199.
5   Taylers, *1715*, p. 95.
6   Baynes, *Jacobite Rising*, p. 141; Barthorp, *Jacobite Rebellions*, p. 7.
7   Reid, *Sheriffmuir*, pp. 125–127.
8   Christopher Sinclair-Stevenson, *Inglorious Rebellion: The Jacobite Risings of 1708, 1715 and 1719* (London: Hamish Hamilton, 1971), p. 114.
9   Szechi, *1715*, p. 196.
10   Patten, *History*, p. 161.
11   Steuart, *News Letters*, p. 69.

Infantry

Unit	Sergeants	Drummers	Rank & File	Total
Forfar	18	18	295	331
Montague	18	12	222	252
Wightman	20	10	253	283
Orrery	22	18	329	369
Shannon	20	10	332	362
Morrison	28	14	323	365
Clayton	20	20	239	279
Egerton	22	20	266	306
Totals	166	122	2,259	2,547

Add 5.5 percent for officers as per Culloden below, which gives an additional 143, so a total of 2,799 infantry (officers and men).

Dragoons

Unit	Sergeants	Drummers	Corporals & Privates
Portmore	6	6	171
Carpenter	6	6	165
Evans	6	6	170
Stair	6	6	151
Kerr	6	6	153
Totals	30	30	810

Add 8 percent for officers as Culloden below which gives an additional 62, so a total of 872 cavalry. Based on figures of 29 October 1715, except for Evans' and these are for 24–31 December 1715, plus the 22 men of Evans' killed and captured at Sheriffmuir.[12]

Artillery

6 x 3 pounder

18 gunners

Rothes' mounted volunteers: 60 or about 150.[13] The Laird of Gorthie wrote 'For want of troops the Duke of Argyle was obliged to make up his line with them, doing just the same service that the dragoons did'.[14]

---

12 TNA, SP54/11/2b, 9/92.
13 Rae, *History*, pp. 308n, 300n.
14 NRS, GD220/5/817/5.

Total strength: 3,749 plus 60–150 volunteer cavalry.

Argyle's strength, therefore, was rather more than previous estimates by contemporaries or historians have allowed for. Yet the figure given is almost certainly incorrect, for numbers of troops were not constant: men died, deserted or fell ill, as well as others being recruited. Thus Argyle had about 3,800–3,900, and though this is not correct, it is probably the nearest we can ascertain with any accuracy.

The army was divided into three brigades: that on the left was led by Whetham and Brigadier Grant, that in the centre by Wightman and Brigadier Clayton, and that on the right by Evans and Forfar.

We now turn to the army led by Mar.

Jacobite Army

As with the British Army, historians differ as to the size of Mar's army at Sheriffmuir. Petrie does not enumerate figures for either side and the Taylers offer 12,000 as a possiblity.[15] This is the highest number that any modern writer gives. Sinclair-Stevenson puts the number at 12,000 minus 200 deserters.[16] Szechi gives about 9,000 as Mar's strength.[17] Fewer numbers are suggested by others. Inglis gives 8,000, Baynes estimates 917 as the number of Jacobite cavalry and 6,255 infantry and allots a numerical strength to each unit.[18] Barthorp gives similar figures, 900 cavalry and 6,200 infantry.[19] The lowest number is given by Reid: 5,800 infantry and 800 cavalry.[20] Thus the figures are even more diverse than those for the British army, between 6,600 and 12,000.

That historians have differed should come as no surprise for contemporaries did likewise, with the enemies of the Jacobites suggesting higher figures. Wightman put Jacobite numbers at 9,100.[21] Lieutenant Alexander Campbell wrote that they were 16,000 well armed men 'with their officers, colours and standards in good order'.[22] Rae gives 9,100 and a reserve of 400 cavalry.[23] Blackader puts it at between 9,000 and 10,000.[24] Jacobite officers suggest lower totals and they were in a better position to know more realistic figures. Sinclair claims it was 8,000 strong.[25] The lowest contemporary figure was that given by Keith, with 6,000 infantry and 800 cavalry, divided into 14 battalions and eight squadrons respectively.[26]

Fortunately there is a 'List of the King's Army' which has never been produced in book form before, as noted in chapter six. It seems to be a basic muster roll, compiled at Perth on 5 November, so just a few days before Mar's march southwards. It would

15   Taylers, *1715*, p. 95.
16   Sinclair-Stevenson, *Inglorious Rebellion*, pp. 113–114.
17   Szechi, *1715*, p. 151.
18   Inglis, *Sheriffmuir*, p. 23; Baynes, *Jacobite Rising*, p. 140.
19   Barthorp, *Jacobite Rebellions*, p. 7.
20   Reid, *Sheriffmuir*, 1715, pp. 127–8.
21   Patten, *History*, p. 158.
22   NRS, RH15/14/149.
23   Rae, *History*, p. 303.
24   Steuart, *News Letters*, p. 69.
25   Scott, *Memoirs*, p. 208.
26   Keith, *Fragment*, p. 16.

appear to be the most reliable account of the Jacobite army at that time. It shows that Sinclair's and Keith's figures are too low, as are some of those offered by previous historians, based on published accounts.

The initial disposition (based on Sinclair's account) was as follows:

Cavalry

Right wing

Earl Marischal's squadrons	120
Linlithgow's squadrons	108
Marquess of Huntley's squadrons	264

Left wing

Earl of Southesk's squadron	74
Rollo's squadron	70
Sinclair's Fife squadron	80

Position unknown

Marquess of Seaforth's	50
Total strength of cavalry	766

Infantry

Line one

MacDonalds

Glengarry	461	
Glencoe	105	
Total		566
MacKenzies		700?
MacLeans		327
Camerons		611
Stuart of Appin		263
Campbell of Glenlyon		no numbers given?
Frazerdale and Chisholm		500
Clanranald		528

Line 2

Marquess of Seaforth's Foot (three battalions)

Applecross	350	
Fairburn	400	
Ballmackie and McKeddin	350	
Total		1,100

Lord Huntley's Foot (four battalions)

Gordon of Glenbucket's	330	
Leith's	303	
Innes'	322	
Cluny McPherson's	207	
Total		1,162

Earl of Panmure's battalion		475
Marquess of Tullibardine's battalion		No numbers given?
Drummond's battalions		
Viscount Strathallan (cmdr)	257	
Logie Almond	366	
Total		623
Strowan Robertson's battalion		223
Position unknown		
Sir Donald MacDonald		650
Lord Ogilvie's		352
Envery's		240
Breadalbane's three battalions		No numbers given

Total infantry: 8,320 plus Breadalbin's men; perhaps a total of about 9,000 infantry.[27]

Artillery

Eleven guns, six brass and five iron. Calibre unknown, probably small; no powder or ball.[28] No known gunners.

It is therefore impossible to ascertain a figure, but it would seem that Mar had just under 10,000 men under his command, with perhaps just over 9,000 infantry and 766 cavalry. Thus Argyle was facing more than twice his own numbers. In terms of infantry he was facing treble his numbers, though had a slight numerical advantage in cavalry. These were conventionally heavy odds: during the War of the Spanish Succession, armies were usually roughly evenly matched numerically and such disparities of numbers, proportionately speaking, were unknown. Yet numbers are not everything. At Narva in 1700 Charles XII's Swedes defeated a vastly numerically superior Russian army.

According to the Laird of Gorthie, the British line was three deep, as was conventional. The Jacobite ranks were eight deep, relying on shock rather than firepower, and so the frontage of the two armies was probably roughly equal. He added, 'The Duke had too few troops'.[29]

Terrain

The district that the two armies had arrived in was sparsely populated. Dunblane had a population of between 1,500–2,000, but of these only about 500 actually lived in the town.[30] According to an anonymous account of the battle, it took place on 'a lonely stretch of moor, interspersed with patches of morass, and so uneven as to be almost hilly'.[31] It was a frosty day and there was fog on the muir.[32] In fact there had been frost

---

27   NLS, MS 1498, ff. 1r, v.
28   Scott, *Memoirs*, p. 200.
29   NRS, GD220/5/817/9b.
30   Inglis, *The Battle of Sheriffmuir*, p. 7.
31   Anon, *Battle of Sheriffmuir*, p. 15.
32   NRS, GD220/5/817/5.

Map 1 – The armies form up, late morning

for several nights prior to the battle, rendering the boggy patches solid and so passable for cavalry.[33]

Contemporary maps often show the disposition of forces arrayed in battle, but the only known map for this one is partial. There have been two interpretations of how they were arranged. Baynes shows the Jacobites and their enemies on a north-east/south-west axis, with Dunblane to their west. More recently the consensus begun under Reid shows them to have faced each other on a west/east axis, with Argyle's army to the east. However, the only contemporary map in existence, that in the National Library of Scotland, suggests that the Jacobite army had its rank flank on a road from Perth, just south of the River Allan and its left flank just south of Whithead's Town hamlet,

33 *Annals*, p. 147.

3. The remnants of a fallen pillar known as 'the Gathering Stone': legend has it that the Duke of Argyle watched the battle from this spot. (Author's photo)

which had hills to its right. It was formed up on a north-west/south east axis on the muir of Kinbuck.[34]

The day of the battle was Sunday 13 November. At sometime before eight in the morning, as day was breaking, the Jacobite army formed itself into two lines, with no reserve, to the left of the road from Dunblane.[35] At sunrise the Jacobites saw a small band of cavalry on the high ground to their south, about a mile away. This could well have included Argyle, who with Wightman joined the advance guard, because he needed to see where his enemy was. Although the two armies were two miles away, hills and broken ground prevented him from seeing them. He had to consider whether the far larger Jacobite force, some of which was close to the River Allan, might flank him on his right. As with Wightman, Argyle was impressed on seeing the Jacobites form up, 'which they did in very good order'. On seeing them the Jacobites sent out their own cavalry to reconnoitre. They returned and reported that Argyle's men were among the enclosures at Kippendavie. There was no general Jacobite advance however. After that, according to Sinclair, 'we lost a great dale of time'. Naturally he blamed Mar, who, according to him, did not expect to see the enemy so close, and despite the discussion on the previous night, did not know what to do, doubted his ability to do anything and so waited whilst his enemy made the next move. Whilst his commander

---

34   Reid, *Sheriffmuir*, pp. 124–126; <http://www.data.historic-scotland.gov.uk/data/docs/battlefields/ sheriffmuir-full.pdf>.
35   Keith, *Fragment*, p. 17.

4. A nineteenth-century drawing of the Earl of Mar holding
a council of war with his officers. (Public domain)

abandoned the initiative, Sinclair put Huntley's two squadrons into order and then discussed the situation with Huntley.[36]

Huntley did not think the army should push south against Argyle because if they did so, and James, who was expected daily, did arrive, he would be lost and out of communication with his army. So they should fall back to Auchterarder. Sinclair was averse to such a cautious, almost defeatist, suggestion, arguing 'for the Duke of Argyle's comeing out was the onlie thing coul doe our business, and the onlie occasion ever we could have to recover our liberties, or force the enemie to give us a peace on our old footing'. Retreat would mean that the Highlanders would desert and the whole cause would be lost forever. It was also suggested that emissaries could be sent to Argyle to ascertain whether he had plenipotentiary powers as regards the Jacobites. Huntley took Sinclair's suggestions to Glengarry and Sir John MacLean.[37] According to one source, 'Huntley as warmly opposed it [i.e. fighting] with such obstinate eagerness that the enemy gain'd no little advantage of time'.[38]

Argyle had remained on the hill observing the Jacobite army's manoeuvres. He could not initially determine what they were going to do and how he should fight them. Eventually, seeing movement on the left of the Jacobite line, he became concerned that it might try and outflank him whilst the Jacobite right attacked his left. Although the marshy ground on his right had hitherto prevented any cavalry action there, it had

---

36 Scott, *Memoirs*, p. 209; TNA, SP54/10/48; Patten, *History*, p. 161; Rae, *History*, p. 303.
37 Scott, *Memoirs*, pp. 209–210.
38 *HMC Stuart Papers*, V, p. 197.

now frozen over and so could be tenable for troops. He decided that he would have to march his troops to the right in order to avoid being partially surrounded. He rode off his hill and at about 11:00 a.m. gave his orders.[39] It is believed that the army took the old west/east road eastwards from Dunblane and towards the hamlet of Dykedale a mile to the east.[40]

Time passed in the Jacobite camp. Hearne later reported that there was 'a sermon in the camp of Mar a little time before the battle on this text, Jos. XXII 22. The Good God of gods, the Lords God of gods, he knoweth, and Israel he shall know, if it be in rebellion, or if in transgression against the Lord (Save us not this day).[41] It was Sunday after all, so a sermon should not have been unexpected amongst Christians. It is not known what the denomination of the speaker was, Catholic or Protestant, or if the latter, presumably Episcopalian.

Sinclair, writing in his memoirs, was pessimistic about success in battle: 'I had no great expectation of the Highlandmen's standing the fire of regular troops … tho' we had more men, they had more fire armes in a condition to fire'. Yet what else was there to be done, 'I saw very clearlie, we had no other chance for our Countrie, our lives, our honour, but by attacking … because after that day, the levitie of the Highlandmen would never give us another opportunitie, tho' I did not think that a victorie could have done our business, for it was not to be doubted, that victorious or beat, they'd go home'.[42]

It was 11:30 a.m. when Mar 'took his resolution', or rather put it to an assembled council of war. He called all unit commanders together on rising ground between the army's two lines. According to Keith, he outlined various possibilities; one being that they could wait, either for the arrival of James, which he daily expected, or for news about the Jacobites in England. He then made a speech, and even Sinclair conceded, 'his Lordship, to doe him justice, which I think I am obliged in conscience to doe, it being the onlie good action of his life, made us a very fine speech'. He spoke of the injustice done to the Stuart family, the misery for Scotland of the Union and the opportunity they now had of righting these wrongs, 'and concluded in very strong and moveing terms'. Keith wrote that 'none daring openly to oppose the current'. In opposition to his earlier sentiments, Huntley suggested 'it wou'd not be fit to remain in unaction till the King's arrival'. Yet Sinclair recalled that Huntley, who was the only other man who spoke at that council of war, asked Mar that if they did win the battle, would that alone serve to recover their liberties and to hold their ground against other forces from England and elsewhere.[43]

Mar ignored Huntley and instead put the question of 'Fight or Not' to a vote, when 'all unanimouslie … with ane unexpressible alacritie, called out, Fight'. They then all went to their posts. The captain of Clanranald, on seeing a squadron of 40 British dragoons, claimed he would take them all prisoners, which Sinclair did not

---

39   Rae, *History,* p. 303.
40   <http://www.data.historic-scotland.gov.uk/data/docs/battlefields/sheriffmuir-full.pdf>.
41   Rannie, 'Hearne's Collections', p. 150.
42   Scott, *Memoirs,* pp. 211–212.
43   Scott, *Memoirs,* pp. 212–213; Keith, *Fragment,* p. 17.

think much of. Keith, on the other hand, wrote that this order was given by Mar to Marischal, to give to Sir Donald MacDonald's Regiment of Foot and his own cavalry, so as to cover the march of their army. This advance went ahead but did not lead to conflict as the outnumbered British dragoons retreated on seeing this advance. Yet according to Cameron, they did not do so, for on moving forward they saw Argyle's army on the march and so returned to let Mar know of this news.[44] Morale was clearly high, for as soon as the officers had got to their posts, and told their men of the council's decision, 'a huzza begun, with tossing up of hats and bonnets and through our whole armie, on the hearing we had resolved to fight; and no man, who had a drope of Scots blood in him, but must have been elevated to see the chearfullness of his countenance on that occasion'.[45]

Half an hour after the end of the council of war, Hamilton at last began to make dispositions for an attack. The infantry, being once in two lines, were now broken up into four columns, presumably to hasten their approach towards the enemy. The four squadrons of cavalry on the right, together with a column of Highland infantry that had been on the right of the front line, were to march and take possession of the high ground from which the British cavalry had been seen. Drummond 'who is always glade to be employed' put himself at the head of the cavalry alongside Marischal. Gordon took command of the infantry. They moved quickly forward. Seeing this happen, Sinclair remarked to Major Balfour that he expected them to be instantly repulsed by the British dragoons. He did not think there could be any enemy infantry there because the scouts had earlier told them that they were all in the enclosure at Kippendavie and that was a long way away.[46] The second infantry column, which had been to the left of the first line, marched by the men who had been to their immediate right, but followed them at some distance. The two other columns advanced and the cavalry squadrons on the right fell into the rear of the last column of infantry. Columns can move faster than line and clearly the intent was to reduce the distance between the two armies as quickly as possible in order to begin the action without further delay. The cavalry of Southesk, Lord Rupert Rollo (1679–1758) and Sinclair was now on the left. By the time the rear units were beginning to move, the foremost ones 'who had made so great haste to the top, were near the enemie, and beginning to form'. Confusingly, though, Drummond and Marischal's squadrons, which should have formed on the right of the infantry, formed on the left instead and so put themselves in the centre of the Jacobite infantry, 'it seems not knoweing their left hand from their right, thought themselves well there'.[47] According to Cameron, 'The horse were call'd all to the right of ye Army; none stayed on the left'. This was not quite true: though there were none on the front line of the left, there were some behind it, which was to prove of no consolation for that part of the Jacobite army.[48] This was noted by the enemy; Sir John Anstruther,

44 Ibid., pp. 213–214; Keith, Fragment, p. 17; <http://www.lochiel.net/archives/arch173.html>.
45 Scott, Memoirs, pp. 213–214.
46 Ibid., p. 214.
47 Ibid., pp. 214–215.
48 <http://www.lochiel.net/archives/arch173.html>.

one of Rothes' volunteer cavalrymen, subsequently wrote, 'the rebels had only Foot upon their left in the first line and some Horse in the second'.[49] The Jacobite army was unable to perform complex drill and so manoeuvres of any type were unlikely to be successful. Such changes in formation were properly ill-advised as they resulted in confusion and disordering the men. Clepham later informed Lord Pitsligo, of 'the first disposition of the battle and how it was broke in the march up the hill, which in all probability deprived us of a complete victory'.[50]

Keith later wrote that Marischal was so eager to attack, having found the enemy, that he wanted Mar to order all of the army forward, to their right. Keith added that the effect was unfortunate, for 'which he did even in too much haste … arrived in such confusion that it was impossible to form them according to the line of battle projected, every one posted himself where he found ground'. On the Jacobite left 'a bog hinder'd them from extending themselves and increased the confusion'. Yet nor was the British army formed into a line of battle: 'The Duke of Argyle was no less embarrassed' wrote Keith.[51] This was despite the confusion among the Jacobite army, for the line of battle as planned had now been torn up, with infantry on the left of the front line where the Camerons should have been. First line troops were in the second line and vice versa and this could not be undone. But morale was high. Cameron claimed, 'never men marched with greater chearfulness towards ane Eneemie'.[52]

The foremost infantry formed up very quickly. The other three columns were 'marching most irregularie at some distance'. They were following each other one by one and then tried to move as fast as possible to the front. These units were running and galloping. An aide of Kilsyth then rode up to Rollo, who was next to the infantry and at the head of the cavalry squadrons. He ordered the cavalry to move to the right of the whole army with all possible haste. Rollo obeyed at once and with speed, and passed the order back to Southesk, who followed Rollo's example. Southesk called back to Sinclair. The latter had no time to think, but followed and then heard a confused Highland cry. He halted his squadron for some minutes and spoke to Balfour, stating that they should obey their original orders, but they had been told otherwise by the aide and so should follow the other two leading squadrons. They then 'gallopt as hard as I could after them'. They were soon all posted together on the right. There was a little hill near their flanks and Sinclair thought it an admirable position for they could not be outflanked.[53]

The British then came into view, 'we saw the enemies' colours, and their heads and screued bayonets, all marching in haste towards our left alonge our front, within two hundred yards of us'. Keith wrote that they were 'marching without beat of drum' and were only twice the distance of extreme musket range from them. Despite the Union flag being visible, apparently many among the Jacobites took these to be Strathmore's

49   NRS, GD220/5/498/4.
50   Henrietta Tayler (ed.), 'The Jacobite Court at Rome in 1719', Scottish History Society, series 3, vol. 31 (1938), p. 87.
51   Keith, *Fragment*, p. 18.
52   <http://www.lochiel.net/archives/arch173.html>.
53   Scott, *Memoirs*, pp. 215–216.

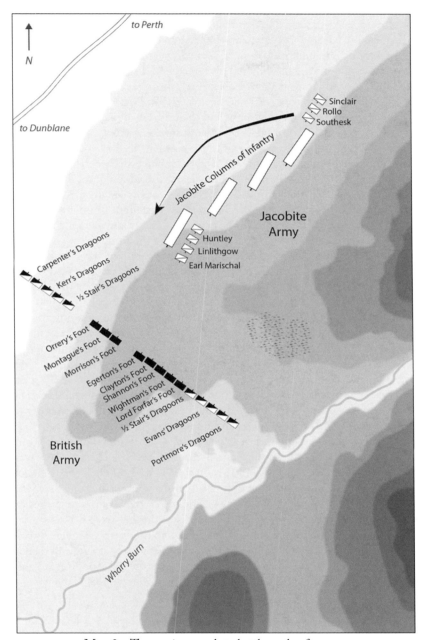

Map 2 – The armies march to battle, early afternoon

Jacobite troops, even though the men they saw were wearing red coats and some had grenadier hats on. Meanwhile, Sinclair told his men that they should shoot him down if he turned to run. He told his men to be silent, look straight ahead and keep together in formation 'without which they could be ruined and disgraced'.[54]

Although Argyle had his drummers beat their drums as soon as he returned to his troops at 11:00, his force's progress had been slow. This was despite the fact that the army had rested on their arms that night and their officers doing their utmost to bring them together. It was not until noon that the army was ready to march. Being in the open on a cold night probably played an important part in this slow pace. A letter to John Stirling noted that movement occurred 'after some debate'. There was nothing more that could be done then, and so 'the Duke was forced to pocket up the Matter'.[55]

Since Argyle had returned from his observation of his enemy, he posted himself on the right of his army, which was formed with six battalions of infantry in the front line, flanked each by three squadrons of cavalry. The intention was for the artillery to be placed in three batteries of two guns in the centre of the front line as was customary, to support the infantry. The second line was of two battalions of infantry and four squadrons of dragoons. Also on the right was the squadron of volunteer cavalry. Argyle marched the troops on the right wing quickly in order to confront the enemy's left wing, believing that was where the Jacobites would try and outflank him, and so it was important that as general he placed himself at the most dangerous point, though this would potentially mean losing control of the overall direction of the battle if he became too much involved in the fight around him. The latter was adjacent to a morass, but the cold weather had frozen it and so it was no longer impassable to troops.[56]

This was a risky manoeuvre, as it exposed the vulnerable left flanks of his marching battalions as they switched from line to columns and marched parallel to their enemy's front line. Argyle was gambling that they would move quickly enough in order to join with his foremost troops and then form up into line again to face the foe.

The battle began at about noon, according to Mar.[57] Cornet John Bennett of Portmore's Dragoons, in command of the advance guard, reported that the Jacobite army was now in full march, but although this was initially on the low ground, they changed tack and began to march up the hill to the right of the British army. It then became a race to reach the top of the hill on the east of the armies' positions. A letter reported that the advance was 'not in a form of Battle going pretty Quick up the hill were a little breathless', probably in columns though this exposed their flanks to the enemy. Argyle's forces were there first; Portmore's Dragoons being at their head, followed by Evans' and then by the volunteer cavalry, and crossed the half mile of the plain at the hill top.[58] It was a shock to see the Jacobites in readiness for them, though as Anstruther wrote, 'When we came up

---

54   *Ibid.*, pp. 216–217; Keith, *Fragment*, p. 17.
55   Rae, *History*, p. 304; NRS, GD220/5/787/A.
56   TNA, SP54/10, 48, 51; Rae, *History*, p. 308n.
57   *Ibid.*, p. 304; NRS, GD220/5/489/4; 220/5/787/A.
58   NRS, GD220/5/787a.

5. A mid-nineteenth century engraving of the battlefield. (Public domain)

the hill we were surprised to find the enemy formed and close', though his commander disagreed with the latter part of this statment.[59]

Once Argyle could see the Jacobite forces moving to his immediate front, he was delighted, as he later wrote, 'finding them not intirley formed, I judged it was necessary to lose no time and accordingly began the action on the right with the dragoons, charged both their horse and foot without fireing one shot, and tho' they received us with a very good countenance, and gave us their fire pretty close, we broke thro' them'. The infantry battalions 'behaved admirably with Captain [Robert] Walkinshaw [of Shannon's] distinguished himself and a great many more'. The Jacobites had disordered themselves by their climb to the hill and their battalions were quite apart from each other. There were casualties among the British troops, too, as the Jacobites fired. Hawley was shot through the shoulder and Forfar was shot in the knee.[60]

It is not certain how many troops were with Argyle and Wightman at this juncture. Without doubt there were the cavalry of Portmore and Evans, some of Stair's and the volunteers. There were also the battalions of Shannon's, Wightman's and Forfar's. Orrery's, Montague's and Morrison's were on the left. The question is where were Egerton's and Clayton's battalions of infantry and this is important in assessing the final phase of the battle. Reid states that they were on the left wing but Szechi states otherwise. Contemporaries were divided: Argyle, Colonel Thomas Harrison (1681–

59 Patten, *History*, p. 161; *The Spottiswoode Miscellany*, 2 (Edinburgh: Spottiswoode Society, 1845), p. 427; NRS, GD220/5/489/4.
60 TNA, SP54/10/48; WO116/3; Patten, *History*, p. 155; Rae, *History*, p. 304; NRS, GD220/5/787A.

6. A view of the battlefield from the Jacobite lines. (Author's photo)

c.1754), Argyle's adjutant, and Torphichen state five battalions were on the right, but Wightman and Rae claim not. These two battalions apparently suffered relatively few casualties – as did those on the right, but this could have meant that they fled rather than fought on the left wing. It would seem probable that Argyle had got it right since this makes the result of the fighting on his weak left wing more probable and adds weight to what was to happen, or rather what did not, at its anticlimax later in the day.

A Jacobite account of this part of the battle was as follows, given by Sinclair:

> In what manner our three colums run away, none of those amongst them could tell, nor where the flight begun, everie corps putting it off themselves, on each other, as is usuall. Most agreed that few of them had ever formed, and those who did, begun to fire at a great distance; that the three columns fell in with one another in that running up the hill, and when they came in sight of the Duke of Argyle's right wing, which was alreadie formed, they were in disorder; and the last confusion, when his dragoons made a mine to attack them through the morass, which happned to be bewixt them; and happie for our foot had they knoun to make the right use of such ane advantage and situation; but instead of that, and falling into forme, they fell into greater confusion, calling for horse against the dragoons, and Generall Hamilton being the onlie officer amongst them, it was impossible for him alone to bring them into order; so they turned their backs that minute we gave the huzza to advance, the Duke of Argyle pursueing them'.[61]

---

61   Scott, *Memoirs*, p. 225.

A later biographer of Argyle wrote that the Jacobites on the left wing had neither 'courage nor inclination to stand'.[62] In all the fighting on this flank lasted half an hour, according to an anonymous letter written to the Provost.[63] Some of the Jacobite infantry here initially put up a good fight, as Anstruther reported, 'the enemy kept up their fire longer than could have been expected, the fire was very hot upon Evans' regiment for a quarter of an hour they had a deep stripe before them which they could not well pass which made them run about in some disorder'.[64] They were helped in this by having a bog to their front.[65]

Jacobite casualties may have been higher than they appeared. Sinclair saw few corpses on that ground, and he put this down to the fact that 'his [Argyle] being obliged to goe about the morass, which gave our people a great advantage in the flight doun hill, and that the frost was strong enough to bear them on foot, when the dragoons' horses sunk deep in the moor's, our's in the mean time getting over the river of Allen'.[66] There was an alternate suggestion. Lieutenant Campbell believed the body count could have been higher still, 'But had we shown as little mercy as they did they had lost thousands instead of hundreds'.[67]

One Jacobite did fight valiantly there. He was Lord Strathmore, who led a battalion of Atholl infantry. According to Sinclair, 'When he found all turning their backs, he seized the colours, and persuaded fourteen, or some such number, to stand by him for some time, which dreu upon him the enemies' fire, by which he was wounded in the bellie, and, goeing off, was takne'. Hearne later reported he received 20 wounds and 'It was done in a cowardly way'.[68] It was also alleged that an unnamed MacDonald woman died fighting, having refused quarter and having killed or wounded several of her enemies.[69]

A number of infantry battalions under Wightman followed their commander. Wightman later wrote, 'The Moment we got to the Top of the Hill, not above half of our Men were come up, or could form; the Enemy, that were within Pistol–Shot, began the attack with all their Left upon our Right … The Enemy were Highlanders, and, as is their custom, gave us a Fire; and a great many came up to our Noses Sword in Hand; but the Horse on our Right, with the constant Fire of the Plattoons of Foot, soon put the Left of their Army to Rout'.[70] The two-gun battery had been pulled up the hill with the right wing, but they had scarce time to unyoke the horses and turn the guns on the Jacobites, before both sides were intertwined in melee and so cannon fire was out of the question.[71]

62 Campbell, *The Life*, p. 191.
63 TNA, SP54/10/47.
64 NRS, GD220/5/489/4.
65 *Ibid.*, 787/a.
66 Scott, *Memoirs*, p. 225.
67 NRS, RH15/14/149.
68 Scott, *Memoirs*, p. 227.
69 *St. James Evening Post*, 77, 24–26 Nov. 1715.
70 Patten, *History*, p. 159.
71 Rae, *History*, p. 308.

An anonymous chronicler gave the following account of the behaviour of various British cavalry units:

> The nobility and gentry of the horse volunteers acted worthy of themselves, and without vanity bore their own share in the victory, and even bore their share of the rebels fire in the attack upon that of Forfar and Wightman's regiments; and tho Evans' dragoons were in some little disorder, it was not throw occasion of the enemy, but through the deepness of the marsh ground, which was near to have bogged their horses.

Evans' Dragoons were able to wheel round and found better ground and then 'performed as could be desired'.[72] Initially this unit had reeled back from the weight of a Jacobite volley (and suffered the highest casualties suffered by any of Argyle's cavalry regiments that day – nearly a third) and had disordered the volunteer cavalry to their rear, but both soon rallied and entered the fray.[73] One reason for Evans' men rallying was because 'Rothes' volunteers call out for Shame to them … [and] took a terrible vengeance'.[74] Anstruther later gave a graphic account of this part of the battle:

> At the time that Evans' Regiment came amongst us my horse got on and his hind part stuck in the marshy ground where we were formed which made him fall back upon me and I concluded that he had been killed dead but he immediately got off me, I kept the reins and got him mounted again with great difficulty for the balls were flying so thick that the horse did not stand long in one posture and I had the good fortune to escape with some bruises occasion'd chiefly by the fall and was so well as to continue on horseback all the pursuit.[75]

Portmore's Dragoons were in the thick of the fighting. Anstruther reported, 'The Greys who are never backward upon these occasions, were the first that cut them to pieces and wherever we got amongst them they fled'.[76] Stair's Dragoons also did well, 'no men under Heaven could doe Better and had a full share in Braking through the enemy's line on their left, and who particularly employed in pursuing the enemy into the River'.[77] Those Jacobite cavalry near their left wing did not take part in the fighting but as Anstruther wrote 'they did not stay till we came up with them and we only saw them flying'.[78] Apparently they were behind the infantry, ironically enough, to prevent the foot soldiers from retreating.[79]

The Jacobites were apparently driven back three miles northwards over the River Allan. Wightman gave it as a mile and a half. Argyle wrote that he 'could not but

72 *HMC 14th Report*, Appendix, III, p. 168.
73 *Ibid.*
74 NRS, GD220/5/787a.
75 *Ibid.*, GD220/5/489/4.
76 *Ibid.*
77 *Ibid.*
78 *Ibid.*
79 *Ibid.*, GD220/5/787A.

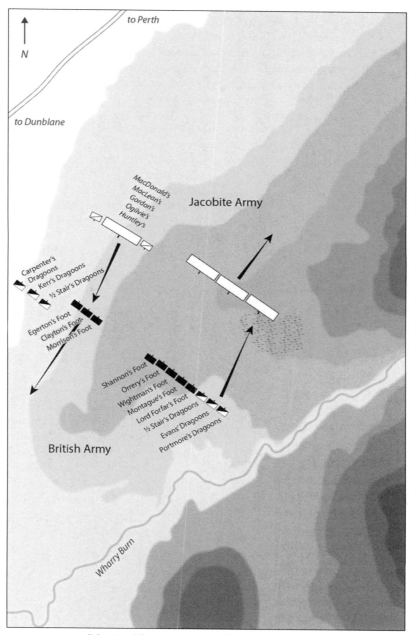

to Perth

N

to Dunblane

MacDonald's
MacLean's
Gordon's
Ogilvie's
Huntley's

Jacobite Army

Carpenter's
Dragoons
Kerr's Dragoons
½ Stair's Dragoons

Egerton's Foot
Clayton's Foot
Morrison's Foot

Shannon's Foot
Orrery's Foot
Wightman's Foot
Montague's Foot
Lord Forfar's Foot
½ Stair's Dragoons
Evans' Dragoons
Portmore's Dragoons

British Army

Wharry Burn

Map 3 – The right wings of both armies attack
the left wing of the other, afternoon

judge it an entire Rout and thought of nothing but pursuing them as long as we had day light'. This action led to officers being taken prisoner, as well as the capture of a standard and 10 colours. The pursuit had taken a long time (possibly three hours) because the Jacobites outnumbered their attackers. The former being allegedly 5,000 strong, repeatedly made attempts to reform their ranks; after all they outnumbered their pursuers, so as Harrison wrote, 'this 'obliged us as often to attack and break them.'[80] According to one report, 80 bodies of Jacobites were later fished up from the Allan.[81] The rout was bloody as is usually the case when exposed infantry are fleeing from the faster moving cavalry: one eyewitness noting that evening that 'For some tyme our dragoons gave no quarter'. Such was the bloody duty of the cavalry. Similar action had taken place after the royalist defeat at Naesby in 1645 and was to occur when another Jacobite army was in flight at Culloden in 1746.[82] At Oudenarde, French infantry when faced with allied cavalry 'met with the usual fate of such, that is, they were cut to pieces'.[83] The eventual rout was utter, Anstruther writing 'they fled in the utmost disorder and there were so very many of them that at first I thought their whole army had been routed and we pursued a good deal too far without knowing what had become of our left'.[84]

Some of the dragoons from Evans' regiment 'made them give little quarter'; perhaps in revenge for being so roughly handled earlier.[85] However, Argyle attempted to minimise enemy casualties, as a contemporary letter noted, comparing his magnanimity to that not shown by the Jacobites elsewhere, apparently he 'treated the enemy in quite a different manner, offering quarter to several gentlemen undesired, and giving it to all who asked; and particularly his Grace parried the strokes of a broad sword aimed by a dragoon at a gentleman who was wounded and begged quarter'.[86]

One Jacobite writer put the defeat of the left wing of the army down to treachery. An officer from Argyle's army, one Drummond, had allegedly gone to Perth a few days before, posing as a deserter. He was made an aide to the Jacobite Lord Drummond. During the battle, Mar sent him with an order to Hamilton, with instructions to attack the enemy, but Drummond (not Lord Drummond) gave him the opposite orders and told Hamilton that since Mar had been beaten on the right of the army, he should 'retire with all haste with as good Order as possible'. Hamilton did as he was told and halted at the very moment that Argyle's force was attacking, resulting in defeat. Drummond then left the Jacobites. The writer of this was unsure of its veracity and added, 'But this I do not affirm for a Truth'.[87] There is certainly no corroborating evidence for this.

80 TNA, SP54/10/48; Patten, *History*, p. 153.
81 *St. James Evening Post*, 77, 24–26 Nov. 1715.
82 TNA, SP54/10/47.
83 Parker, *Memoirs*, p. 147.
84 NRS, GD220/5/489/4.
85 *Ibid.*, 787A.
86 *Spottiswoode Miscellany*, p. 430.
87 Patten, *History*, p. 170.

Another allegation was that Seaforth's men had suffered unduly because of 'the sudden flight of the low county foot posted on the left, whereby their flank was exposed to the Grey Horse … first battalion cut to pieces … by their stout resistance … they prevented the said Duke's right wing from being flanked and routed'.[88]

Lochiel gave a similar account; his clan, impatient to advance and attack the enemy when they came into view, was behind a Lowland battalion, the latter of whom fired a volley, which was returned. Then the British troops:

> Broke in all at once upon my Regiment and carried them off before the half of them were formed, or of Mckinins men who were drawing up wt them, as well as some of the McPhersons. A little before this Regiment broke in upon mine there was a party of the black dragoons came pretty near us, at whom those who were on my right, and the few of my men who were drawen up in the right of my Regiment, fyred and kill'd severalls, and beat them back. I being advanced some few paces before the right of my Regiment, in order to get sight of the Enemy, me being in a hollow ground, which how soon I had got I look'd about to order my men to advance, but to my great surprise saw them caryed away in this manner, and all those who were nixt to me and drawen up on my right and left gone off. All this time we saw no generall officer, neither received any orders; only by the confusion we observed our right had been broke. So finding myself in this situation, with three or four gentlemen of my friends who chanc'd to be nixt me, made off, and found none of my own men until I cross'd the River of Allan where I found some of them with Apin and some of his men.[89]

The Jacobites lost some of their flags. One account has it that the men of Portmore's Dragoons took the Jacobites' royal standard.[90] Another account has it that Colonel Oliver Brook, of Wightman's and a veteran of Alamanza, took this flag as well as a prisoner.[91] The fighting had lasted eight minutes, far less time than it probably took to read this, but the retreat/rout lasted for a lengthier timespan.[92]

Argyle had shown himself at his best and his worst in this part of the battle. Harrison later wrote, 'above all, the great Example of his Grace, the Duke of Argyle, whose Presence not only gave Spirit to the Action, but gained great Success as often as he led on'.[93] Some senior officers did lead by example, as Prince Eugene had at Oudenarde and on other occasions, leading the Dutch troops with his sword in hand; as had Charles XII. Yet the older Marlborough had never done so and had not lost any respect for avoiding personal danger.[94] There was, thus, a different range of command styles; personal bravery was popular in the contemporary media.

---

88   *HMC Stuart Papers*, V, p. 197.
89   <http://www.lochiel.net/archives/arch173.html>.
90   Donald, 'Glasgow', p. 130
91   *Flying Post*, 3730, 29 Nov.–1 Dec. 1715.
92   NRS, RH15/14/149.
93   Patten, *History*, p. 154.
94   John Millner, *A Compendious Journal of all the Marches, Famous Battles, Sieges…* (London, 1733), p. 275.

Another commentator observed, 'His Grace was everywhere in person, made as good a disposition as possible in his circumstances, and charged at the head of several regiments by turns; for nothing but extraordinary courage would have broke the rebels'.[95] This could be dangerous, for Viscount Dundee had been killed in action at Killiecrankie, thus turning what could have been a decisive Jacobite victory into a strategically inconclusive one. Furthermore, by concentrating on this one sector he neglected the other, as was also noted by Parker that Argyle had not been 'considering how matters went with the rest of the Army'.[96] Furthermore, 'The Duke who was on the right and saw not what passed upon the left wing thowght that he had got ane intire victory'.[97] As we shall see, this latter was emphatically not the case. He was not the only one among his command to share this belief, Anstruther writing 'I can give no account of what passed to the left of Shannon's.'[98] Yet he was the commander-in-chief not a brigadier with relatively localised responsibility. However, even if Argyle had been better able to see what was happening, it is not certain whether he could have directed his forces better.

Argyle's attack on his enemy's flank was a common enough tactic in the eighteenth century, having being practised by Marlborough and later Frederick the Great, the latter notably at Rossbach and Leutheun in 1757. At Hohenfriedberg in 1745 the Prussian cavalry had charged the unprotected Austrian flank with devastatingly decisive results. However, having a strong and offensive right wing often meant weakening the army elsewhere.[99] As was proved here.

Elsewhere on the battlefield, the situation was far different. As Wightman was moving his battalions forward against the collapsing Jacobite left, he felt the need to investigate. He sent his aide to enquire,1 and found what had happened there.[100] On the left of the British line, the battalions (Montague's, Morrison's and Orrery's; plus possibly Egerton's and Clayton's) and regiments (Kerr's, Carpenter's and a squadron of Stair's) were not formed up for battle, but were marching to follow the lead of those on their right under Argyle. Parker wrote that this manoeuvre was one 'which should have been done before the Enemy advanced so near him'.[101] Argyle, however, had been taken up with what was happening immediately around him.

The troops on Argyle's left had arrived last onto the field and needed to change their formation from column to line and to wheel to face the enemy. Ahead of them, in a hollow way, were concealed part of the Jacobite right wing, which also outflanked them. Robert Henderson wrote, three days later, that the battalions were 'in a marching poster, not expecting the Highland men so near 'em'.[102]

95   *Flying Post*, 3726, 19–22 Nov. 1716.
96   Parker, *Memoirs*, p. 264.
97   Steuart, *News Letters*, p. 69.
98   NRS, GD220/5/489/4.
99   Dennis Showalter, *Frederick the Great: A Military History* (London: Frontline Books, 2012), pp. 80, 83.
100 TNA, SP54/10/48.
101 Parker, *Memoirs*, p. 264.
102 *Report on the Laing MSS preserved in the University of Edinburgh* (London: HMSO, 1914–1925), p. 180.

At the head of the clans, Mar, seeing the enemy beginning to form their line on their left, decided to attack them, ordering Clepham and Major Ereskine to pass on his wishes. On their return, he pulled off his hat, waved it with a huzza and the men moved forward: the MacDonalds, the MacLeans, the Gordons, the Ogilvies and Huntley's battalions (almost 3,000 men).[103] However Sinclair and Keith reported it rather differently. Sinclair claimed that an elderly gentleman, whom he was told was Captain Livingstone once of Dumbarton's regiment, went up to Gordon 'calling to him, with great oaths, To attack the eneimie before they were formed', and in the exposed flank. Gordon explained that he could not act without orders from Mar. Mar could not be seen or found, so Gordon agreed to attack as Livingstone was 'representing to him that he'd loose his time' if he did not immediately attack.[104]

There was some initial exchange of musketry between each side here. One of the first casualties was Allan Clanranald, who was killed. According to Argyle's biographer, 'which had like to have struck a Damp upon the Rebels as they had a Respect for that gentleman that fell little short of adoration. But Glengarry, who succeeded him, starting from the lines, waved his Bonnet and cried three or four times, Revenge, which so animated the men, that they followed him like furies'.[105]

Sinclair gave a graphic description of what happened next:

The order to attack being given, the two thousand Highlandmen [nearer 3,000], who were then draun up in a very good order, ran towards the ennemie in a disorderlie manner, always fireing some dropeing shots, which drew upon them a general salvo from the eneimie, which begun at their left, opposite us, and turn to their right. No sooner that begun, the Highlandmen threw themselves flat on their bellies; and when it slackened, they started to their feet. Most threw away their fuzies, and, drawing their suords, pierced them everie where with ane incredible vigour and rapidities, in four minutes' time from their receaving the order to attack. Not onlie all in our view and before us turned their backs, but the five squadrons of dragoons on their left, commanded by Generall Witham, went to the right about, and never lookt back till they had got near Dunblain, almost tuo miles from us; while the Highlandmen pursued the infantrie, who run as hard as their feet could carrie them, a great manie of whome threw away their armes to enable them to run the faster, and were sabred by the Highlandmen, who spared few who fell in their hands'.[106]

Keith recorded it more concisely, 'he [Gordon] order'd the troops immediately to charge, which they did with so much vigour that in less than ten minutes they entirely defeated six regiments of Foot and five squadrons of dragoons'.[107] He was exaggerating; Argyle had eight battalions and either five or three were on his left wing.

103 Patten, *History*, pp. 166–167.
104 Scott, *Memoirs*, p. 217; Keith, *Fragment*, p. 18.
105 Campbell, *The Life*, p. 190.
106 Scott, *Memoirs*, pp. 217–218.
107 Keith, *Fragment*, p. 18.

One reason why the Jacobites were so successful is that once they reached their opponents' lines, they 'push'd by the bayonets with their targets, and with their broadswords, spread nothing but Death and Terror'. Although their outnumbered enemies 'behaved gallantly, and made all the Resistance they could make; but being unacquainted with this Savage way of Fighting, against which all the Rules of War made no provision, they were forced to give way'.[108] This was very true: regular troops expected to exchange musketry volleys, possibly aided by adjoining artillery, until one side broke, rather than to engage in melee or even the threat of it. Nor even when in melee, did they expect to fight men with swords, dirks shields and occasionally even Lochaber axes. In fact melee was rare. As a contemporary chronicler noted, 'It is impossible to express the Horror which some of the Gentlemen of the English Regiments say their men were possess'd with at that unusual and savage way of Fighting'.[109]

When Morrison's and Orrery's battalions were attacked, they gave way to superiority of numbers allied to the force of a charge when insufficiently checked by casualties caused by defensive musketry, but only after an intense and bloody struggle. According to an anonymous eye witness, the 'Highland rebels, consisting of the clans who were not only their best, but of triple the number to our left, went quite through them and made a considerable slaughter of our men'.[110]

If the Jacobites had about 3,000 men at this part of the battle they can only have been charging at best three battalions, otherwise the odds would have been far less in their numerical favour. It was here that most of Argyle's casualties occurred: a total, allegedly, of 442 in all (117 from Montague's Foot, 144 from Morrison's and 181 from Orrery's). A few casualties were the result of Jacobite firepower. Lieutenant Colonel Hamars of Morrison's was killed in the first fire. Dennis McMullin, a 28-year-old of Morrison's, a former shoemaker from Coleraine, was shot in his left leg.[111] Most of the injuries, though, came from cutting and stabbing weapons, either in melee or in the running away. George Studders and Robert Thompson, both of Orrery's, suffered numerous cuts to the head.[112]

Lack of artillery support also helped doom the left of the army; grape shot could have helped reduce the impact of the chargers. Yet the four of Argyle's six guns were not fast enough to deploy in the centre but followed up the steep slopes to join the left wing of the army. Just as they were about to unlimber to deploy, they were forced to flee as Carpenter's and Kerr's Dragoons left the field. Apparently they could not be used, 'without doing damage to their own men, as well as the Rebels: so that the officer that commanded, got them very narrowly off, without the Opportunity of firing one shot'.[113]

Finally, there was no support from the two regiments of dragoons to the left. They were interspaced by fleeing infantry men, which 'helped the eneimie to put them in confusion'. Whetham's cavalry then allegedly galloped off the field with news of their

---

108 *Annals of the Reign of George I*, p. 151.
109 Campbell, *The Life*, pp. 190–191.
110 *HMC 14th Report*, Appendix, III, p. 168.
111 TNA, WO116/1–3.
112 Campbell, *The Life*, p. 191.
113 Steuart, *News Letters*, p. 71.

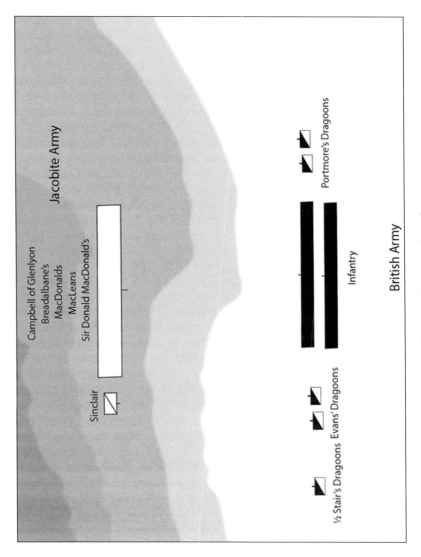

Map 4 – Final confrontation, late afternoon

army's defeat.[114] However, another contemporary stated that Torphichen, lieutenant colonel of Kerr's Dragoons, rallied the troops on the left, eventually, and they were able to retire in good order, being covered by the cavalry.[115] The anonymous narrator agrees with this account, admitting that the two dragoon regiments gave way, but later were able to support the fleeing infantry and 'stopt the clans from further slaughter'. The artillery being never unlimbered and was thus saved, but some colours and standards were lost by the battalions on the left wing.[116]

Torphichen gave his own account of events. His regiment of dragoons had initially been in the second line of the army and on Argyle marching the army to the right, his men were at the rear, despite galloping uphill behind their comrades. Kerr's Dragoons moved between a pass through which they had to travel in order to join the others of the left wing. Yet they did not advance further for the three battalions and the dragoons were running away from the Jacobites. Torphichen had his men make loud cheers, and 'threatened them if they did not stand to treat them as enemies which immediately had the desired effect for both dragoons and Foot rallied under my colour and in the mean time cut down what Highlanders had by their eagerness made too great an advance'.

Whetham, in command of the left wing, then let Torphichen, because of his gallant behaviour, take charge of the rearguard made up of his regiment, and then they took the guns with them back to Stirling, retreating in good order, facing the enemy and thus deterring another attack.[117]

Yet, according to the account given by Argyle, one of the British dragoon regiments on the left charged and took a Jacobite standard, and the reason for their retreat was because they had heard that the right wing of the army had been surrounded and none had escaped, so they thought the best course was to march to Stirling and defend it as long as possible. Whether this was an excuse is another matter.[118]

There was some discussion as to what to do, based on inadequate information as to what was occurring elsewhere on the battlefield, and only seeing their immediate situation. Whetham thought it best to fall back to Stirling in order to secure the place with the fairly unscathed dragoons and what was left of the infantry. Colonel Kerr argued that they should stay on the field of battle until they heard from Argyle. His superior officer, Whetman, 'giving all over for lost', had the troops fall back on Stirling bridge, reaching it at 3:00 p.m.[119] The retreat may have disintegrated into a rout as the men moved further away from the scene of devastation.

According to Blackader, in command of the Glasgow Militia at Stirling, a rout was certainly unfolding when these units neared him:

---

114 *HMC 14th Report*, Appendix, III, p. 168.
115 TNA, SP54/11/95.
116 *Ibid.*, 10/48.
117 NRS, GD220/5/787/A.
118 Andrew Crichton (ed.), *Life and Diary of Lieutenant Colonel John Blackader* (Edinburgh: H. S. Baynes, 1825), pp. 173–4.
119 NRS, GD220/5/787/A.

I saw one of the most melancholy sights ever I beheld in my life – our army flying before their enemies! O Lord, what shall we say when Israel turn their backs and fly before the enemy? But we have sinned. I went down to the bridge and in a heavy heart. Runners away coming fast in, and every one giving a worse account than another, that all was lost and gone. Indeed, seeing is believing, all the fields were covered with our flying troops, horse and foot, all had the appearance of a routed army. O what a distressing view indeed, expecting to see the rebels army at their heels.

Blackader had his militia posted in entrenchments by the bridge to defend it against a Jacobite onslaught, but had no illusions his own force would be successful.[120]

A letter to Sir John Stirling makes a similar point: 'You may easily imagine what consternation we were in to see men and horse running for three hours' time, three miles in length, abundance having thrown away their arms and some their coats, especially all the three regiments that came from Ireland (so far as I can remember)'.[121]

As time went on, those in Stirling realised that not all was lost. An hour after the routers arrived, a gentleman who had been riding hard from Sheriffmuir told them that Argyle retained the field and had obliged the Jacobites to retire. Argyle wanted all his troops to march towards him in order to achieve a complete victory. Captain McBride and another officer on guard at the bridge gave three huzzas and their men echoed the cheer. Yet intelligence was conflicting and another report stated that Argyle was dead and all but six of Portmore's Dragoons had been taken. Then another rider, arriving at 4:30 p.m. gave news that Argyle needed all his men and it was only at this second urging that Whetham gathered what troops he could and returned to the moorland.[122]

Meanwhile, on the battlefield, at least three British officers were injured after trying to surrender. Brigadier Forfar, who, at the onset had dismounted from his horse in order to encourage his men to fight, was soon a casualty himself, being shot in the knee and presumably falling to the ground, where he remained for the remainder of the struggle. He addressed a Jacobite soldier, 'Sir, I am your prisoner, pray take care of me as such and as a reward I give yow this watch'. His enemy took it and then slapped Forfar on the head. Forfar gave his assailant a purse of gold and was assaulted again. He received further injuries 'unmercifully, after he had gotten quarters, [he] received 17 wounds in his head and body (including his right thumb being cut off, his left hand injured, his left arm hurt and several cuts to the head)', which made Henderson reflect on the 'merciless and savage nature of the Highlanders' (Henderson was a Lowland Scot). Richard Henderson referred likewise to his assailants as 'the most savage natives of the Highlands'. Most of Forfar's wounds were suffered after he had surrendered, some inflicted allegedly by 'that ingrained rebel, the Viscount of Kilsyth'. Eventually the Baillie of Dingwell found him and treated him well. Argyle later wrote that Forfar 'Behaved himself as well as man could do' and had led from the front. Yet Forfar was not alone in his initial maltreatment after having surrendered: two officers from

---

120 *Ibid.*
121 *HMC 14th Report*, Appendix, III, p. 169; *HMC Laing*, p. 180; TNA, SP54/11/115B.
122 TNA, SP54/11/97.

Orrery's were likewise harmed. Captain Walter Cheisly, 'after he was taken prisoner was ript up by the rebells'. Likewise, Captain Robert Urquhart was wounded in the belly after having been made prisoner, 'sore as his puddings hang out'.[123]

Although many of his battalion were killed or wounded, Colonel Herbert Lawrence of Montague's 'miraculously escaped and though he was offered Quarter Refus'd it, seeing the cruelty that was us'd to his Men' but eventually he was seized and obliged to surrender.[124] Captain William Lloyd, officially of Wightman's, who took over command of Morrison's once Hamars was dead (killed in the first volley) won his commander's praise, 'he well deserved the majorship'.[125] He also saved one of the battalion's colours.[126]

Of the cavalry, the officers behaved variously: Those officers of Carpenters' Dragoons, according to Argyle, 'did not do their duty'. Yet Lieutenant Colonel John Nicholson of Clayton's 'behaved himself very handsomely, but the regiment extreamly ill'; 'What happened was Mr Whetman's misfortune and not his fault'.[127] Not all officers acted well, however, with Argyle declaring Colonel Egerton to be 'a poor weak man' and that two of the officers of Carpenter's Dragoons had not done their duty.[128]

According to Mar the pursuit of the left wing of the British army lasted as far south as a little hill on the south of Dunblane. Another account has it lasting the distance of a half mile.[129] In either case, it had not lasted long, suggesting great discipline or that the retreat had been effectively covered by Torphichen's dragoons; the latter seemingly most likely.

It seems that the Jacobite right wing cavalry were eager, now that the enemy was broken, to attack them, but Sinclair was against such action, believing that 'there was some more to doe' and so the cavalry needed to be kept together and not loosed against fleeing enemies. One contemporary chronicler suggested that this was a major error, as resolute cavalry action could have cut off all of Argyle's left wing. At this point Major Arthur told him that some of the Jacobite left and centre were in full retreat and Sinclair told him to keep that unfortunate news to himself. Although Sinclair tried to maintain all the cavalry near him together, he was not entirely successful as some men had no regard for their officers and 'folloued in the pursuit, in imitation of Drummond and Marichall's four squadrons'.[130]

The Jacobite cavalry had an undistinguished record on that day. Four squadrons wheeled between the infantry of both armies, 'and in wheeling, came with their flank close to the enemies' foot, who gave them a fire in the flank that brought doun eighteen

123 *Ibid.*, 115b; Edinburgh University Library Special Collections, Laing MSS, III, 375/51.
124 TNA, SP54/11/97.
125 Rae, *History*, p. 308n.
126 Scott, *Memoirs*, pp. 218–219.
127 TNA, SP54/11/115b.
128 *Ibid.*, WO116/1–3; *Annals*, p. 151.
129 Patten, *History*, pp. 161, 167.
130 Scott, *Memoirs*, p. 226.

of Huntlie's two squadrons … and all this to doe nothing'. Huntley's and Marischall's squadrons left the field.[131]

There is a suggestion that Jacobite sympathisers in and around Stirling, on hearing of the victory of the Jacobite right wing, made some effort to stir. That they did not was apparently due to Buchan's presence there, followed by later news of Argyle's success.[132]

As has been said, not all Jacobite troops were present with Mar at Sheriffmuir, but Rob Roy MacGregor, variously described by contemporaries as 'that notorious Robber' and 'a noted Gentleman in former Times for Bravery, Resolution and Courage', terms which are by no means incompatible, was not far away from the battlefield. John Cameron of Lochiel, after rallying his men, saw Rob Roy marching towards him from the town of Doune, a few miles west of Dunblane, with about 250 MacGregors and MacPhersons. Lochiel approached him and 'intreated, he being come fresh wt these men, that we would joyn and cross the River to attack Argyle, which he absolutely refused'. When one of Rob Roy's own men made a similar suggestion, he answered, 'If, they could not do it without me, they should not do it with me'.[133]

Mar then arrived and Sinclair 'wisht him joy of the victorie'. As with Argyle and Whitman, he had no idea of what was happening away from his immediate view. Apparently Mar then rode away to reflect, probably sadly, on what had happened on the bloody field without the pretence of giving orders. Sinclair complained about Mar's incompetence to another officer. He then saw a British squadron on top of a small hill, only 300 yards away. They had taken some of Marischal's squadron prisoner, then surrounded them and 'shot them in our sight', unable or unwilling either to take prisoners or to release them. Sinclair refers to this as 'this small execution' but does not seem to go into the detail of labelling it what would now be termed a 'war crime'. Sinclair's men threatened to advance against the dragoons before they could form up against them, and then 'we made towards them at a trot', but their enemy fled, leaving behind 'some of our's dead or mortallie wounded'. This episode was misreported to Mar as dragoons fighting among themselves.[134]

Sinclair then saw the dragoon squadrons that had been on Argyle's left forming up and returning to the battlefield, but this is probably an error, as Torphichen reported his cavalry only covering the retreat of the left and not returning. There was no sign of either the British infantry from the left wing or of the Highlanders and Jacobite cavalry who had pursued them. It was a potentially dangerous time for Sinclair's cavalry, with enemy in both directions of them, making it imperative that they form up. Later Sinclair sent a message to Mar to inform him that the cavalry and the Highland pursuers had returned to the scene of strife. There then followed a stand-off between Sinclair's cavalry and Portmore's Dragoons.[135]

131 TNA, WO116/1–3.
132 *Flying Post*, 3737, 15–17 Dec. 1715.
133 <http://www.lochiel.net/arch173.html>; Patten, *History*, pp. 170–1.
134 Scott, *Memoirs*, pp. 219–220.
135 *Ibid.*, p. 220.

The cavalry which had been a potential threat to Sinclair's squadrons, seeing that the Jacobites they faced had been reinforced by cavalry and infantry, knew they were now outnumbered. Sinclair ordered his enlarged force to advance and so the dragoons wheeled off and 'made great haste' to return to where Argyle was gathering his men. Apparently some Jacobites believed that Argyle's forces in the distance were their allies, perhaps the forces of Lord George Murray or Invernytie, who had been ordered from Burntisland with their 500 men, and told to join the MacGregors and MacPhersons en route. This was wishful thinking as these troops never took part in the battle.[136]

Afterwards, Mar recovered himself and 'got most of our Horse, and a pretty good Number of our Foot' and reordered them. This was a gradual process, as Sinclair related, 'our foot begun to assemble and draw nere, at least some hundred, I believe three or four; and some few of the horse'. He was ignorant as to what had occurred elsewhere on the battlefield, 'We knew not then what became of our Left'. However, on returning northwards, they saw 'a Body of the Enemy on the North of us consisting mostly of the Grey Dragoons, and some of the Black', whilst some British infantry battalions were further north. He also thought he could see a body of Jacobite infantry to the east. Mar desired to confront the remaining British troops so as to complete his victory.[137] One contemporary chronicler thought that Gordon were then in tactical command of 5,000 men, but probably less (Hamilton had been on the left wing) and could have attacked the British immediately, rather than halting to form up, with the result that they could have destroyed the enemy, though an unformed mass of men might not have been particularly militarily effective. They did not do so.[138]

The sight that lay before the combatants was grim. Wellington wrote, after Waterloo, that the only thing worse than a battle won was a battle lost. As was noted for Sheriffmuir, 'It was an melancholy day to us all that Saboth afternoon, for we saw all the fields covered with those shattered troupes that were broken upon the left'.[139] Haddington noted 'It was ugly work and I don't like it'.[140] The battle was not yet over.

136 *Ibid.*, pp. 221–222.
137 Patten, *History*, pp. 161, 167; Scott, *Memoirs*, p. 221.
138 *Annals*, p. 152.
139 Steuart, *News Letters*, p. 69.
140 Inglis, *Battle*, p. 56.

10

The Battle of Sheriffmuir: Concluding Phase

Argyle had clearly been taken up solely with what lay before him. During the earlier part of the battle, a large gap had opened up between the right and left wings of his army. Not knowing this, he had advanced with the dragoons rapidly and Wightman, with his slower moving infantry, took some time to find him. At some point Wightman was able to converse with him. Although no better informed, his subordinate was at least aware that it was worth considering what was happening on the rest of the battlefield and made this point to his leader. They then halted the pursuit and saw that what had been the right wing of the Jacobite army was now to their rear. Wightman's battalions were no longer in pursuit of the fleeing Jacobite left, but 'not knowing but my Rear might soon be attack'd by the Enemy', he had 'kept what Foot I had in perfect Order'. The Jacobites were now forming up on the top of the hill. No news could be learnt of what had happened to the units on the left of the British army. At this point Argyle had five battalions of infantry and five squadrons of dragoons. He marched them towards the Jacobites, extending his left flank towards Dunblane to allow the units that were now on his right to rejoin him and post themselves there. Both sides were half a mile apart.[1]

The remaining Jacobites on the battlefield were now almost all returned from their limited pursuit of the British left wing. They were formed up 'in tolerable order', with half of the cavalry on each flank of the infantry. The British troops marched towards them and then halted. The Jacobites did likewise and stood looking at one another at about four hundred yards distance, for half an hour.[2]

It is not certain exactly how strong each force now was. Argyle wrote that the Jacobites had 4,000 men and Wightman believed they had a three to one numerical superiority. Sinclair believed there were 2,000 Jacobite infantry and the number of cavalry on both sides was equal (perhaps about 400). Those infantry who charged (Huntley's, the MacLeans, the MacDonalds and Sir Donald MacDonald's men) had been nearly 3,000 strong, but allowing for casualties and men who had left the battlefield, they may have been rather less. A Jacobite alleged Argyle's force were only made up of four squadrons

---

1   Patten, *History*, pp. 159–160.
2   Scott, *Memoirs*, p. 222.

of dragoons and a 'small Battalion of Foot', which is certainly a considerable under-estimate. Sinclair claims there were about 800 British infantry. Another contemporary source states that the British 'were scarce a thousand', with the infantry in the centre, in two lines, but it 'did not bring him to ane equall front with us' and a cannon placed to each side. With Argyle at this point were about 1,550 infantry. Flanking them were the dragoons: Portmore's on the right and Evans' and Stair's on the left (perhaps just over 2,000). It would seem that the Jacobites outnumbered Argyle by a fairly small margin; far less than they had done at the onset of the battle. The Jacobites remained on their hill, 'very prudentially' according to Argyle. This was because he believed that it meant that they could easily withdraw unmolested or if Argyle chose to attack them, it would be the Jacobites who had the advantage of the terrain.[3]

Yet, though Wightman considered that the Jacobites were 'ranged at the Top of a Hill on very advantageous Ground', he thought that his forces were in a better position. He wrote, 'We posted ourselves at the Bottom of the Hill, having the advantage of Ground, where their Horse could not well attack us, for we had the Convenience of some Earth-walls or ditches about Breast high'.[4] These may have been built for agricultural functions, perhaps as sheep pens.

Argyle was certainly at a numerical disadvantage. He needed the remainder of his force to return to him in order to be on an equal or superior footing with the Jacobite force. If he could find these men, 'the victory had been as compleat as ever any was'. So he despatched three officers to locate the other three battalions and the five squadrons of dragoons whose whereabouts he knew not. It was a fruitless search. The rest of his army was too far away to be of any value to him now. Meanwhile, if the Jacobites attacked, the cannon were to fire at them, before the infantry fired at close range. Then the dragoons would charge into the Jacobites.[5]

Mar believed that the British might march towards him, but did not do so according to one account, though another states that two squadrons of dragoons marched towards the top of the hill, but on seeing the Jacobites advancing to the attack, retreated downwards faster than they had ascended it. The Jacobites did little further that was aggressive, except to advance two squadrons of cavalry to observe Argyle's movements. According to Sinclair this was, 'I believe without order, by common consent, for I saw no mortall pretend to give orders that day, the one following the others example'. Linlithgow further advanced his squadron, but Sinclair advised him not to do so for his squadron was not advancing and for Linlithgow to do so unilaterally would be to break the line, though 'he was so vaine of that day's behaviour they had [he] would scarce take advice'. They halted in expectation that the infantry would also advance, following the cavalry's example, but Sinclair 'lookt longe in vaine over our shoulders, for they stood like stakes'. Apparently Mar later explained why the Highlanders had not moved forward, 'Mar told the gentlemen, That the Highlanders were so fatigued they had lost spirits, and would not attack; and to the Highlandmen, That he could not find it in his heart to risque

3   TNA, SP54/10/48; Patten, *History*, pp. 160, 167–168; Rae, *History*, p. 308; Scott, *Memoirs*, p. 223.
4   Patten, *History*, p. 160.
5   Rae, *History*, p. 308.

the gentlemen'. Sinclair merely believed this to be an excuse, that 'Mar had no mind to risque himself' and so 'missed the favourablest [opportunity] that ever offer'd of getting out of the danger he had plunged them in'. He added that it could not be argued that Mar did not know that he outnumbered Argyle.[6]

Keith gave another version of this final confrontation in the afternoon. Mar sent an officer forward to check the enemy's position and then held a council of war:

> To consult whether he should attack them again, but the officer having reported that their numbers were equal to ours, and the Highlanders, who were extreamly fatigued, and, had nothing to eat in two days, being averse to it, it was resolved to keep the field of battle, and to let the enemy retire unmolested, which they had already begun to do under the cover of the earth walls as well as of the night which was now approaching'.[7]

Yet according to Keith, the officer who was sent forward – and never named – had blundered and gave Mar faulty information:

> He having taken his remarks more by the number of colours than the space of ground they occupied, made his report that the enemy was betwixt two and three thousand strong, when in reality there was no more than three battalions not making above 1,000 troops, the other colours being what the Duke had just taken on our left, and being almost the same with his own, he now used them to disguise the weakness of his troops by making a show of four more battalions more than he had, the ground and mud walls by which he had cover'd not allowing to see that he had formed only two ranks deep (usually three ranks deep); this mistake hinder'd us from attacking him in the evening; which its probable we might have done with better success than we had in the morning.[8]

Whether the officer had erred is another question: Argyle may well have had such numbers as he suspected; Keith was presumably further away and so his opinion may be less valid.

Berwick later commented on Mar's inaction at this stage: 'He ought, however, have tried to induce them to it; for it was of great consequence to him to push on and to hazard everything to Argyle'.[9]

Yet the real reason was somewhat different. By this stage of the battle, Lochiel and Strowan had fled with their men and Sir Donald MacDonald was ill at Perth:

> So that the laird of Glengarry was the only chieftain of consequence remaining with the Earl of Mar, who in a most unaccountable manner took it into his head that he could not attack Argile in his return, & said to Mar that he had done enough for one Day, seeing they beat the Enimy and kept the field of Battle, and although Mar used his utmost

---

6   Scott, *Memoirs*, pp. 222–223.
7   Keith, *Fragment*, p. 19.
8   *Ibid.*, p. 21.
9   Parke, *Memoirs*, p. 235.

endeavours to persuade Glengarry to make the Victory compleat, yet nothing could prevail with him to do so. So that Mar was forced to let the enemy with a very inferior Number of Troops march by him and escape the danger they were in.

Argile in the meantime was very sensible of the disadvantage he lay under, and tho he kept his Troops that were with him in good order, yet he retreated in very good order, yet he retreated in very good heart till he gote into the Town of Dunblane where he reassembled a good many of those who had been routed on his left, and a remained all that night. Mar kept the feild of Battle till after sun sett and then marched back to Ardoch, where he encamped that night.

This testimony was from William and Maurice Moray, who formed part of Mar's cavalry escort and were thus better placed than Keith or Sinclair to witness what happened at this crucial juncture of the battle.[10]

Glengarry had about 461 men at the outset of the battle, and so led a sizeable minority of the men who remained with Mar. Without them any attack was even more risky, for the Jacobite's numerical edge was either minimal or non-existent. Furthermore, their holding back may well have discouraged their comrades. Despite all the criticism bestowed on Mar ever since 1715, at least he clearly saw that this was the opportunity to defeat Argyle. It was not his fault that inaction resulted. Instead he was let down by a subordinate. In this he was unfortunate that he was not leading a regular army but an army where most of the officers were volunteers, amateurs and not under any formal discipline. As in 1745, Jacobite officers, as gentlemen, valued their independence and did not always agree with their commander in chief. Glengarry had been an ardent Jacobite, having fought at Killiecrankie in 1689, but his enthusiasm had evidently waned as he did not support the restoration attempt of 1708; by 1715 he was ageing, and though he had vigorously led his clan into battle he clearly thought his men had done all they could.[11]

Unaware of all this, Argyle, finding there was nothing he could do, not having the rest of his men and with darkness now rapidly descending on the moor, marched his troops away from the immediate vicinity of his enemy, whilst still facing the direction of the Jacobites (initially Sinclair thought this was a feint); as did the Jacobites. Wightman later wrote, 'The Enemy behav'd like civil Gentlemen, and let us do what we pleased'.[12] This is not the behaviour expected of enemies in battle. It was about 7:00 p.m. and so was too dark to fight.[13]

Wightman thought that his army had had a lucky escape, writing, 'If they had had either Courage or Conduct they might have entirely destroyed my Body of Foot; but it pleased God to the Contrary. I am apt to conjecture their Spirits were not a little

10   NRS, GD24/1/872/1/3:279.
11   Elcho, *Short Account*, pp. 415–418.
12   TNA, SP54/10/48; Patten, *History*, p. 160; Rae, *History*, p. 308; Scott, *Memoirs*, p. 222.
13   NRS, GD220/5/787/A.

damp'd by having been Witness some Hours before of the firm Behaviour of my Foot, and thought it hardly possible to break us'.[14]

In another respect apart from numbers, Mar had held the advantage if he had but known it. Charging downhill gives additional momentum to the attackers and renders it harder for the enemy to fire uphill with any accuracy. The Jacobite charge down the slopes of Killiecrankie had resulted in a decisive victory in 1689 and they had been outnumbered.[15] Yet Mar had been let down by Glengarry. It is possible that this defensive, even defeatist, mentality also led to Thomas Forster's surrendering another Jacobite army at Preston on that same day. Forster and Glengarry were amateurs, not professionals; and when matters become distasteful the amateur often ceases his labours whereas the professional will continue to the grim reckoning.

A comparison with the final phase of the Battle of Marston Moor may be instructive. The left flank of each army had been victorious against the other's right. At the end of the day the result of the battle still lay in the balance as each side retained forces on the field. As we have seen, the Jacobites withdrew at this point. In 1644 Cromwell pressed home the numerical superiority of the Parliamentary army and won a decisive victory.

Mar's behaviour at this point in the battle was that of the reasonable man. He had tried his best to persuade Glengarry to take the final offensive. Glengarry's attitude was that of a strictly limited mode of warfare. His men had fought and had chased part of their enemy from the field. He may not have wanted to risk the lives of any more of his men now that they had done their duty as he saw it. This was not war to the knife. He could cite reasons for inaction: the day was darkening, his men were tired and he wanted no more bloodshed that day. Jacobite numbers were not that much higher than Argyle's. Yet this was the moment for the final push which could have led to victory and the destruction of their enemy. Montrose or Cromwell would have taken it. There was an opportunity to secure a great victory and should have been seized with both hands. Nothing is certain in war, of course, but failure to take one's chances is disastrous. To attack then would not have been easy, physically or psychologically, but in not doing so any chance of a Jacobite victory was thrown away, though this was only obvious as time passed.

Unlike Argyle, the Jacobite army had to take the role of the aggressor in the battle in order to win opponent. Argyle 'merely' had to prevent his force from being destroyed. The more difficult task fell to Mar. What would have happened had Mar beaten Argyle is hard to ascertain for it would depend on a great number of other variables. It would have been unlikely that it would have been an end to the campaign; Cope's defeat at Prestonpans in 1745 did not result in a Stuart restoration but a prolonged campaign (and ultimate Jacobite defeat). Many of Mar's men would have drifted home as Montrose's had in 1645, and the government would have formed a second army to face him made up of the Dutch forces who were on their way to England and the troops from elsewhere in England, probably headed by General Carpenter or Cadogan (assuming a Jacobite defeat at Preston and the ending of any

---

14 Patten, *History*, p. 160.
15 Pollard and Oliver, *Two Men in a Trench*, II, p. 214.

threat from England). Nor is it certain that the castles of Stirling or Edinburgh would have capitulated to the Jacobites (they did not do so in 1745). Furthermore, as the action occurred in mid November, it was almost at the end of the campaigning season and there was too little time left for further aggressive action in the Jacobites' part. Yet an outright victory at Sheriffmuir would have lifted Jacobite morale and provided an opportunity for later Jacobite success. A repulse of the Jacobites, as unlikely as it may seem, would not have led to a rout as Argyle's forces were too tired to pursue for long.

An hour after the retreat of the Jacobites, some of the units that had been on the left began to rejoin Argyle and explained what had happened there. Argyle's men passed the bridge of Dunblane and posted themselves 'very securely'. As on the night of the 12th, they were lying with their arms ready for any danger.[16] This was a commonplace military practice; Marlborough's troops had done likewise on the night after Oudenarde.[17]

One account claims the Jacobites remained where they were for half an hour before leaving, presumably waiting to see what Argyle would do. Their artillery – never used – had been left where it had initially stood when the rest of the army fled. Some of the carriages were broken, the gunpowder carts were overturned and what little gunpowder there had been was trodden into the wet moor by the horses. Apparently the country people who had charge of the guns and horses fled on being frightened of the sound of the guns. Sinclair suggested burying the artillery which could not be moved, but he was ignored; it is hard to see how this could have been accomplished without a sufficient quantity of the necessary tools even if men could be found who were able and willing to undertake such a menial and physically demanding task at the end of an exhausting day. The Jacobites found that they had lost many of their horses for their baggage carts and artillery, but found a few horses and were thus able to remove some of their material from the field. A total of perhaps six guns were taken away and five abandoned, but as they were pulled away, the horses became exhausted and two of the carriages broke so all the guns were left upon the road. Lacking cover and provisions, they marched away in good order, though Sinclair thought not, with 'everie one shifting for himself … there being no one either to command or obey' in the darkness. They camped that night at Ardoch. The rearguard, Sinclair's squadron, did not arrive until midnight, and when they did, could not find either Mar or a quartermaster to give a report nor to be told where their quarters were. Here Mar expected to be joined by the troops that had been on his left and four other battalions; none of the latter having taken part in the battle itself. These forces joined Mar on the following day.[18]

One group of Jacobite stragglers was led by Lochiel. He ensured his men who had fired their muskets reloaded them, and then wondered what was happening. He later wrote, 'So night coming on, and not knowing what was become of the rest of the

---

16   Patten, *History*, p. 160.
17   John Marshall Deane, *A Journal of the Campaign in Flanders* (John Marshall Deane, 1846), p. 14.
18   Patten, *History*, pp. 162, 168; Scott, *Memoirs*, pp. 224–225; *Annals*, p. 153.

Army, having no word from them, I went to a little village above Bracko and sent to Drummond Castle to know what account was to be got there'.[19]

On daybreak of 14 November Argyle returned to the field of battle, of which he was now undoubted master. He found one of his men who had escaped from the enemy after having briefly being captured. This unknown soldier told Argyle that the Jacobites had retreated to Auchterarder and that some had fled over the Allan. Other wounded men were removed from the field.[20] He also sent out patrols to take any of the dispersed Jacobites that could be found. Colonel Kerr took a detachment of men with him to bury the dead of both sides.[21] It was probably a melancholy sight as Private Deane had noted after the victory at Oudenarde in 1708, 'a heart piercing sight to see ye Dead lyeing in every Hole and Corer; and to hear ye cryes of ye wounded was very dolorouss', though adding that for those with whole skins, 'God has preserved us in a wonderfull manner'.[22]

There was little more that Argyle could do. Provisions were running low, his army was numerically reduced and the weather was bad, so encampment on Sheriffmuir was not practical. Nor was it tenable to advance against the Jacobites because of this. As he wrote, 'as for our advancing, our circumstances would by no means admit of it'. He marched his men back to Stirling, leaving Kerr and a few soldiers there in order to put them under cover again, presumably because of the inclement weather. They were, however, billeted in such a way that they would be able to reassemble within a few hours if the need arose.[23]

The Jacobites were in a doleful plight after the battle, too. Sinclair later wrote, 'We found ourselves without provisions, pouder and men'. Having their army reduced by 5,000 men they could not continue fighting. They lacked food so had no alternative but to retreat to Perth. They marched back to Auchterarder on 14 November and cantoned there that night. They arrived at Perth two days later.[24]

Casualties

The one certainty of a battle is that some of its participants will be killed or wounded. Initially it was not certain what the butcher's bill was, with Wightman opining, 'The Loss on both Sides I leave for another Time, when we have a more exact Account', though he added that Morrison's battalion 'is one of the unfortunate Regiments that were not form'd, and suffered most'.[25] An anonymous chronicler wrote, 'As to the particulars of the slain and wounded on either side is yet uncertain'. Colonel Kerr was sent out to make a return of the fatalities on each side, but regrettably this is not known to have survived.[26]

---

19   <www.lochiel.net/archives/arch173.html>.
20   TNA, SP54/10/48; Patten, *History*, p. 160.
21   *HMC 14th Report*, Appendix III, pp. 168–169.
22   Deane, *A Journal*, p. 15.
23   TNA, SP54/10/48.
24   Scott, *Memoirs*, p. 241.
25   Patten, *History*, pp. 161–160.
26   *HMC 14th Report*, Appendix III, p. 168.

British Army

The casualties inflicted on the British army should be easier to ascertain because regular forces keep records and these often survive. Yet in this instance no record seems to now exist. This has undoubtedly led historians to give widely different numbers, as they have for the size of the army, as has been noted.

Szechi claims Argyle's estimate of the men in his army slain was 500 and the historian suggests another 500 were wounded, bringing the total to 1,000, or over a quarter of the entire army.[27] Others give lower figures: Inglis estimates 500 casualties; Baynes lists 377 dead, 153 wounded and 133 captured.[28] Likewise, Reid has 389 dead, 154 wounded and an unknown number of prisoners.[29]

The losses were certainly perceived by contemporaries as being severe. The Laird of Gorthie wrote on 16 November, 'It was bloody, a good deal of loss on our side'.[30] Another contemporary reported, 'I cannot perfectly learn … what officers are killed tho' there's a pretty many'.[31] Jacobite writers naturally stressed the casualties they had inflicted on their opponents. After all, they were writing for propaganda purposes. An anonymous report gave the British army a total loss of 1,200.[32] Mar referred to Lord Forfar and Captain Urquhart, 'who I'm afraid will die' and 'a good Number of private Men Prisoners; but the Number I do not exactly know'.[33] Lieutenant Campbell provided the lowest estimate, believing that 220 infantry and 45 dragoons were dead.[34] Three days later, the governor of Burntisland noted that there were 110 privates and 10 officers arrived at Perth as prisoners on 15 November. Another Jacobite reckoned on 12–14 officers being taken and about 200 sergeants and other ranks. They were allegedly well treated, 'The Prisoners taken by us were very civilly us'd, and none of them stript'. Some captured officers were allowed to return to Stirling on parole and others were allowed the liberty of walking around Perth.[35] Officers were allowed to keep their swords after having given their parole.[36] This was in line with Mar's charity towards his enemy.[37]

Sinclair thought that 15 officers had been taken and perhaps 200 privates, but of these, some escaped on the night of the battle and some died of their wounds.[38] Another added that 'the Enemy lost on the Spot above eight hundred Men', with another Jacobite estimate at being 'We compute that there lay killed upon the Field of Battle above 7 or 800 of the Enemy; and this is certain, that there lay dead upon the Field of Battle above fifteen of the Enemy to one of ours: Besides the Number of the

27 Szechi, *1715*, p. 159.
28 Inglis, *Sheriffmuir*, p. 56; Baynes, *Jacobite Rising*, p. 152.
29 Reid, *Sheriffmuir*, p. 144.
30 NRS, GD220/5/817/7.
31 *Ibid.* 787/a.
32 Patten, *History*, p. 169.
33 *Ibid.*, p. 162.
34 NRS, RH15/14/149.
35 Patten, *History*, pp. 162, 168.
36 NRS, GD220/5/787A.
37 *Ibid.*, GD2/171.
38 Scott, *Memoirs*, p. 228.

Wounded must be very great'.[39] Sinclair claimed that he did not see above 200, but stated that Jacobite accounts at Perth gave 'near to eight hundred killed'.[40]

Rae gives the following figures:[41]

	Killed	Wounded	Prisoners	Total
Infantry	241	120	110	471
Dragoons	25	53	12	80
Officers	14	11	10	35
Sergeants	10	3	1	13
Total Men	290	187	133	610
Horses	42	75	40	157

There are no numbers of casualties among State Papers for Scotland. Figures, broken down by unit, were published in the press a few weeks after the battle. Their accuracy can be doubted, however.

Infantry Killed

Unit	Field Officers	Capts.	Lieuts.	Ens.	Sergts.	Others	Total
Forfar			1			11	12
Morrison	1	2	3	4	4	97	111
Montagu	1	3	2			87	93
Clayton			1			6	7
Wightman						7	7
Orrery's		1	2		3	85	91
Shannon		1				5	6
Egerton						21	21
	2	7	9	4	7	319	348

39 Patten, *History*, pp. 162–3.
40 Scott, *Memoirs*, p. 228.
41 Rae, *History*, p. 310.

Infantry Wounded

Unit	Field Officers	Capts.	Lieuts.	Ens.	Sergts.	Others	Total
Forfar	1						1
Morrison		1				13	14
Montagu			2			19	21
Clayton						14	14
Wightman						5	5
Orrery		1			1	24	26
Shannon						5	5
Egerton					1	14	15
	1	2	2	0	2	94	101

Cavalry Killed

Unit	Officers	Lieuts.	Cornets	Q'mrs.	Sergts.	Others	Total
Portmore						2	2
Carpenter						17	17
Evans			1			19	20
Stair						7	7
Kerr						0	0
							46

Cavalry Wounded

Unit	Officers	Lieuts.	Cornets	Q'mrs.	Sergts.	Others	Total
Portmore	1			1		2	4
Carpenter					1	8	9
Evans	2	2			1	28	33
Stair						6	6
Kerr						1	1
	3	2	0	1	2	45	53

Horses

	Killed	Wounded
Portmore	3	8
Carpenter	11	4
Evans	13	44
Stair	11	15
Kerr	1	14
	39	85

Troops Captured

Unit	
Portmore	2
Carpenter	3
Evans	3
Stair	1
Kerr	0
Forfar	0
Morrison	19
Montagu	3
Clayton	1
Wightman	0
Orrery	64
Shannon	0
Egerton	16
Total	112

To sum up, according these figures, the British army had lost 404 dead, 154 wounded and 112 prisoners; a total of 670 casualties; roughly a fifth of their total force. A disproportionate loss was suffered by Montague's, Morrison's and Orrery's, who had borne the brunt of the Jacobite onslaught.[42] These may be underestimates. They were significant, but worse had happened: at Blenheim the victorious allies lost a quarter of their men. At Mollwitz in 1740, both sides lost about a fifth of their strength. Such was not unusual.[43]

---

42 *Flying Post*, 3732, 3–6 Dec. 1715.
43 Showalter, Frederick the Great, p. 50.

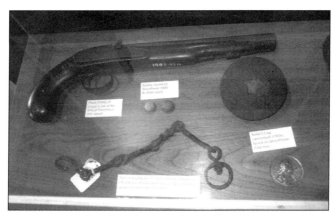

7. Artefacts from the battle, Dunblane
Museum. (Author's photo)

It is impossible to know with accuracy how many men the British Army lost. The figure of 120 prisoners seems reasonable; as noted below there were at least 245 wounded who survived for years later (and there may have been an overlap between this figure and the previous one), so the figure above of 154 wounded is certainly an underestimate. Some men were killed and some men may have gone missing, but these numbers are unrecorded. Argyle wrote on 15 November, 'My Lord, I have but this moment received the Return of the killed, wounded and missing, which are in so much confusion, that I cannot send them, but I judge that killed, wounded & missing we are 500 men weaker now than the day we marched to the Enemy'.[44] The Return mentioned does not survive, and though commanders often exaggerate the enemy's losses and minimise their own, Argyle's correspondence shows him as a plain speaker in whom duplicity was not a part of his mentality. So his assessment of casualties may be the least inaccurate there is.

At least 245 men later claimed to have been wounded at the battle and later claimed disability pensions (from 1716–1746), in part at least because of these wounds. Some of these men wounded would have been among the prisoners taken. Whilst it is impossible to know in which units most of these men served because they were in a different unit at the time of their claim, it is possible to ascertain some details of the wounds inflicted. It must be borne in mind that these wounds were the ones that were recoverable from, not all those inflicted, for some men would die of wounds received.

Of those with recoverable wounds, 122, or 50 percent, had received injuries from cutting weapons, which would almost all have been inflicted by swords and perhaps occasionally Lochaber axes. Nineteen men (8 percent) had been injured by stabbing weapons, probably swords and dirks. Nearly a quarter of them, 54 men, had been injured by musket balls. Horses trampled on 11 men; five received bruises, two were

44   TNA, SP54/10/51.

wounded by bayonets; one by each of the following – a sword pommel, the butt of a gun and the butt of a pistol. For 29 men, or 12 percent, the cause of injury is unknown.[45] These injuries are very uncharacteristic of those inflicted in conventional warfare at the time; in the Invalides, in 1762, the overwhelming proportion of wounds had been inflicted by muskets balls, some by cannon and only a very small number by hand-to-hand weapons.[46] The majority of these wounds, where their location is known, was to the head, 93 (40 percent), with there being 50 (31 percent) leg wounds and 39 (24 percent) arm wounds.[47]

The officers were listed individually in various accounts of the battle; four were killed outright; six wounded, 15 were captured. Two were taken prisoner and subsequently died and another wounded officer was made prisoner.[48] These are listed in appendix I.

Lest we become distanced from the human cost of battle through these statistics, recall the words of contemporaries. Captain John Farrer of Evans' Dragoons, who later wrote, 'that unfortunate Day I had the misfortune to Receive a Musquett shott into my left Thigh which broke and shattered all the bone to pieces I lay madam 24 weeks upon my back end'. He was also taken prisoner and lost £200 worth of belongings including his horse, cloak and bag with £70 of cash. On 15 June 1716 he wrote from Stirling 'I could have wished madam that I had escaped that wound that I might have been with ye Regiment when at Brechin.[49]

Anstruther wrote a week after the battle about four officers who had been wounded, that they were 'much better than could be expected, the surgeons are in no apprehension about the three last but they can't as yet be certain about Forfar who's good heart and strength of constitution will contribute very much to his cure'.[50] Cockburn also wrote of the wounded a few days later; 'Poor Forfar is dead. James Dormer is in all ill way. I hope my poor brother is out of danger but I am afraid he has lost ye use of his arm; many pieces of bone are already come out and others are coming it will be sometime before he is well'.[51] Campbell thought that Forfar, wounded in 17 places, was 'a sample of their [the Jacobites'] mercy'.[52]

Hospital facilities were rudimentary: there was a regimental surgeon and his mate, but there was no monetary vote for medical services. Such costs usually came out of contingencies and extraordinary expenses. Yet payments were made. Just after the battle, £215 was paid for surgeons at a makeshift hospital at Stirling and one Robert Watson claimed £22 19s 9d for hospital utensils (Patrick Crawford later supplied more at £8 15s 5d). Robert Crawford, Peter Lapange and Mr Sutherland, surgeons, were paid £226 for their attendance at the hospital from November to January. Andrew

45   TNA, WO116/1–3
46   Christopher Duffy, Warfare in the Age of Reason (London: Routledge and Kegan, 1987), p. 245.
47   TNA, WO116/1–3.
48   TNA, SP54/11/45A: RA, SP5/97; NRS, GD220/5/481/4; HMC Appendix III, p. 169; Patten, History, p. 155; Flying Post, 3727, 22–24 Nov. 1715.
49   NRS, GD45/14/263.
50   Ibid., GD220/5/489/5.
51   Ibid., GD/37/6.
52   Ibid., RH15/14/149.

Vinielle, master surgeon, supplied medicines and nurses from late January to late February at the cost of £17 4s. Nurses were employed from early December and were paid on a monthly basis of about £8 16s from then until April 1716.[53] Horses were also killed or injured; perhaps 42 and 75 respectively. After the battle, £1,344 was given in total to the colonels of the regiments of Evans, Carpenter and Stair to reimburse them for the horses lost at the battle; £204 was given to the colonel of Portmore's.[54]

Then there were the material losses. The British army had also lost one flag, though another statement gives it as being four.[55] Mar added 'We have taken a great many of the Enemy's Arms'. Three days later his colleague at Burntisland elaborated; 'forty good Horses and one Thousand five Hundred Stand of the Enemy's Arms'. Another Jacobite put captured small arms at 1,400–1,500.[56] Sinclair thought it was 1,200.[57]

Jacobite Casualties

No known list of Jacobite casualties survives either; even assuming one was ever compiled. Various figures are given by historians. Sinclair Stevenson refers to Mar's stated figure of 60 Jacobite dead but then cites an unreferenced government report of 600 Jacobite dead, stating that this 'has the stamp of truth'.[58] Reid suggests the total was between 60 and 800.[59] The lowest total is given by Baynes, who accepts Mar's figure of 60 dead and cites 90 wounded, with 82 prisoners; and so 232 casualties in all.[60] Inglis suggests 500, but adds, rightly, that it is difficult to be precise.[61] The highest known estimate by a historian of Jacobite losses was made by Szechi; 1,500 killed, wounded or captured, or about 17 percent of those involved.[62]

Argyle wrote 'I count their dead my lord to be 500 and believe the number of their wounded to be considerable' (some of whom had drowned in the Allan) as well as having captured 21 Jacobite officers (out of 82 men taken; for a list of names, and fates where known, see appendix V).[63] Harrison put the figure as higher but was uncertain, 'We have as yet no certain Account of the Numbers killed, but its reckoned they may be about 800, amongst whom are several Persons of Distinction'. He counted 15 officers and numerous subalterns that had been captured.[64] Rae gives two figures for Jacobite dead: 600 and 800, admitting that the Jacobites gave lower figures.[65] Jacobites minimised their losses, Mar writing, 'We have lost, to our Regret, the Earl of Strathmore, and the Captain Clan-Ranald. Some are missing; but their Fate we

---

53   Chandler, *Marlborough*, p. 75; *Journal of the House of Commons*, 1718, pp. 551–553,
54   *Journal*, p. 554.
55   TNA, SP54/10/48; Patten, *History*, p. 168.
56   *Ibid.*, p. 168.
57   Scott, *Memoirs*, p. 228.
58   Sinclair-Stevenson, *Inglorious Rebellion*, p. 121.
59   Reid, *Sheriffmuir*, pp. 144–145.
60   Baynes, *Jacobite Rising*, p. 152.
61   Inglis, *Sheriffmuir*, p. 56.
62   Szechi, *1715*, p. 159.
63   TNA, SP54/10/48, 54.
64   Patten, *History*, p. 154.
65   Rae, *History*, p. 310.

8. Memorial to members of Clan MacRae who were killed at Sheriffmuir. Erected by the Clan in 1915. (Author's photo)

are not sure of. The Earl of Panmure, Drummond of Logy and Lieutenant Colonel Maclean are wounded'.[66] Another writer gives Jacobite losses as 60 dead and 'very few wounded'.[67] In addition, there were 80 Jacobites taken prisoner, the most exalted being Viscount Strathallan (see appendix IV for a list).[68] In contrast to the lenity allowed the Jacobites' prisoners, captured Jacobite prisoners were 'close confined'.[69] The injured Panmure was left in a cottage, guarded by a dragoon, but at nighttime the peer was rescued.[70]

It is impossible to ascertain which of these figures is correct, except that the Jacobites' own figures are certainly far too low. Men fleeing the field and being pursued by enemy cavalry as occurred on the Jacobite left are likely to take severe losses, so the figures given by Argyle and Harrison are more probably nearer the truth. In any case, they were present on the battlefield on the following day and so were more likely to be able to give fairly accurate figures. Yet, proportionately speaking, the Jacobite battlefield losses were fewer than those of their enemy.

Both sides, therefore, lost approximately the same number of men; proportionately Argyle had lost far more, one fifth compared to the tenth of the Jacobite forces which had been lost. On the face of it, Argyle could simply not afford such losses.

Jacobite losses went beyond manpower. Argyle stated that they had lost four cannon, ammunition carts, baggage carts, 13 flags and the royal standard, titled the Restoration. Harrison confirmed these numbers.[71] Furthermore, Argyle's soldiers apparently returned from the field loaded with booty.[72]

Both generals have come in for censure among historians. Mar comes in for the majority of blame on the grounds that he had overwhelming superiority of numbers

66 Patten, *History*, p. 162.
67 *Ibid.*, p. 169.
68 Rae, *History*, pp. 309–310.
69 NRS, GD220/5/787A.
70 *An Account of the Battel of Dunblain in a Letter from a Gentleman at Stirling to his friend at Edinburgh* (Edinburgh, 1715).
71 TNA, SP54/10/48; Patten, *History*, p. 154.
72 *An Account of the Battel of Dunblain*

and yet could still not achieve a decisive victory. His control over his subordinates, especially Glengarry, the cavalry and the units which lay off the field but could have been engaged, has also attracted criticism. Argyle has also been attacked for indecision, for not showing 'the intelligence to be expected of a general trained under Marlborough' and for being apparently reluctant to attack his fellow countrymen.[73] Mar has also been criticised for desisting from fighting, with one historian stating, 'There was no need for tactical skill on Mar's part. All he had to do was to attack and keep on attacking. Two days' fighting would have finished off Argyll'.[74] Ashby McGowan, in an article in a wargames magazine, gives a view more favourable to the Jacobites than any other, writing, 'Mar and (his officers), who is usually portrayed as an incompetent commander, sought the initiative and outmanoeuvred Argyle'.[75]

So who won the battle? Clearly this was not a clear cut result, as were Blenheim or Poltava, though in both cases the wars which these were part of were far from at an end because of their results. Neither army was destroyed and neither was wholly routed. Often it is described as being indecisive for these very reasons. Yet most historians point out that the battle was 'strictly speaking a drawn contest' but that 'the rising lay in ruins' and was 'as good as lost' for the Jacobites.[76] Inglis is certain of the result, writing, 'There is no doubt that the Jacobites failed in their aim and that Argyle succeeded'.[77] McGowan, characteristically describes it as a 'tactical victory' for the Jacobites but even he admits it was a strategic defeat.[78]

Following the battle of guns and swords there came a battle of words. Both sides claimed the victory. Argyle, typically modest, informed his political masters in London that 'The Victory we have got is owing to Providence, for my own part, I pretend no further merit than having done my best'. He bestowed praise on the troops, stating that they 'deserve His Majesty's favour' and commended the behaviour of his officers and that of the squadron of volunteers. He was downbeat about the immediate prospects of the campaign, though, writing, 'we cannot hope always to beat three times our number' and looked forward to the arrival of the Dutch auxiliary forces. Colonel Harrison was despatched to London to tell Townshend the news.[79] Yet a contemporary letter stated, 'Our troops, who are very hearty and desirous of meeting the rebels a second time'.[80]

Harrison also paid tribute to the soldiers in the army in which he had fought:

The Courage of the King's Troops were never keener than on this Occasion; who, though the Rebels were three times the Number, yet attacked and pursued them with all the Resolution imaginable. The Conduct and Bravery of the Generals and inferior officers

---

73   Sinclair-Stevenson, *Inglorious Rebellion*, p. 120.
74   Lenman, *Jacobite Risings*, p. 153.
75   Ashby McGowan, 'Sheriffmuir, 1715, Part 2', *Miniature Wargames* no. 143, April 1995, p. 10.
76   *Ibid.*, p.122.
77   Inglis, *Sheriffmuir*, p. 57.
78   McGowan, *Sheriffmuir*, p. 10.
79   TNA, SP54/10/48, 51.
80   *Spottiswoode Miscellany*, p. 430.

9. Memorial cairn at Sheriffmuir, erected by the 1745 Association. (Author's photo)

contributed much to this Success; But above all, the great Example of his Grace the Duke of Argyle, whose Presence not only gave Spirit to the Action, but gained Success as often as he led on.[81]

There was a royal bounty of £500 for Harrison on his bringing the news to the court five days later. The brigade majors were given a gratuity to disperse to the rank and file soldiers who captured the Jacobite flags. A bounty for the private men totalled £188 9s 6d.[82] Loyalist Scots agreed with Harrison. The Laird of Gorthie wrote 'Argyle mett with the rebels and has had a victory'.[83]

The Jacobites also did their best to publicise the fact that they had won. On the evening of the battle Mar penned a letter for publication, beginning 'I thought you would be anxious to know the Fate of this Day'. He later stated, 'And had our Left and Second Line behaved as our Right, and the rest of the first line did, our Victory had been complete: But another Day is coming for that, and I hope 'e'er long too'.[84] At Burntisland, 'Upon Receipt of this News the Governor acquainted the Magistrates, whereupon they went to Church and thanked God for the victory'.[85] At Perth a pamphlet was printed with this title, 'An Account of the Engagement on the Sheriff-Moor near Dunblain, Novem. 13 1715 betwixt the King's Army, commanded by the Earl of Mar, and the Duke of B-k's commanded by Argyle'.[86]

Mar portrayed the battle to the world as a victory. As well as various published accounts at Perth, when he returned there on the 16th he caused thanksgiving sermons to be read out from the pulpits. A *te deum* was sung in the cathedral and the evening ended with bell ringing and other public demonstrations of rejoicing.[87] He also sent a message to the French court via James Murray, telling them of the victory

81 Patten, *History*, p. 154.
82 *Journal*, p. 551.
83 NRS, GD220/5/817/5.
84 Patten, *History*, p. 162.
85 *Ibid.*, pp. 163–164.
86 *Ibid.*, p. 164.
87 Rae, *History*, p. 311.

at Sheriffmuir.[88] Ormonde was clearly aware of this for he wrote to Mar, 'I take this opportunity of congratulating your Grace on the victory that you have gained over your enemys and hope you will have all the success you desire'.[89]

This version was also learnt of by the agents of the British government in Paris. Thomas Crawford wrote on 11 December (New Style), 'The news here are that the Duke of Argyle is beat and the Town of Edinburgh is in my Lord Mar's hands. We cannot contradict them not having seen any letters from England since those of the 17th November (i.e. 28 November New Style)'.[90]

Yet when Mar wrote to James 11 days after the battle, he was less upbeat in private, in part because of what had happened in the days following the battle, which will be explained in the next chapter, though even here he put a positive spin on events: 'Our left behaved scandalously and run away, but our right routed the enemies left and most of their body. Their right follow'd and pursued our left, which made me not adventure to prosecute and push our advantage on our right so far … wee kept the field of battle and the enemies retired to Dunkeld [Dunblane]'.[91]

James was no fool and clearly appreciated what had happened, as much as Mar had attempted to put a favourable gloss on events, writing a few days later after having read a published account: 'tis plain we have not lost, tho' what related to our left wing is not well explained. The gaining the camp de battaille is but a fruitless honour when one can reap no other advantage, and at best that advantage can only make of even a victory if want of provisions force one not to advance'.[92]

Two Jacobite officers, in their memoirs, gave less enthusiastic verdicts about the battle. Sinclair noted that it was a case of 'our not gaineing ane intire victorie' and that 'People raison'd differentlie of the causes … as is usuall on such occasions. He argued that Mar and his supporters apportioned the blame on Hamilton's cowardice. Sinclair thought that Hamilton's putting the infantry into four columns meant time was lost and that they moved forward at an inconsistent pace, with the cavalry being unable to screen the infantry in their changes of formation that were carried out so close to the enemy. Drummond's moving his cavalry from the left to the centre was also condemned, for having cavalry on the left could have prevented a rout on the left wing. Sinclair thought that the Jacobites should have advanced in two lines and not have changed into columns. He also condemned Seaforth and Tullibardine for not leading their men's advance on foot.[93]

Keith was more forthright than Sinclair and also assigned the battle the status of a defeat for the Jacobites, 'thus ended the affair of Dunblane in which neither side gained much, however, but which was the entire ruin of our party'.[94]

88   *HMC Mar and Kellie*, p. 515.
89   *HMC Stuart Papers*, I, p. 480.
90   TNA, SP78/160, 159.
91   *HMC Mar and Kellie*, I, p. 514.
92   *HMC Stuart Papers*, I, p. 473.
93   Scott, *Memoirs*, pp. 229–231.
94   Keith, *Fragment*, p. 20.

Argyle's political masters were enthusiastic about his endeavours. Townshend wrote to him on 19 November in most fulsome terms:

> This Evening Mr Harrison arrived and brought me your Grace's of the 14th inst which was immediately laid before the King, who has ordered me to return you his hearty thanks for the good service you have done His Majesty and your Country by this victory you have obtained over the rebels, the good consequences of which His Majesty doubts not will appear every day, and your Grace must allow Mr Secretary Stanhope and me to congratulate you on this good success, which we do both very sincerely. I have also His Majesty's orders to desire your Grace to give thanks in his name to all the officers and other under your Grace's command, who have on this occasion given proof of their bravery and fidelity.[95]

On 22 November, Pulteney wrote a similar letter to Argyle:

> I wish I cou'd express my joy to your Grace upon an occasion so happy to your self and Country; in which you have given the Enemys to His Majesty's Crown strong occasion to understand that they are to expect from you when you shall be augmented by the forces designed for you. The Blow you have given them with your small Numbers having already dampen'd their fire, no question but the next will extinguish the last support of the Rebellion.[96]

At the end of the day or very shortly afterwards, some Whigs had already broadcast the battle as a victory. An anonymous and optimistic government supporter wrote on the evening of the battle, 'I am very hopeful tomorrow may in a great measure put an end to this rebellion'.[97] James Anderson, the Edinburgh postmaster, wrote two days later, 'Where, bless'd be God we had the better, and hope soon to hear, that what remains of the Rebels are intirely routed or fled'.[98] Colonel Aird, in charge of the Glasgow Militia stationed at Stirling wrote on the evening of the battle, 'We are still confirmed that the Duke of Argyle is master of the field'.[99] Blackader, despite recording the rout of the left wing, was put in a more positive frame of mind by the end of the day, writing:

> We got intelligence that the Duke was still on the field of battle, and after having been victorious, where he first was. O what a surprising turn! We could not believe it; we were as men dreamed; but it was soon confirmed to us by eye witnesses. O how hast thou turned our fears and griefs into joys and songs of praise! Providence had managed it so that no flesh could boast.[100]

95 *HMC Townshend*, p. 179.
96 TNA, WO4/17, p. 285.
97 *Ibid.*, SP54/10, 47.
98 *Ibid.*, SP54/11/49.
99 T. F. Donald, 'Glasgow and the Jacobite Rebellion of 1715', SHR, XIII, 1915–16, p. 130.
100 Crichton, *Life and Diary*, pp. 174–175.

More distant observers made comments about the outcome. Parker wrote, 'both sides claiming the victory, which indeed both had a right to … The Battle however had this good effect, that it prevented Mar from marching into England, though the other gained but little honour by it'.[101] Predictably, a diametrically opposite view came from Thomas Hearne, noting in his diary on 5 December, 'The Duke of Mar (for King James hath made him a Duke) hath got a victory (as tis said) over the Duke of Argyle'.[102]

Reactions to the differing accounts of the battle certainly varied. Lady Cowper wrote that, along with the news of the Jacobite surrender at Preston, it 'filled the Town with Joy, which was augmented by the News of a Victory in Scotland. The Illwill which was borne the Duke of Argyle made it to be mighty lessened, and even reported to have been none but a Defeat; but the consequences showed plainly that he had the Advantage, for the Rebels dispersed after it'.[103]

Ryder was also fascinated by news of the campaign in Scotland. On 18 November, the express from Argyle had reached London and it was being eagerly devoured among the politically conscious of its citizens. Although the accounts were of a victory over the Jacobite army, 'The particulars are not very clear and the victory seems not to be very complete'. Apparently the capital's armchair generals, ever ready to be wise after the event, argued that Argyle should have kept on the defensive, stayed south of the Firth and denied the Jacobites the opportunity for battle 'because that is what must be that which they desire. As long as they can do nothing they lose and it is a victory to us'.[104] Instead Argyle had gambled and won.

Ryder seemed to have shared an animus against Argyle which Lady Cowper touched on. He held strongly Whig and Hanoverian views and so presumably supported George I and his ministry against its critics, whether Tory or otherwise. He imputed cynical motives to Argyle's allegedly aggressive defence which had led to battle: 'the Duke of Argyll is an ambitious man and perhaps was afraid lest the honour of conquering the rebels and reducing them should be given to others or shared with others if he had stayed until the Dutch troops came, which seems to have been the occasion of his going out of his camp to fight the rebels'.[105] As noted in chapter six, this is a travesty, possibly born out of prejudice and ignorance; Argyle having been reluctant to fight and most desirous of the Dutch troops' arrival in order to even up the odds.

More news came on the following day and it enabled Ryder to have a more positive impression of Argyle's achievement:

> It seems to have been a very bloody one and the loss of each side seems to be pretty equal, but the Duke of Argyll gained the field of battle and took prisoners and carried away the cannon and baggage of the rebels who seem to be dispersed. They have disappeared and are unwilling to come to another engagement.[106]

---

101 Parker, *Memoirs*, p. 265.
102 Rannie, 'Hearne's Collections', p. 150.
103 Cowper, *Diary*, p. 57.
104 Matthews, *Diary*, p. 139.
105 *Ibid.*
106 *Ibid.*, p. 140.

News of the battle seems to have been slower reaching Chester. It was on the 22nd that Henry Prescott referred to it, having learnt that Mar had been defeated, with many flags and cannon having been captured, as well as an impossible figure of 5,000 Jacobite dead. Official responses in the city to this apparently decisive victory were positive, as Prescott recorded, 'Hence Joy in the Town inexpressible'. Two days later, with additional newspaper reporting, the battle seemed to Prescott to have been rather more indecisive, 'Almost equal success even in the Gazet is given to the right wing of Marrs Army … so that *inter utrumque, volat dubiis Victoria pennis* [victory flies between the two sides on uncertain wings]'.[107]

Later news came of the battle in the following days. Prescott read that though the newspapers reported a victory for Argyle, they also stated that the Jacobites believed that they had won, too, for there were 'bonfires and rejoiceing made by Lord Marr'. Prescott surmised that another reason suggesting a Jacobite victory was that the whole of the Dutch troops were ordered to march northwards. On 2 December, he reported reading additional accounts of the battle, 'Wee are today dejected, and transported with different relacions of the Event of the Battle in Scotland … both very improbable, nothing giving any credit to support the victory on Marr's part'.[108] Prescott was a Tory with Jacobite sympathies and clearly was hoping that Mar had been triumphant – he was clutching at straws in reasoning that the government sending Argyle reinforcements was proof that he had been the loser in the fighting, which was not really the case.

Some government supporters saw the battle as being a very close call and with the benefit of hindsight suggested that the Jacobite army was but a marginal threat at best. Defoe later wrote, on visiting the battlefield, 'how it was possible, that a rabble of Highlanders armed in haste, appearing in rebellion, and headed by a person never in arms before, not of the least experience, should come so near to the overthrowing an army of regular, disciplined troops, and led on by experienced officers, and so great a general'.[109]

Others gave thanks to God for the outcome of the battle. Given that this was very much a Christian age of near universal belief, this should not be unexpected. God's hand was seen everywhere in human affairs, both for good and for necessary chastisement (e.g. the Fire of London of 1666). For instance, John Evelyn wrote after hearing of the allied victory at Blenheim in 1704, 'God Almighty promote and improve this Great News, to him be the glory'.[110] Likewise, Parker wrote that this success had been 'Under Divine Providence'.[111]

Joseph Symson, a Kendal merchant and a supporter of George I, wrote to Peter DeSitter, 'God be thanked the Duke of Argyll obtained a victory over them in Scotland and it is very remarkable it was the very same day that they were defeated

---

107 Peter McNiven (ed.), 'The Diary of Henry Prescott, L.L.B., Deputy Registrar of Chester Diocese, II', Record Society of Lancashire and Cheshire (1994), pp. 475–6.
108 *Ibid.*, pp. 476–477.
109 Rogers, *Daniel Defoe's Tour*, p. 647.
110 Esmond S. de Beer (ed.), *The Diary of John Evelyn* (London: Everyman, 2006), p. 949.
111 Parker, *Memoirs*, p. 110.

at Preston. Gloria Dea'.[112] Likewise Defoe praised the result: 'we blessed the Good Protector of Great Britain ... who gave that important victory to King George's troops and prevented the ruin of Scotland from an army of Highlanders'.[113]

The financial markets greeted the news of the battles favourably. In early November they registered 90 5/8 to 89 for the South Sea Company and from 118¾ to 119 for the Bank of England. Late that month, following the battles they registered 94½ to 94¾ and 124¼ to 124½ respectively. This clearly shows that investors treated the results of the battle as a sign that the government and dynasty were more stable than they had been. A defeat for Argyle would probably have resulted in a deterioration in these figures as investors withdrew funds as their confidence in the status quo waned.[114]

Predictably historians sympathetic to the government claimed the battle as a victory, being able to view the matter in retrospect. Rae wrote:

> By this Battle the Heart of the Rebellion was broke, the Earl of Mar was baulked of his Design; his Undertaking for a March to the South was laid aside, and never attempted afterwards; and his Numbers daily decreased, so that he could never gather such an Army again. We must own it indeed a great Victory to our rightful Sovereign King George.

Rae added that it was providence which kept the rebellion alive for a few more weeks in order to let everyone know the failings of James Stuart.[115] Rather agnostically, Patten's *History* prints both Jacobite and Hanoverian accounts of the battle.[116]

The medium and long term impacts of the battle were even more important to the campaign's outcome than what happened on the field of battle, though these eventualities would not have resulted had the fighting taken a different turn. We shall now examine the battle's other results which only became apparent in subsequent days and weeks.

---

112 David Smith (ed.), *Letter Books of Joseph Symson, 1711–1720* (Oxford: Oxford University Press, 2003), p. 345.
113 Rogers, *Tour*, p. 647.
114 *Daily Courant*, 4376, 2 Nov. 1715; 4391, 19 Nov. 1716.
115 Rae, *History*, p. 311.
116 Patten, *History*, pp. 151–171.

11

The Consequences

After the battle there was a period of uncertainty for both armies, but both knew that the conflict was far from over. Patten later wrote that once Argyle had returned to Stirling and Mar to Perth, 'both continued quiet the remaining Part of November, and all the next Month', but this is to understate matters and to equate the lack of military action with inaction.[1] The campaign was unfinished. The Jacobite cause was not at an end and nor was their army no longer potentially threatening. As noted, Argyle had been constantly downbeat even both he had arrived in Scotland as commander-in-chief. Although he acknowledged that he had triumphed at Sheriffmuir, he impressed on his masters that this did not mean that they were out of the woods yet. He observed on 15 November that the Jacobites were 'just in the same situation as they were, before they advanced'. He believed that they were at Perth and Auchterarder, gathering together their forces as a prelude to a second advance against Stirling. Indeed, he had heard intelligence that such a move was imminent. He had, he wrote, 500 men less than he had had on 12 November and so they would be insufficient to beat them again. He could hardly expect a second 'miracle'. All he could do was to implore the government that the Dutch forces arrive and so an end to the campaign be made, 'I most heartily wish for His Majesty's service that they may arrive in time'.[2]

This fear continued on the following day. Argyle's intelligence was that 8,000 Highland infantry and cavalry would be attacking in the next day or two. He also believed that the Jacobites were increased in numbers and he had too few men to prevent them. He needed more than 3,000 Dutch soldiers: 'I wish to God my Lord the Dutch Troops had not been countermanded [to march into England]'. Meanwhile, on the morning of the 16th he had been putting his forces together in the best possible order. If he were not reinforced and as soon as possible, 'depend upon it my Lord the consequences would be very bad'.[3] Argyle wrote a similar letter to Pulteney, fearing an imminent and devastating Jacobite onslaught.[4]

---

1   Patten, *History*, p. 171.
2   TNA, SP54/10/51.
3   *Ibid.*, 54.
4   NRS, GD244/624/71.

Yet when the Dutch arrived they would need to recover from a seaborne voyage before they could be of service. Private Deane had recorded, when travelling by ship from the Continent to Scotland seven years previously, 'while we lay on board we had continual Distraction in ye foretops; ye pox above board; ye plague between decks: hell in ye forecastle, and ye Devil att ye helm'.[5]

Argyle's pessimism was unrelieved by the news he received of the surrender of the Jacobite army at Preston on 14 November, despite hopes elsewhere that it would lead to the end of the campaign. Argyle was less than confident that the Battle of Preston would have any decisive result for the Scottish campaign, He told Townshend on 19 November:

> I received last night a letter from Mr Carpenter with the good news of the Rebells at Preston being all Prisoners but he makes a Reflection at the end of his letter wch is a very wrong one, he imagines those at Perth may upon this news desire to capitulate. I hope His Majesty's ministers have not been of this opinion, because it would literally very greatly danger the whole.[6]

Cornet William Kennedy of Stair's dragoons wrote about Townshend thinking it odd that Perth was not taken, despite a lack of heavy artillery, 'generals here differ in opinion from those who make war in a warm room in London to whom everything may seem easy'.[7]

Cockburn was more optimistic, writing about the Jacobite surrender at Preston, 'this will putt ane end I hope to the rebellion in England, and must have good consequences as to us'.[8] Not all in the government's camp in Scotland shared Argyle's views. Cockburn added that the 'agreeable news … of the Rebels in Lancashire being entirely subdued wch will we hope put a stop to any further Insurrection in England'. This had been a very decisive battle in which the entire Jacobite army in England capitulated. He had heard that the Jacobites were gathering themselves together again at Perth, 'but we do not fear of their offering to move forward again'.[9] An anonymous correspondent of John Sterling wrote 'I believe this affair almost over now'.[10]

Instead, Argyle was insistent on the 19th that an advance of 7,000 Jacobites (1,000 less than the previous day's estimate) was imminent. He referred to the 'order and discipline' of his enemy's army. His difficulty – to fight a numerically superior army or to flee – was 'as miserable a dilemma as I think can be possibly imagined'. This was no mob that he faced, but a superior army. On the 20th he wrote, 'it is not in nature for this handful of Troops to defend themselves against such regular Multitudes'.[11]

5   Deane, *A Journal*, p. 6.
6   TNA, SP54/10/64.
7   Henrietta Tayler (ed.), *Seven Sons of the Provost: A Family Chronicle of the Eighteenth Century complied from Original Letters, 1692–1761* (London: Nelson and Sons, 1949), p. 76.
8   TNA, SP54/10/60.
9   *Ibid.*, SP54/10/71.
10   NRS, GD220/5/787A.
11   TNA, SP54/10/64, 70.

Anstruther wrote that reinforcements were crucial: 'its probable there will be no more action until the Dutch Troops come which have been looked for. We have no prospect of forcing the Rebels from Fife until we get more troops'.[12] Lieutenant Alexander Campbell agreed with Argyle's assessment of the situation, writing, 'The Duke all this time was in no condition to attack them having but the remains of the 3000 ... nor no guns excepting the small artillery pieces that were not fit to batter a garden wall'.[13] Gorthie elaborated on this theme and explained it:

> I have reason to believe that our ministry in England have had but a very mean opinion of the Highlanders and that for this reason, they have always opposed the reinforcing of the Duke with more troops. I shant say if this ill will some of ym likely bear to his Grace was any art of this reason, but if it is, their reasoning from that despicableness of the enemy, will not hold good.[14]

Ironically, the Jacobites' intelligence was equally poor; they thought that there might be an offensive against them, Sinclair writing, 'we had several alarmes of the Duke of Argyle's comeing to attack us ... which frightened us prodigiouslie'.[15] On 22 November, Mar wrote that he had heard that Argyle was about to take the offensive, adding 'He certainly knows our condition and tis not unlikely that the severeness of our numbers may make him attempt it'. Yet he was wrong in his beliefs, which included the notion that Argyle had gathered militia to take part in the attack and that he expected no reinforcement from England because his Jacobite allies there 'are in a prosperous way'.[16]

Reliable intelligence of the Jacobites was scarce, as Anstruther wrote on 22 November, 'I don't pretend to send your Grace any news from Perth than can be relayed on'.[17] On the other hand, a writer from the government camp noted 'We are pretty credibly informed of great Desertions and some say not 3,000 are at Perth'.[18] This was indeed the case.

Unbeknown to Argyle, matters in the Jacobite camp made it impossible for them to have mounted an offensive. They just did not have the manpower after Sheriffmuir to have done so. Mar complained:

> Amongst many good Qualities, the Highlanders have one unlucky Custom, not easy to be reform'd; which is, that generally after an action they return Home. Accordingly, a great many went off after the Battle of Sheriffmuir; so that the Earl of Mar not being in a Condition to pursue the Advantage he had by it, was forc'd to return to Perth'. Such had happened in the previous century as was to do so again. They did not return, in part

---

12 NRS, GD220/5/489/5.
13 NRS, RH15/14/149.
14 NRS, GD220/5/817/9B.
15 Scott, *Memoirs*, p. 256.
16 NLS, ADV MS 13.1.8/44.
17 NRS, GD220/5/489/5.
18 *Ibid.*, 220/5/787a.

because the much promised supplies from abroad did not appear, nor had the Duke of Berwick. Many of the leading Jacobites went home because their money was running out and some went without asking leave.[19]

Sinclair wrote, 'The greatest part of our two thousand Highlanders, who stay'd with us at the battle went home with the enemies' plunder, and the Chiefs of the neighbouring Clans were sent out to bring back what they could of their men, but with very bad success'.[20]

Breadalbane's 300 men also went home, as did most of Marischal's. Strathmore and Auchterhouse being killed at Sheriffmuir, their men left the army, as did Panmure's, though he was only badly wounded. Some cited their lack of money as a reason for leaving. Sinclair wrote, 'It was easie to see, by no complaints being made of these gentlemen who left us, and as few endeavours to bring them back, and our recruiteing onlie in Perth from one another, that our dissolution was drauing near'.[21] Argyle's biographer reasoned that the desertions occurred because the Highlanders 'not seeing any Likelihood of coming to a Action; as it is a custom with these People never to remain long from Home unless they are kept in constant Employ, a life of uncertainty and Inactivity not suiting with their fiery and restless Disposition'.[22]

Likewise, Colonel Sir Robert Pollock, in charge of the garrison at Fort William, reported on 23 November, 'I am informed that a great many have deserted the Rebels and are now return'd home, particularly the MacDonalds and the Stewarts of Appin'.[23] However, as we shall note in the next chapter, some of the MacDonalds and Appin Stewarts remained with the Jacobite army at Perth.

Mar urgently wrote to those who had left the army with their men. On 19 November he told Strowan, 'the principle thing now is for you all to haste up wt yr people a quick rendezvous being what must give life to our affairs ... For God's sake hast up wt yr people'.[24] Three days later he repeated himself, stressing that it was 'absolutely necessary for all the King's friends to get together their men immediately and join us forthwith, else it may be too late'.[25]

A slight straw against this wind was MacDonald of Keppoch arriving with 240 men, who had not been to Perth previously. They believed that there was much spoil to be gained. Mar greeted him with great glee, offering the clan leader pay and provisions. Yet though he remained, his men left after a few days, taking what they liked from others on the way back.[26]

Historians who have complained that Mar should have attacked Argyle again until by means of attrition he would have been victorious, have clearly not grasped the

19   Patten, *History*, p. 212.
20   Scott, *Memoirs*, p. 244.
21   *Ibid.*, pp. 260–264.
22   Campbell, *The Life*, p. 231.
23   TNA, SP54/10/77.
24   NLS, ADV MS 13.1.8. 43.
25   *Ibid.*, 44.
26   Scott, *Memoirs*, pp. 266–267.

points made above. Mar's army was in no condition to take the offensive in the near future because of its vastly reduced numbers.

Rather, it was standing on the defensive. Work took place on Perth's defences, but to little effect. Mar tried to keep up morale by reminding his men, yet again, of promises of French arms, gunpowder and ammunition and the eventual arrival of James. Possibly these promises were beginning to sound hollow. Divisions among the Jacobites also began to make their appearance, perhaps unsurprisingly in the light of the setback at Sheriffmuir. Meetings which had hitherto been held regularly were no longer being held, such as the Court of General Officers and the committee which dealt with arms and ammunition. The Council of Finance was still in being, however, headed by Francis Stuart, the Earl of Moray's brother, as treasurer, as money still needed to be levied and warrants given to him for payments. The Committee for Fourage and Vivers was maintained 'for neither horses nor men could live on wind'.[27]

The Jacobites, or at least some of them, heard the news of the surrender at Preston shortly after their return to Perth. Mar tried to pretend it was a victory and ordered public celebrations, which took place. He wrote to Strowan thus, 'The government gives out that our Friends in England have been defeated but I am sure their accounts are not true, tho' it is very likely there has been some action there: Lord Nairn disbelieve it'.[28]

The reality was soon widely known. Keith recalled the demoralising effects of the result of the news of the surrender at Preston. Several leading Jacobites at Perth, 'seeing that the English, which we always looked on as our principal strength, were quelled … began to think of making terms for themselves'.[29] Others did, too 'the melanchollie account was confirmed from all hands' as Sinclair wrote, adding, 'One might imagine that all this storm threatening to break upon us, at a time when we were abandoned by the whole world.'[30] Eventually Mar wrote to James that the surrender at Preston, 'I'm afraid will putt a stop to any more riseings in that country at this time'.[31]

The news from England meant that the British state could now, if it chose, turn its full resources against the Jacobites in Scotland: both in terms of British units, though in the end only two regiments of dragoons were despatched to Scotland, and also all of the Dutch troops as none of the latter would be needed in England. By 27 November Pulteney had ordered Newton's dragoons, who had not been engaged at Preston, to join Argyle. Colonel William Stanhope (c.1683–1756) had pressed for his own regiment of dragoons to go there and General Charles Wills (1665–1741), whose command they and Newton's were part of, wrote to Marlborough that as these 'being the best mounted regiment of the whole', he had them go, too.[32]

It was not only the news of the surrender of the Jacobite army at Preston that was disconcerting for the Jacobite cause. Sir John Mackenzie, who was in command of the Jacobite garrison at the castle and town of Inverness, had been threatened by

27   *Ibid.*, pp. 244, 246–247, 249.
28   NLS, ADV MS 13.1.8.43.
29   Keith, *Fragment*, p. 23.
30   Scott, *Memoirs*, pp. 251–252, 256.
31   *HMC Mar and Kellie*, p. 514.
32   British Library Add. MSS. 61315, f. 231r.

the Earl of Sutherland with men of his own clan, and those of Ross, Fraser, Munro, Forbes and Mackays. On 10 November Mackenzie was summoned to surrender the city. Although he initially refused and withdrew his small garrison of 300 men to the castle whilst they occupied the city, he clearly realised the position was untenable and left on the following day.[33]

The loss of manpower in terms of desertions and the Jacobite defeats elsewhere were grim news for those still at Perth. Worse was to come as some Jacobites clearly saw that defeat and all that implied was staring them in the face and there was no plausible military solution open to them any more. According to Keith, Huntley headed the faction in the Jacobite army which wanted to ask for terms. Some also suspected that Mar, contrary to his pronouncements in public, had also made overtures towards the government, too. Some did not believe that James would ever arrive and so pressed Mar to negotiate.[34]

A letter from Stanhope to Stair of 15 December showed another gloomy insight of the Jacobite camp. Apparently, as regards the long awaited James: 'his friends there despair of seeing him and are in such a confusion as cannot easily be described … several of the leaders there actually keep centinels upon Lord Mar least he should make his escape and abandon them; tis certain they intend to abandon Perth the minute the Dutch Troops shall be got to Stirling'.[35]

Morale was low. Sinclair, on being asked by Hamilton for his opinions, suggested, 'There was no other to be proposed but to endeavour to get terms, and make a fair capitulation with the Gouvernment', though was not inclined to surrender without conditions and stated that many other gentry had a lot to lose. Mar was aware of potential dissension and so proposed that an Association be formed which would bind the leading Jacobites together, to stand as one man, or as Sinclair put it, for the officers 'to be hoodwinkt into a blind submission to his arbitrarie will'. Huntley refused to have anything to do with it.[36]

In order to avoid a potentially disastrous split in what remained of the army, a meeting of officers was held. Mar announced that 'we should enter into new tyes and bonds, obliging us never to desert one another'. Huntley proposed the signing of a shorter version. There was discussion over the wording of the documents. Mar admitted that the Jacobite cause was not progressing as well as it might but stated that it was not hopeless either. The meeting was far from unanimous; and a later meeting of some of those present led to a motion that a capitulation would be preferable, in part because James had not arrived and the cause seemed hopeless, with 1,400 men against Argyle's alleged 10,000. Mar was told of this and accused them of deserting their King and Country. They replied that they had already done all they could and were unconvinced by his pleading.[37]

---

33   Patten, *History*, p. 171.
34   Keith, *Fragment*, p. 23; NLS, ADV MS 13.1.8.44.
35   TNA, SP78/160, 169.
36   Scott, *Memoirs*, pp. 257, 268, 272.
37   *Ibid.*, pp. 272–286.

There followed much discussion, arguments and lobbying. Argyle was aware of this, writing 'I am in hopes tho cannot answer for it that there are some differences among the rebels which may prove fortunate'.[38] Cameron argued, 'it would be the greatest hardship imaginable to enter into any termes with the Government till once we were assured what had become of the King'.[39] Eventually Mar surprised his detractors by proposing that Colonel Lawrence, the most senior British officer taken by the Jacobites at Sheriffmuir, should be sent from Dundee to Argyle with proposals for negotiation.[40] At the same time, Mar, despite his public utterances, was involved in securing his own safety by employing one Methuen to 'use his credit to get terms from the enemy in favour of Mar' and continued to do so until the end of the year.[41]

On the morning of 27 November, almost a fortnight after Sheriffmuir, Lawrence came into Argyle's camp at Stirling. He was on his parole and told Argyle that Mar and his officers wanted to know what terms Argyle was able to grant them and whether these could be discussed. Argyle could not answer without consultation. He talked to his brother Roxburghe about it and they concluded that they would need to seek the King's permission to do so. Lawrence also told them that he had been informed privately by Huntley, Rollo and Gordon that they asked for a separate peace, suggesting that if so they could take their men home. The other Jacobite leaders, apparently, wished to remain with Mar. Lawrence told Argyle that these three Jacobites thought that the published account of the Jacobite victory at Sheriffmuir 'was only to keep their people in heart'.[42]

All this must have been very encouraging for Argyle. Far from having to fear another battle against a numerically stronger force, he had now learnt that the Jacobites wanted to sue for the peace. He also had confirmation that they were divided among themselves. However, he lacked the plenipotentiary powers to negotiate with the Jacobites, though he fully realised that if he could reduce the numbers in the Jacobite army it would be highly beneficial and so recommended this to his masters, 'it would be His Majesty's interest to show them mercy'.[43] Lawrence was sent to London with a letter concerning the potential submission of the Jacobite leaders.[44]

There was no immediate definitive reply from Westminster. The prognosis was not optimistic, for on 26 November Townshend had already told him that the King had made no statement as to the exchange of prisoners. It may not have come as an entire surprise to Argyle that, a week later, on being told of Mar's offer of a negotiated settlement, Townshend still could not tell Argyle the King's resolution. Nor could he in the next letter, of 6 December. At some time Argyle told Mar that he had no powers to negotiate, for, three days later, Townshend assured Argyle that the King 'approves very much of your declining to enter into any treaty on the proposals made by Huntley

38 TNA, SP54/10, 84.
39 <www.lochiel.net/archives/arch173.html>.
40 Scott, *Memoirs*, p. 298.
41 *HMC Stuart Papers*, II, p. 169.
42 TNA, SP54/10/86b.
43 *Ibid.*, 96a.
44 *St. James Evening Post*, 82, 6–8 Dec. 1715.

and others'. Surrender would have to be unconditional. The reasoning behind this was, as Townshend explained on 15 December, 'It is not consistent with the Honour and Dignity of his Crown ... that any treaty should be entered into ... upon other terms or conditions, than surrendering themselves at discretion'.[45]

After all, General Wills had had no such powers during the campaign in England and when the subject of a negotiated surrender was broached at Preston he declared that this could not be done, for the Jacobites were deemed rebels against their lawful monarch rather than honourable and legitimate enemies, such as the French had been viewed during the War of the Spanish Succession. Any government or regular army dealing with insurgents in the eighteenth century would have had similar views, as would be made very clear in 1746 with the different treatment meted out to captured French and Spanish troops and those Scottish and English Jacobites taken in arms.

Argyle's proposals have usually been applauded by historians, seeing his actions as being purely that of a soldier, motivated by the wish to end the conflict as soon as possible without further lives being lost. Not all contemporaries agreed with such an opinion as a letter of Cockburn's revealed. Argyle was also a politician as well as a soldier. He believed that Argyle's eagerness for negotiations was because he wanted the Jacobites to have a dependence on him, and this would increase his client range and thus his political leverage when peace returned. He knew that once his military colleague, Cadogan, arrived with the Dutch, Argyle's hand would be weakened as 'Cadogan will be for going through entirely with itt ... all this makes his Grace very uneasie'.[46]

Mar had other matters on his mind. He later stated that a resolution had been taken in late November to abandon Perth if Argyle moved against it. Despite the fact that 'this Resolution was known to a good Number in our Army', none made it public. Therefore this led to Argyle delaying his offensive until he had built up sufficient strength. Yet, as Mar conceded, 'in reality, our Condition was then such, as obliged us to take that Resolution, having neither a sufficient Number of Men, Ammunition nor Arms'.[47] Gorthie reasoned similarly, 'Earl Marr is not in a condition to stir from Perth, even against the troops we have' and that was before the Dutch had arrived.[48]

His army continued to haemorrhage. Huntley and Seaforth, who led two of the larger Jacobite contingents, were concerned that Sutherland's loyalist forces might threaten their lands as they now had the upper hand in the north. They promised, however, that they would return to Perth after having resolved matters there. Mar tried to dissuade them, but was unable to do so and therefore reluctantly consented to their departure.[49] So almost 2,500 men had left. Tullibardine also departed during this month.[50] Lord Stewart arrived at Stirling on 26 November and asked for mercy and was sent to Glasgow under guard; Argyle hoped that others might do likewise.[51]

---

45   Patten, *History* pp. 201–202.
46   NRS, GD3/37/4.
47   LUL, Townshend, 49r, 55r, 57r, 60v.
48   NRS, GD220/5/817/21.
49   Keith, *Fragment*, pp. 23–24.
50   Campbell, *The Life*, p. 231.
51   TNA, SP54/10/107b.

Frustration with absent allies led Mar to make a grim jest to Strowan when writing to him on 4 December, 'I fancie you must be waiting to hear of our capitulation to see if there be occasion for you or not'. After adding 'Railery apart', he stated that the presence of Strowan's men was 'absolute necessity'. Yet it seems that Strowan's men were too few and lacked pay. By 5 December, Mar still hoped they would arrive and as we will note in the next chapter that a few did so.[52] Other attempts at recruiting were of little success. Gordon of Glenbucket had been told by Mar on 18 November to go into Aberdeen and Banffshire to levy all fencible men, preferably armed and equipped. Yet he later replied, 'It took time before the vassals would condescend to give a man' and that 'these people that will not own none of your orders, nor consider our hazard'.[53]

Further dissension continued in the Jacobite ranks and there were even suspicions of violence against those who distrusted Mar. This was because they despaired of the Jacobite cause. Sinclair wrote, 'I could be of no further use to the cause, which was now not onlie desperate, but sunk'. He left but many of his men remained. Mar tried to persuade men not to leave, but without success.[54] The remaining Jacobite leaders had entered into another association in order to stem the haemorrhaging of their strength, 'to take all the same fate, and to destroy any who shall attempt to desert them'.[55]

Money and supplies were still needed. Gordon was ordered to take all arms, ammunition and horses from any in Aberdeen and Banffshire who supported George I. Likewise tax collectors there were instructed to send their money to Perth. Those supporting George I had to pay double rates.[56] Somehow, enough was raised to keep the men that remained in and around Perth, however. Clearly, though, the Jacobites' situation was not a happy one, as even Mar admitted. Jacobite hopes now rested on James himself.[57]

Mar wrote a despondent letter to James on 24 November, concerned that his master should know the worst before his arrival to a potentially disappointing situation. He tried to present, as ever, an optimistic future, however: 'I have been doing all I can ever since to get the armie together again, and I hope considerable numbers may come in a little time'. Yet, fearing the imminent arrival of the Dutch troops to reinforce Argyle, the immediate military prospects for the Jacobites looked grim: 'I am afraid we shall have much difficultie in making a stand anywhere, save in the Highlands, where we shall not be able to subsist'. He looked forward to James' arrival, which he believed would 'certainly give new life to your friends and make them do all in their power for your service'. But this alone might not be enough, 'but how far they would be able to resist such a form'd body of regular troops as will be against them I must leave your Majesty to judge'. Such a disparity of numerical strength 'unless your Majesty have troops with you, which I am afraid you have not, I see not how we can oppose them'.[58]

---

52 NLS, MS ADV 13.1.8, 46–47.
53 *HMC Stuart Papers*, I, pp. 470, 478–9.
54 Scott, *Memoirs*, pp. 316–318, 323.
55 TNA, SP54/10, 107b.
56 *HMC Stuart Papers*, I, p. 471.
57 *Ibid.*; *HMC Mar and Kellie*, p. 515; NLS, ADV MS 13.1.8.47.
58 HMC Mar and Kellie, p. 515.

Meanwhile, after the initial despondency in the week after the battle, even Argyle's spirits rose. On the 21st Argyle was far more optimistic, because of news received of reinforcements, writing, I 'am very glad that the Dutch Troops are ordered to come hither, for upon their arrival in time depends the saving of the country'. If they arrived, the Jacobites would not attack. He did not think the latter was a phantom menace because he was still hearing accounts of a plan for a Jacobite advance, 'whose vigilance and furious zeal is inexpressible'. His further concern was over the imminent lack of subsistence for his troops, as it would expire in three days' time and he had heard no further news.[59]

Argyle's optimism continued. He was pleased to hear of the success of Scots loyalists at Inverness. According to him, Lovat's retaking of the town was 'of infinite service to His Majesty'. Meanwhile, he learnt that Cadogan would be sent to Scotland, which would be 'very agreeable to me' and was glad to hear that the Dutch troops were on the march towards him.[60] Cornet Kennedy was glad of his arrival: 'I believe he will have this good effect and that his account of things will be more credited at court'.[61] Townshend told him that with the Jacobites in Lancashire defeated, the Dutch could be wholly sent northwards. This would make a considerable force in Scotland and so an additional British lieutenant general should be sent – Cadogan – 'as the person who is best acquainted with the Dutch Troops, and who His Majesty judges will be most acceptable to your Grace'. After all, he had played a leading role in the negotiations at The Hague as to their despatch.[62]

Townshend, as ever, had the job of trying to reassure Argyle. Writing on 26 November, he stated, 'It is with Great Concern that His Majesty observes the uneasiness you are under' and that 'Nothing is wanting' as regards governmental support for him. He reiterated that 'it was not possible to spare any more Troops from hence till ye Dutch Troops should arrive'. He could now tell him that two regiments of dragoons from Lancashire could be sent as well as all the Dutch. He suggested that the militia could be drafted into the regulars.[63] Cockburn was convinced the Jacobites would not stand, 'so soon as our troops march I believe we shall hear of their running away'.[64]

The march of the Dutch and Swiss forces was a lengthy business. After their arrival in England on 15 November, four blue-coated battalions were briefly encamped around London. It was on 21 November that they were given marching orders to depart northwards. By 9–13 December, four battalions had reached as far north as Leeds.[65]

Meanwhile, just off the Continent, William Rowley (1690–1768), a naval officer at Le Havre was reporting that James was in Lower Normandy, and was eager to depart for Scotland. Two ships of the Royal Navy were ready to stop him.[66] James was

59   TNA, SP54/10, 74b.
60   *Ibid.*, 84, 86a.
61   Tayler, Seven Sons of the Provost, p. 76.
62   *HMC Townshend*, p. 179.
63   LUL, Townshend, 47r.
64   NRS, GD3/37/6.
65   TNA, WO5/20, pp. 157, 159; Leeds Local and Family History Library, *Memoranda Book of John Lucas*, p. 34.
66   TNA, SP54/10, 90.

reported to have boarded the *Neptune*, an eight-gun boat captained by one Harris at St. Maloes on 17 November.[67] However by 13 December it was reported that he was at Bar le Duc.[68] Bolingbroke had been advocating that he not depart 'at a season when your navigation is very uncertain and in a conjuncture when I apprehend that little progress can be made'. Yet on the next day he had made a volte-face, urging the young master that 'nothing but the impracticability of the navigation ought to hinder you from going to the north west of Scotland'.[69] James' arrival, constantly reported as being imminent, was held up as being an event of huge significance. Argyle, naturally, feared its consequences, believing that it would lead to a Jacobite army of 20,000 men being created subsequent to his arrival.[70]

As well as awaiting reinforcements, Argyle was trying to increase the number of troops under his command, but without much hope that they would be effective, explaining that 'Recruits just raised are of very little service'. There were no uniforms for them and they were expensive to feed, too. He likened them to the militia, 'a thousand of the best of the Highlanders would drive the whole militia of Scotland before them'. He stressed his own worth, 'no man has been a more faithful servant to those employed by His majesty at the helm of affairs than myself'.[71]

Additional troops were only arriving at a trickle. It was on 4 December that the first of the Dutch troops were sighted. Argyle reported that part of the Dutch contingent, Swiss soldiers, had arrived by ship at Leith on that day. Yet another six days passed and there was no sign of any more, nor of Cadogan. Although there was no intelligence about a further Jacobite advance, and given the news from Lawrence there was no obvious indicator of any immediate aggression, what Argyle learnt made him despondent. Firstly, he heard that the Jacobites had finished making their entrenchments at Perth and had been laying in magazines both there and at Dunkeld. Furthermore, there was the ever-present fear of the arrival of James. Lord Drummond's brother had arrived from France, allegedly with a large sum of money, and there were rejoicings at Perth for the news he had brought. This was not known to Argyle, but there was a rumour that James had arrived in Scotland. Argyle's only crumb of comfort was the news that Newton's dragoon regiment was expected in Edinburgh on the 15th.[72]

His worries were slowly assuaged, however. Cadogan, who was to receive £1,500 for his work in Scotland, reached Edinburgh on the evening of 12 December and was at Stirling on the following day. Stanhope's dragoons were at Linlithgow on 13 December and Newton's were at Edinburgh on the following day. Another 1,200–1,500 Dutch troops disembarked at Edinburgh. It was not all plain sailing for the seaboard Dutch, for two companies had to be rescued at sea by, presumably, the sailors on their ship. Yet he believed it would be some time before the campaign would be over. After all, it had taken two years to subdue the earlier Jacobite rebellion of 1689–1691. Argyle wrote

67 *Ibid.*, 126.
68 *Ibid.*, 127.
69 Mahon, *History*, I, Appendix, pp. xxxviii–xxxvix
70 TNA, SP54/10, 86a.
71 *Ibid.*, 101.
72 *Ibid.*, 119.

10. A nineteenth-century engraving of the Royal Navy bombarding
Jacobite positions on Burntisland. (Public domain)

that 'the soonest that the rebellion can be entirely crush'd' was the summer of 1716. In any case, they could not act aggressively against the Jacobites until the weather improved and all the Dutch troops had arrived. Both Cadogan and Argyle wished that they could offer terms to the Jacobites still in arms in order to reduce their numbers, for there were mixed messages about arrivals and departures from the Jacobite base at Perth, but this was not to be.[73]

There was a proactive step taken, and that was to seize Burntisland from the Jacobites. The commodore in charge of the ships on the coast battered the castle there and the Jacobite garrison of 150 men promptly abandoned it. A party from Edinburgh was then despatched to hold it on 20 December. This new garrison numbered 150 Dutch infantry and 60 militia. Wightman heard of a Jacobite plan to send 700 men to retake it, but there was a change of plan and so the attempt never took place.[74] The Jacobites' remit was slowly contracting and a rebellion on the defensive is inevitably doomed.

The politicians in London, as often the case, out of touch with practical realities on the ground, were eager for an offensive on Argyle's part. On 15 December, Townshend told Argyle, 'as soon as you are joined by that reinforcement … dislodge them from Perth, and even follow them amongst the hills'. He added, 'The situation of affairs in your parts does indeed require your Grace's presence, that no time may be lost, no measure neglected for suppressing this unnatural rebellion and for restoring to His Majesty's

73   *Ibid.*, 130, 133, 139; *Journal*, pp. 553, 554.
74   TNA, SP54/10, 139, 162.

good and faithful subjects that peace and quiet it has deprived them of'.[75] When the King had seen Cadogan's plan for attack by 27 December, Townshend urged Argyle to have it put into operation without loss of time, though he acknowledged that the weather and supplies were issues that needed addressing. If James had landed, then it was all the more imperative that an attack on Perth take place.[76] Oddly enough Bubb, in distant Spain, wrote on 30 December to the effect that due to the Scottish climate the campaign could not be over until the summer of 1716, mirroring Argyle's thought.[77]

Argyle also crossed swords with another at Westminster: Sir Robert Walpole, now First Lord of the Treasury and so effectively 'Prime Minister'. Walpole had been secretary at war and paymaster of the forces under Anne and was reinstated as a minister in 1714, so was no novice in matters of military expenditure. On 20 December Walpole wrote to Argyle to let him know that he was unhappy with the demands for excessive levels of money for the troops. These sums exceeded the Parliamentary allowances and the campaign had seen an increase in military spending. Walpole also pointed out that sending large amounts of specie northwards was dangerous. Argyle's colonels had desired large sums and Argyle had forwarded the requests to the Treasury. Walpole stated that these figures included sums for 'non-effectives' and so he was suggesting that the colonels, who were proprietors of their regiments after all, were inflating the numbers in their units in order to claim additional funds for non-existent men. Walpole emphasised that he had genuine regard for 'these brave men who venture their lives in the defence of their King and Country' but would not be a party to frauds perpetuated by their officers on the public purse.[78] Such corruption was not unknown.

At least the balance of forces was now in favour of the government. There had certainly been a diminution of Jacobite strength in and around Perth since the brief high-water mark of early November. Cockburn's reports gave the Jacobites 3,000 men at Perth, 200 on the bridge of Earn, with Panmure's battalion at Dunkeld and Strathmore's at Dundee. Their cavalry was housed on the north side of the Tay. Keith estimated their strength was 4,000 infantry and 500 cavalry. Huntley who had left was believed might now be raising men in the north. But Mar's attitude was defensive, with a ditch and pallisade being built around Perth.[79]

Mar was, however in a more optimistic mood in early December, having heard that Bolingbroke had finally secured financial support from Spain. He was also buoyed up by the alleged imminent arrival of James (the effect of which would 'I make no doubt of your having very soon an army together of 10,000 men'), the news that the Dutch troops had not arrived for Argyle and that Cadogan's arrival there was unpopular with Argyle. He even downplayed the impact of additional enemy troops, for 'I have very good hopes of a good part of the army coming over to you'. The notion that the enemy troops would declare for him was one shared by Monmouth in 1685

75   LUL, Townshend, 60r.
76   *Ibid.*, 65v-r.
77   TNA, SP94/84, letter, 30 Dec. 1715.
78   *Calendar of Treasury Books*, XXIX, Part 2, 1714–15, pp. 857–8.
79   TNA, SP54/10, 140; Keith, *Fragment*, p. 24.

and Derwentwater on the eve of the battle at Preston, and was to be entertained by Charles Stuart in 1746; in all cases these hopes were very largely disappointed. Finally, despite the recent attempts to negotiate an end of the armed struggle, Mar was now convinced that these were at an end, 'I hope the danger of that is over and that you shall not want people to stand by you to the last drop of their blood'.[80]

There was Jacobite concern that Argyle would receive substantial reinforcements and that by the following year would have 12,000 men. Yet there was also some optimism, in that a fortified Perth and poor weather would give them enough breathing space so that in the following spring the Highlanders would return and fresh recruits might come in. Others pinned their hopes on the claimant to the throne. Keith later wrote that he hoped that when James did arrive, he would come, 'with whome we expected a recruit of officers and a quantity of arms and ammunition from France, of which we stood in great need, having lost most of our powder, which was, even then in a very small quantity, at the affair of Dunblane'.[81]

Perhaps the Jacobites' greatest ally was the weather. Conventionally armies did not fight in the winter; Marlborough's campaigns ended in the autumn and did not commence again until the spring. There were many good reasons for this: forage, food and shelter were hard and expensive to procure, roads and water froze making movement very difficult, slow and dangerous. Days for campaigning were shorter. Scotland in 1715 was no different and this was an exceptionally bad winter; the Thames famously froze for a few days in December. Ships with heavy artillery were still stranded in the Thames due to the ice at the end of the year.[82]

Hearne gave a graphic description of the weather in that winter of 1715–1716:

This has been such a severe winter that the like hath not been known since the Year 1683. In some respects it exceed that … there was a much greater snow yt ever I knew: as it was also ye severest frost yt ever I have been sensible of. It began on Monday December 5th & continued 'till Friday, February 10th following, which is about 10 weeks, before there was an intire thaw. Indeed it began to thaw 2 or 3 times, but then the frost soon began again with more violence, & there was withal a very sharp and cold and high wind for some Days. When it first began to thaw & afterwards to freeze again.[83]

Argyle, as the one who would need to lead the winter offensive, was well aware of this. Logistics were difficult enough at the best of time for a large army on the move, as the Jacobites had found out in October and November 1715. Argyle pointed out that any march towards Perth would be expensive. There was no forage, provisions or firewood within seven miles of the city and very little within 16 miles of it. If the Jacobites retreated that would be problematic too, for it would be 'impossible for an army to follow the Highlanders amongst the hills in winter time and very hard to

80 HMC Mar and Kellie, I, p. 516.
81 Keith, Fragment, p. 24.
82 TNA, SP54/10/165.
83 Rannie, 'Hearne's Collections, 1714–1716', p. 174.

do it even in the summer'. In the latter, Argyle was being unduly pessimistic, for Cumberland's forces were able to penetrate the Highlands in the spring of 1746, though he was hardly in a position to be aware of what lay three decades away.[84]

The poor weather certainly put a brake on the progress of Argyle's operations. Artillery from the Tower of London was on board ships in the Nore but could not leave the ice-bound ports. Therefore a train of artillery (10 cannon and four mortars, with ammunition and other accoutrements) was fetched from Berwick by 1,500 draught animals with 500 men.[85] Guns could not be taken from ships because they could not be moved very far on land without carriages. Naval gunners were not of use because they were not 'versant in leading the artillery'.[86]

It was certainly an expensive business. From 23 December to 3 February, Cadogan spent £11,000 on provisions, £1,500 on transporting bread, and £500 for the horses hired to pull the bread wagons. The cost of hiring horses and civilians on the march from Stirling onward cost £2,585 9s 6d. Cadogan had to employ bakers and workmen to provide the bread and forage for the men and horses at an additional cost of £560 16s. Overall the costs of provisioning had been extensive as well as being expensive. For the horses this had been 160,000 tonnes of hay (£3,000) and 10,000 bolls of oats (£5,833 6s 8d). For the men there had been 300,000 biscuits (£2,145 12s 6d) and corn to the value of £2,342 12s 7 1/2d. For these the soldiers had to contribute out of their meagre pay, a total of £6,072 11s 7 1/2d.[87] There were other necessities: Thomas Blackman was paid £60 for the use of his oxen, and straw was bought for soldiers to lie on at the cost of £70. Extraordinary forage and baggage costs for the nine battalions of British infantry totalled £4,114 9s 4d.[88] Pulteney was concerned about the heavy expenditure involved and on 5 January urged Argyle 'to prevent the great and unnecessary charge of sending more money to Edinburgh than the service there absolutely requires'.[89]

---

84 TNA, SP54/10, 150.
85 Patten, *History*, p. 184.
86 TNA, SP54/11/7a.
87 *Journal*, p. 550.
88 *Ibid.*, pp. 553–554.
89 TNA, WO4/18, p. 6.

12

Endgame in the Highlands

Meanwhile, Mar had been awaiting James' presence for many a long month and had made many promises about his imminent arrival. In early December a ship arrived at St. Andrews with Hay, Sir John Areskine and Dr Patrick Abercomby, who had been to France to ask when James might arrive and told Mar that his coming would be not long delayed. In mid December he received a letter from Mary of Modena, thanking him for his good service and promising aid.[1] The decision for James to go to Scotland was made in late November, and when Ormonde returned a few days later to tell of the failure of his endeavours in England ('I am mortified, to have met with disappointments that have hindered me from endeavouring to make a diversion in the south'), the die was cast. On 5 December James wrote, 'I shall be soon with my friends'. He had a little good news to set across the failure of the English venture: the Spanish court had decided to give the Jacobites financial support, at least, though there was the inevitable chasm between the taking of the decision and the receipt of the goods.[2] He put his delay down to accidents, misfortunes, hopes of a universal rising and of his arriving with a strong force of troops.[3] However, there is no evidence that Stair planned to have him assassinated as is occasionally noted.[4]

On 22 December James finally set foot on Scottish soil, for the first time in his life. He had travelled incognito through Normandy and embarked at Dunkirk with the Marquess of Tinmouth, Berwick's son, Lieutenant Cameron, and several others, on a former French privateer of eight guns. They had initially set sail for Tetneuse in Norway, but changed course and after seven days arrived at Peterhead, 'a good market town, and a port with a small harbour for fishing vessels, but no considerable trade'. James and six gentlemen alighted and the ship was sent back to France with news of his arrival. One of the six, Cameron, then rode to Perth to tell Mar of his master's arrival. The others, dressed incognito as naval officers, spent the night in lodgings at Peterhead.[5]

1 *St. James' Evening Post*, 82, 6–8 Dec. 1715; 87, 17–20 Dec, 1715.
2 *HMC Stuart Papers*, I, pp. 471, 473, 479.
3 *Ibid.*, p. 505.
4 Parker, *Memoirs*, p. 239.
5 Rae, *History*, pp. 351–352; Defoe, *Tour*, p. 656.

Initially James was upbeat, writing to Bolingbroke, 'I am at last, thank God, in my own ancient kingdom ... I find things in a prosperous way; I hope all will go well, if friends on your side do their part as I shall have done mine'.[6] Later James was to write what he thought: 'The dismall prospect I found here at my arrival did not discourage me'. He was resolved to remain with his followers to the 'last extremity' in order to make Scotland 'a free and happie people'.[7]

He was described as being in buoyant spirits before departing, as an observer noted, 'I never knew any to have better temper, be more familiar and good, always pleased and in good humour ... never the least dispirited, but with ye greatest courage and fermness resolved to goe through what he designed on' and had 'all ye qualityes of a great prince'.[8] Travelling to Scotland in a small boat with few companions in winter was at least the sign of a brave or foolhardy young man.

The ship was followed by two others, one carrying James' baggage and the other his servants. One arrived safely at Dundee but the other sank near St. Andrews, though those aboard were saved. Another ship with men and money sank near Arbroath. Meanwhile on 23 December, James and his companions stayed at a house belong to Marischal, at Newburgh. On the following day they passed through Aberdeen with two baggage horses, again their true identities unbeknown to onlookers. That night they stayed at Fetteresso. It was here that James fell ill and was unwell for a few days.[9]

Mar, Hamilton and Marischal, with 20–30 other gentlemen met him there. They kissed his hand and announced his identity at the door of the house he was staying in. Hamilton then took a boat to France to implore supplies. The plan at Fetteresso was that they should then all travel to Perth, but because James was unwell their departure was delayed.[10] Yet he behaved as if he was King, appointing officers of state, and creating peers.[11] He also wrote to Cardinal Gualterro, asking him to request that the Pope assist with supplies vital to the success of the campaign, ('with supplies of every kind I feel assured that by the spring we shall be in a position to take the offensive, without them we shall be overwhelmed') and stressing that there was 'not a moment to lose'.[12] James contacted Huntley, hoping that he would return to the fold, writing on 28 December, that 'my presence will inspire, I do not doubt, new life and vigour into the troops you command'.[13]

It was not until 2 January 1716 that James was well enough to travel. By this stage his initial optimism had worn off and he wrote a lengthy letter to Bolingbroke on this day, 'our present circumstances, which, to speak plain, are none of the best'. Any attack on Perth would have to result in a Jacobite retreat for 'it is impossible we can meet the advantages the enemies have over us in all particulars'. He implored assistance of

---

6   Mahon, *History*, I, Appendix, p. xxxix.
7   *HMC Stuart Papers*, I, p. 505.
8   W. Seton, 'The Itinerary of King James III', SHR XXI, 84, 1924, p. 266.
9   Rae, *History*, p. 352.
10   *Ibid.*
11   Campbell, *The Life*, p. 239.
12   *HMC Stuart Papers*, I, p. 485.
13   *Ibid.*, p. 484.

men, money and arms from abroad; the arrival of Berwick 'would really work miracles'. Hamilton was sent to France as 'there is much odium against him as cannot be wiped off' due to his failure at Sheriffmuir and so 'one of our only two experienced officers' who was 'certainly brave and honest' would be gone. Mar, too, was exhausted, 'he himself is very weary of that burden' and no longer wanted command of the army. James had faith him and his achievements: 'I never met with a more able nor more reasonable man ... It is wonderful how he arranged matters here, and with what dexterity he has, till now, managed all parties and kept life in so many spirits'.[14]

The small cavalcade went onto Brechin, then to Kinnard on the 4th, and arrived at Glamis on 5 January. He reached Dundee on the late morning of 6 January, making a public entry at the head of 300 horsemen, flanked by Mar and Marischal. For an hour in the marketplace there was the opportunity for the crowd to kiss his hand. In the evening he dined at Stuart of Grantdully's house. On 7 January they travelled from Dundee to Castle Lyon, seat of Lord Strathmore, dining there but lodging at Sir David Triplin's. James was at Scone, and on the 9th made a public entry into Perth where he inspected some of the troops and returned to Scone for the night. Apparently he expressed his pleasure at seeing Highland dress.[15] Yet Berwick later noted that the troops were ill-armed, badly ordered and in want of everything.[16] Mar issued a circular letter stressing James' popularity and regal bearing:

People everywhere as we have come along are excessively fond to see him and express that Duty they ought ... he is really the finest gentleman I ever knew: He has a very good Presence, and resembles King Charles a great deal...He has fine Parts and despatches all his Business himself with the greatest Exactness ... He is affable to a great degree, without losing that Majesty he ought to have, and has the sweetest Temper in the World. In a word he is every way fitted to make us a happy people.

Mar claimed he looked forward to a speedy improvement in Jacobite fortunes.[17] Mar later wrote:

Upon the Cheavalier's Arrival, we expected that our Friends would then have certainly joined us; both those who had formerly been with us and were gone Home, and those who before had given, the Chevalier not being come, as the only Reason of their not joining the Army; and also that those, to whom the reducing of Inverness, the Lord Sutherland, and those with him was committed, would have vigorously performed that Service, and then have joined us; and we had no reason to doubt, but Money, Ammunition, and Arms would immediately be sent after the Chevalier'.[18]

---

14   Mahon, *History*, I, Appendix, pp. xl–xli.
15   Rae, *History*, p. 355; Campbell, *The Life*, p. 241.
16   Parker, *Memoirs*, p. 246.
17   Patten, *History*, pp. 180–181; TNA, SP54/10/166.
18   Patten, *History*, p. 202.

Keith was less sanguine about the impact of James' arrival:

The King indeed arrived safely in the end of December 1715, after a great many dangers, but came in a very small fishing boat, with only two servants and without any of the things which we had so depended on, so what should have given our affairs the greatest life was rather a discouragement to them. Every one plainly saw that we had no assistance to hope for from France; the English were entirely suppressed, and we were in too bad a condition to be able long to resist the power of those who were combined to destroy us.[19]

Mar was to eventually agree with this verdict:

But, to our great misfortune, we were disappointed in all those our Hopes, though never so well grounded in Appearance.

The Rigour of the Season, and the great Fall of the Snow on the Hills, kept in some Measure the rest of the Highlanders from joining us. Most of those who before had excused themselves upon the Chevalier's not being come, kept still at home, now that he was come, waiting perhaps to see how his Affairs were like to succeed. Those employed for reducing of Inverness, were so far from acting with Vigour, that they made, what they called it, a Cessation of Arms with the Enemy. Some gold was sent to us in lingos [from Spain]; but the ship in which it came was stranded, and the Gold lost. Several ships came with Officers, but neither Arms nor Ammunition in any of them; so that our condition after the Chevalier's Arrival, was no ways better'd, except by the new Life his Presence gave us.[20]

Throughout January there were complaints about the severe weather. Argyle wrote of 'extreamly severe [weather], the frost is great and there is deep snow upon the ground'. Yet it hindered the Jacobites, too, with Cockburn writing, 'They get daily some few people more into Perth, but they are not considerably augmented. The badness of the weather is some hindrance to them'.[21]

Opponents were at first uncertain whether James had arrived, presumably because of the number of false alarms over the previous months and because intelligence of activity deep in Jacobite heartland was difficult to obtain. Furthermore he had shown himself to few and did not appear in public for a few days. Argyle, on 29 December, believed that he had arrived. Cockburn was less certain because he had heard conflicting accounts. As late as 3 January, Cadogan was writing that the reports were 'so various, and so contradictory in the circumstances'.[22]

Townshend was dismissive about the results of his arrival, 'thinking that he might well be discouraged by news of Preston and Sheriffmuir and even if he landed and was

19 Keith, *Fragment*, p. 24.
20 Patten, *History*, pp. 202–203.
21 TNA, SP54/11/41, 48.
22 *Ibid.*, 10/165, 169; 11/5.

to lead 20,000 men, that 'Providence which has hitherto so visibly blessed the Justice of his [George I's] cause, will continue to do it, to the Destruction of his enemies'.[23]

Scone was where Kings of Scotland had been traditionally crowned. Defoe later wrote:

> The Pretender found it very well in repair for his use. Here he lived and kept his court, a fatal court to the nobility and gentry of Scotland, who were deluded to appear for him; here I say he kept his court in all the state and appearance of a sovereign and received honours as such; so that he might say he reigned in Scotland, though not over Scotland, for a few days.[24]

It was thus apt that he played the part of King and issued several proclamations. One was for a general thanksgiving for his safe arrival, another that prayers be said for him in public, another concerning the currency, another for a meeting of a Convention and finally one for summoning all men aged 16–60 to flock to his royal standard. He also sent a declaration to be read out by all clergymen in their parish churches, though this only occurred in some of those in northern Scotland. This declaration was similar to those issued by Mar on his behalf in August and September: namely that he was the rightful king, here to save his subjects from the religious and political calamities that had ensued following the Hanoverian Succession. The Episcopalian clergy and the magistrates of Aberdeen responded positively by sending him loyal addresses on 29 December and James replied, 'I am very sensible of the Zeal and Loyalty you have expressed for me, and shall be glad to have Opportunities of giving you Marks of my Favour and Protection'.[25]

Meanwhile, Argyle was readying his army to march and assembling heavy artillery for a siege of Perth. He had, by 3 January, two 18-pounders with a further two at Edinburgh Castle. However he had to find gunners for these. Cadogan wrote, 'We only want artillery to put it into execution'. A request was sent to Berwick-upon-Tweed for ten 12-pounders and he hoped these would arrive by the 16th, and sent an aide there. He also asked Marlborough for these guns. He set 15 January as the date for the beginning of the offensive, but Cadogan put it back two days. All this artillery, he wrote, 'will in my opinion be sufficient for our enterprise on Perth'.[26] All this time he was receiving letters from Townshend, with comments on 6 January such as the necessity of 'putting in Execution, without the least loss of time, the project I then mentioned'.[27]

There had already been much discussion about whether the Jacobites could be granted any terms whatever. Townshend wrote on 27 December to allow Argyle to assure them that they would be mercifully dealt with, but could not offer any specific terms. This was better than what had happened at Preston on 13–14 November, when

---

23   LUL, Townshend, 59r.
24   Defoe, *Tour*, p. 649.
25   Patten, *History*, pp. 172–180.
26   TNA, SP54/11/4–5.
27   LUL, Townshend, 69r.

the Jacobites could surrender (and did) at the King's pleasure. This only meant that they would not be put to the sword immediately, but would be tried, and these trials for those who had surrendered at Preston, began in January and February; trials which in a minority of cases would lead to the scaffold or block. Argyle lamented that he had not had these instructions from London earlier when the Jacobites had first put out peace feelers. Had it been so, Argyle was convinced that the campaign would have ended there and then. However, now it was too late, he thought. James had landed and with his arrival very few Jacobites still in arms would now surrender themselves.[28]

There were numerous difficulties facing the government's forces. Cadogan and Argyle had had a falling out, with the former claiming that the latter lacked any plan of offensive. Argyle denied this and stated that the troops were ready once the weather was less inclement. He intended that the first objective would be Dunblane; troops would march from their various quarters rendezvousing there.[29] There were also problems with the commissariat: William Burroughs, the commissary, was unavailable leading to delays.[30] Argyle, characteristically, pleaded 'without the power of working miracles I am unable to proceed no faster than I do'.[31]

Argyle was also fearful that when he advanced, the Jacobites would send a powerful force to Strathallan and then threaten Glasgow directly. He explained to Marlborough that 'if they should put this artfully in execution, it would Disconcert us very much'. Yet this credited the Jacobites with more men and more initiative than they possessed.[32]

Argyle was being criticised by others on his own side. Rothes had written to a friend in London criticising his commander, but the substance of the letter is unknown and Argyle asked Townshend to use his influence against it. He complained to the latter about:

[The] unfortunate Dilemma that I who have the name of commanding here am reduced to, that either I must make steps that in my judgement are detrimental to the service of His Majesty and my Country, and which afterwards must appear in the eyes of the world, to be faults of mine, or by Refusing, to act by the opinion of others, draw complaints against me, that I am afraid are not without weight.[33]

He also feared that the Jacobites were far stronger than they had been, because of the impact of James' arrival. There were other reports elsewhere in Scotland about a renewed Jacobite threat. At Fort William it was noted that 'this country are now all in arms and ready to march out by the Marquis of Huntley's particular commands'. The Stewarts of Appin and 200 of Donald MacDonald's men were allegedly on the march back to Perth.[34] So they did, but at reduced numbers compared to the case on the eve of

---

28 TNA, SP54/11, 7a.
29 *Ibid.*
30 *Ibid.*
31 *Ibid.*
32 British Library Add. MSS. 61632, f. 147v.
33 *Ibid.*, Add. Mss 61136, f. 183v.
34 TNA, SP54/11, 7a, 9.

11. Statue of Rob Roy MacGregor, Stirling. Erected by a descendant. (Author's photo)

Sheriffmuir. James ordered Cameron to return home to raise all the men he could and also those of the adjoining clans. Cameron went but on his return, a few weeks later, learnt that it was too late.[35]

There was some limited aggression on the part of the British forces. Dunfermline was taken and garrisoned with 200 infantry and 80 dragoons. By 7 January it was reinforced by another 150 troops, for the county militia there were slow in rising.[36] Cadogan had troops stationed in Kinross and Burleigh House as well as having men in houses between Queensferry and Perth in order to secure communications.[37] Meanwhile, Jacobite posts were being pulled back to Perth; on 12 January Mar wrote to Gordon, 'I do not see how any of our people can be safe in Fife, and tis hard to lose our men at this time'.[38]

Not all expeditions against the Jacobites were successful. Thirty of Rothes' volunteers and a company of Dutch infantry went to Falkland Palace. They were led into a trap and surrounded, leading to the Dutch surrendering.[39] This may have been the same incident as that where Rob Roy decoyed troops at Merkins, when a total of a dozen Swiss infantry and 18 militia found themselves trapped in an enclosure and barnyard. Rob Roy had 60 men, and though two were killed, two of the Swiss were wounded and the remainder surrendered.[40]

Argyle was not certain how easy it would be to take Perth from the Jacobites. He thought that it would only be simple if they 'do not act with common prudence' but otherwise, if they 'take the measures which I would do if I were in their place' it could be so much different. The Jacobite record of military achievement to date had not been impressive and Mar's military acumen was rather less than Argyle's, so Argyle was being, once more, unduly pessimistic.[41]

Supply was another difficulty. Biscuit for the troops and forage for the horses and artillery had to be moved to Stirling with a 'proper person' to manage this. Burroughs

35 <www.lochiel.net/archgives/arch173.html>.
36 TNA, SP54/11, 7a, 16, 18.
37 Ibid., 19.
38 HMC Stuart Papers, I, p. 487.
39 Campbell, The Life, p. 247.
40 Steuart, News Letters, pp. 97–8.
41 TNA, SP54/11, 19.

was still absent. Money to pay the troops was about to run out.[42] Cadogan went to Edinburgh to deal with these issues, though it meant a delay of advancing by about five or six days.[43]

Although Cadogan was still in doubts over James' arrival as late as 7 January, by the 10th even he was convinced that it was a reality. Yet unlike Argyle, he was not perturbed, writing, 'in my humble opinion his arrival all this time will doe us very little prejudice'.[44]

The troops at their disposal were nine battalions of British infantry, which numbered on 2 January 2,895 men plus officers; seven regiments of cavalry, numbering 864 men plus officers, and then Lieutenant General Reiner Vincent van der Beck's Dutch and Swiss troops, theoretically 6,000 strong but numbering 'not over 5,000 men'. Some of these battalions were 'very compleat' but others were 'very weak'.[45] An order of battle was drawn up. They were divided into seven brigades; the first being led by Major General Evans (Kerr's Dragoons and Carpenter's Dragoons); then Brigadier Chambrier (Schlippenbach's dismounted dragoons (Dutch), Pallandt's Foot (Dutch), Chambrier's Foot (Swiss) and Sturler's two battalions of Foot (Swiss)); Brigadier Morrison (Forfar's Foot, Orrery's, Egerton's Foot and Clayton's Foot); Brigadier Stanwix (Portmore's Dragoons, Evans' Dragoons and Newton's Dragoons); Brigadier Grant (Morrison's Foot, Montague's Foot, Shannon's Foot, Grant's Foot and Wightman's Foot); Brigadier Cronstrom (Cronstrom's Foot, Rantzow's Foot (both Dutch) and Meymey's Foot and Stanhope's two squadrons of dragoons); and a reserve under Brigadier Lalande (Stair's Dragoons, Welderen's Foot (Dutch), Zoutland's Foot and Schmidt's two battalions of Foot (Swiss)).[46] All in all, there were about 9,000 men, the largest army seen in Scotland since 1650, saving Mar's at Sheriffmuir.

Argyle's British forces on 2 January 1716, were as follows:[47]

Infantry

Unit	Sergts.	Drums.	PoWs	Sick	Wounds	Ready	Total	Deserted
Forfar's	20	20	0	14	0	350	366	0
Morrison's	24	14	19	28	24	207	275	2
Montague's	20	20	13	13	13	200	232	2
Clayton's	20	20	1	6	0	232	241	0
Wightman's	20	10	0	14	1	282	297	1
Fusiliers	20	21	64	19	16	289	403	1
Shannon's	24	24	0	5	6	377	406	0
Egerton's	20	20	16	10	0	229	263	1
Grant's	20	17	0	24	4	384	412	1
Total	188	166	113	133	64	2,550	2,895	8

42 Ibid.
43 Ibid., 24a.
44 Ibid.
45 Ibid., 2a, 19.
46 Ibid., 32.
47 Ibid., 2A

Dragoons

Unit	Sergts.	Drums.	PoWs	Sick	Wounds	Ready	Total	Horses
Portmore's	6	6	2	3	2	167	177	177
Carpenter's	6	6	2	5	0	163	170	178
Evans'	6	6	3	10	7	148	168	157
Stair's	6	6	1	6	0	163	173	161
Kerr's	6	6	0	3	0	167	174	179
Total	30	30	8	27	9	808	862	852

There were, however, a few signs of dissension among the regular army. Twenty soldiers deserted, including some of the grenadiers and a sergeant from Grant's regiment from Edinburgh. Two Dutch soldiers deserted, having been bribed with two guineas each. They were caught, taken to Edinburgh Castle on 31 December, and there shot.[48] Mar was also encouraged by the deserters from both enemy armies.[49]

Against these forces, the Jacobites, having lost Seaforth's and Huntley's men, as well as many others from desertion and death, could only offer a vastly depleted force, as calculated in December/January 1715:

Infantry

Unit Commander	Strength
Sir Donald MacDonald	345
Marquess of Drummond	320
Envery	428*
Strathmore	134†
Panmure	203
Ogilvie	253
Struan	166
Invernytie	321
Cameron of Lochiel	288
Glengarry	258
Maclean	372
Appin	101
Clanranald	347
MacGregors	134
Total	3,670

* 170 at Dundee, 108 at Burntisland

† at Dundee

48   Steuart, *News Letters*, pp. 96, 128.
49   *HMC Stuart Papers*, I, p. 490.

Cavalry

Unit	Strength
Marischal	40
Linlithgow	78
Southesk	44
Rollo	67
Fife	40
Total	269

The Jacobites were outnumbered a little more than 2:1, with 4,393 men to oppose about 9,000. The odds were poor and the boot was firmly on the other foot compared to the situation at Sheriffmuir.[50]

Other concerns for the British Army were with Jacobites in the west and north of Scotland. Sutherland needed money to keep his men together. Captain Lewis Grant of Grant's was in Inverness and was worried about Seaforth and his 2,000 men, though the latter had agreed to disperse them and to cease the struggle against King George. This was soon to be confirmed.[51] There were reports that the MacDonalds of Glengarry were at Perth, and that Huntley's men were in arms again (untrue), but the movements of the Appin Stewarts and MacLeans were unclear (some were at Perth). Some of the Camerons were certainly back in their own lands.[52] Meanwhile, for the Jacobites, supply-wise, matters looked bleak, with a mere 700 weight of gunpowder at Perth.[53]

Mar wrote to Huntley on 18 January, and it is hard to know whether he really believed what he wrote or whether it was merely an optimistic spin in an attempt to regain Huntley's support. The latter is probably nearer the truth. He wrote that the French were ready to send troops and that war between England and France was imminent (Hamilton was in Paris lobbying hard, leading him to write that 'it seems they are in no want of generals at Perth'). He referred to stocks in London plummeting and mass desertions from Argyle's army. Hamilton wrote that the French would send substantial amounts of gunpowder and there were hopes for hundreds of troops and officers to be sent over. Meanwhile, James contacted Charles XII of Sweden to update him with the news of the campaign. Both were too late, however.[54] Huntley was certainly trying to gather troops and put a brave face on matters on 10 January, writing to the Lord of Carnonlie, 'I make no doubt but this will find you in a readiness to march whithersoever the King's service requires. I intend to move soon … I have reason to expect our numbers will augment'.[55]

---

50 Blair Atholl, Bundle 45, 12/97.
51 TNA, SP54/11, 30b–c, 39b.
52 *Ibid.*, 34
53 *HMC Stuart Papers*, I, p. 502.
54 *Ibid.*, pp. 490, 492, 504; TNA, SP78/160, 212.
55 NRS, RH15/1/24/13.

With the delays of artillery from the Tower, guns were assembled from locations rather nearer at hand. On 3 January, Brigadier Lewis Petit (1665–1720), an engineer, was sent to Edinburgh and Berwick by Argyle to assemble a train from the guns in the castle. These were to be 12 heavy guns (nine-, twelve- and eighteen-pounders) and six field guns of four to six pounds in calibre. With the six three-pounders, four mortars and two howitzers already at Stirling, this would make 30 guns in total. There were 20 gunners available from the pre-1707 Scottish artillery establishment as well as 50 men from the British and Dutch forces under Argyle who claimed knowledge and experience of using artillery. On 8 January Cadogan went to Edinburgh to organise the supply of 1,500 horses to drag the guns and wagons north of Stirling.[56] It was clearly envisaged that the Jacobites would make a stand at Perth and that heavy guns would be needed to make breaches in its defences prior to an attack by the infantry.

On 9 January Argyle's and Cadogan's council of war was convened to have everything ready for marching as soon as the artillery was assembled together. An order of battle was settled and copies were distributed to all field officers.[57] The Jacobites gave the appearance of confidence that the weather would be beneficent towards them, with Mar writing to Huntley that 'we have the stormiest weather and greatest snow I ever saw and that it is impossible for the enemy to attempt anything against us as long as it lasts'. That was on 18 January.[58]

It was at this juncture that James, described as a man 'with the sweetest Temper in the World' was about to put his name to another document, issued from Scone, which resulted in anything but blessings for some of his people. Stressing that it was 'absolutely necessary' in order to incommode the march of his enemies towards Perth to destroy all the corn and forage, he instructed James Graham the Younger of Braco, to 'burn and destroy the Village of Auchterarder, and all the Houses, Corn, and Forage, whatsoever within the said Town, so they may be rendered entirely useless to the Enemy'. This was obeyed. It was not only Auchterarder that was destroyed, but also Blackford, Dalreach, Crieff, Dunning and Muthill which suffered likewise between 25–28 January.[59] Such activity, of course, was to deny Argyle's forces shelter or food on their way to attack the Jacobites at Perth. It should be said that, as Mar wrote, 'I never put my hand to a paper so unwillingly' and he wrote of James, 'The burning goes mightily against his mind, but there is no help for it'.[60]

Was this a war crime? No one was killed and so it is not comparable to the massacre of Glencoe in 1692 when 38 people were slain. However, it was an operation that brought suffering to the inhabitants, especially as it occurred in the middle of winter when cold and hunger would increase the plight of those who lost their homes. Yet it was not unusual for armies to destroy civilian property as a method of attempting to make their enemy's campaigning more difficult. Marlborough had villages in

56 Rae, *History*, p. 362.
57 *Ibid.*
58 *HMC Stuart Papers*, I, p. 490.
59 Patten, *History*, pp. 182–183.
60 *HMC Stuart Papers*, I, p. 496.

Bavaria destroyed in 1704 in order to force his enemies to weaken their main army by detaching troops to defend their countryside. Recalcitrant Jacobite clans had their property destroyed by Cumberland in 1746. Dorput in Estonia was a town utterly destroyed by the Russians in 1708.[61] Naturally the Whigs made much of these burnings in their anti-Jacobite propaganda; as will be noted, Argyle was furious.[62] Perhaps the best testimony comes from Parker, commenting on the destruction of the hamlets, homesteads and villages in Bavaria a decade previously: 'Such are the effects of war, the innocent suffer for the guilty. But let those ambitious men, that occasion such things, take care how they will account for it another day'.[63]

The advance of the Anglo-Dutch army could not be long delayed. On 21 January Guest took 200 dragoons with him from Stirling to reconnoitre the roads leading to Perth as a prelude to the army marching in that direction.[64] The roads were covered with deep snow. Three days later Argyle and Cadogan took the same route for the same reason, taking 200 dragoons with them. This caused some concern among the Jacobites and so they began to pull back their forward posts in Fife and to retreat behind the River Earn. This was despite the fact that the main Anglo-Dutch army had not yet left Stirling. Argyle took the opportunity to increase his hold on the country by posting troops at both Dunblane and at Down.[65] Meanwhile, frantic efforts were made at Perth to strengthen the defences there by planting artillery, making breastworks, and digging trenches.[66]

On the same day as Argyle's ride north, there was a sudden thaw. This was followed by a great snow which, on the roads, lay between two and three feet deep. It then froze again, rendering them almost impassable. Some officers suggested waiting until less inclement weather but Argyle had orders for an almost immediate advance. He arranged with Buchan to have countrymen clear the roads from Stirling to Dunblane as much as was possible. By the 26th, most of the guns from Berwick and Edinburgh had arrived. The train was ready to move on the 28th, and on that day Colonel Albert Borgard (c.1656–1751) and the artillery from London finally reached Leith. They decided it was pointless to unload those guns, so Borgard and his artillerymen went to Stirling and arrived on the next day.[67] The advance guard of 700 infantry and 200 dragoons under Grant were posted at Dunblane on 27 January.[68]

It was on 29 January that Argyle led the main army northwards from Stirling. According to Townshend, the importance of taking Perth lay in the fact that it would force the Jacobites into the hills 'where it will be impossible for them to keep together in a Body'.[69] Other observers thought that an advance by Argyle would lead

61 Frost, *Northern Wars*, p. 303.
62 Patten, *History*, p. 183.
63 Parke, *Memoirs*, pp. 98–99.
64 Patten, *History*, p. 184.
65 *Ibid.*
66 Rae, *History*, p. 364.
67 *Ibid.*, p. 365.
68 *HMC Stuart Papers*, I, p. 498.
69 LUL, Townshend, 73r.

to a Jacobite retreat; though one thought this would be towards Murray.[70] There was certainly impatience in London with the perceived delays, with Liddell writing, 'We long to hear off the march off our army towards Perth, which if itt please God to prosper with success will be a vast strengthening off the K's friends'.[71] This was easy to say, and William Kennedy wrote thus to a relative: 'Wee thought it very strange that our army should march at a time when the weather made it almost impossible for men to attempt anything … I am apt to think the cold will kill as many of our men as the enemy, but the court thinks it proper we should immediately dislodge them and Mr Cadogan thinks it practicable'.[72]

They reached Dunblane as first port of call, and this day being a Sunday, rested there for the remainder of the day. Meanwhile another party, with two cannons, approached Braco Castle, causing it to be abandoned by the Jacobites without a struggle. Argyle regretted this, as he had hoped to make an example of them, 'upon account of the cruell barbaritys' inflicted by them at Auchterarder and the adjacent villages. Yet because of the weather the heavy artillery, over which there had been so much anxiety and correspondence, was not taken northwards anyway; only the light guns. On the following day, the advance continued. Two hundred dragons and 400 infantry, with two cannons, marched to Tullibardine and took that post from the Jacobites. The main body of the army marched from Dunblane to Ardoch and Auchterarder. This was the closest that they had got towards Perth so far. The struggle was very much brought home to the Jacobite army. That night they were obliged to lie in the open air as the village had been mostly burnt down. This caused Argyle much concern, in part because of his worry for the welfare of his men which would impair their combat efficiency.[73]

Argyle considered what the Jacobite response to his advance would be. He thought that there were three main possibilities. Firstly they could fight his army outside Perth in open battle. Secondly, they could defend Perth, as Forster's Jacobite army had done at Preston the previous year. Or they could try to elude his own army and slip past to threaten Stirling, which would have been a bold move. Of the three alternatives he preferred that the Jacobites would fight him there and then, presumably because, with his outnumbering them (he thought that the Jacobites had 6,000 infantry and cavalry as an absolute maximum, which was an overestimate) he was confident he could decisively defeat them in battle.[74] He did not foresee what actually did happen.

Mar was aware on 26 January that Argyle planned to march on the 29th, and on 27 January that probing forces had been making their way north of Stirling, yet he concluded that they had found movement impracticable and that baggage horses had been sent back. Although he could not tell how long the snow and frost would last, he thought it would delay Argyle by at least 10 days. He thought that this would give the Swiss long enough to desert in significant numbers and apparently there was a

---

70   Cowper, *Diary*, p. 66.
71   Ellis, 'Liddlell-Cotesworth Correspondence', p. 220.
72   Tayler, *Seven Sons of the Provost*, p. 81.
73   Patten, *History*, p. 185; TNA, SP54/11/68.
74   *Ibid.*

Jacobite agent spreading dissension and disaffection among them, though at this time there was only one, and he a prisoner, who definitely had done so.[75]

Despite all Argyle's difficulties, the Jacobites had many of their own. With an army reduced to perhaps 3,000 infantry and of those 1,000 'very indifferent', and allegedly but almost certainly far fewer than 700–800 cavalry, 'and for these not ammunition for one day's action', it was thought best not to make a stand at Perth. Mar put Jacobite numbers at 4,000 and of these, only 2,500 were 'good fighting Men'. As Keith later wrote, 'neither our troops nor our half raised fortifications being in a condition to resist him'. James however, was in favour of defending the city or marching out for battle.[76]

James was woken at two in the morning of the 30th January with news that Argyle was marching towards Perth. A council of war was thus held, interrupting any discussion of James convening a Parliament or planning a coronation. The question was whether to fight or to retreat. Most of the officers and soldiers were enthusiastic for a clash of arms, 'so keen for fighting that they could not be restrained'. Mar disagreed with this and with his king, explaining that the great expectations of support from Ormonde's projected rising in the south-west had come to nothing and that there had been no aid from abroad.[77]

He also thought that the city was indefensible, 'little better than an open Village' and whilst there was a river on one side and a ditch on the other, both were frozen over and so passable by troops. Berwick later noted that the city had 'no other fortifications than a simple wall'. Frost had put the mills out of operation so the defenders only had two days worth of bread, and there was little in the way of fuel. They were outnumbered and 'the Highlanders are not used to defend Towns', though their allies in the south had initially repelled the attack on the first day of the fighting at Preston three months previously. Sinclair wrote 'where they are invested and see no retreat, I am of opinion that none are capable to make a more vigorous defence in a breach, for they fire as well as any, from under cover against attackers, and in the melee, which must happene in a storm, their sabres are dangerous weapons'. To fight in the open was also impractical because there was no advantageous position or pass to defend and so the numerically superior enemy could have surrounded them and prevented all chance of a retreat.[78]

So, as Mar concluded, 'All this put us into an absolute Necessity of leaving Perth and retiring Northwards, which we did in good order'. Instead, the stated aim was to march to Inverness and retake the city, which it was deemed an easy matter to have done, then fight there, 'and so put the affair to the decision of a battle'.[79]

Apparently 'warm debates' followed among the advocates for fighting immediately. The council was adjourned. A few hours later, Mar brought a select few together. He still advocated retreating, but suggested letting the army know that this was in order

75 Rae, *History*, pp. 486–487; *HMC Stuart Papers*, I, p. 497.
76 Keith, *Fragment*, p. 26; Patten, *History*, p. 203.
77 Rae, *History*, p. 366; *HMC Laing MSS*, p. 183.
78 Parker, *Memoirs*, p. 246; Patten, *History*, pp. 203–204; Scott, *Memoirs*, p. 130.
79 Keith, *Fragment*, p. 26.

to fight later at a more favourable moment; at Aberdeen, where supplies were expected from abroad.[80] James later rationalised the decision made there:

> Many friends at home were slow of declaring, the defeat at Preston and the securing of many loyal nobility and gentry deprived us of all succour from the south, and at the time we wanted so much necessaries from abroad for the men by ourselves here, the delay of them and the want in equalities twixt us and the enemie made our retreat from Perth unavoidable … to have stood it then would have only served to sacrifice you all without any possibility of success.[81]

Ironically on the same day, the government feared that 600 French officers were about to board ship at Calais for Scotland, with money and other equipment. They subsequently instructed naval vessels to attack any such ship, but in the event none ever came.[82] They were ordered back to their regiments.[83]

The Jacobites departed from Perth at 10:00 a.m. of the morning of 31 January. As the Tay was frozen, they were able to march over the ice without difficulty, thus hastening their departure. James and Mar were among the last to leave, exiting at about noon.[84] Apparently James had tears in his eyes, 'complaining that instead of bringing him to a Crown they had brought him to his Grave'. When he told this story to Prince Eugene of Savoy in later years, the Prince replied that 'weeping was not the way to conquer Kingdoms'.[85]

Yet the plan for a subsequent offensive in the north relied on Argyle's pursuit being slow and thus allowing the Jacobite army time to rest and regroup. This did not happen: on 31 January Argyle's men crossed the River Earn without any opposition and advanced to Tullibardine, only eight miles from Perth. There was a small Jacobite garrison there of an officer and 50 men. They fired a few ineffectual shots at Argyle's men. The Duke had two four-pounders brought up to cannonade them, as well as an officer and 10 grenadiers, but on seeing this they surrendered and were sent as prisoners to Stirling. At 4:00 p.m. that afternoon Argyle learnt of the Jacobite flight from Perth, so ordered an advance guard of 400 dragoons and 1,000 infantry to proceed towards the Jacobites' former headquarters, and they arrived at 10:00 a.m. on the morning of the first day of February. Cadogan and Argyle arrived the same day. The remainder of the army, because of the poor weather and atrocious roads, did not reach Perth until the evening. A few Jacobites had remained, drunk on brandy, and so were made prisoner.[86] Anything heavy or difficult to move quickly had been abandoned by the

80   Rae, *History*, p. 367.
81   *HMC Stuart Papers*, I, p. 506.
82   Hill, 'Side Light', p. 232.
83   NRS, GD220/5/624.
84   Patten, *History*, p. 185.
85   Rae, *History*, p. 367.
86   Keith, *Fragment*, p. 26; Patten, *History*, p. 185; Rae, *History*, p. 367.

Jacobites, including 18 iron and three brass cannon, which were thrown into the river, as well as carriages and baggage.[87]

Both Argyle and Cadogan sent the news of the possession of Perth to London independently of one another. Argyle sent the news to Major James Stewart (*c*.1681–1743), who had been his ADC at Sheriffmuir, and he received a bounty of £500, whilst Cadogan sent one Captain Rowland Lewis Morton of Rich's dragoons, who received only £200.[88]

This was all of great interest to newspaper readers and others in England. Jacobites found initial consolation in rumours such as those told to Henry Prescott of Chester: 'Mr Yates comes and reads us probable letters of Lord Marrs success, Argyle defeated, the Swiss cut in peeces'. Similar stories persisted for a few days in early February.[89]

Later misinformation had the Jacobites defeated and Mar a prisoner. On 6 February Townshend wrote to Argyle to pass on to him George I's 'great satisfaction' with his taking Perth, and the pursuit of the Jacobites.[90] Liddell was also pleased with the news, writing that 'Cadogan was in pursuit and doubted not giving a good account off them'. In Newcastle, Liddell's friend, William Cotesworth, had the church's 'great bells' rung through the night 'which sufficiently proclaims our success throwout that neighbourhood'.[91] Similarly at Chester on 10 February, 'The Bells presently publish the success. Joy and despair part the Town'. Apparently Chester Jacobites consoled themselves that the Jacobite retreat was part of a highly cunning strategy and it took several days until the truth sank in.[92] Monsieur d'Iberville, the French envoy in London, 'says amongst his Cronies that the Pretender's Retreat from Perth is all a Feint, and was concocted in France only to prolong the Time till the Regent if France can succour him openly'.[93] In London 'there was not a word that was loyal but what met with the greatest Acclamations'.[94]

It had been envisaged that the campaign would be lengthy. Sir Robert Anstruther provided 50,000 rations of hay and corn for the army marching to Perth. Yet, because the Jacobites had rapidly abandoned Perth, Anstruther's provisions were largely wasted.[95]

Should the Jacobites have stood their ground at Perth? The men seemed to be resolute but would have been outnumbered two to one – and at Sheriffmuir had not been able to win outright when they had twice their opponents' numbers, so to fight in the open and to win looked unlikely. Whether a siege might have been ultimately more successful is another question. Argyle's light artillery might have taken a few days to batter away at the Jacobite defences and by then would the attackers have been in a fit state to take the offensive? Argyle's men would have had little to cover

---

87 Steuart, *News Letters*, p. 119.
88 *Calendar of Treasury Books*, XXX, part 2, 1716 (London: HMSO, 1958), pp. 123–4.
89 McNiven, 'Prescott's Diary', pp. 490–491.
90 LUL, Townshend, 77r.
91 Ellis, 'Liddell-Cotesworth Correspondence', p. 223.
92 McNiven, 'Prescott's Diary', II, pp. 492–494.
93 Cowper, *Diary*, p. 70.
94 *Ibid.*, p. 69.
95 *Journal*, p. 553.

themselves on the icy nights, so their fighting ability would have been reduced. On the other hand, the limited quantity of supplies would have made the Jacobites' ability to hold out to be a mere two days, even without any fighting. As ever in war, nothing can be certain. The decision to retreat, though, rendered the burning of the Perthshire villages as pointless as it was ruthless.

At Perth Argyle was met by loyalists from his own clan under Colonel Alexander Campbell, and Argyle sent these men forward to Dundee; they arriving at Perth before he had.[96] On 2 February there was no let up of the pursuit. Leaving Wightman at Perth with 900 men, Argyle advanced with six squadrons of dragoons, three battalions of infantry and a further 800 infantry from various battalions (possibly from grenadier companies). They reached Errol that day. On the next day this advance guard was at Dundee, which their fellows reached on 4 February. On the 3rd, Argyle had sent a detachment forward to Arbroath, within eight miles of Dundee. Next day Major General Joseph Sabine (c.1661–1739) with three battalions, 500 infantry from various battalions and 50 dragoons, took two routes to Montrose: one via Brechin the other via Arbroath. Colonel Jasper Clayton, with a further 300 infantry and 50 dragoons, marched to Brechin. Both officers were authorised to set the country people at work to clear the roads for the main forces behind them.[97]

Argyle did not think he would be able to overtake the Jacobites, for they could march three miles to his men's one. At least the weather was fine, but deep snow had prevented the heavy artillery, over which there had been so much fuss, from being moved northwards, so he hoped that the guns would not now be needed. Carts loaded with ammunition for the infantry were also slow moving so their supply was thus limited. Yet he would pursue the Jacobites until they dispersed, noting that 'they desert daily' and 'their Highlanders desert very much'. Yet some of the men under his command went over to the Jacobites, including Captain Elphinstone of Grant's. Argyle also believed that James would embark for France. Fort William should be reinforced, he thought, in order that the garrison could act offensively against the Jacobites.[98]

Montrose was not a place easily defended, but it did possess an excellent harbour. It had been near here that the French ships carrying troops and James himself had arrived in 1708, in what proved to be an abortive invasion attempt. The town was 'a sea port' and had 'a considerable trade'. It could have been somewhere to receive aid from abroad and if the Jacobites had desired to stay there, believing that Argyle would halt for a considerable time at Perth, they could have done so. In the meantime, the wounded Panmure was advised by James at Dundee to take ship to France, and finding a ship at Arbroath, he did so.[99]

At Montrose on 4 February, Mar had evidently come to the conclusion that the army's military prospects were minimal. He therefore advised James to depart to France while he still could. Mar believed that support from the north was uncertain

---

96   Rae, *History*, p. 368.
97   Patten, *History*, p. 186; Rae, *History*, p. 368.
98   TNA, SP54, 11/68, 81, 89.
99   Patten, *History*, p. 204.

for Huntley and Seaforth had probably already come to terms with the government and even if this were not the case neither's forces were well provided with arms and ammunition. To take to the mountains at the present inclement season of the year was not an option either, for there would be neither cover nor provisions for the army there, nor any forage for the horses. James must either take ship at Montrose or risk capture. Once he had gone, the British might lose their ardour and so give the army respite and thus time to regroup. James could then return with foreign support in the spring when the campaigning season began again. Or if worst came to worst, the Jacobites could seek reasonable terms from their enemy, which would not be possible if James remained on British soil.[100] Mar also thought that because Argyle did not cease his march at Perth that he meant to follow them to the end, and that because Inverness was in loyalist hands the Jacobites would not be able to seize it before Argyle reached them.[101] Not all were so despondent: Gordon of Glenbucket wrote, 'so for God's sake let us do something worthy of memory, if we fall, let us die like men of honour and reputation. Our cause is good and just'.[102]

James 'was still extremely unwilling to leave his Loyal people, who had sacrific'd their All with so much Zeal and Alarcity for his Service', but was impressed by the force of Mar's arguments, though he sought the counsel of others. 'He therefore at last told them, that he was sorry to find himself obliged to consent to what they desired of him'. Marischal and Mar also conversed on this matter and the former disagreed with Mar's assessment of the situation. He admitted that it was serious, but not critical. He believed that the Jacobite army would gain support in the north to the extent it would soon have an additional 7,000 infantry and 400 cavalry, which would make them equal in numbers to Argyle's forces. They could procure additional ammunition at Aberdeen (though if this really were the case then why had it not been found months earlier?) If the army fought they might win and even if they lost they would be in no worse a state than they were now. He added that James was not in any danger because he could always escape from the west of Scotland. In conclusion, he told Mar, that 'he did not think it for the King's honour, nor for that of the Nation, to give up the same without putting it to a tryall'.[103]

Mar initially agreed with Marischal and said he would try to dissuade James from leaving. Yet there was a ship, the *Maria Teresa* of St. Malo, of 90 tonnes, bound for France in the harbour and was designed to convey a Jacobite messenger to a foreign court. It was small and could take only a few passengers. James had to decide who would go with him. He named Mar, who initially refused, but James argued that if he did not leave then the others might obtain better terms, and 'as Things now stood, he could be no longer of any use to them in that Country', so he submitted. James also ordered Drummond, then lame from a horse fall, to accompany them. He also desired that Tullibardine and Linlithgow come along, but both were several miles away, as

100 Keith, *Fragment*, p. 27.
101 *HMC Stuart Papers*, I, p. 508.
102 *Ibid.*, p. 507.
103 Keith, *Fragment*, p. 28; Patten, *History*, p. 206.

were Clepham, Marischal and others that James wanted to go with him. Eventually the master of the ship, becoming fearful, put to sea.[104]

Mar was despondent, and dwelt on his own role in the campaign in a revealing letter to Strowan written at some point in that day. He wrote of his military incapacity, 'I wish His Majesty had a general more capable to serve him than I wch I hope he will have soon'. He claimed that when he had met James a few weeks ago, he asked him to give the command 'to some other who had more knowledge of these matters and how soon he gets anybody who he thinks fit for it I will assure you I will render my request'. He also wrote, self-pityingly perhaps, 'During my having this honour I endeavoured all I could to please everybody, but it seems I have been not so happie to succeed in this'.[105]

There were a few final matters to be settled before departure. James wrote a commission to Gordon to be commander-in-chief, with powers to negotiate with the enemy. He also explained why he was leaving and left him with all remaining money from the paymaster. He wrote orders that compensation be paid to those who had lost their property when the Perthshire villages had been burnt, and wrote to Argyle to compensate those who had suffered in this way. James regretted the necessity for such an action 'which had been thought necessary to be done to prevent the Enemy's March'. He also left a letter for Argyle, explaining how the money should be distributed.[106]

At 9:00 p.m. that night James and Mar took a small boat out to the ship, which by now lay a mile off the coast. Marischal and Clepham arrived at the shore but were unable to leave, not finding a boat. James waited until 11:00 p.m. for them but dared not stay any longer, fearing that Royal Navy vessels might intercept them, so the little ship left Scottish waters by daybreak of the 5th.[107] A few others left with James and Mar: the Earl of Melford, Drummond, General Sheldon and another 10 gentlemen. They arrived seven days later at Waldam near Gravelines between Dunkirk and Calais.[108] Once in France they arranged for two ships to be sent to Scotland to bring off any Jacobites who wished to leave; more oddly a ship with arms and ammunition was finally despatched.[109] Yet a ship with officers from Calais was stopped by winds.[110] Orleans, however, had already declared that France wished to be at peace with Britain and in the following month even sent congratulations to the Dutch on the Jacobite defeat.[111]

Their departure went unannounced. Gordon marched both infantry and cavalry six miles apart from one another, with the cavalry as a rearguard. The command was executed quickly but with great confusion as rumours flew throughout the men. Some believed that an attack by Argyle was imminent and others were nearer to the mark in thinking that perhaps James had departed from them. It was not until they reached

104 *Ibid.*, pp. 206–207.
105 NLS, ADV MS 13.1.8/48.
106 Patten, *History*, pp. 207–208; *HMC Stuart Papers*, I, p. 505.
107 Patten, *History*, p. 208.
108 Rae, *History*, p. 369.
109 *HMC Stuart Papers*, II, p. 3.
110 *Daily Courant*, 4462, 8 Feb. 1716.
111 *Daily Courant*, 4459, 4 Feb. 1716; *Weekly Remarks*, 17 March 1716.

Stonehaven that it was known for definite that James had left Scotland. A general meeting was held that afternoon, and it was controversial. In the letter that James had left them, he thanked his followers for their services and wished them well, but explained that disappointments, especially from abroad, had led him to reach the decision that he had taken. Matters were now worse than they had been because they were locked up in a corner of the country without bread, money or hope of foreign aid. James said he had not wanted to leave Scotland, but thought it the only way to save the lives of his followers and that he declared that he hoped to return to them.[112] He would, in fact, never return.

Gordon had more news: there was no money left to pay the soldiers. According to Keith, at this revelation, 'The consternation was general and in the whole body so dispirited'. There was anger and despair and talk that they had been betrayed. Apparently, the clans were 'very unwilling to part with him but Desired he might run the same fate with them'. Had Argyle arrived at that point with a mere 2,000 troops, he could have taken them all, believed Keith.[113]

A council of war was held at Aberdeen and they discussed their options. They could, as had been decided a week previously, march to Inverness and give battle there (this is what did happen to another Jacobite army 30 years later, with, for them, unhappy results). The alternative was to march into the mountains and disperse. They decided, unanimously, to march to Castle Gordon and there consult with Huntley. If he agreed to join them, they would then march on Inverness. Otherwise they would disperse. Artillery and baggage were left at Aberdeen.[114] That night 'great numbers of the gentlemen who served in the horse dispers'd, being extreamly discouraged'.[115] No one suggested making a stand at Aberdeen.

Meanwhile, Argyle had divided the remainder of the army into two columns in order that they might march all the more quickly. On 5 February he went with the cavalry by the upper road to Brechin, whilst Cadogan took the infantry to Brechin by Arbroath, the two forces uniting at Montrose on 6 February. It was on this march, at noon on the 5th, that Cadogan learnt of James' flight. This news led him to hasten his men's march and they arrived at Montrose that afternoon. Argyle reached Aberdeen on 8 February with 50 dragoons and 400 infantry; the bulk of the army also being in that neighbourhood on that same day. Learning that a number of Jacobite officers were seeking transport to France, he sent out detachments to various seaports to try to intercept them. Evans was sent with 200 dragoons and 400 infantry on this task, along with Colonel Campbell with 40 dragoons and 400 infantry, but their only capture was James' doctor at Fraserburgh.[116]

The Jacobite army had marched from Aberdeen on the morning and early afternoon of 7 February, in three columns for Keith, which they reached, via Strathbogie, on

112 Rae, *History*, p. 371.
113 Keith, *Fragment*, pp. 29–30; TNA, SP54/11/90; Rae, *History*, p. 370.
114 Keith, *Fragment*, p. 30.
115 Charles Stanford Terry (ed.), 'Allan Cameron's Narrative', SHR v, 1907–8, p. 138.
116 Patten, *History*, pp. 187–188.

9 February. Gordon sent Marischal to communicate with Huntley but received a negative response; an attack on Inverness had been considered had Huntley agreed to it. In fact, the marquess was seeking the best terms he could get from Argyle. By the 10th they were at Rhynie and then went to Strathdon on the following day, and on the 12th were at Kincairn and Badenoch. It was 'a very severe march, considering the great snow that lay on the mountains and the bad weather which came on'.[117] Two days later the army reached Ruthven in Badenoch, in the Highlands, as this site was 'judged the fittest place to dismiss our troops'. The army, which by then only numbered 400 cavalry and 500 infantry, then ceased to exist. The chiefs wrote a letter to Argyle, seeking clemency, which was never answered. It was 14 February. Keith added, 'From there every one took the road pleased him best'. About 100–120 of the officers, who had most to lose and least chance of forgiveness, rode to Burgh in Murray in the Western Isles and eventually took ship to France on 20 April. On 19 February Sir Robert Pollock at Fort William could announce that the Jacobites had wholly dispersed and had returned home.[118]

On 13 February Colonel Alexander Grant of Grant's battalion informed Argyle that he had taken possession of Castle Gordon and that Gordon and the main body of the Jacobite army had marched up Strathspey and Strathdon, which made him believe that they were dispersing. There were some final acts of resistance: on Skye, Brigadier Campbell formed a body to resist the British troops, but on the advance to the latter, his men fled and so he surrendered his sword and thus became a prisoner.[119]

Some, still hoping for aid from Huntley and Seaforth, however, had wanted to fight on by taking Inverness and these included Sir Donald MacDonald and the Appin Stewarts. Their wishes came to nothing, however.[120]

Once Argyle was at Aberdeen, and on hearing reports of the dispersal of the Jacobites either to their homes or in the case of numerous officers, to France, he decided that he did not need to march all the army to Aberdeen. Over the next few days he received in person and by letter several offers of surrender, and requests for mercy. As before he could only reply that he personally could not give any assurances. Troops and civil magistrates were to search for and arrest any Jacobites found still to be in arms. Four regiments of dragoons were ordered to Inverness, and castles (including those of Seaforth and Mackintosh) were garrisoned by troops and militia. Sutherland would disarm the Seaforth men and troops began to march to numerous towns in the Highlands. The task now was to disarm the Jacobites and return the country to obedience to George I. For once Cadogan was in agreement with Argyle.[121]

Argyle's work was over. He was feeling unwell, not surprisingly after five months of a physically and mentally demanding campaign and requested that he might return to London. Permission was granted on 17 February as it was deemed by Townshend

---

117 Keith, *Fragment*, pp. 30–32.
118 Keith, *Fragment*, pp. 30–32; Patten, *History*, p. 188; TNA, SP54/11/132; *HMC Stuart Papers*, II, pp. 111–112.
119 TNA, SP54/11, 144A, 156B
120 Terry, 'Narrative', p. 140.
121 TNA, SP54/11, 96, 106, 120, 126B.

that the King's affairs there had been settled, and he left Aberdeen on 24 February, arriving at Edinburgh two days later.[122] In April 'His Grace has been receiv'd at court with much esteem and the little artifices wch were us'd by his Enemys in his absence to extenuate the Glory his Services might expect, have hade no other effect, than lessening their own interest'.[123]

Although many Jacobites continued to surrender in February and March, some did not. There was a report of some hiding in the Braes of Mar at the end of February; Marischal, Sir Donald MacDonald and Linlithgow allegedly had small parties with them still. Some chiefs prevented 'the meaner sort of peoples submitting and bringing in their arms'. Few officers surrendered their weapons. It was not easy to deal with them for as Cathcart wrote, 'they shift about amongst their tenants never having nights together in one place' in Perthshire. The season did not make such searches any easier, but Wightman on 10 March was planning to make an incursion into the Highlands against them. Those who resisted could be dealt with severely.[124]

Although progress was made with the business of disarming (the Camerons handed in weapons and elsewhere, guns and swords were surrendered) by the assistance of the clergy, who preached the need to do so from the pulpit, other measures were also needed. Some of the MacDonalds were reluctant to comply and they assembled to the number of 200–300. Colonel Zoutland took 300 men against them and they dispersed to the mountain. Zoutland's men then burnt the laird's house and took his sheep and cattle, to be distributed among his men. According to Cadogan, 'This Example has had a very good effect'. Other MacDonalds later surrendered to Cadogan in early April.[125]

There was a report about a French ship seen off the Isle of Uist and a rumour that it had 1,500 stand of arms, as well as money for the Jacobites from Spain, and this was taken by a naval vessel. Cadogan did not think this would encourage the Jacobites to make a stand, but if they did he would oppose them. Troops marched to the Isle of Skye, Bernera and elsewhere to show the Jacobites that they meant business and Cadogan urged them to take fire and sword to villages near Morvern, Sunart and Ardnamurchan if they continued in rebellion. Towards the end of April Cadogan could confidently write, 'There remains now not one single clan in rebellion and the Highlands being so intirley reduced that a subaltern with 30 men might with safety go all over them'. All that was needed now was to have forts built in the Highlands.[126]

By the end of February, Dutch and British troops had been stationed in various towns in Scotland to ensure that the rebellion was at an end. Aberdeen had two battalions of British and two of Dutch infantry there and two squadrons of dragoons. Inverness had two battalions of British and Dutch stationed there. Glasgow, Perth, Dunkeld, Dumbarton, Fort William, Stirling, Dundee, Elgin, Montrose, Fife, Edinburgh, Arbroath, and Brechin were also garrisoned. Cadogan returned to

122 LUL, Townshend, f. 81r.
123 NRS, GD27/6/15.
124 TNA, SP54/11. 169, 170, 173A; NRS, GD44/51/167/4.
125 *Ibid.*, 215, 219.
126 *Ibid.*, 224, 236, 241.

Edinburgh on 1 May, thinking his job there done.[127] By that time the Dutch and Swiss were withdrawn from Scotland, Cadogan noting, 'there was no further occasion for them there' and by June they had left Britain.[128]

The Dutch forces had been expensive, costing £126,033 4s 9d, as well as a further £14,662 14s 7d for purchasing 998 tents and other equipment for them and transporting them to England. The return trip cost another £3,661 15s 9d, including provisioning. Some had died and some had deserted and it was reported that 'The said Troops at their Return, were extremely lessn'd in their numbers'. There were also allegations that the contractor and agents employed by the government in equipping and provisioning them had been corrupt, but the enquiry urged by the Parliamentary opposition in 1717 was dropped.[129]

Yet the end to unrest in the Highlands was not yet in sight. In September, there were reports that in the Highlands, 'many partys have been sent after them, which have generally ended in our People plundering the Country, and making the King more enemys than he had before, of which I have many complaints, and am endeavouring to address them'. General Carpenter had to deal with them. He suggested a similar solution to that proposed unsuccessfully by Argyle in the previous year, 'really my lord here will continue a petite Guerre till such a power is lodg'd in one or more persons … to promise that such as come in, submitted and gave up their arms should live quietly thereafter'. He also wanted permission to release Jacobite prisoners from gaol because if treated with clemency they might return to their previous trades and not disturb the peace.[130] Some of the 'disorders' caused by the soldiers were apparently due to faulty supervision on their officers' behalf.[131]

Throughout Britain and its colonies, celebrations took place for the defeat of the Jacobites. Often these took the form of sermons. Most focused on the iniquity of the Catholic rebels and the justness of the Protestants, liberty, and George I, but they also referred to the Battle of Sheriffmuir. The unfortunately surnamed Michael Pope's sermon at Glasgow included the following reference: 'The Surprizing success at DUNBLAIN … were by divine order. The conduct and valour of our Victorious Generals, as well as the Fidelity and Courage of the loyal Soldiery, must be remember'd with Gratitude and Joy'.[132]

On 13 November 1716, Dudley Ryder noted in his diary: 'Supped at sister's. Whilst we were at supper there passed by through the streets a mob with the effigy of the Pretender holding a taper in one hand and a gallows in the other, with a pair of wooden shoes hanging on them. It seems this is the day that the rebels were beat last year at Dunblane'.[133]

---

127 Rae, *History*, pp. 372–373, 375.
128 TNA, SP54/11/236.
129 *Political State*, XIII, pp. 695–698, 704.
130 TNA, SP54/12, 160A, 179, 171a.
131 NRS, GD248/46/7/50.
132 Michael Pope, *A Thanksgiving Sermon for the Suppression of the late Rebellion* (Bristol/Glasgow, 1716), p. 25.
133 Matthews, *Diary*, p. 363.

Recently historians have stressed that the government was neither weak nor savage in its treatment of the Highlands in 1716, as was not the norm hitherto. What retribution there was fell mainly on the Catholics in northern England, and even this was less than that meted out to the unsuccessful rebels in south-western England in 1685. This policy was dictated by the good sense that civil society needed to be knitted together after the traumatic experience of rebellion. Clemency was thus indicated. Furthermore, Scottish Whig elites were Scottish as well as Whig and were ready to come to terms with their Jacobite neighbours.[134]

Jacobite prisoners taken in Scotland at Dunfermline, Sheriffmuir, and at other places were housed in various castles, including those of Edinburgh, Stirling and Blackness, and were also held at Glasgow, Perth and Fife. In January Argyle had been concerned about these men and thought they were very troublesome and potentially dangerous, so wanted them moved to England, but nothing came of this. At the end of March there were over 250 in Edinburgh and 343 in Glasgow. They were told that they could petition to be transported to the American colonies and the Caribbean islands, but only 28 took up this offer. Most claimed to have been pressed into the Jacobite army and then to have deserted. Prisoners became sickly and infection was feared, so many wanted them moved away.[135]

Surgeons were employed to provide medical care for the Jacobite prisoners. John Knox, surgeon, provided £55 15s worth of medicines to the prisoners at Edinburgh. Patrick Crawford, who had aided the wounded of the regular army, also provided medicine for the prisoners at Stirling and was later paid £32 15s 10d.[136]

The British state was not geared to hold large numbers of men in captivity for any length of time, and had not done so since 1685, but that is what it had to deal with in 1715–1717. By October 1716 all of the Jacobites captured in England had been tried, at Liverpool (in February and October 1716) and in London (in February and June 1716), and many had been transported to the Americas. A few had been executed.[137]

On 20 January 1716, John Bowman pointed out what was the matter with the prisoners in Scotland:

> We wish how soon something were done with them and they brought to a tryall and we released of the burden of them and so much on account of the charge of their maintenance which we are very unable to bear. As that they being so crowded together in rooms, and the weather hot, are generally very sickly and nasty and many of them have ulcers which may prove dangerous and infectious.[138]

Many prisoners held in Scotland were released without trial throughout 1716. In May and June those Jacobite prisoners taken in November 1715 on their desertion

---

134 Szechi, *1715*, pp. 198–250; Sankey, *Prisoners*, pp. 59–156; Oates, *Last Battle*, pp. 165–181
135 TNA, SP54/12/31, 194A, 236.
136 *Journal*, p. 554.
137 Sankey, *Prisoners*.
138 TNA, SP54/12/35.

12. Carlisle Castle. Jacobite prisoners were held here after the battle. (Author's photo)

from the Anglo-Scottish army in late October and subsequently held in Glasgow and Edinburgh were set at liberty. On 16 August, a further 70 Jacobite prisoners held in Edinburgh and Stirling were ordered to be set free. These men were described as being of the 'common sort'. More were released in October, 35 from Edinburgh and 30 from Stirling. This was probably on the grounds that holding them in gaol was expensive (Stirling residents complained of this in August about the 34 men sent from Tullibardine on 31 January to the Tolbooth Prison in Stirling), and might cause an outbreak of disease.[139] Some were taken to London, being guarded by a sergeant Baugh and 91 men.[140]

Others escaped. On 11 September Carpenter noted that some had escaped from the Tolbooth Prison. Eleven were recaptured by his soldiers. Carpenter referred to the would-be escapees as 'wretched creatures, almost starved … neither worth hanging or keeping'.[141]

Some of the Scottish prisoners were then sent to Carlisle Castle for trial (including 19 taken after Sheriffmuir, named in appendix IV): those from Stirling and Blackness on 3 September, and those from Edinburgh two days later. Horses were provided for the elderly and infirm. They were also given a few days notice so they could have money, horses and other comforts with them. Carpenter was to supervise their voyage.[142]

As with the other Jacobite prisoners, they were tried outside the assize courts by a special commission of oyer and terminer which was appointed to sit there in November. The judges were Mr Baron Sir Robert Price (1665–1733) of the Exchequer,

---

139 *Ibid.*, SP55/5, 162, 173–174, 209–211; SP55/6, pp. 1–4; SP35/6, f. 11r.
140 *Journal*, p. 553.
141 TNA, SP54/12/171A.
142 *Ibid.*, SP54/12/133, 135, 152C.

Mr Justice Robert Tracy (1655–1733) of the Common Pleas and the Lord Chief Baron Smith.[143] To assist them in the prosecution were Robert Craigie and Alexander Gairden, advocates.[144]

It was not envisaged that this would be what the state's enemies could define as a bloody assize as had occurred during James Stuart's father's reign in 1685 after an unsuccessful rebellion then. Stair had written earlier that year, 'Some examples and severe ones are necessary, but I hope it won't be carried so far as yt justice may have no air of cruelty or revenge'.[145] Townshend wrote to the judges on 19 November thus: 'there should be examples made of three of the most notorious of those who will be condemned, and that those three should, if possible, be persons of different conditions … as to all the rest of the prisoners in general, who may be condemned … you are to reprieve them until such time as His Royal Highness' pleasure shall be known'.[146] Sir Thomas Calder wrote that there would be very few at Carlisle, if any, who would suffer the lot of traitors, for there was insufficient evidence against them and that they were favourably represented to the King.[147]

The trials opened at Carlisle on 7 December. Since Price was ill, Tracy made a short charge to the grand jury, stating both the legality and reasonableness of the trials taking place. Carlisle being near Scotland made it easy and inexpensive for Scottish witnesses to attend, and the jury at Carlisle could be relied upon to be free of Jacobite sympathy. A true bill was found against 11 of the defendants. They were encouraged to plead guilty so as to hope for mercy, but in doing so their lands would be forfeit. The trials began three days later and the grand jury found the indictments.[148]

The Scottish advocates who were defending the prisoners made use of several arguments. They contested that the court's jurisdiction was invalid and that the trials were contrary to the judicial provisions of the Act of Union, which was to preserve the separation of the English and the Scottish legal systems. Moving Scottish prisoners who were accused of crimes in Scotland to an English jurisdiction was surely invalid because English treason legislation did not apply to Scotland. Bills of ignoramus were beginning to be found. The judges discussed this matter with the King's solicitors.[149]

Thirty-four of the prisoners were released without trial by royal clemency, even though there were witnesses against them. Of these, John Paton of Grandham made a speech praising the King's merciful nature. Thirty-two were brought to trial. William Hay complained about the legality of the court's jurisdiction, but later withdrew his complaint. All but one of the prisoners pleaded guilty. Tulloch of Tanachie pleaded not guilty and could bring witnesses to show that he had been forced into the rebellion. On 24 December the grand jury was dismissed and so no further bills were presented to the prisoners. Of the others, 24 were sentenced to death, but no date for the sentences

143 Rae, *History*, p. 387.
144 TNA, SP55/5, p. 110.
145 NRS, GD220/5/624.
146 TNA, SP44/118, p. 332.
147 NRS, GD205/38/8/1.
148 Henry Paton (ed.), 'Eight letters by William Nicholson of Carlisle', SHS, *Miscellany*, 1893, pp. 523–525.
149 *Ibid.*, pp. 526–531.

was announced. In June 1717 an indemnity was passed and so all the prisoners at Carlisle were released, as were those in gaols elsewhere in England. The only man hanged in Scotland for his part in the rebellion was former sergeant Ainsley, for his attempt in trying to assist in the seizure of Edinburgh Castle. He was executed on 24 December 1716, after confessing that he had given into greed rather than being motivated by any loyalty towards James Stuart.[150]

After 1716 the government was still apprehensive about a future insurrection in Scotland. Additional forts were built near Inverness: Fort George, and to the west, Fort Augustus. General Wade built an extensive network of military roads and bridges throughout the Highlands. A Highland regiment named the Black Watch was founded. The victory in 1715–1716 had not been a definitive one, but merely one more knock-back to Jacobite hopes which were not to be wholly extinguished until 1746, though the support for that cause was far weaker then than it had been 30 years previously.

As to the campaign's participants: Mar died in exile, and though MacIntosh escaped gaol he was later imprisoned for life. Bolingbroke and Ormonde were pardoned. Other Jacobite officers took part in the Forty Five and some perished on the battlefield or on the scaffold; others, such as Sinclair, lived quietly. Keith went into the Prussian service and rose to the rank of field marshal. Wightman defeated the Jacobites at Glenshiel in 1719 and ended the next Jacobite campaign. Others' subordinates met with mixed fortunes in Scotland decades later. Lord George Murray became Charles Stuart's premier lieutenant general. Hawley rose to the rank of lieutenant general though was defeated at the Battle of Falkirk in 1746; fellow colonel Joseph Guest became a major general and helped keep Edinburgh Castle from the Jacobite army in 1745. As for the man who would be King: 1716 was the last time James ever stepped foot in the land he wished to rule, though by fathering Charles Edward Stuart he paved the way to the final round of bloodletting on his family's behalf.

---

150 *Ibid.*, p. 535; Rae, *History*, pp. 387–388, 198; Steuart, *News Letters*, p. 152.

Conclusion

Many receive their impression of a conflict or a battle from popular culture such as films, songs or poetry. The popular impression of the First World War largely derives from a handful of poems and some popular shows, which is at odds with a more complex version of events as known to historians. The poetry of the Battle of Sheriffmuir (see appendix V) suggests that the battle was inconclusive. As is often the case, this is highly misleading.

For all the comments that the Battle of Sheriffmuir was indecisive, the conclusion to be reached must be that it was the battle which decided the campaign. This was where the armies were concentrated in Scotland under their respective commanders-in-chief. It was where a decision would be reached. Either the outnumbered Argyle would be left with an army that would no longer be in a position to act aggressively and he might be slain, or Mar would fail to do so. The former did not happen and there is no doubt about that.

The arguments that it was indecisive can be given as follows. Neither army destroyed the other; both remained intact, though inevitably battered. The left wing of both had been routed. Both commanders remained with their successful troops, and alive. This was not a Blenheim or a Killiecrankie, a Marston Moor or a Sedgemoor. The Jacobite campaign did not come to an end after the battle as it was to do at Glenshiel or Culloden. It was to be nearly another three months before Mar would concede defeat and Argyle needed more troops before he could finish the job.

It was not a tactically decisive battle. Yet strategically it was otherwise. In the two months prior to the encounter, the Jacobites had been building up their military strength in order to convert their dominance of the Highlands of Scotland into that of the dominance of the whole country. The next step would be England, as it was to be in 1745, though of course, that would be another chapter in the campaign. The Jacobites needed to move from one stage to another in order to have an opportunity for the most difficult stage of them all.

Mar had brought together a sizeable force without any need for a successful military encounter. He had achieved the first stage towards a Jacobite restoration. In part this was because he had been allowed to do so unimpeded by the forces of the British state. This was because the same state, centred on London, believed that the

13. The sign outside the Sheriffmuir Inn, close to the battlefield. (Author's photo)

main thrust of the Jacobite threat would be in England, possibly aided by France, not in Scotland. Thus the majority of its forces were stationed in England even after the Jacobite army in England had surrendered at Preston. Argyle only possessed a force that could stand on the defensive.

Initially this was not a problem while Mar amassed forces. When it came to the latter using them it was another story. Outnumbered by 2:1, Argyle was in a difficult position and one not of his making. The question is whether Mar could have been successful at Sheriffmuir. Both generals made tactical mistakes, especially in the opening phases of the battle. Argyle allowed his units to be strung out, leading those at the back to be isolated and almost unformed when attacked. His artillery was never able to fire. Mar's initial manoeuvres were confused. He was unable to use artillery or cavalry and his left flank was overwhelmed by a numerically weaker opponent. Argyle, as a professional leading professionals, made fewer mistakes whilst the amateur general, leading amateurs (enthusiastic and brave though many were) made rather more and was crucially let down by one of his subordinates. Argyle led from the front and set an example to his men but in doing so risked being killed, as had occurred at Killiecrankie for Dundee, whereas Mar kept out of the firing line. Yet perhaps Argyle felt he needed to take that gamble to be in with a fighting chance of a victory, given the odds against him.

Victory conditions and goals were never explicitly stated by contemporaries. They were different for each army. Argyle had to prevent the Jacobite army from marching south whilst keeping his own forces reasonably intact. Strategically he was, as ever, on the defensive. The Jacobites had to destroy his army or render it *hors de combat*, in order to press southwards, whilst not losing a serious proportion of their own men. They had the offensive role, strategically.

Argyle's defence was an aggressive one. He felt he needed to turn his flank to the Jacobites in order to match their line's dispositions on his right flank. This was taking a risk that the Jacobites might attack his forces in the undefended flank, but clearly thought the risk worth taking. Because troops move at different speeds and those at the fore tend to march fastest, it was another risk that the army's components would be spread apart from each other and thus some become isolated and vulnerable. The ground, too, was no parade ground in which visibility was perfect. The result was that whilst Argyle's right was in the optimum order to attack, his left was struggling to catch up as per orders, and not entirely certain where its immediate enemies were. On the left, cavalry and infantry, let alone artillery, were not in a position to support one another in defence nor attack, and though Argyle's guns on his right were equally unable to offer supporting fire, he was able to use both foot and horse to combine in what was a devastatingly successful attack, with minimum casualties to his own side against a vastly superior number of unformed troops. This was a great achievement and did much to even up the disparity in numbers between the two sides.

Mar's left was rushing forward, after a number of changes of formation over rough ground. To ask any troops to perform such manoeuvres would have been asking a lot, and Mar's partly disciplined forces were unable to do so. They were thus in a vulnerable condition to face the onslaught that awaited them and the result was bloody ruin. Yet on the left of Argyle's force there was a similar scenario, and one, too that the Jacobite right was able to exploit without any tactical skill. Raw courage and impetuosity won the day in this sector and nearly half of Argyle's army was put out of commission for the remainder of the day.

The final test was yet to come, and here professionalism scored the victory. It is not certain what the balance of forces here were. Mar had more men but quite possibly the numerical advantage was not so great. For Mar to have continued the fight would have meant taking an immediate gamble. This, to his credit, he realised. Mar was no fool. But he was let down by one of his key subordinates. Lacking the discipline of a regular army, Mar had no means to compel Glengarry to act, and failed to persuade him. As at Derby in 1745, Jacobite officers saw the campaign as a limited liability exercise when the decision was to risk all or to withdraw and postpone the final decision. As with 1745 the easier option, which might make short term sense (saving the lives of their men), but made none in the long term, was taken. Similar decisions had been taken during the campaign in England in 1715. Of course, it is easy for armchair generals three centuries hence, far away from the bloody reality of the killing grounds to make such judgements (barring time travel, they can do nothing else). Yet warfare and rebellion are violent and unsettling events in which a good many people will die. Mar was unable, but not unwilling, to exercise the necessary ruthlessness. The chance had passed and would not come again. Yet he was not to blame for this. Let down by an insubordinate, his pleadings for a final assault went unheeded and now the balance of numbers was possibly no longer in his favour or was such a small margin that a successful attack would be problematic.

Having survived the battle, Argyle only needed to wait and to accrue the additional strength that the far stronger British state could bring to bear on its opponents. Mar's numbers drained away – which they would have done in any case even in the event of a victory. By failing to win those who left would be less likely to return. There would be even less prospect of help from abroad now. Foreign powers wanted to back the winning side and before Sheriffmuir that was less easy to predict. The fact that the Jacobites in England surrendered at Preston on the day after Sheriffmuir was another big nail in the Stuarts' coffin. James' arrival, much hoped for, could not alter the strategic realities in Britain. Whether it would if he had arrived earlier is another matter, but quite possibly not. The arrival of Berwick may well have done, if he could have adapted his command to leading irregular troops, which would have been another big 'if'.

To sum up, Sheriffmuir was important for what did not happen on the battlefield, namely that Argyle was not beaten, and for what happened afterwards when Mar was. However, even a Jacobite victory would not have meant an immediate Stuart restoration, but would have made that event less unlikely and would have kept that window of opportunity open. That this did not happen meant that the Hanoverian dynasty and their Whig governments would continue to rule without any major internal military challenge until 1745, when they would be in a far stronger position vis-à-vis their Stuart rivals, despite the latter being led by the more dynamic Charles Edward Stuart. And – if this is not to sound wholly Whiggish – with nearly three decades of peace, commerce, agriculture, and population could flourish unchecked; though with restrictions on the rights of Dissenters and, more so, Catholics, as well as many discontented Scots. Whether a Jacobite restoration would have led to an independent Scottish kingdom and religious toleration for all, is an unanswerable question, though brokering religious harmony would have been difficult at best. Yet its baptism would have only been possible with an additional effusion of British blood and that was more or less checked for three decades by the sacrifices made at Sheriffmuir.

Appendix I

The British Army

Rank and file wounded at Sheriffmuir and claiming disability pensions, 1716–1746 (TNA, WO116/1-3). Where parish of origin and former occuation not known

* In years, at the time of Battle of Sheriffmuir
† Pension granted

Name	Unit	Age*	Service*	Wound	Year†
William Hughes	Montague's	24	5	Lost left arm and wounded in the head	1716
William Chambers	Montague's	33	12	Wounded in his right knee and right breast	1716
Neale Mackay	Orrery's	?	20	Cut over the nose; right arm shattered with 9 wounds	1716
Samuel Coupland	Guards	56	18½	Shot in ye left leg	1717
David Scott	Orrery's	36	9	Shot through ye neck in ye left ear	1718
Robert Lewis		41	21	Lost use of his right hand	1718
James Dawson	Montague's	19	6	His left thigh shot and miserably disabled	1718
David Gordon	Stair's	21	0	Cut in his left hand and cut in two places ye left side of his head	1718
Donald MacNaughton	Orrery's	34	13	Four cuts on his head done on ye right side of his face.	1719
Andrew Boswell	Orrery's	40	17	A bad cut on ye side of his right arm	1719
Robert Bond	Clayton's	53	12	Stabbed in the left thigh	1719
Richard Billiatt	Clayton's	46	24	Dislocation of the left shoulder	1719
Evan Jones	Egerton's	48	21	Cut on his head at his back	1719

Name	Unit	Age*	Service*	Wound	Year†
John Reynolds	Kerr's	49	16	Much bruised	1719
Peter Murdoch	Stair's	45	21	?	1719
John Young	Kerr's	47	21	Disabled in the right hand … ye thumb and middle finger	1720
Francis Rae	Montague's	42	16	Trod on left foot by a horse	1720
James Terry	Carpenter	47	25	Run along ye ribs by a sword or spade	1721
George Studders	Orrery's	32	7	Cut in five places on the head	1721
Robert Thompson	Orrery's	30	2	Six cuts on the head and stabbed in his right leg	1721
Simon Parry	Clayton's	30	1	A bruise on the right hip and a cut over his left wrist	1721
John Colson	Evans'	27	3	Shot in ye left arm	1722
John Clayton	Evans'	57	33	Cut over his right elbow, left side of his head, shot in ye calf of his leg	1722
Lawrence Hayes	Kerr's	34	15	Cut through the left side of his head	1723
Thomas William	Kerr's	41	24	Cut at the top of the little finger. Several bad wounds on his head, cut on his left shoulder	1723
John Creswell	Morrison's	40	13	Disabled in ye left arm	1723
Richard Mclaughlin	Stair's	52	21	Lost his right eye	1723
Arthur Cease	Carpenter's	45	10	Wounded in the calf of the left leg	1723
Edward Pilgrim	Montague's	34	8	Cut left side head	1723
David Powell	Morrison's	44	15	Cut in the middle of the right hand and shot in the left arm and shoulder	1723
Alexander Ogilvie	Portmore's	54	9	Wounded in ye left groyne by a Lochaber axe	1724
Hugh Highley	Carpenter's	45	13	His horse fell on his left arm and disabled that and his collar bone	1724
Samuel Severn	Carpenter's	40	9	Scar by a sword above his left wrist	1724
Donald MacKenzie	Orrery's	36	12	Cut in ye left cheek	1724
George Warren	Carpenter's	53	21	A cut in his forehead	1724
William Macgagten	Portmore's	40	15	Cut ye back part of his left leg	1724
William McKay	Orrery's	46	17	Shot below ye elbow his right arm	1724
Hugh Smith	Orrery's	24?	2?	Cut ye left side of his neck very bad	1724

Name	Unit	Age*	Service*	Wound	Year†
John Whalley	Clayton's	49	11	Ridden down by ye horse	1724
Thomas Johnston	Kerr's	47	12	Cut on his head in 2 places	1724
John Reynolds	Whetham's	53	7	Cut on ye left hand by a broadsword	1724
William Flood	Stair's	49	10	Bruise on his right knee by a fall of his horse	1726
David Syme	Forfar's	50	12	Forefinger on his right hand contracted by a shot	1726
John Baill	Clayton's	43	10	Cut across his left hand	1726
Hugh Browne	Guards	29	10	Cut up right side of his head	1726
Jacob Worth	Montagu's	41	11	Cut on his hand	1726
John Kelly	Kerr's	46	18	Cut across ye head	1726
William Bloomer	Morrison's	32	13	Cut over ye forehead	1727
William Evans	Morrison's	45	15	Shit in the forehead above the left eye	1727
Patrick McLaughlin	Montagu's	37	17	Shot through ye upper part of his left thigh and cut up	1727
Magnus Harris	Montague's	38	10	Much bruised by ye horse	1727
James Sked		29	9	Stab by a dirk in the crown of his head	1727
William McBain		38	14	Cut on the head, cut through the indent of his right thigh	1727
John Morrison		39	12	Cut at the top of his nose, and a stab to the right	1727
Thomas Gordon	Orrery's	43	22	Wounded in his head	1727
James McKay		38	9	Wounded on left side of his neck, shot	1727
David Dunbar		37	9	Small scar under his lip	1727
Duncan Campbell	Orrery's	29	9	Shot in ye left shoulder	1727
James Brown	Orrery's	37	10	Shot in ye right thigh	1727
Lachlan Ross	Orrery's	42	9	Cut on the thumb of his left hand and on the right side of his mouth	1727
Allan McClain	Orrery's	38	16	Cut on ye back side of his head also on ye right shoulder	1727
Thomas Forrest	Orrery's	48	13	Trod on by a horse near his navel	1727
Daniel McGregor	Orrery's	35	17	Cut on his left temple	1727
Alex. Abernethie	Orrery's	43	10	Bruise on his mouth by ye butt of a piece, knockt out his teeth, bruised in the breast by a horse	1727

Name	Unit	Age*	Service*	Wound	Year†
Robert Brown	Orrery's	48	24	Stabbed in the breast towards the left side, cut over the left elbow	1727
George Hutcheson	Morrison's	46	13	Bruised	1727
Hugh Cunningham	Morrison's	41	16	Wounded left side of head	1727
Patrick Garvan	Morrison's	36	11	Left arm disabled by dirk thrown, cut on right hand	1727
Robert Lindsay	Orrery's	27	8	Shot by musket ball at right side head	1727
Andrew Grierson	Orrery's	33	8	Shot in right leg	1727
William Sommcobell	Kerr's	32	10	Head wounds	1727
Michael Burk	Guards	31	10	Shot through left arm	1727
John Allison	Montague's	41	7	Stabbed by a bayonet under left side of chin	1728
John Creighton	Anstruther's	42	21	Right hip shot	1728
Walter Barr	Middleton's	41	23	Cut on ye right side of forehead	1728
Edward Lewis	Clayton's	36	6	Kick of horse	1728
William Sinclair	Montague's	43	11	Cut on forefinger of left hand and on crown of ye head	1728
James Moreton	Montague's	50	26	Left hand cut and thumb also cut off	1728
Fergus Gunnion	Stair's	47	11	Cut	1728
William Creede	Montague's	47	9	Cut	1728
John Swann	Evans'	46	7	Cut?	1728
George Brown	Evans'	35	26	Cut ye left side of head	1728
Thomas Brennan	Stair's	29	8	Left collar bone broke, cut over crown of the head	1728
Godfrey McNeil	Stair's	32	9	Right hand disabled by fall from his horse, several cuts on head	1728
Patrick McConnell	Stair's	37	9	Cut in five places in his head, also stabbed in his right hand	1728
Michael Peake	Forfar's	42	13	Shot under ye right eye, also cut under it	1728
John Sharp	Grove's	37	11	Cut on right side of his forehead	1728
Thomas Ashmal	Hartford's	37	7	Cut on ye left knee	1728
Walter Templeman	Portmore's	50	15	Shot in right leg	1728
Christopher Petty	Stair's	41	13	Cut above ye left temple and shot in the left shoulder	1728
William Atkinson	Carpenter's	44	12	Cut through left jaw	1729
Richard Gittens	Portmore's	46	26	Cut across ye left	1729
Robert Devens	Clayton's	50	15	Cut through left side of head	1729

Name	Unit	Age*	Service*	Wound	Year†
William Smith	Delamain's	36	8	Shot ye ne side of his right ankle	1729
David Ballis	Stair's	34	8	Cut ye left side of ye head, his horse shot under him	1729
Archibald Douglas	Stair's	33	8	Cut on the head, his back hurt by a fall	1729
William Hitchcock	Guards	36	13	Cut on his right cheek	1729
Joshua Scarborough	Guards	55	19	Cut through right side of his head	1729
John Mcewe	Stair's	35	8	Shot above elbow of left arm, horse shot under him	1729
John Englesham	Forfar's	45	16	Left arm bruised, right leg bruised by fall from horse	1729
William Mearns	Evans'	27	6	Disabled by cut across left hand	1729
John White	Clayton's	26	6	Shot in left thigh	1729
William Butterfield	Montague's	42	5	Wounded in ye crown of his head	1729
John Grives	Delamain's	26	8	Shot the outside of his left leg	1729
Thomas Hinds	Carpenter's	36	9	Cut through right wrist and shot through inside right leg by pistol	1729
Charles Baird	Kerr's	31	7	Wound in left arm below elbow and cut on right eyebrow	1729
William Dunn	Kerr's	24	6	Cut in his left wrist	1729
William Mclean	Kerr's	25	7	Cut in his left wrist	1729
James Napier	Portmore's	31	10	Cut on ye back of his head	1729
John Bellamy	Pocock's	29	12	Cut in ye forehead and on left shoulder	1730
John McLaughlin	Carpenter's	30	7	Cut over his left wrist, a kick of a horse	1730
Alexander Cockram	Carpenter's	42	6	Cut in the right side of his cheek and right arm	1730
Joseph Harris	Kerr's	25	6	Cut the left side of his head	1730
Thomas Stagg	Cadogan's	30	5	Cut on his left hand by a broadsword	1730
Richard Farrall	Tyrawley's	34	8	Wounded ye left side of his hand	1730
James Brae	Stair's	33	6	Cut by a sword on ye right leg	1730
Daniel King	Stair's	31	6	Cut on upper part of head	1730
James Whetham	Carpenter's	44	23	Bad cut on right wrist	1730
Thomas Johnson	Portmore's	39	15	Stab of bayonet at left side	1730
John Mcconnell	Stair's	40	7	Shot in right leg	1730
Thomas Pearson	Stair's	31	5	Cut on forehead	1730
Andrew Hentley	Stair's	31	7	Cut on right side of cheek	1730
Archibald Dunlop	Stair's	35	9	Cut over right temple	1730

Name	Unit	Age*	Service*	Wound	Year†
John Mcffanis	Stair's	26	6	Scar on corner right eye by sword pommel	1730
Duncan McGregor	Guards	35	10	Wounded left knee	1730
Tobias Tully	Stair's	31	6	Cut both sides head	1730
Thomas Graham	Montague's	31	5	Stabbed back of left hand	1730
Crawley	Carpenter's	36	13	Horse trod on him	1730
John Wilson	Carpenter's	42	8	Cut left side of head	1730
Thomas May	Stair's	26	6	Shot in ye left arm and cut left side chin	1730
John Fazakala	Montague's	34	6	Cut on left wrist	1730
Charles Wall	Stair's	33	8	Cut on his left hand and finger	1730
Henry Richardson	Stair's	32	6	Right hand quite disabled by cut of broadsword	1730
William Wiggins	Stair's	35	9	Small cut right side of forehead	1730
William Hyde	Whetham's	34	10	Shot right leg	1730
Alexander Davidson	Middleton's	45	11	Scar right side hand	1730
George Sutherland	Middleton's	46	15	Cut under right hand and shot in side of thigh	1730
Thomas Johnston	Stair's	26	6	Shot under right breast and wounded under right ear	1730
Archibald Lecky	Kerr's	26	7	Cut left side belly by a broadsword	1730
Robert Allen	Montague's	35	8	Disabled by cut	1730
William Watt	Middleton's	30	8	Shot	1730
John Asplee	Newton's	45	13	Bad cut to right side of head by a broadsword	1730
Joseph Barker	Stair's	30	5	Cut on nose and left side lip	1730
John Smith	Carpenter's	31	5	Bad cut on right wrist	1731
James Wilson	Carpenter's	39	14	Kick of horse on left shin	1731
John Griffiths	Stair's	42	5	Shot in small of left leg	1731
Thomas Singleton	Stair's	33	5	Cut in 2 places right side of head	1731
William Thompson	Stair's	46	7	Cut on right wrist	1731
James Martin	Middleton	46	13	Cut by broadsword on right leg	1731
John Fidler	Kerr's	24	0	Cut on left wrist and horse fell with him and bruised him	1731
John Dixon	Morrison's	34	7	Wounded on right leg by a broadsword, and on left thigh and on left hand	1731
John Hare	Stair's	44	13	Shot in left shoulder	1731
James Perrell	Guards	41	4	Cut on left cheek	1732

Name	Unit	Age*	Service*	Wound	Year†
George Meldrum	Portmore's	32	8	Right hand disabled	1732
William Robinson	Whetham's	29	4	Second finger of left hand split by a broadsword	1732
Ephriam Cample	Stair's	27	3	Cut ye hind part of ye head	1733
Daniel Cameron	Montague's	42	3	Back part of left hand cut	1733
James Terrey	Morrison's	20	0	Shot in right elbow and left leg	1733
James Forrest	Stair's	32	7	Wound on left side of head	1733
James Woollard	Stair's	31	1	Left hand disabled and bad cut on wrist	1733
John Atkinson	Stair's	30	7	Cut down ye tip of nose and lips and lost left eye	1733
Barnaby Harrison	Guards	34	9	Cut on ye head	1733
Robert Graham	Montague's	21	4	Left arm disabled by cut of a sword	1733
Hugh Cameron	Handasyde's	38	10	Shot in right thigh	1733
Benjamin Pinder	Cornwallis'	37	4	Shot in right arm	1733
William Scott	Carpenter's	31	7	His left hand lame by cut between his forefinger and thumb	1734
Jeremiah O'Bryan	Rothes'	37	1	Shot in ye left shoulder	1734
Richard Rowles	Clayton's	35	11	Wounded in ye forehead by ye blow of a back of a pistol	1734
William Smith	Evans'	35	7	Cut between ye wrist and elbow of his right arm	1735
James Hearne	Stair's	25	1	Cut on ye left cheek and upper lip	1735
Adam Rutherford	Rothes'	36	7	Stabbed in ye right wrist	1735
William Atkins	Morris'	23	0	A bad cut on ye back of his head and shot in ye left shoulder	1735
John Hutchins	Drummond's	36	9	A ball; scar on forehead	1735
Thomas Patty	Shannon's	31	9	Wounded in the shoulder	1735
Samuel Wilson	Kerr's	25	1	Shot in the left leg and cut on right hand	1736
William Mearing	Guards	26	0	Cut on ye right side of his head	1736
John Hill	Evans'	22	4	Cut on ye head	1736
Abraham Marks	Evans'	29	5	Cut over his left hand	1736
John Carr		42	5	Shot in ye right shoulder	1736
Andrew Johnson		20	7	Cut on the left side of his head	1736
James Higgins	Hargraves'	40	10	Cut in both legs	1736
John Holt	Page's	30	7	Cut on the left side	1736

Rank and file wounded at Sheriffmuir where parish of origin and former occupation recorded

* In years, at the time of Battle of Sheriffmuir
† Pension granted

Name	Unit	Age*	Service*	Occup.	Parish	Wounds	Year†
Robert Richardson	Montague's	35	16?	Smith	Northallerton	Shot in his left thigh and cut in ye finger	1736
John Donaldson	Stair's	34	11	Taylor	Perth	Stabbed on left arm	1736
Richard Dore	Morrison's	29	0	Husbandman	Nantwich	Shot on ye crown of his head	1736
Dormis Boyd	Morrison's	33	15	Taylor	Islay	Cut behind right ear	1736
Dane Lawler	Clayton's	41	7			Shot in ye right thigh	1736
John Stratton	Morrison's	22	2		Yorkshire	Cut on ye wrist	1736
John Pikeman	Morrison's	26	9	Glover	Draycott, Staffs	Cut	1736
Robert Rapin		28	8			Cut on the head and on right hand	1736
Denis McMullin	Morrison's	28	0	Shoemaker	Colerain	Shot in left leg	1736
William Fullhan	Kirke's	30	4		Monmullick, Ireland	Left hand disabled by a cut on ye wrist	1736
Joseph Langhorn	Whetham's	27	0	Shoemaker	Richmond, Yorkshire	Stabbed in his right wrist	1736
Samuel Carr	Rich's	25	0			Cut on right side of face	1736
Joseph Hopp	Wightman's	39	7	Labourer	Richmond, Yorkshire	Cut on right side of nose	1736
William Beardon	Hamilton's	26	0		Airshire	Shot in left leg	1736
Alex. Reyney	Hargrave's	19	0		Bamff	Shot in right leg and thigh	1736
James Morrison	Cope's	33				Cut on left side of head	1736
Patrick McCombe	Morrison's	34	7	Weaver	Dublin	Cut in belly	1736

Name	Unit	Age*	Service*	Occup.	Parish	Wounds	Year†
John Malone	Montague's	34	9	Clothier	Galloway	Disabled in right wrist	1737
John Davis	Harrison's	32	5			Cut on left side of head, stabbed in breast	1737
Thomas Watts	Harrison's	28	5			Stabbed in right shoulder	1737
Robert Flemming	Grant's	26	7	Taylor	Hamilton	Shot in right thigh	1737
Robert Moor	Montague's	28	2	Weaver	Glasgow	Bruise don right foot by horse tread	1737
Simon Fraser	Rothes'	27	8		Inverness	Finger of left hand contracted by a sword	1738
Alex. MacDonald	Rothes'	38	14		King's Shire, Murray	Wounded under the right breast	1738
John Wright	Rothes'	26	6		Burton upon Trent	Cut over ye left eye	1738
Archibald Grey	Rothes'	28	0		Argyleshire	Bad wound on right leg	1738
Henry Nailor	Rothes'	31			Killeath, Tipperary		1738
William Miller	Kerr's	37	3		Fyforth, Roshard	Shot in knee	1738
George Mires	Guards	29	1			Wounded in head and cut on left shoulder	1739
Thomas Nelson	Newton's					Cut on head	1739
William Wilson	Shannons?	33	0			Wounded several palces on head and in left arm	1739
Thomas Score	Forfar's	35	4	Weaver	Bridgnorth	Lost his left eye and wounded in right hand	1739
William Allen	Rothes'	29	1			Cut between his eye brows	1739

Name	Unit	Age*	Service*	Occup.	Parish	Wounds	Year†
Frederick Hay	Portmore's	25	5			Upper part of his head cut by broadsword	1740
Robert Jarvis	Portmore's	25	1	Barber	Stirling	Convulsion in right side	1741
John Cockran	Clayton's	22	2	Weaver	Dublin	Cut in left knee	1742
Daniel Martin		27	0	Taylor	Lanark	Shot in two places under chin and in belly	1743
Thomas Clayton		21	0	Taylor	Macclesfield	Shot in ye head and right arm	1743
John Walls	Montague's	37	8	Mason	Bristol	Cut on head	1743
George Cook	Clayton's	24		Weaver	Nottingham		1746
John Johnston	Clayton's	29		Weaver	Creitch near Worksop		1746

Officers Wounded[1]

Name	Rank	Unit	Wound/s
Patrick Robertson	Captain	Portmore's	Finger left hand shot off
Dudgeon	Quartermaster	Portmore's	Breast
John Farrer	Captain	Evans'	Thigh bone broken
Henry Hawley	Lieutenant Colonel	Evans'	Shot in shoulder
Forfar	Lieutenant Colonel	Forfar's	Shot in knee and cut to head
Mark	Ensign	Wightman's	Unknown
Robert Urquhart	Captain	Orrery's	
John Dancer	Captain	Egerton's	Bruised by a horse
Islay		Volunteers	Arm wound
Charles Cockburne		Volunteers	Shot in arm
Peter Robinson			Wounded in hand

---

1   *Flying Post*, 3727 22–24 Nov. 1715; *HMC Appendix III*, p,169; NRS, GD220/5/489/4.

Officers Captured[2]

Name	Rank Unit	Unit
Herbert Lawrence	Colonel	Montague's
John Edwards	Captain	Montague's
William Barlow	Captain	Clayton's
Edward Gibson	Lieutenant	Clayton's
Michael Rennet	Captain	Kerr's
Walter Chiesley	Captain	Orrery's
Thomas Michaelson	Lieutenant	Orrery's
Lord Richard H/ Kenneway	Lieutenant	Orrery's?
John Oldman	Ensign	Morrison's (dead)
Michael Moret	Captain	Clayton's?
Glenkindy		Morrison's?
Andrew Hay	Lieutenant	Orrery's
Keith Kenney	Lieutenant	Morrison's?
Robert Urquhart	Captain	Kerr's
John Semple	Lieutenant	Morrison's
A Riding Master		Carpenter's
Laird of Glenkindy		Carpenter's

Officers Killed[3]

Name	Rank	Unit
William Branch	Ensign	Forfar's
William Barlow	Captain	Clayton's
Arnot	Captain	Shannon's
Francis Armstrong	Captain	Aide to Argyle
Hammar	Major	Morrison's
Forfar	Colonel	

2   TNA, SP54/11/45A; RA, SP5/97.
3   *Flying Post* 3727, 22–24 Nov. 1715, *HMC Appendix III*, p.169; Patten, *History*, p.155.

Rank and file later claiming disability pensions 1716–1746 and who were members of units which fought at Sheriffmuir

Age at Time of Battle	Number	Age at Time of Battle	Number	Age at Time of Battle	Number
27	12	39	13	51	1
28	17	40	16	52	0
29	17	41	20	53	0
30	23	42	11	54	1
31	33	43	15	55	0
32	25	44	8	56	1
33	17	45	14	57	0
34	38	46	15	58	0
35	25	47	8	59	1
36	25	48	9	60	2
37	20	49	6		
38	11	50	9		

Length of Service

Length of Previous Service	Number	Length of Previous Service	Number	Length of Previous Service	Number
0	10	13	16	26	3
1	10	14	19	27	2
2	12	15	14	28	3
3	11	16	6	29	0
4	17	17	8	30	0
5	22	18	3	31	0
6	58	19	0	32	0
7	55	20	3	33	0
8	42	21	5	34	0
9	27	22	1	35	0
10	25	23	3	36	0
11	17	24	4		
12	11	25	5		

Parish of Origin

England		
Parish	**County**	**Number**
Nottingham		4
	Yorkshire	2
Richmond	Yorkshire	2
Wolverhampton		2
Nantwich		2
Litchfield		2
Birmingham		2
Chipton on Stowe		2
Alton		1
Barnard Castle		1
Berwick		1
Blockley		1
Bridgewater		1
Bristol		1
Bungay		1
Burton	Devon	1
Burton	Lincolnshire	1
Burton	Nottinghamshire	1
Burton		1
Canslea	Wiltshire	1
Canterbury		1
Charlbury	Oxfordshire	1
Chesterfield		1
Creith		1
Cornwall		1
Dowars		1
Draycott	Staffordshire	1
Easlan	Warwickshire	1
Falmouth		1
Hasted	Essex	1
Ledsworth		1

England		
Parish	**County**	**Number**
Litchfield		1
Lizard	Cornwall	1
London		1
Long Compton	Warwickshire	1
Lostwhithel	Cornwall	1
Macclesfield		1
Marlborough		1
Newcastle		1
Neyland	Staffordshire	1
Northallerton		1
Northumberland		1
Norwich		1
Onslow		1
Ormskirk		1
Oxford		1
Petchester		1
Preston		1
Ridgely		1
Rowcester		1
Rugby		1
Sailsbury		1
Selby		1
Shippen Malett		1
Skipton		1
Stamford	Lincolnshire	1
Uxbridge		1
Walsall		1
Wellington		1
Whitby		1
Widmisbury		1
Wolverhampton		1

Ireland		
Parish	County	Number
Dublin		5
Antrim		2
Colerain		2
Galloway		1
Armagh		1
Belfast		1
Belturbitt		1
Boscommon		1
Carlow		1
Channon	Armagh	2
Colerain		1
Downpatrick	Down	1
Drumcliff	Sligo	1
Dungeroon		1
Fermanagh		1
Killeath	Tipperary	1
Lisborn		1
Malliom	Cork	1
Mannaghan		1
Mommulick		1
Newton Forbes	L	1
Portmanney	Gallaway	1
Sligo		1
Waterford		1
Wexford		1
Wicklow		

Wales		
Parish	County	Number
Holywell	Flintshire	1
Welshpool	Monmouthshire	1
Haverford		1

Scotland		
Parish	County	Number
Glasgow		3
Air		3
Edinburgh		2
Aberdeen		2
Argyleshire		1
Arbroath		1
Beggar		1
Banff		1
Dumbarton		1
Fyforth		1
Haddington		1
Hamilton		1
Inverness		1
Islay		1
Kintyre		1
King's Shire	Murray	1
Lawther		1
Lanark		1
Leith		1
Stirling		1

Other	
Place	Number
Frankfurt, Germany	1
Blacks	2

Wounded at Previous Engagements

Battle/Siege	Number
Londonderry	1
Limerick	1
Aughrim	1
Killiecrankie	2
Steinkirk	1
Namur	4
Alamanza	19
Ramillies	4
Malplaquet	3
Other	12

Occupations

Occupation	Number
Husbandman	12
Weaver	11
Shoemaker	10
Labourer	8
Tailor	6
Servant	5
Apprentice	4
Glover	3
Cooper	2
Hatmaker	2
Barber	1
Bricklayer	1
Brusher	1
Bucklemaster	1
Butcher	1
Carrier	1
Coalworker	1
Cooper	1

Occupation	Number
Draper	1
Farmer	1
Farmer's son	1
Glassworker	1
Linen draper	1
Linen weaver	1
Mason	1
Miller	1
Nailor	1
Ostler	1
Pedlar	1
Plaster	1
Publican	1
Roper	1
Smith	1
Soldier's son	1
Tiner	1
Turnner	1
Woolcomber	1
Clothier	1

Appendix II

Panmure's Battalion[1]

Captain	Lieutenant	Ensign	Sgts.	Cpls.	Mus	Oth
The Earl of Panmure, Colonel	Patrick Ouchterlony	George Nairn, brother of Lord of Baldovan	2	2	1	40
Patt. Lyon of Auchhterhouse, Lieutenant Colonel	Andrew Fotheringham, son of laird of Powrie	Robert Lyon	2	2	0	39
Alex Leslie, Major	James Pitscottie	Gilbert Robertson	2	2	0	32
William Crichton	Francis Erskine, son of laird of Kirkkuddo	William Colvill, son of laird Kincardin	2	2	0	31
Alex. Duncan of Ardounnie	Harry Auchinleck, brother to lord of Auchinleck	Gilbert Auchinleck, son of laird Auchinleck	2	2	0	29
David Grant of Latoun	Charles Gairn	James Pantom	2	2	0	36
Malcom Gregorie	Charles Carnaigie, son of late Sheriff Depute	John Gregorie	2	2	0	32
John Blair	Robert Dell	Patrick Cold	2	2	0	31
William Nairne of Baldowan	Patrick Gordon	James Auchterlony	2	2	0	31
Alex. Arbuthnot of Findaurie	David Ramsey of Cairnloun	Alex. Ouchterlony, son of laird Guino	2	2	0	33

1   NRS, GD45/1/201

Captain	Lieutenant	Ensign	Sgts.	Cpls.	Mus	Oth
James Carnegy of Findheaven	Adam Urquhart	0	2	2	0	44
John Oliphant of Baytrie in Dundee (Grenadier Company)	Gilbert Cowper and James Duncan, brother to Ardourie	0	2	2	2	39
12	12	10	24	24	3	417

Plus:

Harry Auchinleck, quartermaster

George Nairne, chirurgeon

Charles Gairne, adjutant

Appendix III

List of British Army officers deserted to Jacobites in 1715[1]

Name	Rank	Former Unit
Hamilton	Lieutenant General	Kerr's
James Urquhart	Lieutenant Colonel	Kerr's
John Nairne	Major	Kerr's
Philip Lockhart	Captain	Kerr's
Simon Fraser	Lieutenant	Kerr's
William Clepame	Lieutenant Colonel	Grant's
Alexander Lessines	Captain Lieutenant	Grant's
James Lindsay	Ensign	Grant's
Walkinshaw	Captain	Wynn's
David Erskine	Lieutenant	Wynn's
Lord Charles Murray		Orkney's
Dalziell	Ensign	Orkney's
Kielle	Captain	Hyndford's
James Innes	Captain	Pocock's
Lord George Murray	Cornet	Ross'
David Nairn	Lieutenant	Forfars'
Hepburn	Captain	Douglas'
Patrick Small	Ensign	Douglas'
Wedderburn	Ensign	Lauder's
Fleming	Ensign	Lauder's
Calderwood	Ensign	Lauder's
Chalmer	Ensign	Lauder's

---

1   NRS, SP13/215

Appendix IV

Jacobite Prisoners taken at Sheriffmuir and fates where known[1]

Name	Castle held at	Date of Trial in 1716	Plea	Verdict
Robert Murray	Stirling	10 December		Guilty
Captain David Gardin	Edinburgh			
William Hay	Edinburgh	10 December	Guilty, 19 December	Guilty
Colonel Mackenzie	Blackness			Discharged
John Ratray	Blackness	7 December	Guilty	
George Taylor	Blackness	12 December	Guilty, 19 December	
Ensign Alexander Garrioch	Blackness			Discharged
Patrick Stewart	Blackness			Discharged
Charles Garden	Blackness	7 December	Guilty, 10 December	Guilty
Lieutenant William Adamson	Blackness			Discharged
Thomas Robertson	Blackness			Discharged
John Stewart	Blackness	13 December		Acquitted
Alexander Mackenzie	Edinburgh	15 December		Guilty
William Nairn	Stirling			
Patrick Auchtermay	Stirling	7 December		Guilty
William Stewart	Stirling			Discharged
Dr James Carnegie	Stirling	10 December		Guilty
Dr James Gordon	Stirling			Discharged
Lieutenant Archibald Fotheringham	Stirling	7 December		

---

1   Rae, *History*, pp.309–310; *Faithful Register of the Late Rebellion* (London: T. Warner, 1718); TNA, SP55/6.

Name	Castle held at	Date of Trial in 1716	Plea	Verdict
Thomas Drummond	Edinburgh			Guilty
Dr James Gordon	Stirling			Discharged
Viscount Strathallan	Edinburgh			
John Walkinshaw				
Logie Drummond				
Mr Drummond				
Mr Murray				
Captain William Creighton				
John Ross				
John Forbes				
James Peddie				
Captain John Gordon				
Lieutenant William Forbes				
Ensign Nicholas Donaldson	Stirling			Discharged, 1716
Alexander Stuart				
Nicholas McGlasson				
Lieutenant James Stuart	Stirling			Discharged
Alexander Stuart	Stirling			Discharged
Lieutenant John Robertson				
Kenneth McKenzie				
Captain Charles Chalmers				
Adjutant John McLean				
Captain Colin McKenzie				
Peter Stuart				
Donald Mitchel				
James Lyon				
Lewis Crammond	Stirling			Discharged
John Richie				
George Mear	Stirling			Discharged
Hector McLean	Stirling			Discharged
Alexander Mill				
John McIntosh				
Hugh Calder				
James Innes	Stirling			Discharged
Donald McPherson				

Name	Castle held at	Date of Trial in 1716	Plea	Verdict
John Morgan				
John Menzies	Stirling			Discharged
Robert Menzies	Stirling			Discharged
William Menzies	Stirling			Discharged
John Cattinach	Tolbooth, Edinburgh			Discharged, 1716
Alexander McLachlan				
Patrick Campbell	Stirling			Discharged
Hugh McRaw				
Donald McRaw				
Christopher McRae				
John Lesley				
James Edgar				
James Mill				
James Moody				
James Gordon				
Donald McMurie				
Murdoch McPherson				
Alexander Cameron				
Donald Mack-Naughtie				
Ewan McLachlan	Stirling			Discharged
Ewan MacDonald				
Donald Robertson	Stirling			Discharged
James Kench				
Francis Finlay	Stirling			Discharged
Alexander Morrison				
Andrew Jamison	Stirling			Discharged
Robert Miller	Stirling			Discharged
Adam Grinsel	Stirling			Discharged
Angus Stuart				
John Robertson				
Duncan McIntosh				

Appendix V

Poetry and Songs inspired the Battle of Sheriffmuir

THE BATTLE OF SHERRAMUIR

O, can ye here the fight to shun,
Or herd the sheep wi' me, man?
Or were ye at the Sherra-mmor,
Or did the battle see, man?
I saw the battle, sair and teugh,
And reekin-red ran monie a sheugh;
My heart for fear gae sough for sough,
To hear the thuds, and see the cluds
O'clans frae woods in tartan duds,
Wha glaum'd at kingdoms three, man.

The red-coat lads wi' black cockauds
To meet them were na slaw, man:
They rush'd and push'd and bluid outgush'd,
And monie a bouk did fa', man!
The great Argyle ed on his files,
I wat they glanc'd for twenty mikes,
They hough'd the clans like nine-pin kyles,
They hack'd and hash'd, while braid-swords clash'd,
And thro' they dash'd, and hew'd and smash'd,
Till fey men died awa, man.

But had ye seen the philibegs
And skyrin tartan trews, man,
When in the teeth they daur'd our Whigs
And Covenant trueblues man!
In lines extended lang and large,
When baig'nets o'erpower'd the targe,
And thousands hasten'd to the charge,
Wi' Highland wrath they frae the sheath
Drew blades o'death, till out o'breath
They fled like frighted dows, man!

O, how Deil! Tam, that can be true?
The chase gaed frae the north, man!
I saw myself, they did pursue
The horsemen back to Forth, man:

And at Dunblane, in my ain sight,
They took the brig wi' a' their might,
And straight to Stirling wing'd their flight;
But, cursed lot! The gates were shut,
And monie a huntit poor red-coat,
For fear amaist did swarf, man!

My sister Kate cam up the gate
Wi' crowdie unto me, man:
To Perth and to Dundee, man!
Their left-hand general had nae skill;
The Angus lads had nae good will
That day their neevbors' bluid to spill;
Fir fear by foes that they should lose
Their cogs o'brose, they scar'd at blows,
And homeward fast did flee, man.

They've lost some gallant gentlemen,
Amang the Highland clans, man!
I fear my Lord Panmure is slain,
Or in his en'mies' hands, man.
Now wad ye sing this double flight,
Some fell for wrang, and some for right,

But monie bade the world guid-night:
Say pell and mell, wi' muskets; knell
How Tories fell, and Whigs to Hell
Flew off in frighted bands, man.[1]

WHEN WE GAED TO THE BRAES O'MAR

When we gaed to the braes o'Mar,
And to the weapon-shaw, Willie;
Wi' true design to serve the king
And banish Whigs awa, Willie.
Up, and warn a',
For lords and lairds came there bedeen,
And wow! But they were braw, Willie.

Chorus:
Up, and warn a', Willie
Warn, warn a;
To hear my canty Highland sang
Relate the think I saw, Willie.

But when the standard was set up,
Right fierce the wind did blaw Willie,
The royal not upon the tap
Down to the ground did fa', Willie.
Up, and warn a', Willie,
Warn, warn a';
Then second-sighted Sandie said
We'd do nae gude at a', Willie.

But when the army join'd at Perth,
The bravest e'er ye saw Willie,
We didna doubt the rogues to rout,
Restore our king an' a', Willie.
Up, and warn a', Willie,
Warn, warn a';
The pipers play'd frae right to left
O whirry Whigs awa, Willie.

---

1   Robert Burns, *Complete Poems and Songs of Robert Burns* (Glasgow: Harper Collins, 1995), pp. 518–519.

But when we march'd to Sherramuir
And there the rebels saw, Willie;
Brave Argyle attack'd our right,
Our flank, and front and a', Willie;
Up, and warn a', Willie,
Warn, warn a';
Traiter Huntly soon gave way,
Seaforth, St. Clair and a', Willie.

But brave Glengarry on our right
The rebels' left did claw, Willie;
He there the greatest slaughter made
That ever Donald saw, Willie;
Up, and warn a', Willie,
Warn, warn a';
And Wittam fyled his breeks for fear,
And fast did rin awa, Willie.

For he ca'd us a Highland mob,
And soon he'd slay us a', Willie;
But we chas'd him back to Stirling brig-
Dragoons, and foot, and a', Willie.
Up, and warn a', Willie,
Warn, warn a';
At length we rall'd on a hill,
And briskly up did draw, Willie.

But when Argyle did view our line
And them in order saw, Willie,
He straight gaed to Dunbane again,
And back his left did draw, Willie.
Up, and warn a', Willie,
Warn, warn a';
Then we to Auchterairder march'd
To wait a better fa', Willie.

Now if ye spier wha wan the day,
I've tell'd you what I saw, Willie,
We baith did fight, and baith did beat,
And baith did rin awa, Willie.

Up, and warn a', Willie,
Warn, warn, a';
For second-sighted Sandie said
We'd do nae gude at a', Willie.[2]

A RACE AT SHERIFFMUIR

There's some say that we wan and some say that they wan,
And some say that none wan at a' man,
But of one thing I'm sure that at Sheriff Muir,
A Battle was fought on that day man.
And we ran and they ran and they ran and we ran,
And we ran, and they ran awa' man.

Now Trumpet McLean whose breeks were not clean
By Misfortune did happen tae fa' man
By saving his neck his trumpet did break
He came off without music at a' man
And we ran and they ran and we ran
And we ran and they ran awa' man

Whether we ran or they wan or they wan or we wan
Or if there was winnin' at a' man
There's nae man can tell save our brave general
Wha first began runnin' awa' man
And we ran and they ran and we ran
And we ran and they ran awa' man

Pray come ye here the fight tae shun or keep the sheep wi' me man
Pr was you at the Sheriffmuir and did the battle see man
Pray tell which o' the parties won for weel I know saw them run
Both south and north when they began
Snell pell and mell and kill and fell wi' muskets snell and pistols knell
And some tae hell did flee man
But my dear Will I kenna still which o' the twa did lose man

---

2   *Ibid.*, pp. 456–458.

For weel I know they had good skill tae set upon their foes man
The Redcoats they are trained you see the Highland clans disdain tae flee
Wha then shall gain the victory
But the Highlands race all in a brace with a swift pace to the Whigs' disgrace
Did put to chase their foes man

But Scotland has not much to say for such a fight as this is
For baith did fight baith did ran away the devil take the misses
For every soldier was not slain that ran that day and was nae ta'en
Either flying from or to Dunblane
For fear of foes that they should loose the bowels of brose all crying woes
Yonder them goes d'ye see man
And we ran and they ran and they ran and we ran
And we ran and they ran awa' man.[3]

WILL YE GO TO SHERIFFMUIR?
(Traditional Song)

Will ye go to Sheriffmuir?
Will ye go to Sheriffmuir, Bauld John O' Innisture,
There to see the noble Mar, And his Highland ladies.
A' the true men o' the north; Angus, Huntley, and Seaforth,
Scouring on to cross the Forth, wi' their white cockadies?

There you'll see the banners flare,
There you'll hear the bagpipes rair,
And the trumpets deadly blare,
Wi' the cannon's rattle.
There you'll see the bauld McCrows,
Camerons and Clanranalds raws
And a' the clans, wi' loud huzzas,
Rushing to the battle.
There you'll see the noble Whigs,
A' the heroes o' the brigs,
Rawhides and wither'd wigs,
Riding in array man.
Ri'en hose and raggit hools,
Sour milk and girin gools,
Psalm- beats and cutty stools,
We'll see never mair, man.

---

3   Rev. McLellan, *The Battle of Sheriffmuir*.

Will ye go to Sheriffmuir?
Bauld John o'Innisture?
Sic a day, and sic an hour.
Ne'er was in the north, man.
Siccan sights will there be seen;
And, gin some be nae mista'en
Fragant gales will come bedeen,
Frae the water o'Forth, man.[4]

---

4   James Hogg, *Jacobite Relics* (1813), p. 297.

Bibliography

Primary Sources

Manuscript
Blair Atholl Castle, Bundle 45, 12/97

British Library
Additional MSS. 47028, 61315, 61316, 61636, 61632
Stowe MSS. 228

The National Archives
KB8/66
State Papers Military 41/5
State Papers Naval 42/14
State Papers Scotland 54/7–12
SP55/3, 5, 6, 12.
SP57/29
SP78/160
SP84/253
SP94/48
WO4/17–18
WO5/20
WO116/1–3

National Records of Scotland
GD2/17
GD3/24
GD5/489
GD158/2880
GD27/6
GD30/1724
GD38/2/2
GD220/5/, 787a, 816
GD241/380

GD248/561/53
RH15/14/149

National Library of Scotland
ADV MS 13.1.8.
MSS 489
MS 902
MS 7104

University of Edinburgh Library Special Collections
Laing MSS III, 375/51

University of Leeds Special Collections
Townshend – Argyle official despatches

Published
A Collection of Original Letters and Authentick papers relating to the Rebellion, 1715 (Edinburgh: 1730).
Allardyce, James (ed.), *Historical Papers relating to the Jacobite Period, 1699-1750* (Aberdeen: New Spalding Club, 1895)
Anderson, John (ed.), *The Papers of the Rev. John Anderson* (Dumbarton: Bennett and Thomson, 1914)
The Annals of King George the second Year (London: A. Bell, 1717)
Anon, *A Compleat History of the Late Rebellion* (London: Hinchliffe, 1716)
Anon, *A Faithful Register of the Late Rebellion* (London: T. Warner, 1718)
Anon, *The Case of John Kynaston* (London, 1716)
An Account of the Battel of Dunblain in a Letter from a Gentleman at Stirling to his friend at Edinburgh (Edinburgh: 1715)
Armet, Helen (ed.), *Edinburgh Burgh Records, 1702–1718* (Edinburgh: Oliver & Boyd, 1967)
Memoirs of the Marshal Duke of Berwick, II, (London: T. Cadell, 1779)
Beer, Esmond Samuel de (ed.), *The Diary of John Evelyn* (London: Everyman, 2006)
Blaikie, Walter Biggar (ed.) , 'Origins of the '45', *Scottish Historical Society*, 2nd series, 2, (1916)
Campbell, Robert, *The Life of the Most Illustrious Prince, John Duke of Argyle and Greenwich* (Belfast: F. Joy, 1745)
Cowper, Spencer (ed.), *Diary of Lady Cowper*, (London: John Murray, 1864)
Crichton, Andrew (ed.), *Life and Diary of Lieutenant Colonel John Blackader* (Edinburgh: H.S. Baynes, 1825)
Daily Courant, 1714–1716
Deane, John Marshall, *A Journal of the Campaign in Flanders* (John Marshall Deane, 1846)
Dickson, William Kirk (ed.), 'Warrender Letters: Correspondence of Sir George Warrender, Bt., Lord Provost of Edinburgh, and Member of Parliament for the City, with Relative Papers, 1715', (Edinburgh: Scottish Historical Society, 3rd series, 21, 1935)

Donald, T.F., 'Glasgow and the Jacobite Rebellion of 1715', *Scottish Historical Review* XIII (1915–6)

Drake, Peter, *Amiable Renegade: The Memoirs of Captain Peter Drake, 1673–1753* (Stanford: Stanford University Press, 1955)

Elcho, Lord, *A Short Account of the Affairs of Scotland, 1744–1746* (Edinburgh: David Douglas, 1907)

Ellis, Joyce (ed.), 'Liddlell-Cotesworth correspondence', (Durham: Surtees Society, 1985)

Flying Post, 1715

Forbes, James, *Jacobite Memoirs* (Edinburgh: William & Robert Chambers, 1834)

Grant (ed.), 'Mrs Warriston's Diary; Mar's legacies to his son, 1639–1746', Scottish Historical Society, 26 (Edinburgh: T.A. Constable, 1896)

Hardy, William John (ed.), *Calendar of the Middlesex Sessions, 1689–1709* (London: Sir Richard Nicholson, 1905)

Hibbert-Ware, Samuel (ed.), 'Memorials of the Rebellion of 1715', Chetham Society, 5 (1845)

Hill, Ninian (ed.), 'A Side Light on the 1715', *Scottish Historical Review*, XVII (1919-20).

Historical Manuscripts Commission:

Calendar of the Stuart Papers, I, II, V, VII (London: HMSO, 1902–1920)

Manuscripts of the Marquess of Townshend (London: HMSO, 1887)

14th Report, Appendix III (London: HMSO, 1894)

Report on the Manuscripts of the Earl of Mar and Kellie preserved in Alloa House (London: HMSO, 1904)

Report on the Laing Manuscripts preserved in the University of Edinburgh (London: HMSO, 1914–1925)

Hogg, James (ed.), *The Jacobite Relics of Scotland* (Edinburgh: Blackwood, 1819–1821)

Home, John, *History of the Rebellion of 1745* (London: T. Cadell jun,. and W. Davies, 1802)

Johnstone, James, *A Memoir of the Forty Five* (Oxford: Alden Press, 1970)

Keith, James, *A Fragment of a Memoir of Field Marshal James Keith, 1714–1734* (Edinburgh: Spalding Club, 1843)

London Gazette, 1715

MacBane, Donald, *The Expert Sword-Man's Companion* (Fallen Book Publishing, 2015)

Mackay, Hugh, *Memoirs of the War carried out in Scotland and Ireland, 1689–1691* (Edinburgh: Bannantyne Club, 1833)

McNiven , Peter (ed.), 'The Diary of Henry Prescott, L.L.B., Deputy Registrar of Chester Diocese', II, Record Society of Lancashire and Cheshire, 1994

Mahon, Lord, *History of England from the Peace of Utrecht until the Peace of Versailles*, I, (London: John Murray, 1854)

Mathews, William (ed.), *Diary of Dudley Ryder, 1715–1716* (London: Methuen & Co., 1939)

Maxwell, James, *Narrative of the Expedition of Prince Charles* (Edinburgh: T. Constable, 1841)

Millner, John, *A Compendious Journal of all the Marches, Famous Battles, Sieges…* (London, 1733).

Murdoch, Rev. Alexander (ed.), 'The Grameid: an heroic poem on the Campaign of 1689', Scottish History Society, I, vol. 3 (1888)

Parke, Gilbert (ed.), *Letters and Correspondence of Bolingbroke*, IV (London: G.G. and J. Robinson, 1798)

Parker, Robert, *Memoirs of the Most Remarkable Military Transactions from the year 1683–1718* (London: S. Austen, 1747)

Patten, Robert, *History of the Rebellion* (London: J Baker & T. Warner, 1745)

Paton, Henry (ed.), 'Eight Letters of Bishop Nicholson', *Miscellany of the Scottish Historical Society*, I, 1893

Political State of Great Britain, IX (1715), XIII, (1717)

Pope, Michael, *A Thanksgiving Sermon for the suppression of the Late Unnatural Rebellion* (Bristol/ Glasgow, 1716)

Rae, Peter, *History of the Late Rebellion* (London, 1746)

Rannie, (ed.), David Walter, 'Hearne's Collections', Vol. V, 1714–1716', Oxford Historical Society, XLII, 1901

Rogers, Pat (ed.), Daniel Defoe, *Tour of the Whole Island* (Harmondsworth: Penguin, 1971)

Scott, Walter (ed.), *Memoirs of the Insurrection in Scotland in 1715* (Edinburgh: Abbotsford Club, 1845)

Journal of the House of Commons, Vol. 18

Post Boy, 1714

St. James' Evening Post, 1715

Seton, Walter (ed.), 'The Itinerary of King James III', *Scottish Historical Review*, XXI (1924)

Shaw, William and Slingsby, F.H. (eds.), *Calendar of Treasury Books*, XXIX, Part 2, 1714–1715 (London: HMSO, 1957); XXX, 1716 (London: HMSO, 1958)

Smith, David (ed.), *Letter Books of Joseph Symson, 1711–1719* (Oxford: Oxford University Press, 2003)

The Spottiswood Miscellany, 2 (Edinburgh, 1845)

Steuart, Archibald (ed.), *News Letters of 1715–1716* (London and Edinburgh: W. and R. Chambers, 1910)

Stuart, John (ed.), *Extracts from the Records of the Burgh of Aberdeen, 1643–1747* (Edinburgh: Scottish Burghs Records Society, 1872)

Tayler, Alastair (ed.), *1745 and After* (London: Thomas Nelson & Sons, 1938)

Tayler, Alistair and Henrietta (eds.), 'Lord Forfar and the '15', *Journal of the Society for Army Historical Research*, 15 (1936)

Tayler, Alistair and Henrietta (eds.), *Cess Roll for the County of Aberdeen in 1715* (Edinburgh: Spalding Club, 1932)

Tayler, Henrietta (ed.), *Seven Sons of the Provost: A Family Chronicle of the Eighteenth Century complied from Original Letters, 1692–1761* (London: Nelson and Sons, 1949)

Tayler, Henrietta (ed.), 'The Jacobite Court at Rome in 1719', Scottsh History Society, series 3, vol. 31 (1938)

Terry, Charles Sanford (ed.), 'Allan Cameron's Narrative', *Scottish Historical Review*, 5 (1907–8).

Thomson, Katherine (ed.), *Memoirs of the Jacobites* (London, 1845)

Secondary Sources

Books

Anon, *The Battle of Sheriffmuir* (Stirling: Eenas MacKay, 1898)

Arnot, Jean Gordon and Seton, Bruce Gordon, 'Prisoners of the '45', Scottish Historical Society, 3rd series, vols. 13–15, 1928-1929

Barthorp, Michael, *Marlborough's Army, 1702-1711* (London: Osprey Publishing, 1980)

Barthorp, Michael, *The Jacobite Risings, 1689-1745* (London: Osprey Publishing, 1982)

Baynes, John, *The Jacobite Rising of 1715* (London: Cassell, 1970)

Blackmore, David, *Destructive and Formidable: British Infantry Firepower, 1642-1765* (Barnsley: Pen and Sword, 2014)

Chandler, David, *Marlborough as Military commander* (London: Batsford, 1984)

Cruickshanks, Evelyn (ed.), *Ideology and Conspiracy: Aspects of Jacobitism, 1689-1759* (Edinburgh: John Donald, 1982)

Dalton, Charles, *Army of George I*, I (London: Eyre and Spottiswoode, 1930)

Dalton, Charles, *English Army Lists and Commission Registers, VI, 1707-1714* (London: Eyre and Spottiswoode, 1904)

Doyle, William (ed.), *Old Regime France* (Oxford: Oxford University Press, 2001)

Duffy, Christopher, *The '45* (London: Casell, 2003)

Duffy, Christopher, *Warfare in the Age of Reason* (London: Routledge & Kegan, 1987)

Earle, Peter, *Monmouth's Rebels: The Road to Sedgemoor* (London: Weidenfeld & Nicolson, 1977)

Frost, Robert, *The Northern Wars, 1558-1721* (Pearson: London, 2000)

Henshaw, Victoria, *Scotland and the British Army, 1700-1750: Defending the Union* (University of Birmingham, 2014)

Holmes, Geoffrey and Szechi, Daniel, *Making of a Great Power, 1660-1722* (London: Longman, 1993)

Houston Rab, and Knox, William (eds.), *Penguin New History of Scotland* (London: Allen Lane, 2000)

Inglis, William, *The Battle of Sheriffmuir* (Stirling: Stirling Council Libraries, 2005)

Israel, Jonathan, *The Dutch Republic: Its Rise, Greatness and Fall, 1477-1806* (Oxford: Clarendon Press, 1995)

Keay, John and Julia, *Encyclopedia of Scotland* (London: Harper Collins, 1994)

Lenman, Bruce, *The Jacobite Risings in Britain and Europe, 1688-1746* (London: Methuen, 1980)

Oates, Jonathan, *The Jacobite Campaigns* (London: Pickering and Chatto, 2011)

Oates, Jonathan *The Last Battle in England: Preston* (Farnham: Ashgate, 2015)

Oxford Dictionary of National Biography (Oxford, 2004)

Petrie, Charles, *The Jacobite Movement* (London: Eyre and Spottiswoode, 1932)

Plumb, John, *The First Four Georges* (Glasgow: William Collins and Sons, 1956)

Pollard, Tony and Oliver, Neil, *Two men in a Trench*, II (London: Michael Joseph, 2003)

Reid, Stuart, *Culloden* (Barnsley: Pen and Sword, 2005)

Reid, Stuart, *Sheriffmuir, 1715: The Jacobite War in Scotland* (London: Frontline Books, 2014)

Rowlands, Guy, *The Financial Decline of a Great Power* (Oxford: Oxford University, 2001)

Sankey, Margaret, *Jacobite Prisoners of 1715: Preventing and Punishing Rebellion in Early Hanoverian England* (Farnham: Ashgate, 2005)

Sedgwick, Romney, *History of Parliament: The Commons*, II, (London: HMSO, 1970)

Singleton, Charles, *Famous by My Sword: The Age of Montrose and the Military Revolution*, (Solihull: Helion, 2015)

Showalter, Dennis, *Frederick the Great: A Military History* (London: Frontline Books, 2012)

Smith, Lawrence Bartlam, *Spain and Britain, 1715-1719: The Jacobite Issue* (London/New York Garland, 1987)

Speck, William, *Stability and Strife: England, 1714-1760* (London: Edward Arnold, 1977)

Stevenson-Sinclair, Christopher, *Inglorious Rebellion: The Jacobite Risings of 1708, 1715 and 1719* (London: Hamish Hamilton, 1971)

Szechi, Daniel, *1715: The Great Jacobite Rising* (New Haven, CT: Yale University Press, 2005)

Szechi, Daniel, *Britain's lost Revolution, Jacobite Scotland and French Grand Strategy, 1701-1708* (Manchester University Press, 2015)

Szechi, Daniel, *Jacobitism and Tory politics, 1701-1714* (Edinburgh: Donald, 1984)

Tayler, Alastair and Henrietta, *1715: The Story of the Rising* (London: Thomas Nelson & Sons, 1936)

Articles

McGowan, Ashby 'Sheriffmuir, 1715, Part 2', *Miniature Wargames*, no. 143 (April 1995)

Szechi, 'Towards an Analytical Model of Military Effectiveness for the Early Modern Period: the Military Dynamics of the 1715 Jacobite Rebellion' in *Militargeschichliche Zeitschrift*, 72 (2013), Heft 2

Electronic

<http://www.data.historic-scotland.gov.uk/data/docs/battlefields/Sheriffmuir-full.pdf>
<http://www.lochiel.net/archgives/arch173.html>
<http://www.nls.uk/exhibition/jacobites/1715/sheriffmuir>

Index

INDEX OF PEOPLE

Aikman, James 86, 95

Anne, Queen of England 13, 15–17, 21–22, 24, 26, 28–29, 118, 134, 207

Anstruther, Sir Robert 153, 156, 159–160, 162, 164, 185, 197, 199, 225

Areskine, Sir John 93, 210

Argyle, John Campbell 2nd Duke of xi, 15, 21, 23–24, 39, 44–45, 50, 54–57, 63–64, 67–71, 74–82, 88, 90–105, 108–114, 117, 119, 121, 130–132, 134, 136–138, 141, 143–145, 146–148, 150–150, 155–156, 158–162, 164–168, 170–182, 186, 188–211, 215–219, 221–232, 234–235, 239–242

Arthur, Thomas 85–86

Atholl, John Murray 1st Duke of Atholl 24, 36, 41, 56, 69, 87, 89, 104, 110

Balfour, Major 55, 153–154

Barthorp, Michael 144, 146

Baynes, John viii–ix, xi, 116, 129, 144, 146, 149, 180, 186

Belhaven, John Hamilton 3rd Baron 68, 141

Berwick, James Fitzjames 1st Duke of 17, 22, 24–25, 31, 33–37, 40, 45–47, 49–50, 57, 65, 104, 116, 175, 189, 198, 209–210, 212, 220, 223, 240

Blackader, Colonel John 144, 146, 168–169, 191

Bolingbroke, Henry St John 1st Viscount 17–18, 20, 25–27, 30, 32, 35–36, 41, 43, 45–46, 63, 73, 140, 205, 207, 211, 236

Breadalbane, John Campbell 1st Earl of 24, 83, 103, 106, 111, 148, 198

Bubb, George 81, 207

Buchan, David Erskine 9th Earl of 111, 171, 221

Burroughs, William 80, 215–216

Byng, Admiral Sir George 34, 78

Cadogan, Major General William 22, 62–64, 177, 202, 204–207, 209, 213–217, 220–22, 224–225, 229–232

Cadogan 22, 62–64, 177, 202, 204, 206–207, 209, 211, 213–217, 220–222, 224–225, 229–232

Calder, Sir Thomas 49, 235

Cameron of Lochiel, John 24, 119, 153–154, 171, 201, 210, 216

Campbell, Colonel Alexander 67, 226, 229–230

Campbell, Lieutenant Alexander 146, 197

Campbell, Lieutenant Colonel James 131–132

Campbell, Robert 62, 117

Carpenter, General George 101, 177, 232

Cathcart, Colonel Charles 102–103, 132, 231

Charles Edward Stuart 33, 236, 240

Charles II 15, 18, 62, 118, 134, 136

Charles XII of Sweden 34–35, 141, 148, 163, 219

Claverhouse, Colonel John 12–13

Clayton, Brigadier Jasper 131, 146, 226

Clepham, William 118, 154, 165, 228

Cockburn, William 37, 41, 51, 61, 65, 68, 75, 77, 80, 85, 88, 91, 95, 108, 185, 196, 202, 207, 213

Cotesworth, William 87, 225

Cowper, Lady Mary 22, 76, 192

Crawford, Patrick 185, 233

Cromwell, Oliver 177, 279

Deane, Private 179, 196

Defoe, Daniel 16, 62, 87, 89, 193–194, 214
Derwentwater, James Radcliffe 3rd Earl of 90, 140, 208
Douglas, Robert 97, 100, 119, 122
Drummond of Logie 51, 187
Dundee, Viscount 83, 142, 164

Egerton, Colonel 170
Elphinstone, Arthur 140, 226
Eugene, Prince of Savoy 163, 224
Evans, Major General William 96, 117, 131, 146, 217, 229

Findlater, James Ogilvy 4th Earl of 39, 41
Forfar, Douglas Archibald 2nd Earl of 45, 54, 79, 95, 97, 102–103, 108, 111, 131, 146, 157, 169, 180, 185
Forster, Thomas 45, 56, 71, 73, 82, 90–91, 100, 103, 108, 115–116, 177, 222

George I vii, 16–30, 32, 34, 37, 39–43, 45, 57–58, 63, 65, 67–68, 70–72, 74, 76, 79, 81, 83, 88, 130, 140, 188, 191–194, 201, 203, 207, 214–215, 219, 225, 230–232, 235
Glengarry, Laird of 23, 25, 38, 67, 99, 123, 147, 151, 165, 175–177, 188, 219, 239
Gordon of Glenbucket, John 48, 50, 107, 147, 203, 227
Gordon, George 1st Duke of 20, 38, 53
Gordon, Major General Alexander of Auchintoul 20, 51, 100, 105
Gordon, Sir William 66–67
Gorthie, Laird of 145, 148, 180, 189, 197, 202
Graham, Major Thomas 102–103, 118
Grant, Colonel/Brigadier General Alexander 69, 131, 146, 217, 221, 230
Guest, Joseph 131–132, 170, 221, 236

Haddington, Thomas Hamilton 6th Earl of 68, 141, 172
Haddock, Captain 66, 78
Hamars, Lieutenant Colonel 166, 170
Hamilton, Major General George 37, 117

Harrison, Colonel Thomas 111, 157, 162–163, 186–189
Hawley, Henry 131, 157, 236
Hay, Colonel John 88, 105
Hearne, Thomas 73, 152, 159, 192, 208
Henderson, Colonel Robert 164, 169
Holland, Private John 12–13, 17, 20, 34, 63–64, 85–86
Home, Rev. John 124–125
Huntley, Alexander Gordon 5th Marquess of 20, 24, 38–39, 42, 48–51, 54, 83, 89, 99, 110–112, 117, 121, 151–152, 165, 171, 173, 175, 200–202, 207, 211, 215, 218–220, 227, 229–230

Ilay, Archibald Campbell, 1st Earl of 18, 74, 85, 106
Inglis, William 144, 146, 180, 182, 186, 188
Invernytie, John Stewart of 51, 99, 107, 172

James VII and II vii, 12–15, 17, 19, 25, 27, 44, 46–47, 71, 85, 117–118, 235
James VIII and III (James Francis Edward Stuart; later, 'the Old Pretender') 12–43, 45–52, 54, 57–58, 65–67, 74–75, 82, 88–89, 92–93, 104, 142–143, 152–154, 189, 192–194, 196, 198, 201–202, 205–207, 209–210, 212–219, 221–222, 225–227, 229–231, 237–238, 241

Keith, James 32, 38, 40, 59, 113, 117, 146–147, 152–154, 165, 174–176, 190, 199–200, 207–208, 213, 223, 229–230
Kenmure, William Gordon 6th Viscount 38, 56, 91, 97–98
Kennedy, Colonel Cornelius 23, 81
Kennedy, Cornet William 196, 204, 222
Kerr, Colonel Mark 168, 179
Kynaston, John 73, 133

Lawrence, Colonel Herbert 170, 201, 205
Lenman, Bruce viii, x, 27, 116
Liddell, Henry 71, 73, 222, 225
Linlithgow, James Livingston 5th Earl of 128, 174, 227, 231
Lockhart, George 59, 66, 116

Loudoun, James Campbell 2nd Earl of 132, 141

Louis XIV 13, 19, 24, 32–33, 35, 37, 47, 62, 83, 132, 136

Lovat, Simon Fraser 11th Lord 110, 204

MacDonald of Clanranald, Allan 119, 165, 186

MacDonald, Sir Donald 49, 107–108, 148, 153, 173, 175, 215, 230–231

MacGregor, Rob Roy xi, 51, 59, 109, 171, 216

Mackay, Major General Hugh 13, 126, 142

Mackenzie, Sir John 199–100

Mackintosh of Borlum the Younger, William 24, 83, 89, 92

MacLean, Sir John 56–57, 151

Mar, John Erskine 6th Earl of ix–x, 12, 21, 23, 27–30, 32–33, 36–42, 44–57, 69, 61, 65, 69–70, 74–76, 80–83, 85, 88–112, 115–118, 12–124, 128–131, 146, 148, 15–154, 156, 162, 165, 170–172, 174–178, 180, 186–190, 192–193, 195, 197–203, 207–208, 210–214, 216–220, 222–228, 231, 236–240

Marischal, George Keith 10th Earl of 36, 38, 50–51, 83, 99, 110, 119, 153–154, 171, 198, 211–212, 219, 227–228, 230–231

Marlborough, John Churchill 1st Duke of 21, 25, 27, 42, 60, 71, 76, 80, 91, 129–130, 133, 136–137, 139–140, 163–164, 178, 188, 199, 208, 214–215, 220

Mary II, Queen of England 12, 14

Mary of Modena 19, 32, 210

Monmouth, James Scott 1st Duke of 31, 36, 39, 44, 60, 62, 96, 113, 136–139, 141, 207

Montrose, James Graham 1st Duke of 18, 21, 23, 56, 65, 77, 86–87, 89, 104, 128, 177, 179

Montrose, James Graham 1st Marquess of (d.1650) 128, 177

Murray, James 33, 41, 189

Murray, Lord Charles 92, 107, 120

Murray, Lord George 89, 99, 107, 118, 143, 172, 236

Nairn, Lord Charles 92, 120, 122, 199

O'Sullivan, Colonel John 137–138

Ogilvie, Brigadier James 39, 51, 111.

'the Old Pretender', see James VIII and III

Orleans, Phillipe duc d' 33–34, 41, 46, 67, 82, 93, 228

Ormonde, James Butler 2nd Duke of 21, 25, 27, 30–31, 35, 37, 39, 41, 46, 140, 190, 210, 223, 236

Packington, Sir John 71, 73

Panmure, James Maule, 4th Earl of 52, 66, 83, 89, 99, 107, 117, 122, 187, 198, 226

Patten, Rev. Robert viii, 30, 38, 55, 83, 86, 89, 94, 98, 100, 116, 121, 124, 126–127, 194–195

Pollock, Colonel Sir Robert 198, 230

Prescott, Henry 193, 225

Preston, Brigadier General George 69

Price, Mr Baron Sir Robert 234–235

Pulteney, William 61, 65, 80, 119, 133, 136, 191, 195, 199, 209

Rae, Rev. Peter viii, 19, 33, 144, 146, 158, 181, 186, 194

Reid, Stuart ix–xi, 115, 129, 144, 146, 149, 157, 180, 186

Robertson of Struan, Alexander 13th Baron 46, 51, 99, 107, 119, 148, 175, 198–199, 218, 228

Rollo, Rupert, Lord 107, 153–154, 201, 219

Roxburghe, John Ker 1st Duke of 23, 141, 201

Ryder, Dudley 68, 130, 140, 192, 232

Seaforth, William Mackenzie 5th Earl of 24, 38, 50–51, 54, 105–106, 108, 117, 121, 147, 163, 190, 202, 218–219, 227, 230

Sibbitt, John 87, 100, 123

Sinclair, John 14, 16, 41–42, 48, 50, 52–56, 59, 88–90, 92–94, 99–100, 105–106, 109, 111–113, 116–119, 121–123, 125, 127–128, 130, 138, 144, 146–147, 150–154, 156, 158–159, 165, 170–176, 178–181, 186, 190, 197–200, 203, 223, 236

Sinclair-Stevenson, Christopher 144, 146

Sophia, Electress of Hanover 15–16

Southesk, James Carnegie 5th Earl of 42, 52, 83, 112, 154

Stair, John Dalrymple 2nd Earl of 34, 58, 64, 67–68, 81, 97, 200, 210, 235

Stanhope, Colonel William 64–67, 70, 74, 76, 80–82, 97, 130, 199–200, 205, 217

Stanhope, James 21, 60

Stewart, Daniel 69, 103

Stewart, Major James 33, 85, 225

Strathallan, William Drummond 4th Viscount 24, 51, 148, 187, 215

Strathmore, Lord 93, 98, 119, 122, 159, 186, 198, 212

Strowan (or Struan), Lord, *see* Alexander Robertson

Sutherland, John Gordon 16th Earl of 54, 102, 200, 202, 219, 230

Szechi, Professor Daniel viii–x, xi, 31, 44, 115–116, 129, 144, 146, 157, 180, 186

Tayler, Alastair and Henrietta ix, 116, 146

Thomson, Private James 85–86

Torcy, Jean-Baptiste Colbert Marquis de 20, 32

Torphichen, James Sandilands, 7th Baron of 99, 132, 158, 168, 170–171

Townshend, Charles 2nd Viscount 60, 63, 67–68, 70, 74–77, 81–82, 84, 86–87, 95–96, 130, 188,

191, 196, 201–202, 204, 206–207, 213–215, 221, 225, 230, 235

Tullibardine, William Murray Marquess of 42, 50–51, 83, 89, 119, 190, 202, 227

Tweeddale, John Hay 4th Marquess of 24, 68, 78, 95

Urquhart, Captain Robert 170, 180

Wade, Major General George 73, 236

Wales, George Prince of 79, 130

Wales, Princess of 22, 130

Walpole, Sir Robert 21, 60, 64–65, 76, 207

Warrender, Sir George 38, 62, 65–66, 78, 84–86, 93

Whetham, Major General Thomas 50, 59, 61–62, 66–67, 84, 88, 98–99, 130, 146, 166, 168–169

Wightman, General Joseph 18–19, 60, 67, 96, 100–101, 110, 127, 130, 132, 144, 146, 150, 157, 158, 159–160, 164, 173–174, 176, 179, 206, 226, 231, 236

William III (William of Orange) 12–15, 18, 22, 25, 36, 62, 77, 118, 134, 141

Wills, General Charles 82, 201, 204

INDEX OF PLACES

Aberdeen 22, 36, 52–53, 59, 65, 83–84, 123, 203, 211, 214, 224, 227, 229–231, 256, 273, 275

Aberdeenshire 37, 42, 66, 120

Allan (River) 24, 112–113, 119, 149–150, 160, 162–163, 165, 179, 186

Alloa 28, 56, 69, 102

Angus 36, 38, 50–51, 88, 93, 112, 120

Anstruther 54, 93

Arbroath 211, 226, 229, 231

Ardoch 99, 176, 178, 222

Atholl 48, 88, 119, 159

Auchterarder 51, 53, 99–100, 109, 111, 151, 179, 195, 220, 222

Badenoch 48, 50, 230

Bar le Duc 24–25, 92, 205

Bath 46, 70, 73

Bavaria 13, 135, 221

Berwick-upon-Tweed 36 61 87 90 94 209 214 220–221

Blackness 233–234

Blair 69, 120, 259

Boyne (River) 13, 62

Braco 53, 220, 222

Braemar 37, 39–41, 43, 48, 65, 83

Brechin 83, 185, 212, 226, 229, 231

Bristol 36, 70, 73, 94, 96

Burntisland 54–55, 78, 92–93, 109, 122–123, 172, 180, 186, 189, 206, 218

Calais 224, 228

Carlisle 234–236

Castle Campbell 55, 102

Cherbourg 46, 131

Chester 101, 193, 225, 274
Coupar 19, 51, 54
Crail 37, 54, 92–93
Crieff 22, 53, 220
Cumberland 26, 209, 221

Derby x, 239
Drummond Castle 24, 51, 179
Dumbarton 165, 231
Dumfries 16, 19, 60, 91, 101
Dunblane vii, xi, 81, 94, 98–99, 109–113, 148–150,
    152, 170–171, 173, 176, 178, 184, 190, 208,
    215, 221–222, 232, 266, 270
Dundee 22, 27, 52, 54, 83–84, 106, 109, 127–128,
    201, 207, 211–212, 218, 226, 231, 238
Dunfermline 93, 102, 104, 216, 233
Dunkeld 49 51 83 190 205 207 231
Dunkirk 210, 228
Dunning 53, 102, 110, 220
Dunottar Castle 106, 127

Earn (River) 207, 221, 224
Edinburgh viii, 16, 18–20, 23, 27, 37–38, 54,
    58–62, 65, 67–69, 75, 78–79, 81, 84–85, 87–88,
    90–91, 94–100, 102, 106, 110, 119, 134–135,
    178, 190–191, 205–206, 209, 214, 217–218,
    220–221, 231–234, 236
Edinburgh Castle 19, 59–60, 67–69, 84–85, 98,
    106, 135, 214, 218, 236
Elie 37, 93
Exeter 36, 70

Falkirk 79, 103
Fifeshire 37, 65, 88, 99
Firth of Moray 78
Firth of Forth 78, 81–82, 91–94, 98, 100–101,
    122, 192
Flanders 63, 118–119, 130–131, 137, 139, 273
Fort William 24, 51, 60–61, 66, 79, 198, 215, 226,
    230–231
Forth (River) 54, 56, 76, 80, 91, 109, 111
France vii, 12–13, 15, 17–18, 21, 24–25, 30–35, 40,
    43, 46–47, 59, 68, 74, 78, 82, 93, 102, 123, 135,
    205, 208, 210–213, 219, 225–230, 238

Glamis 120, 212
Glasgow 16, 24, 59–60, 68–69, 80–81, 97, 101,
    106, 110–111, 134, 168, 191, 202, 215, 231–234

The Hague 20, 63–64, 204
Hanover xi, 15–16, 19–22, 34, 36, 39, 45, 89
the Highlands 20, 24, 33, 36, 38, 43–44, 51, 60–61,
    65–66, 74, 83, 87, 101, 124, 169, 203, 209–210,
    230–233, 236–237
Holland 12–13, 17, 20, 34, 63–64, 85–86
Humber 64, 82

Inverness 23, 25, 83, 120, 199, 204, 212–213, 219,
    223, 227, 229–231, 236
Ireland 12–13, 19, 21, 23, 43–44, 46, 60, 68, 76,
    78–80, 82, 91, 93, 99, 101, 105, 118, 126, 134,
    136, 139, 169

Jedburgh 23, 91, 101

Kelso 22–23, 100–101
Kendal 132, 193
Kildrummy 48–49, 120
Kilsyth 79, 103, 110, 154, 169
Kinbuck 112–113, 150
Kinross 19, 74, 102, 216
Kippendavie 111, 150, 153

Lancashire viii, x, 26–27, 36, 45, 71, 82, 101, 109,
    196, 204
Le Havre 24, 204
Leeds 26, 61, 204
Leith 19, 23, 37, 54, 78, 92, 94, 96–100, 205, 221
Linlithgow 68, 205
London x, 16–20, 23–24, 26, 30, 37, 56, 61–65, 67,
    69, 71, 73–75, 81, 88, 90, 101–102, 130, 133,
    140, 188, 192–193, 196, 201, 204, 206, 209,
    215, 219, 221–222, 225, 230, 233–234, 237
Lothian 92–93, 96
Low Countries 131, 136
the Lowlands 20, 60–61, 92, 94, 96, 100

Manchester 26, 61
Montrose 53, 83, 226–227, 229, 231

Moulin 83, 120
Moy 93, 98, 120
Murray 222, 230
Muthill 53, 220

Newcastle 37, 57, 71, 91, 94, 100–101, 225
Normandy 204, 210
North Berwick 94, 97
Northumberland 27, 36, 45, 90, 92, 96, 100–101

Ostend 63–64
Oxford 25–26, 70, 73–74

Paris 13, 18–19, 25, 70, 190, 219
Perth x, 48–51, 54–57, 60, 76, 80–81, 83, 87–90,
     92–94, 96, 98–101, 103, 105–109, 119, 121, 127,
     146, 149, 162, 175, 179–181, 189, 195–200,
     202–203, 205–208, 210–216, 219–227, 231, 233
Perthshire 51, 83, 99, 120, 226, 228, 231
Pittenweem 54, 93
Portsmouth 19, 62
Preston vii, ix–xi, 26, 77, 120, 126–127, 133, 137,
     140, 144, 177, 192, 194, 196, 199, 202, 208,
     213–215, 222–224, 238–239

Reading 22, 193
Ross 65, 131, 200

Scone 212, 214, 220
Seaton House 98–100

Skye 23, 230–231
Spain 13, 18, 31–32, 35, 46, 81, 130–131,
     135–137, 139, 207, 213, 231
St. Germain 13, 33
St. Malo 34, 227
Stirling x–xi, 16, 19, 22, 28, 48, 52, 54, 56–57,
     59–62, 68–70, 75, 79–81, 84, 88–90, 92, 94, 96,
     98–104, 109–111, 113–114, 144, 156, 168–169,
     171, 178–180, 185, 191, 195, 200–202, 205,
     209, 216, 220–222, 224, 231, 233–234
Stirling Bridge 109, 168
Stirling Castle xi, 28
Stirlingshire 51, 99, 128
Strathbogie 50, 229
Strathdon 48, 230
Sweden 31–32, 34–35, 43, 74, 219

Tay 37, 87–88, 105, 207, 224
Thames 37, 64, 208
Tower of London 209
Tullibardine 53, 104, 111, 222, 224, 234

Utrecht 25, 32, 34, 60, 63

Wales 22, 36, 71, 76, 79, 130, 134
the West Country 36, 46, 70–71
West Indies 130, 134, 137
Western Isles 102, 230
Westminster 22, 31, 60, 62, 201, 207
Yorkshire 26, 67

MILITARY UNITS

Black Dragoons, see Stair's

Carpenter's Dragoons 61, 68, 75–77, 90, 96, 101,
     131, 137, 164, 166, 170, 217
Clayton's Battalion 74, 79–80, 157, 164
Clayton's Regiment 132, 135, 139, 170, 181–183,
     217
Edinburgh City Guard 27, 86–87, 96
Egerton's Battalion 79, 157, 164
Egerton's Regiment 79–80, 135, 139, 164, 217

Evans' Dragoons 68, 70, 74, 78, 79, 110, 131, 137,
     145, 156, 159–160, 162, 174, 185, 217

Foot Guards 60, 62, 118, 130–131, 140
Forfar's Battalion 76, 96, 157
Forfar's Regiment 23, 60, 61, 75, 131, 139, 140, 217
French Army 23, 34
Glasgow Militia 69, 111, 168, 191
Grant's Battalion 76, 79, 230
Grant's Regiment 61, 75, 118, 217–219, 226

Grey Dragoons, *see* Portmore's

Horse Guards 62, 119, 129
Huntley's infantry 51, 110–111, 147, 165, 173, 218
Huntley's cavalry 51, 99, 147, 151, 171

Kerr's Dragoons 61, 68–69, 75–77, 79, 90, 99, 132, 135, 137, 140, 164, 166, 168, 217

Linlithgow's cavalry 51, 107, 128, 147, 219
Logie Drummond's Regiment 92–93, 119, 122
Lord Nairn's Regiment 92, 94, 120–122

Mackintosh's Battalion 51, 91, 93, 97, 100, 103, 106, 120, 122–123
Mar's Battalion(s) 51, 98, 120–122
Mar's Regiment 92, 94, 118, 131
Marischal's cavalry 51, 99, 147, 153, 171, 198
Militia 17, 60, 62, 69, 73, 78, 91, 95–96, 99–102, 111, 168–169, 191, 197, 204–206, 216, 230
Montague's Battalion 76, 113, 157, 164
Montague's Regiment 61, 75, 79, 132. 139, 145, 166, 170, 183, 217
Morrison's Battalion 79, 135, 157, 164, 166, 179
Morrison's Regiment 139, 145, 181–183, 217
Murray's Regiment 121–122

Nairn's 92, 94, 120–122
Newton's Dragoons 199, 205, 217

Ogilvie's Battalion 148,165
Ogilvie's Regiment 99, 107, 218
Orrery's Battalion 60, 76, 96, 157, 164, 166

Orrery's Regiment 61, 75, 139, 145, 166, 170, 182–183, 217

Panmure's Battalion 51, 89, 122, 148, 198, 207
Pocock's 69, 73
Portmore's Dragoons 61, 74–76, 79, 96, 102–103, 118, 131–132, 137–138, 156–157, 160, 163, 169, 171–172, 174, 182–183, 186, 217
Preston's Battalion 77, 86

Rich's Dragoons 73, 225
Royal Navy 14, 17, 62, 78, 93–94, 101, 119, 204, 206, 228

Scots Fusiliers 131–132
Shannon's Battalion 61, 76, 84, 96, 157, 164
Shannon's Regiment 75, 79, 131, 135, 139–140, 217
Southesk's cavalry 128. 147
Stair's Dragoons ('the Blacks') 61, 75–76, 79, 96, 103, 135, 137, 157, 160, 164, 174, 196, 217
Strathmore's Battalion 51, 120–122, 156, 207
Strathmore's Regiment 51, 92, 107, 122
Strowan's Regiment 51, 203
Swiss 63, 204–205, 216–217, 222, 225, 232

Trained Bands 17, 19, 60, 62
Tullibardine's Battalion 51, 148

Wightman's Battalion(s) 74, 157, 173
Wightman's Regiment 79, 135, 139, 160, 163, 170, 217
Windsor's 73, 77

CLANS

Appin Stewart 111, 123, 147, 198, 215, 218–219, 230, 263

Cameron 13, 51, 111, 121, 147, 154, 219, 231
Of Lochiel 24, 110
Campbell 29, 67, 130, 147

MacDonald 13, 15, 51, 111, 121, 147, 159, 165, 173, 198, 219, 231. Of Clanranald 108, 119, 122–123, 147, 152; of Glengarry 23, 123, 147, 219
MacGregor 56, 108, 171–172, 218
MacLean 13, 123, 147, 165, 173, 218–219
MacPherson 171–172

GENERAL TERMS

Act of Union vii, 12, 28, 235
Alamanza (battle, 1707) 47, 131–132, 135–136, 163
anti-Catholicism 18, 29, 141

Bank of England 64–65, 194
Barons of the Exchequer 67, 77
Barrier treaties 17, 63
Blenheim (battle, 1704) 42, 131, 136–137, 140, 144, 183, 188, 193

Catholicism 15, 18, 27, 29, 45, 141
cess tax 52–53
Church of England 17–18, 23, 26–27
Culloden 23, 137–139, 145, 162

Darien disaster 15–16
Dunkeld (battle, 1689) 13, 119, 128
Episcopalianism 14–15, 17

Falkirk (battle, 1746) vii, 126, 236
the Forty Five viii–x, 42, 125, 236

General elections 17, 23, 25
Glenshiel (battle, 1719) 144, 236–237

Hanover (House of) xi, 15–16, 20–22, 34, 36, 45, 89
Hanoverian Succession 15, 17, 20, 26, 28, 67, 130, 214
Highlanders 23–24, 41, 43, 55, 65, 68, 74, 78, 85, 88–89, 96, 106, 116, 120–124, 126–127, 138, 141–142, 151, 159, 168–169, 171, 174, 193–194, 198, 205, 208, 223, 226

Killiecrankie (battle, 1689) 13, 62, 119, 126, 128, 135, 138, 141, 144, 164, 176–177, 237–238

Lochaber axes 53, 123–124, 166, 184
Lowlanders 100, 123

Malplaquet (battle, 1709) 117, 129, 131, 135–137, 139
Massacre of Glencoe 15, 220
Monmouth rebellion 60, 137, 139

Namur (siege, 1695) 131–132, 135
National Library of Scotland viii, 113, 149

Oudenarde (battle, 1708) 162–163, 178–179

Parliament 15–17, 22–23, 25, 28, 42, 58, 117, 130, 133, 223
Presbyterians 13–14, 29
Preston (battle) vii, ix–xi, 23, 26, 69, 77, 86, 120, 126–127, 133, 137, 140, 144, 177, 192, 194, 196, 199, 202, 208, 213–215, 222–223, 238–239
Prestonpans (battle, 1745) 98, 126–127, 138, 177
Protestants 12, 15, 17–18, 20, 23, 34–35, 39, 63, 95, 133, 152
Ramillies (battle, 1706) 132, 135–137
regency 18, 46

the Restoration xi, 14, 30, 41, 44, 48, 136, 176, 187

Sedgemoor (battle, 1685) 113, 144, 237
South Sea Company 64, 194
States General 20, 63–64

Tories 17–18, 21, 25–27, 45
the Treasury 63, 65, 67, 207
Treaty of Utrecht 25, 32, 34, 60, 63

the Union 14–16, 23, 28–29, 40, 42, 130, 136, 141, 152, 154

War of the League of Augsburg 130, 135
War of the Spanish Succession 13, 17, 21, 25, 31, 33, 63–64, 129, 131–132, 134–137, 148, 202
Whigs 17, 21–23, 25–26, 39, 88, 191, 221

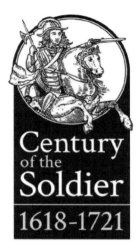

The Century of the Soldier series – Warfare c 1618-1721

www.helion.co.uk/centuryofthesoldier

'This is the Century of the Soldier', Falvio Testir, Poet, 1641

The 'Century of the Soldier' series will cover the period of military history c. 1618–1721, the 'golden era' of Pike and Shot warfare. This time frame has been seen by many historians as a period of not only great social change, but of fundamental developments within military matters. This is the period of the 'military revolution', the development of standing armies, the widespread introduction of black powder weapons and a greater professionalism within the culture of military personnel.

The series will examine the period in a greater degree of detail than has hitherto been attempted, and has a very wide brief, with the intention of covering all aspects of the period from the battles, campaigns, logistics and tactics, to the personalities, armies, uniforms and equipment.

Submissions

The publishers would be pleased to receive submissions for this series. Please contact us via email (info@helion.co.uk), or in writing to Helion & Company Limited, 26 Willow Road, Solihull, West Midlands, B91 1UE.

Titles

No 1 *'Famous by my Sword'. The Army of Montrose and the Military Revolution*
Charles Singleton (ISBN 978-1-909384-97-2)*

No 2 *Marlborough's Other Army. The British Army and the Campaigns of the First Peninsular War, 1702–1712*
Nick Dorrell (ISBN 978-1-910294-63-5)

No 3 *Cavalier Capital. Oxford in the English Civil War 1642–1646*
John Barratt (ISBN 978-1-910294-58-1)

No 4 *Reconstructing the New Model Army Volume 1. Regimental Lists April 1645 to May 1649*
Malcolm Wanklyn (ISBN 978-1-910777-10-7)*

No 5 *To Settle The Crown – Waging Civil War in Shropshire, 1642–1648*
Jonathan Worton (ISBN 978-1-910777-98-5)

No 6 *The First British Army, 1624–1628. The Army of the Duke of Buckingham*
Laurence Spring (ISBN 978-1-910777-95-4)

No 7 'Better Begging Than Fighting'. The Royalist Army in Exile in the War
against Cromwell 1656–1660
John Barratt (ISBN 978-1-910777-71-8)*

No 8 Reconstructing the New Model Army Volume 2. Regimental Lists April 1649
to May 1663
Malcolm Wanklyn (ISBN 978-1-910777-88-6)*

No 9 The Battle of Montgomery 1644. The English Civil War in the Welsh
Borderlands
Jonathan Worton (ISBN 978-1-911096-23-8)*

No 10 The Arte Militaire. The Application of 17th Century Military Manuals to
Conflict Archaeology
Warwick Louth (ISBN 978-1-911096-22-1)*

No 11 No Armour But Courage: Colonel Sir George Lisle, 1615–1648
Serena Jones (ISBN 978-1-911096-47-4)

No 12 Cromwell's Buffoon: The Life and Career of the Regicide, Thomas Pride
Robert Hodkinson (ISBN 978-1-911512-11-0)

No 14 Hey for Old Robin! The Campaigns and Armies of the Earl of Essex During
the First Civil War, 1642–44
Chris Scott & Alan Turton (ISBN 978-1-911512-21-9)*

No 15 The Bavarian Army during the Thirty Years War
Laurence Spring (ISBN 978-1-911512-39-4)

No 16 The Army of James II, 1685–1688: The Birth of the British Army
Stephen Ede-Borrett (ISBN 978-1-911512-39-4)*

No 17 Civil War London: A Military History of London under Charles I and Oliver
Cromwell
David Flintham (ISBN 978-1-911512-62-2)*

No 18 The Other Norfolk Admirals: Myngs, Narbrough and Shovell
Simon Harris (ISBN 978-1-912174-22-5)

No 19 A New Way of Fighting: Professionalism in the English Civil War
Serena Jones (editor) (ISBN 978-1-911512-61-5)

No 20 Crucible of the Jacobite '15: The Battle of Sheriffmuir 1715
Jonathan Oates (ISBN 978-1-911512-89-9)

Books within the series are published in two formats: 'Falconets' are paperbacks, page size 248mm
x 180mm, with high visual content including colour plates; 'Culverins' are hardback monographs,
page size 234mm x 156mm. Books marked with * in the list above are Falconets, all others are
Culverins.